ASCETICS, AUTHORITY, AND THE CHURCH

ASCETICS, AUTHORITY, AND THE CHURCH

In the Age of Jerome and Cassian

SECOND EDITION

PHILIP ROUSSEAU

University of Notre Dame Press

Notre Dame, Indiana

Paperback printed in 2010 by the University of Notre Dame Press
Notre Dame, Indiana 46556
www.undpress.nd.edu

First edition published in 1978 by Oxford University Press

Published in the United States of America

Library of Congress Cataloging-in-Publication Data

Rousseau, Philip.
Ascetics, authority, and the church in the age of Jerome and Cassian / Philip Rousseau. — [2nd ed.]
p. cm.
Includes bibliographical references and index.
ISBN-13: 978-0-268-04029-1 (pbk. : alk. paper)
ISBN-10: 0-268-04029-X (pbk. : alk. paper)
1. Asceticism—History—Early church, ca. 30–600. 2. Monastic and religious life—History—Early church, ca. 30–600. 3. Authority—Religious aspects—Christianity. I. Title.
BV5023.R68 2010
248.4'709015—dc22

2010008789

∞ *The paper in this book meets the guidelines for permanence and durability of the Committee on Production Guidelines for Book Longevity of the Council on Library Resources.*

AILEEN, HUBERT,

and **ROGER**

CONTENTS

Introduction to the Second Edition ix

Abbreviations xxxvii

Introduction 1

PART ONE: THE DESERT

I. Discovering the Desert Fathers
1. Contemporary Judgements 9
2. The Evidence Today 11

II. Masters and Disciples
1. The Dialogue 19
2. The Basis of Authority 21

III. The Growth of Ascetic Society
1. From Hermit to Coenobite 33
2. Power within the Community 49

IV. Ascetics in the Church 56

V. The Written Word 68

PART TWO: WESTERN BEGINNINGS

I. Exiles and Pilgrims 79

II. Ascetic Literature 92

PART THREE: JEROME

I. Antioch, Constantinople, and Rome 99

II. Letters from Bethlehem 114

III. Jerome on the Priesthood and Episcopate 125

IV. Jerome's *Lives* 133

PART FOUR: MARTIN OF TOURS

I. A Bishop and his Biographer
1. Sulpicius the Disciple 143
2. Martin the Master 148

II. An Apostle in Gaul 152

III. Martin's Audience 161

PART FIVE: CASSIAN

I. An Exile in Reverse 169

II. Hermits or Coenobites? 177

III. Adapting Egypt to the West 183

IV. Authority
1. The Decline of the Charismatic Master 189
2. Discipleship within the Community 194

V. Monks and the World
1. The Monastic *Élite* 199
2. Wealth and Patronage 205
3. A Pastoral Role 212

VI. Cassian the Writer
1. Books 221
2. The Church as a Monastery: Cassian's *De Incarnatione* 227
3. The Thirteenth Conference: Portrait of an Abbot 231

Epilogue: the Next Generation 235

APPENDICES

I. Greek, Coptic, and Latin Lives of Pachomius 243
II. Greek and Latin Versions of the *Historia Monachorum* and the *Life of Antony* 248
III. The Monastic Teaching of Evagrius of Pontus 251
IV. Cassian's Dependence on Oral Tradition: Some Examples 254

Bibliography 257

Index 273

INTRODUCTION TO THE SECOND EDITION

More than thirty years after publication, it is useful to lay out the chronology of the original enterprise and to assess where it did and did not lead. *Ascetics, Authority, and the Church in the Age of Jerome and Cassian* was published in 1978, but I changed very little the text of the doctoral thesis upon which it was based (defended in March 1972); it was essentially ready for publication by the end of 1973. Indeed, important components of the argument had already been published towards the end of 1971,[1] and the first version of the book itself was completed just a few weeks later. Subsequent delay was related only to the series in which the book eventually appeared. Meanwhile, I published two short pieces on eastern ascetics in 1972 and 1974 and a paper on Cassian in 1975.[2]

I think it is important not to imagine in retrospect that such a pattern of research was predictable. The steps taken seemed rational enough at the time. I wanted (this was in 1968) to explore the western aftermath of Augustine's career, so vividly and so recently disclosed in Peter Brown's biography; attention to Possidius and Prosper of Aquitaine was obviously necessary; and Prosper led me back to Cassian. It was at that point that my curiosity took a new turn, and I journeyed to Egypt via the *Conferences*. As a result, the western churchmen with whom I had planned to spend my thesis years took on a surprisingly "eastern" appearance.

It is also important to recognize the company I was keeping as a student. Some people are lucky in their moment, and I was certainly lucky in mine. In addition to Peter Brown, I shared a "late Roman" enthusiasm with classicists such as John Matthews and Timothy Barnes and with medievalists such as Patrick Wormald and Alfred Smyth. We pursued our interests in a world

1 "The Spiritual Authority of the 'Monk-Bishop.'" Full references, including those alluded to in the text, are provided in the additional bibliography at the end of this introduction.

2 "Blood-Relationships among Early Eastern Ascetics," "The Formation of Early Ascetic Communities," and "Cassian, Contemplation, and the Coenobitic Life."

dominated by giants of the century—Arnaldo Momigliano, Richard Southern, and Ronald Syme. Geoffrey de Sainte Croix, Michael Wallace Hadrill, and Karl Leyser were familiar figures. I was also blessed with friends in the world inspired by Isaiah Berlin, president of my own college (this book is dedicated to them and still recalls for me their style, sensitivity, and affection). None of this says much about me personally, but it speaks volumes about the formation of a scholarly movement—interdependent, inventive, and tolerant. I often felt slightly odd and out of place in this vibrant circle—indeed, my ancient ascetic acquaintances *were* odd companions at the seminar table in those days; but I always knew that, if I talked about them with what clarity I could muster and with respect for the disciplinary skills and interests of others, my immediate colleagues would find a common interest in those apparently fringe figures of the Mediterranean world. Few of us anticipated how soon our own inquiries would make them central players on the late antique stage.

By the time *Ascetics* appeared in 1978, I had begun work on a second book, *Pachomius*. Published in 1985 but completed by 1982, *Pachomius* represented my first major misgiving about the argument of *Ascetics* itself—namely, its relative neglect of the Pachomian material taken as a whole. This new and narrower focus was to be significant, since it weaned me from the Latin West, made me appreciate more fully the riches of Egypt, and developed my understanding of the Greek East in general. If, moreover, I had known more in the early 1970s about what was afoot in Upper Egypt after Pachomius' death (in the era of Shenoute of Atripe), I would almost certainly have modified my assessment of ascetic authority and its wider impact.

Pachomius had its own shortcomings. The book overlooked major points that we now appropriately associate with the name of James Goehring (as I admit in the preface to the later paperback edition). Goehring published his work on the *Letter of Ammon* only shortly after my *Pachomius* first appeared, and it was a pity that I had not learned of his interests sooner.[3] Somewhat graver, however, was my ignorance of his earlier study of the Pachomian "tradition," which might have warned me to be less

[3] Goehring, *Letter of Ammon.*

trusting of the surviving biographies.[4] In the years that followed, Goehring also emphasized Pachomius' proximity to village and town life.[5] Both *Ascetics* and *Pachomius* are explicitly aware of that need for hermeneutic caution and of the mythologized character of the "desert" (particularly evident in the epilogue of *Ascetics*), but it took me a few more years to do such matters fuller justice.[6]

Ascetics was also about bishops (or at least what I thought of as "ascetic" or "monk" bishops), and here we come across another shortcoming. The difficulty resides in my having essentialized monks and bishops as distinct social categories. I took up older notions about charism and office[7] and then focused on what I perceived as a passage from the first to the second. I would say in my own favor that I did identify an axis of influence (from the "desert," in a sense, to the "city"), in the East as well as in the West, not to mention the breadth of context required to make sense of that development. This is probably the book's most useful contribution, again, summed up succinctly in the epilogue. I could have been more forthright, however, in recognizing and describing what was in fact a *single arena* available to *all* my protagonists. It was within that newly constituted space that the boundaries, the circumscriptions of religious authority, were at once marked out and constantly renegotiated. I hinted at this "single arena" by my use of the phrase "the Church" in my title; but the notion of "boundary" was more fully explored in my biography of Basil of Caesarea, and that of "negotiation" in

[4] Goehring, "Pachomius' Vision of Heresy."

[5] See the collection of his papers on these and other topics, *Ascetics, Society, and the Desert.* Two other studies imply much about centers of ascetic settlement: Gilbert Dagron, "Les Moines et la ville," and Ewa Wipszycka, "Le Monachisme égyptien et les villes."

[6] Crucial for me, in this regard, was the stunning paper by Dagron, "L'Ombre d'un doute." But the seed had been sown by Evelyne Patlagean's foundational study, "Ancienne hagiographie byzantine et histoire sociale." A more literary but equally sturdy arch of insight reached from Ludwig Bieler, *Theios Anēr,* to Patricia L. Cox (now Patricia Cox Miller), *Biography in Late Antiquity.* Miller has continued this emphasis in, for example, "Desert Asceticism and 'The Body from Nowhere,'" and "Jerome's Centaur." The degree to which we have shifted from a social to a textual view (and in that sense from Peter Brown's famous paper "The Rise and Function of the Holy Man") is evident from the essays in, for example, James Howard-Johnston and Paul Antony Hayward, eds., *The Cult of Saints in Late Antiquity.*

[7] See especially Hans von Campenhausen, *Kirchliches Amt und geistliche Vollmacht.*

a subsequent treatment of ascetic historiography. The arena was, I now believe, essentially urban.[8]

I had begun to sense, in other words, a need to understand bishops and their settings *as such.* I happily confess that I did not fully appreciate the force of the inquiry until the appearance of Peter Brown's *Body and Society* in 1988 (which seemed to me at the time to neglect exactly that need). But I produced earlier small-scale studies on Sidonius, Augustine, and Hilary of Poitiers;[9] and, even before 1988, I had begun my work on Basil (who is almost entirely absent from *Ascetics*). The resulting *Basil of Caesarea* was designed precisely to portray a fourth-century bishop—not in a role that was "typical" (for there was as yet no post-Constantinian "type"), but rather in one governed by insecurity and experiment and invented very much "on the hoof."[10] A question that interests me now is whether Martin of Tours could sustain a similar analysis (I shall mention Martin again shortly), or indeed Augustine himself (hints of how that may well be the case occur in Peter Brown's epilogue to the new edition of his *Augustine*).[11]

Episcopacy soon preoccupied a number of scholars.[12] One has to acknowledge the pioneering work, for our generation, of Rita Lizzi, both on the late antique East and more specifically on the world of Ambrose.[13] J. N. D. Kelly produced in 1995 a much delayed and not wholly successful portrait of John Chrysostom

[8] The line of thought can be observed in not only "The Historiography of Asceticism: Current Achievements and Future Opportunities," but also "'The Preacher's Audience,'" "Ascetics as Mediators and as Teachers," and the forthcoming "Homily and Asceticism in the North Italian Episcopate," in the conference proceedings *Cromazio di Aquileia e il suo tempo,* edited by Alessio Persic and Pier Franco Beatrice.

[9] "In Search of Sidonius the Bishop," "Augustine and Ambrose," and "The Exegete as Historian."

[10] The text was essentially complete by the end of 1991. Since I mention her later work below, I must draw attention to Andrea Sterk's unpublished Princeton doctoral thesis, "Basil of Caesarea and the Rise of the Monastic Episcopate: Ascetic Ideals and Episcopal Authority in Fourth-Century Asia Minor" (1994). I am sorry that we found no opportunity at the time to share our views and findings.

[11] For a newer picture of the world in which the question arises, see Erika Hermanowicz, *Possidius of Calama.*

[12] Note the landmark lecture (1979) by Henry Chadwick, "The Role of the Christian Bishop in Ancient Society."

[13] Rita Lizzi (now Rita Lizzi Testa), *Il potere episcopale nell'Oriente romano* (the tension between ideal and reality remains central to her analyses), and *Vescovi e strutture ecclesiastiche.* See her important summary, "Ambrose's Contemporaries and the Christianization of Northern Italy."

(also mentioned rarely in *Ascetics*), a figure now being redesigned from the ground up, especially by Wendy Mayer.[14] A year previously, we had been given Neil McLynn's *Ambrose of Milan*; and Dennis Trout's *Paulinus of Nola* appeared in 1999.[15] Attention soon turned to a more challenging figure, Gregory of Nazianzus. John McGuckin produced a predominantly theological portrait; Susanna Elm's more contextualized account is on the brink of appearing;[16] and Neil McLynn is completing a study that will be interesting to compare with his *Ambrose*. Several themes are adumbrated in a recent collection, based on a conference in Bergen, which includes papers by Elm and McLynn.[17]

Works broader in scale have been equally important. Peter Brown made a crucial move beyond his *Body and Society* by publishing in 1992 his lectures on "power and persuasion"—in my opinion, his best book since *Augustine of Hippo*. I have mentioned already the work of Rita Lizzi,[18] and Italian scholarship is rich on this topic.[19] The link between bishop and city now occupies center stage: the specifically religious ambitions of the pastor are seen to be not only enfolded within the broad institutions of the late Roman state but also dependent on systems of patronage and social hierarchy at the more local level. The conjunction was already evident in the studies referred to above (by Kelly, Mayer, McLynn, and Trout); but one must be careful not to assume that the Christian city *was* the bishop's city, that he succeeded in claiming it entirely for himself.[20] The same

[14] Kelly, *Golden Mouth*; Mayer, *The Homilies of St. John Chrysostom*, and, with Pauline Allen, *John Chrysostom*.

[15] See also Catherine Conybeare, *Paulinus Noster*.

[16] The proposed title for Elm's work is *Sons of Hellenism, Fathers of the Church*.

[17] Jostein Børtnes and Tomas Hägg, eds., *Gregory of Nazianzus*; Elm, "Gregory's Women," and McLynn, "Among the Hellenists." See also Elm, "Hellenism and Historiography." Developing work by Suzanne Abrams Rebillard and Dayna Kalleres will also contribute to the picture.

[18] To which one should add her paper "The Bishop, 'Vir Venerabilis.'" Some implications are explored more fully (not least in relation to the Rome of Damasus) in her *Senatori, popolo, papi*.

[19] See, for example, Lellia Cracco Ruggini, "Prêtre et fonctionnaire." This was scholarship in which Peter Brown shared: see his "Dalla 'plebs Romana' alla 'plebs dei.'"

[20] See Éric Rebillard and Claire Sotinel, eds., *L'Évêque dans la cité*, and Mark Humphries, *Communities of the Blessed*. These studies provide a fine context for Sotinel's more recent work on Aquileia, *Identité civique et christianisme*; but note the judicious, broader, and slightly earlier caution expressed in her "Évêques italiens dans la société de l'antiquité tardive."

links have come to affect the study of whole provinces, as in Raymond Van Dam's trilogy on the Cappadocian Fathers and Ralph Mathisen's monographs on fifth-century Gaul.[21] More fine-grained analysis and a sharper degree of definition have revealed a genealogy of episcopal embroilment reaching, especially in the West, into the early Middle Ages.[22] I was clearly conscious, even in the early 1970s, that this was where *Ascetics* would logically lead (see the epilogue once more). The earliest work that struck me as realizing the possibilities was that of William Klingshirn on Caesarius of Arles. The story continues well into the sixth century, into the world of Gregory of Tours.[23] Beyond that, of course, looms the figure of Gregory the Great—simply too big a topic to expand upon here, although one has to mention the influence during my own career of at least Claude Dagens, Robert Markus, and Carole Straw. Conrad Leyser and Susan Wessel have shown in broad analyses how much is still to be done on the intervening period.[24] The greatest step forward has been taken, however, by Claudia Rapp in her study of "holy bishops." She was not directly inspired with that purpose; but she has made the most forceful attempt in recent years to address the problem I grappled with more than thirty years before.[25] Engagement with Rapp's arguments must now govern any development of my own. Crucially, her bishops *were* the "ascetics" with "authority," although neither of us supposes that

[21] Van Dam had already ventured into the Gallic field in his *Leadership and Community in Late Antique Gaul.* It was not just in the towns that "blind spots" persisted, where the episcopal eye was less penetrating: we shall hear a lot more of what Kim Bowes implies about the countryside in her *Private Worship, Public Values, and Religious Change.*

[22] I have been particularly impressed by Eva Elm, *Die Macht der Weisheit.* Meanwhile, there is much to look forward to in the developing work of both Lisa Bailey and Albrecht Diem. See also Henry Chadwick, "Bishops and Monks," especially in its closing pages.

[23] See Martin Heinzelmann, *Gregor von Tours (538–594).* Heinzelmann was building here on his earlier work, *Bischofsherrschaft in Gallien,* a book that reached back to the political and economic historiography of Roman Gaul in the previous generation, such as the work of Karl Friedrich Stroheker (the co-founder of *Historia*) recorded here in my original bibliography. Whether Heinzelmann is right in the pedigree he identifies is another matter.

[24] In his *Authority and Asceticism,* Leyser deliberately, I think, follows the leads identified at the end of this book. In her *Leo the Great,* Wessel adds much that is fresh (and more inclusive of the East).

[25] One needs to take note also of Sterk, *Renouncing the World Yet Leading the Church.*

bishops exhausted the species. Nor, as I say, were they always assuredly masters of the cities to which they preached.

Work on the specifically Egyptian front did not stand still during the 1980s and 1990s. In addition to broader studies, religious or otherwise,[26] there has been significant progress in three major fields of inquiry: Shenoute, already mentioned briefly above; Manichaeism in Egypt; and monastic archaeology. Work on Shenoute has been at once furthered and channeled by the textual labors of Stephen Emmel.[27] As far as the themes of *Ascetics* are concerned, one would have to note in particular the status of biographical evidence (in this case, the portrait associated with the name of Besa); the degree to which Shenoute was "faithful" to the Pachomian tradition (which forces us to ask to what degree such a notion of fidelity would have made sense in the later fourth century anyway); and Shenoute's relations both with secular patrons and critics and with ecclesiastical authorities. Similar issues are raised within the context of Palestinian monasticism, a central preoccupation for Derwas Chitty, but hardly touched upon here in *Ascetics*.[28] The omission is in some ways a comment on the very structure of the book, a book "written backwards." Because I began my doctoral research in Gaul and with Cassian, no matter how far backward I was prepared to go, I always wanted to hurry forward to Cassian again, with whom I knew the book was going to end. Even Cassian the Palestinian, as it were, made hardly any impression upon me.

The "Manichaean connection" relates especially to both the social structures of that sect's ascetic endeavor and the attitude to the body and to materiality in general that the endeavor re-

[26] Elm, *Virgins of God*; David Brakke, *Athanasius and the Politics of Asceticism*—but note the shift in his preoccupations in his *Demons and the Making of the Monk*; David Frankfurter, *Religion in Roman Egypt*; and Wipszycka, *Études sur le christianisme dans l'Égypte* and *Moines et communautés monastiques en Égypte*.

[27] Emmel, *Shenoute's Literary Corpus*. His bibliography points back to years of work, and the commentary itself makes clear how much remains to be done. A clear account of how matters stood at the time my *Pachomius* appeared is presented by Janet Timbie, "The State of Research on the Career of Shenoute of Atripe." See now Rebecca Krawiec, *Shenoute and the Women of the White Monastery*, and Caroline T. Schroeder, *Monastic Bodies*.

[28] The subtitle of Chitty's famous *The Desert a City* is "an introduction to the study of Egyptian and Palestinian monasticism under the Christian Empire." I made amends only in my chapter "Monasticism" in *The Cambridge Ancient History*, vol. 14. See Yizhar Hirschfeld, *The Judean Desert Monasteries*; John Binns, *Ascetics and Ambassadors of Christ*; and Joseph Patrich, *Sabas, Leader of Palestinian Monasticism*.

flected. I still suspect that attitudes counted for more than structures: the fear of being thought a Manichee in one's theology was more real to a Christian ascetic than any risk of confusion between a monastery and a *mānistān*.[29] In terms of organization, the Melitians (rigorists but not necessarily dualists) were more serious rivals.[30] That does not lessen, however, the real possibility that a "monastic" emphasis in the modern sense—the development of a specifically coenobitic sociology—was, because of its visibility and its hierarchy of command and formation, an important safeguard against imputations of heretical thought and practice.[31] Probably the most interesting development in the study of Manichaean Egypt has emerged in the context of the Dakhleh Oasis, the scene of some decades of excavation. Specifically at Ismant el-Kharab (ancient Kellis), there is now abundant evidence of a Manichaean community, literarily productive and highly self-conscious, yet wholly (and apparently unobtrusively) embedded in the surrounding Christian township.[32]

If one takes into account Egyptian archaeology more generally, one soon comes up against multiple investigations, not all of them relevant to early Christianity in the province, but many of them associated as well with work on papyri and late antique art. The bibliography becomes enormous. In the specifically monastic sphere, however, recent work has borne considerable fruit. This is due not least to ventures such as the Egyptian Delta Monastic Archaeology Project, directed by Stephen J. Davis (Yale University), with Darlene L. Brooks Hedstrom (Wittenberg University) as its co-director and director of excavations. Various teams in different seasons have worked in a variety of places in Lower Egypt, including the long familiar Wadi el-Natrun area but also sites associated with Shenoute. The

[29] These matters are touched on both here in *Ascetics* and in *Pachomius*. See also Bo Utas, "Mānistān and Xānaqāh."

[30] The contrasts are dealt with by both Brakke in his *Athanasius* and Annik Martin, *Athanase d'Alexandrie*.

[31] I explored this notion in my "Orthodoxy and the Coenobite."

[32] A general picture is most easily gained via the stunning websites of the Dakhleh Oasis Project and in the editorial work of Colin A. Hope and the project's director, Anthony J. Mills. Of special importance in our own context are the publications of Iain Gardner—for example, "The Manichaean Community at Kellis," the similarly titled "The Manichaean Community at Kellis," in Mirrecki and BeDuhn, eds., *Emerging from Darkness* (a volume with much else of interest), "Personal Letters from the Manichaean Community at Kellis," and, with S. N. C. Lieu, "From Narmouthis (Medinet Madi) to Kellis (Ismant el-Kharab)."

effect of this endeavor has been to expand our understanding of place, of the physical (and particularly the domestic) circumstances of the ascetic life. It has also made possible a more detailed link between buildings and the texts and artistic depictions that were created within and around them.[33] Although it has broader concerns, including the restoration of later art in existing monastic buildings, the antiquities section of the American Research Center in Egypt has analyzed comparable relicts, first at St. Antony's Monastery by the Red Sea, subsequently at the monastery of St. Paul (the "first hermit") nearby, and also at the Red Monastery at Sohag (associated originally with Shenoute and his successors). A notable contributor here has been the art historian Elizabeth S. Bolman (Temple University). Her published work on the Red Sea sites bears witness to a long surviving tradition but also to the hazards its survival has to overcome. More recent work at Sohag promises a different and perhaps a greater reward, since the site (in Bolman's words) may include the only standing ensemble of architecture, sculpture, and paint left from the late antique period in the entire Mediterranean. Nowhere else in Egypt, certainly, do we know of a monument of the late antique and early Byzantine period whose architectural sculpture is *in situ* up to the highest level of the building.[34]

My own work on Egyptian themes, following upon *Pachomius,* focused at first on Antony. I made some early general assessments,[35] but I became chiefly interested in Antony as a teacher.[36] This shift (begun in 1996) coincided with my introduction to the work of Samuel Rubenson[37] and marked the development

[33] Useful introductions to the topic are provided by Brooks Hedstrom, "Redrawing a Portrait of Egyptian Monasticism," and "Divine Architects: Designing the Monastic Dwelling Place." See also Davis's recent reports in *Mishkah.*

[34] Statements here are drawn from the several striking websites to be discovered under "Red Monastery." For Bolman's work at the Red Sea, see her *Monastic Visions.* The volume contains several introductory and technical essays by other scholars. On Sohag, we await her forthcoming *Chromatic Brilliance in Upper Egypt: The Red Monastery Church.* See also her "Veiling Sanctity in Christian Egypt," and "Depicting the Kingdom of Heaven."

[35] "The Desert Fathers: Antony and Pachomius," and "Christian Asceticism and the Early Monks." Pachomius has not been forgotten: see my "The Successors of Pachomius and the Nag Hammadi Library."

[36] "Antony as Teacher in the Greek Life."

[37] Rubenson, in his *Letters of St Antony,* famously allowed Antony more erudition and a place in the Christian philosophical tradition: the writer of the *Vita Antonii* was not the sole player here. It is an emphasis he has resolutely maintained.

of a new emphasis on the "ascetic master," which I had already set in motion in 1993,[38] and which continues to govern my current research. I turned more to Theodoret of Cyrrhus (whose *Historia religiosa* had been central to Peter Brown's famous "Rise and Function" article);[39] but I allowed the inquiry to reflect back on *Ascetics* by appealing to similar traits in studies of Jerome and Cassian.[40] The effect has been to redefine the link between asceticism and the pastoral life of the church, particularly in relation to homilies, to the rhetoric of moral formation; and *pari passu* to swing back to the urban sphere, to the political and municipal setting within which ascetically inspired teachers of many stripes, clerical and otherwise, applied their skills and created their audiences. Inquiry should now be rooted, in my view, in a developing critique of both Peter Brown (*Power and Persuasion*) and Claudia Rapp (*Holy Bishops*).

Ascetics is about individuals as well as themes. Pachomius I have discussed at length. Samuel Rubenson, James Goehring, and Janet Timbie have been my more recent guides and critics. Thirty years of reading and reflection have led us all to appreciate more the importance of an ascetic culture and tradition, of a literary envelope (almost always tendentious) around the individual life, of a heritage that invites understanding of succession but also of mythology, and above all the importance of a setting in no way restricted to any "desert," real or imagined. To that extent, ascetics were not members of either an enclosed or a static society. We are not trying to describe, therefore, the *internal* development of a *system,* and certainly not of a coenobitic system outgrowing eremitic origins. I came in for some criticism here. The text of *Ascetics,* especially in its earlier sections ("From Hermit to Coenobite," for example), suggests, I agree, that I accepted such a development. Currently, I am inclined to stick to my guns, but in a carefully defined way. It would be ridiculous to suppose that coenobites entirely supplanted more solitary enthusiasts, and I do not think I did so. What does seem incontro-

[38] Leading to "Eccentrics and Coenobites in the Late Roman East."

[39] "The Identity of the Ascetic Master in the *Historia Religiosa* of Theodoret of Cyrrhus," "Moses, Monks, and Mountains in Theodoret's *Historia religiosa,*" and "Knowing Theodoret: Text and Self." For a specific contrast to Brown, see my "Ascetics as Mediators and as Teachers."

[40] "'Learned Women' and the Formation of a Christian Culture in Late Antiquity," "Cassian: Monastery and World," "Jerome's Search for Self-Identity," and "Christian Culture and the Swine's Husks."

vertibly the case is that the coenobitic life gained some prominence, which needs explaining, and gained it among ascetics previously accustomed to a less corporate order. The crucial point is made on p. 41: "one is dealing not merely with contrasting types of asceticism, but with moments of change in the lives of individuals" (and note the summary on pp. 42–3). What follows, in my original account, is equally important: first, the accompanying element of interiority—apparently paradoxical but, to those familiar with corporate asceticism, in no way surprising—and second, the presentation of coenobitic ideals in texts that gloss over the untidiness of actual development. By critical reading, we immediately unmask the writers and do greater justice to the ambiguity, the constant shifts that characterized the careers of Jerome, Cassian, and, indeed, Pachomius himself. We are also reminded of how much there is yet to do, if we wish to make clear the circumstances, the purposes, and the progressive development of such texts as the *Apophthegmata patrum*. Response to contemporary but changing demands—contemporary with the writers or compilers themselves, and involving demands expressed and felt far away from Egypt—was always the governing factor.[41]

Jerome figures prominently in both the title and the structure of *Ascetics*; but I wonder whether I asked directly enough and answered with sufficient detail the question why he is here at all. I do not doubt that he flirted with the notion of a leadership role in the church, which his temperament and lack of tact forced him to fall back from, and I am equally certain that his ascetic inclinations both heightened his reluctance and antagonized his critics; but I said far too little here about the alternative views of pastoral responsibility and personal abnegation against which he was compelled to take a sometimes ineffectual stand. Jovinian and Pelagius are the most obviously absent players.[42] One

[41] Graham Gould, in his *The Desert Fathers on Monastic Community*, was particularly forceful in his censure, some of which I attempted to counter in my "Orthodoxy and the Coenobite." Gould's book, like Douglas Burton-Christie's *The Word in the Desert*, illustrates well the dangers of the "enclosed" and "static" view; but we have to remember that few other scholars had attempted as much on such a scale. For a keener sense of openness and elasticity, see Daniel Caner, *Wandering, Begging Monks*, and Jennifer Hevelone-Harper, *Disciples of the Desert*, as also Maribel Dietz at n. 54 below.

[42] On Jovinian, we are now blessed with David Hunter's *Marriage, Celibacy, and Heresy in Ancient Christianity*. See also Yves-Marie Duval, *L'Affaire Jovinien*. Matters have progressed much less on the Pelagian front.

has to say that Jerome failed in any bid he may have ventured in the cause of defining priesthood, let alone episcopacy. As far as *Ascetics* is concerned, my attempt to make him part of a bridge between a "desert" culture and churchmanship in Gaul boiled down to his hagiography, some of his letters, and his less easily documented contribution to our understanding of Sulpicius Severus. The story of Priscillian also has some relevance here, pitting moral rigor against episcopal authority and embroiling Gaul as well as Spain, and the attentions of Ambrose.[43]

Mention of Priscillian (and of Escribano's essay in my previous note) points to another area demanding more inquiry. At the time of his execution (385), the disputes over the teaching of Arius and his followers were still a fresh memory, indeed raw; and Athanasius' enlisting of ascetics (Antony most famously) in his personal intrigues and campaigns in the cause of Nicene orthodoxy was only one example of an empire-wide alliance, to which ascetics were not reluctant to subscribe. Jerome, let us not forget, was in Constantinople at exactly the time when the Arian conflict was reaching a certain climax (in the council of 381). He had already betrayed his taste for confrontation by his involvement in Antioch's schism, choosing to receive ordination at the hands of Paulinus. Martin of Tours' attachment to Hilary of Poitiers (more on that in a moment) reflected the same *rapport*. It is a pity, therefore, that I said so little about the Origenist Controversy, which did not appear to me in the early 1970s to call for immediate connection with the theme of the book—a miscalculation, obviously.[44] Jerome's understanding of the body—of both its redemption and its discipline—was central to his ambiguous assessment of both Origen and Rufinus. He saw the great Alexandrian as claiming too easy a "likeness to God," which he then attempted to link with both a Pelagian view of "nature" and a false understanding of the incarnate Christ. Equally important to the theme of the book, the controversy pitted him against bishops: for all his vaunted friendship with

[43] Virginia Burrus, *The Making of a Heretic*. See also Henry Chadwick, *Priscillian of Avila*, and more recently, Victoria Escribano, "Heresy and Orthodoxy in Fourth-Century Hispania: Arianism and Priscillianism."

[44] See Ilona Opelt, *Hieronymus' Streitschriften*, given a wider context by her *Die Polemik in der christlichen lateinischen Literatur*; Elizabeth A. Clark, *The Origenist Controversy*.

Gregory, Damasus, and Epiphanius, he lost ground significantly against John in Jerusalem and Siricius in Rome.

I tried to make amends for some of these omissions (although I still think that the Jerome of *Ascetics*, if incomplete, is yet true to character);[45] but I was agreeably overtaken not only by the study of J. N. D. Kelly, already referred to, but also by that of Stefan Rebenich. The latter's biography, *Hieronymus und sein Kreis*, surely the most astute since Cavallera and worthy of comparison with the more disparate essays of Yves-Marie Duval, illustrated the enduring problem that Jerome's "circle" is more accessible than his *persona*.[46] Wise after the event, I now think that Gregory of Nazianzus—so anxious a priest, so self-consciously a "man of the church," and so polished a philosopher and *littérateur*—gives us more to compare him with, when set beside his aristocratic lady-friends and his doomed association with Damasus. It also makes him—rightly, I think—less easily thought of as an isolated Westerner.

The least successful portrait in *Ascetics* may be that of Martin, bishop of Tours. I knew too little about the world of Sulpicius Severus (strikingly distant from Tours), not to mention the church in Gaul more generally. I am not even sure that I provided a convincing explanation of why Sulpicius wrote about Martin in the first place. Who were the friends who needed assurance, and who the enemies who needed defeating? I have mentioned already Martin's association with Hilary of Poitiers, which was specifically directed against Arian opponents—a feature of their relationship just as important as Hilary's acquired taste for eastern ascetic devotion. In later years, and well after Hilary's death, the shock of Priscillian's popularity and misfortune both would undoubtedly have worried Martin's episcopal critics. His personal disdain for convention and comfort could

[45] In addition to essays already cited (especially "Jerome's Search for Self-Identity"), see my earlier "Jerome: His Failures and Their Importance."

[46] See, more recently, Andrew Cain, *The Letters of Jerome*, and Andrew Cain and Josef Lössl, eds., *Jerome of Stridon*. The essays of Mark Vessey, many now collected in his *Christian Latin Writers*, have been of great importance in portraying Jerome as a self-designing writer, but the fullest recent (and excellent) treatment is by Megan Williams, *The Monk and the Book: Jerome and the Making of Christian Scholarship*. A broader context is explored by Catherine Chin in her *Grammar and Christianity in the Late Roman World*; but she will bring us back closer to Jerome in her proposed study of Rufinus, *The Momentum of the Word*.

have seemed to some of them little more than symptoms of a deeper tendency to error. The chief sign of my inadequacy is the relative absence of reference to the *Dialogues*. Dependence on the judgments of Jacques Fontaine kept me firmly in the biographical groove, too little ready to subject the biography to the necessary cautious critique—exactly the difficulty I would experience with Pachomius.[47] I also found myself working on Martin alongside Clare Stancliffe—a privilege, of course, rather than an inconvenience. We worked with different supervisors—I with Peter Brown, she with Michael Wallace-Hadrill—but we shared the academic milieu of Oxford graduate life, and it was necessary to map out the territory between us. Stancliffe's published thesis made fuller and greater sense of Martin's story. But there has been precious little else published in the intervening decades: it is necessary to turn to more contextual studies.[48]

Finally, we come to Cassian. Nearly half the book is a study of the great ascetic theorist, and I attempted to fill some of the gaps that I felt had been left by Owen Chadwick's dual (in effect) portrayal in his *John Cassian*. Since 1978, the major contribution has been made by Columba Stewart, who was kind in both his acknowledgment of my opinions and his response to my omissions.[49] In more recent years, three important studies have appeared. Two in a sense look backwards (to Palestine, Egypt, and the work of Evagrius of Pontus).[50] Here one brushes against the work of Adalbert de Vogüé, before he engages with the "Lérins tradition."[51] The other looks forward into Gaul

[47] Fontaine, in his recent Sources Chrétiennes edition, has since done for the *Dialogues* what he did for the *Life*.

[48] Most notably, perhaps, Aline Rousselle, *Croire et guérir*. A useful assessment of what has been achieved is included in Martin Happ's *Alte und neue Bilder vom Heiligen Martin*. See also Jean Honoré, Michel Laurencin, and Guy-Marie Oury, eds., *Saint Martin de Tours*. As suggested above, Burrus's *Making of a Heretic* also offers useful comment on Sulpicius' necessary caution; and any work on Jerome or Paulinus of Nola is bound to touch upon his world.

[49] In addition to his *Cassian the Monk*, it is important to take into account his earlier book, *"Working the Earth of the Heart."* See also Gerd Summa, *Geistliche Unterscheidung bei Johannes Cassian*.

[50] Steven D. Driver, *John Cassian and the Reading of Egyptian Monastic Culture*; Augustine Casiday, *Tradition and Theology in St John Cassian*.

[51] De Vogüé, *De Saint Pachôme à Jean Cassien*. See also Andreas E. J. Grote, *Anachorese und Zönobium*. I do not make my allusion to De Vogüé's inquiries into later developments in any way dismissively. I am thinking immediately of his *Règles des saints pères*, which traces what is still a controversial pedigree through the fifth and sixth centuries; but the succession of volumes in his *Histoire littéraire du mouvement monastique* provide a brilliant and indispensable account of early medieval monasticism.

and beyond (following, although not necessarily consciously, the path marked out by Leyser's *Authority and Asceticism,* which picked up in its turn some elements in the work of Robert Markus).[52] All three suggest where the thrust of research has been leading: towards theological roots and components, and towards *Nachleben* and the influence of texts and ideas.

An attempt to decide who Cassian was and what he was actually doing is, in other words, less evident, although Goodrich takes the surest strides, reaching into the world explored by Mathisen, as mentioned above (and previously by Prinz). Unfortunately, the "real" Cassian does seem to disappear, virtually at death, into a tunnel of silence. What then emerges in the surviving evidence is an almost entirely written Cassian, and not always assuredly written by himself. I had my own stab at "contextualizing" the man in my "Cassian: Monastery and World," but a more recent examination of literary traditions has shown me how difficult it is to keep him anchored in his western lair. Even fresher reading, in an unrelated cause, has brought home to me what an enduringly Greek figure he was. It calls, no doubt, for a steely temperament to think the same of Jerome (Jerome in relation to Jerusalem and Caesarea, as well as to Bethlehem); but there is a broader chain of events that may encourage us to make such an adjustment. We too easily forget, for example, that the movement of Gothic settlers into the western provinces—first of the Visigoths and then of the Ostrogoths—was a movement *ex oriente,* by routes long familiar in Roman Mediterranean geopolitics (from the Balkans and through Italy; a route then followed by the Lombards). Only the Vandals and the Alans, Burgundians, and Franks were truly "northerners." So, if we can bring into one framework of analysis the careers of Jerome, Rufinus, Sulpicius, and Cassian, not to mention Athanasius earlier and Honoratus (of Lérins) towards the end, then, in the age of Ammianus and Claudian, we can really begin to see how Antioch and Alexandria, western Syria and Egypt, recolonized the imagination of the Latin West. This is what makes Susan Wessel's Leo, already mentioned, both possible (then) and convincing (now), and what makes Fergus Millar's "Greek empire" less self-contained than I take him to infer. The military interventions of

[52] Richard J. Goodrich, *Contextualizing Cassian.* I am thinking in particular of Markus's *The End of Ancient Christianity.* For a similarly broader sweep, see Heinrich Holze, *Erfahrung und Theologie im frühen Mönchtum.*

Theodosius II and his immediate successors, and of Justinian decades later, are intelligible only within a single *oikoumenē*, and prepare us for a "Greek" (or certainly an "imperial") Gregory the Great.[53]

If one were to sum up, therefore, the ways in which subsequent scholarship has affected the argument of *Ascetics*, it would be, first, that a fuller context has been provided. Within this context, however, the argument itself survives—namely, that ideals appropriately labeled "ascetic" were injected into the pastoral mainstream of the church. There is a sense, of course, in which they had always been present: to fulfill the Christian vocation was necessarily to adopt a disciplined, even rigorist, and certainly abstinent life. We are dealing, however, with a specific phase of the Christian story: the period following upon the toleration decreed by Constantine; the period within which the clerical leaders of Christian communities enjoyed new opportunities to develop new social goals; the period within which the "monastic" culture, however we define it, began to grow; the period also during which an increased mobility enabled Christians to explore and transport their practices over great distances.[54] Where we need to adjust the diagonal line I invoked in my original introduction is in realizing that those two developments—the episcopal and the monastic—were intertwined, and were intertwined within the urban setting that we normally associate with the episcopal endeavor.

A second effect is closely connected, for it is heightened awareness on this front that makes the first perception possible: I mean, our understanding of the texts upon which we depend—indeed, our understanding of what "texts" actually are. Here, I need to discuss in more general terms what I have so far touched upon in a variety of narrower contexts. An overwhelming feature of the written material that survives is the way in

[53] A point not lost on Markus: see his *Gregory the Great and His World*. At this point the frame of reference becomes enormous (which is very much the point); but see especially Averil Cameron, "Old and New Rome," and Celia Chazelle and Catherine Cubitt, eds., *The Crisis of the Oikoumene*.

[54] Here we touch upon my "pilgrims and exiles" theme, which has been enormously developed since 1978. A recent study that enables one to trace that scholarly development is Maribel Dietz, *Wandering Monks, Virgins, and Pilgrims*; but see also her earlier, briefer, but broader essay, "Itinerant Spirituality and the Late Antique Origins of Christian Pilgrimage."

which much of it deceives us in its handling of what Evelyne Patlagean called "l'espace." My strongest sense is of what I have called "displacement"—a displacement of the author, who is often removed from the scenes he (almost always a "he") describes; but a displacement of the reader also, in that he or she is transported by the text into a setting other than that where the reading takes place. Ascetic texts so often, therefore, exalt a "desert" in the eyes of those who live in the "city." But this sleight of hand was practiced for city purposes—for purposes associated with the growing Christian *polis*. Within the texts themselves, in other words, the ascetic came to town: the texts were designed, often by urban authors, to evoke and reinforce implications, not least about spiritual authority, that were to be realized within the urban milieu, no matter how withdrawn, how anchoretic in the literal sense, the exemplars might seem to be. The texts made, to that extent, a "political" point—a point, as I say, about the episcopal milieu, about the milieu of the church's pastoral endeavor.

This is partly what I meant by my earlier comment, in note 6, that we have "shifted from a social to a textual view." It is a shift in some degree from the world of Mary Douglas—the Mary Douglas at least of *Purity and Danger*—to the world of Jacques Derrida.[55] Indeed, anthropology itself has made the same move, away from the amassing of supposedly realist *réportage* to an interest in the interplay between reporter and audience. The denizens of the "field" have been deeply affected by the scrutiny of outsiders; but the scrutineers themselves have been transformed by the ideology and behavior of those "elsewhere," which they import and apply for their own purposes in settings entirely different. This is the "cultural turn" that Dale Martin and Patricia Cox Miller helped to describe in a crucial collection by that name, and it mirrors with a pleasing irony the sleight of hand effected by the ancient hagiographer. It makes sense to insist, therefore, that *Ascetics* did begin to explore that transportation of an image—or, rather, of a potency—from one setting to another (and hagiography was, in this early phase, the vehicle of transportation *par excellence*). Those essays on the "cultural turn" were written in honor of Elizabeth Clark, and she has been

[55] Derrida's *Grammatologie* appeared just before I began my doctoral research.

preeminent in her insistence on the centrality of reading itself as a key to not only the formulation but also the imposition of the ascetic ideal.[56] In this respect the bibliography becomes suddenly enormous and reaches well beyond the scope of *Ascetics.* As soon as one begins to pick out examples—Georgia Frank's *Memory of the Eyes,* or Derek Krueger's *Writing and Holiness*—it becomes obvious that one is talking about a generation of inquiry. But Frank and Krueger, like Elizabeth Clark, were most interested in asceticism; and it was a good topic with which to start a scholarly career, for I found myself standing on the threshold of "late antiquity" as we now understand it. It is difficult to remember how new and unpredictable it all was; and its unfolding was entirely bound up with contemporary reflections on gender as well as textuality and self-discipline.

But let us not forget that society did exist, and that social structures were the source and outcome of ascetic ideals. We need to look for their traces, especially since the force of ascetic textuality did not always achieve its goal. For there is a third component, even to the surviving narratives. Those intent upon "intertwining" the ascetic and the pastoral were not the only players on the scene. There were always some who believed too readily the histories they created, but who failed to translate them effectively into an urban agenda. There were also those who never believed them in the first place, and who were never in a position to need to believe them. They built futures as well. Many a monastery and many a solitary cell, across the changing Roman landscape, bore witness to a different sense of authority, a different understanding of legacy, a different deployment of power. Writing always runs the risk of merely preserving what it hopes to redefine.

[56] The crucial text is *Reading Renunciation*; but see also her later and broader treatment, *History, Theory, Text: Historians and the Linguistic Turn,* and her earlier work on gender, typified by the classic *Ascetic Piety and Women's Faith.*

ADDITIONAL BIBLIOGRAPHY

Bagnall, Roger S., ed. *Egypt in the Byzantine World, 300–700* (Cambridge: Cambridge University Press, 2007).

Bailey, Lisa. "Building Urban Christian Communities: Sermons on Local Saints in the Eusebius Gallicanus Collection," *Early Medieval Europe* 12 (2003): 1–24.

———. "Monks and Lay Communities in Late Antique Gaul: The Evidence of the Eusebius Gallicanus Sermons," *Journal of Medieval History* 32 (2006): 315–32.

Bieler, Ludwig. *Theios Anēr: das Bild des "göttlichen Menschen" in Spätantike und Frühchristentum* (Vienna: Höfels, 1935–1936; repr. Darmstadt: Wissenschaftliche Buchgesellschaft, 1967).

Binns, John. *Ascetics and Ambassadors of Christ: The Monasteries of Palestine, 314–631* (Oxford: Clarendon Press; New York: Oxford University Press, 1994).

Bolman, Elizabeth S. "Depicting the Kingdom of Heaven: Paintings and Monastic Practice in Early Byzantine Egypt," in Bagnall, ed., *Egypt in the Byzantine World*, 408–33.

———. *Monastic Visions: Wall Paintings in the Monastery of St Antony at the Red Sea* (New Haven, CT: American Research Center in Egypt/Yale University Press, 2002).

———. "Veiling Sanctity in Christian Egypt: Visual and Spatial Solutions," in Sharon E. J. Gerstel, ed., *Thresholds of the Sacred: Architectural, Art Historical, Liturgical, and Theological Perspectives on Religious Screens, East and West* (Washington, DC: Dumbarton Oaks Research Library and Collection, 2006), 73–104.

Børtnes, Jostein, and Tomas Hägg, eds. *Gregory of Nazianzus: Images and Reflections* (Copenhagen: Museum Tusculanum, 2006).

Bowes, Kim. *Private Worship, Public Values, and Religious Change in Late Antiquity* (Cambridge and New York: Cambridge University Press, 2008).

Bowes, Kim, and Michael Kulikowski, eds. and trans. *Hispania in Late Antiquity: Current Perspectives* (Leiden and Boston: Brill, 2005).

Brakke, David. *Athanasius and the Politics of Asceticism* (Oxford: Clarendon Press; New York: Oxford University Press, 1995).

———. *Demons and the Making of the Monk: Spiritual Combat in Early Christianity* (Cambridge, MA: Harvard University Press, 2006).

Brooks Hedstrom, Darlene L. "Divine Architects: Designing the Monastic Dwelling Place," in Bagnall, ed., *Egypt in the Byzantine World*, 368–89.

———. "Redrawing a Portrait of Egyptian Monasticism," in David Blanks, Michael Frassetto, and Amy Livingstone, eds., *Medieval Monks and Their World, Ideas and Realities: Studies in Honor of Richard Sullivan* (Leiden: Brill, 2006), 11–34.

Brown, Peter. *Augustine of Hippo: A Biography*, new edition with an epilogue (Berkeley and Los Angeles: University of California Press, 2000).

———. *The Body and Society: Men, Women, and Sexual Renunciation in Early Christianity* (New York: Columbia University Press, 1988).

———. "Dalla 'plebs Romana' alla 'plebs dei': aspetti della cristianizzazione di Roma," in Brown, Cracco Ruggini, and Mazza, eds., *Governanti e intellettuali,* 123–45.

———. *Power and Persuasion in Late Antiquity: Towards a Christian Empire* (Madison: University of Wisconsin Press, 1992).

———. "The Rise and Function of the Holy Man in Late Antiquity," *Journal of Roman Studies* 61 (1971): 80–101.

Brown, Peter, Lellia Cracco Ruggini, and Mario Mazza, eds. *Governanti e intellettuali, popolo di Roma e popolo di dio (I–VI secolo)* (Turin: Giappichelli, 1982).

Burrus, Virginia. *The Making of a Heretic: Gender, Authority, and the Priscillianist Controversy* (Berkeley and Los Angeles: University of California Press, 1995).

Burton-Christie, Douglas. *The Word in the Desert: Scripture and the Quest for Holiness in Early Christian Monasticism* (Oxford and New York: Oxford University Press, 1993).

Cain, Andrew. *The Letters of Jerome: Asceticism, Biblical Exegesis, and the Construction of Christian Authority in Late Antiquity* (Oxford and New York: Oxford University Press, 2009).

Cain, Andrew, and Josef Lössl, eds. *Jerome of Stridon: His Life, Writings and Legacy* (Farnham and Burlington, VT: Ashgate, 2009).

Cameron, Averil. "Old and New Rome: Roman Studies in Sixth-Century Constantinople," in Philip Rousseau and Manolis Papoutsakis, eds., *Transformations of Late Antiquity* (Farnham and Burlington, VT: Ashgate, 2009), 15–36.

Caner, Daniel. *Wandering, Begging Monks: Spiritual Authority and the Promotion of Monasticism in Late Antiquity* (Berkeley and Los Angeles: University of California Press, 2002).

Casiday, Augustine. *Tradition and Theology in St John Cassian* (Oxford and New York: Oxford University Press, 2007).

Cavadini, John C., ed. *Gregory the Great: A Symposium* (Notre Dame, IN: University of Notre Dame Press, 1995).

Chadwick, Henry. "Bishops and Monks," *Studia Patristica* 24 (1993): 45–61.

———. *Priscillian of Avila: The Occult and the Charismatic in the Early Church* (Oxford: Clarendon Press, 1976).

———. "The Role of the Christian Bishop in Ancient Society," in Edward C. Hobbs and Wilhelm Wuellner, eds., Protocol Series of the Colloquies 35 (Berkeley, CA: Center for Hermeneutical Studies in Hellenistic and Modern Culture, 1980), 1–14.

Chazelle, Celia, and Catherine Cubitt, eds. *The Crisis of the Oikoumene: The Three Chapters and the Failed Quest for Unity in the Sixth-Century Mediterranean* (Turnhout: Brepols, 2007).

Chin, Catherine. *Grammar and Christianity in the Late Roman World* (Philadelphia: University of Pennsylvania Press, 2008).

Chitty, Derwas J. *The Desert a City: An Introduction to the Study of Egyptian and Palestinian Monasticism under the Christian Empire* (London: Blackwell, 1966).

Clark, Elizabeth A. *Ascetic Piety and Women's Faith: Essays on Late Ancient Christianity* (Lewiston, NY: Edwin Mellen Press, 1986).
———. *History, Theory, Text: Historians and the Linguistic Turn* (Cambridge, MA: Harvard University Press, 2004).
———. *The Origenist Controversy: The Cultural Construction of an Early Christian Debate* (Princeton, NJ: Princeton University Press, 1992).
———. *Reading Renunciation: Asceticism and Scripture in Early Christianity* (Princeton, NJ: Princeton University Press, 1999).
Conybeare, Catherine. *Paulinus Noster: Self and Symbols in the Letters of Paulinus of Nola* (Oxford and New York: Oxford University Press, 2000).
Cox, Patricia L. *Biography in Late Antiquity: A Quest for the Holy Man* (Berkeley and Los Angeles: University of California Press, 1983).
Cracco Ruggini, Lellia. "Prêtre et fonctionnaire: l'essor d'un modèle épiscopal aux IVe–Ve siècles," *Antiquité Tardive* 7 (1999): 175–86.
Dagens, Claude. *Saint Grégoire le Grand: culture et expérience chrétiennes* (Paris: Études Augustiniennes, 1977).
Dagron, Gilbert. "Les Moines et la ville: le monachisme à Constantinople jusqu'au concile de Chalcédoine (451)," *Travaux et Mémoires* 4 (1970): 229–76; reprinted as Paper VIII in his *La Romanité chrétienne en Orient: héritages et mutations* (London: Variorum, 1984).
———. "L'Ombre d'un doute: l'hagiographie en question, VIe–XIe siècle," *Dumbarton Oaks Papers* 46 (1992): 59–68.
Davis, Stephen J. *The Early Coptic Papacy: The Egyptian Church and Its Leadership in Late Antiquity* (Cairo and New York: American University in Cairo Press, 2004).
Davis, Stephen J., et al. "Yale Monastic Archaeology Project [various reports]," *Mishkah: The Egyptian Journal of Islamic Archeology* 3 (2009): 47–57.
De Vogüé, Adalbert. *De Saint Pachôme à Jean Cassien: Études littéraires et doctrinales sur le monachisme égyptien à ses débuts* (Rome: Pontificio Ateneo S. Anselmo, 1996).
———. *Histoire littéraire du mouvement monastique dans l'antiquité* (Paris: Éditions du Cerf, 1991–).
———. *Les Règles des saints pères,* introduction, texts, French translation, and notes, Sources Chrétiennes 297, 298 (Paris: Éditions du Cerf, 1982).
Diem, Albrecht. "Monks, Kings, and the Transformation of Sanctity: Jonas of Bobbio and the End of the Holy Man," *Speculum* 82 (2007): 521–59.
———. "The Rule of an 'Iro-Egyptian' Monk in Gaul: Jonas' *Vita Iohannis* and the Construction of a Monastic Identity," *Revue Mabillon* 19 (2008): 5–50.
Dietz, Maribel. "Itinerant Spirituality and the Late Antique Origins of Christian Pilgrimage," in Ellis and Kidner, eds., *Travel, Communication, and Geography,* 113–22.
———. *Wandering Monks, Virgins, and Pilgrims: Ascetic Travel in the Mediterranean World, AD 300–800* (University Park: Pennsylvania State University Press, 2005).

Driver, Steven D. *John Cassian and the Reading of Egyptian Monastic Culture* (New York: Routledge, 2002).

Duval, Yves-Marie. *L'Affaire Jovinien: D'une crise de la société romaine à une crise de la pensée chrétienne à la fin du IVe et au début du Ve siècle* (Rome: Institutum Patristicum Augustinianum, 2003).

Ellis, Linda, and Frank L. Kidner, eds. *Travel, Communication, and Geography in Late Antiquity: Sacred and Profane* (Aldershot and Burlington, VT: Ashgate, 2004).

Elm, Eva. *Die Macht der Weisheit: das Bild des Bischofs in der Vita Augustini des Possidius und anderen spätantiken und frühmittelalterlichen Bischofsviten* (Leiden and Boston: Brill, 2003).

Elm, Susanna. "Gregory's Women: Creating a Philosopher's Family," in Børtnes and Hägg, eds., *Gregory of Nazianzus,* 171–91.

———. "Hellenism and Historiography: Gregory of Nazianzus and Julian in Dialogue," in Martin and Miller, eds., *The Cultural Turn in Late Ancient Studies,* 258–77.

———. *Virgins of God: The Making of Asceticism in Late Antiquity* (Oxford and New York: Oxford University Press, 1994).

Emmel, Stephen. *Shenoute's Literary Corpus,* 2 vols., Corpus Scriptorum Christianorum Orientalium 599–600; subsidia, 111–12 (Louvain: Peeters, 2004).

Escribano, Victoria. "Heresy and Orthodoxy in Fourth-Century Hispania: Arianism and Priscillianism," in Bowes and Kulikowski, eds. and trans., *Hispania in Late Antiquity,* 121–49.

Fontaine, Jacques. *Sulpice Sévère, Gallus: Dialogues sur les "vertus" de Saint Martin,* introduction, text, translation, and notes by Jacques Fontaine, with the collaboration of Nicole Dupré, Sources Chrétiennes 510 (Paris: Éditions du Cerf, 2006).

Frank, Georgia. *The Memory of the Eyes: Pilgrims to Living Saints in Christian Late Antiquity* (Berkeley and Los Angeles: University of California Press, 2000).

Frankfurter, David. *Religion in Roman Egypt: Assimilation and Resistance* (Princeton, NJ: Princeton University Press, 1998).

Gardner, Iain. "The Manichaean Community at Kellis," in P. Mirrecki and J. BeDuhn, eds., *Emerging from Darkness: Studies in the Recovery of Manichaean Sources* (Leiden, New York, and Cologne: Brill, 1997), 161–75.

———. "The Manichaean Community at Kellis: Progress Report," *Acta Orientalia Belgica* 8 (1993): 79–87.

———. "Personal Letters from the Manichaean Community at Kellis," in Luigi Cirillo and Alois Van Tongerloo, eds., *Atti del Terzo Congresso Internazionale di Studi "Manicheismo e Oriente Christiano Antico"* (Turnhout: Brepols, 1997), 77–94.

———, ed. *Kellis Literary Texts I* (Oxford: Oxbow Books, 1996).

Gardner, Iain, and S. N. C. Lieu. "From Narmouthis (Medinet Madi) to Kellis (Ismant el-Kharab): Manichaean Documents from Roman Egypt," *Journal of Roman Studies* 86 (1996): 146–69.

Goehring, James E. *Ascetics, Society, and the Desert: Studies in Early Egyptian Monasticism* (Harrisburg, PA: Trinity Press International, 1999).

———. *The Letter of Ammon and Pachomian Monasticism* (Berlin and New York: Walter de Gruyter, 1986).

———. "Monasticism in Byzantine Egypt: Continuity and Memory," in Bagnall, ed., *Egypt in the Byzantine World,* 390–407.

———. "Pachomius' Vision of Heresy: The Development of a Pachomian Tradition," *Muséon* 95 (1982): 241–62.

Goodrich, Richard J. *Contextualizing Cassian: Aristocrats, Asceticism, and Reformation in Fifth-Century Gaul* (Oxford and New York: Oxford University Press, 2007).

Gould, Graham. *The Desert Fathers on Monastic Community* (Oxford: Clarendon Press, 1993).

Grote, Andreas E. J. *Anachorese und Zönobium: der Rekurs des frühen westlichen Mönchtums auf monastische Konzepte des Ostens* (Stuttgart: Thorbecke, 2001).

Happ, Martin. *Alte und neue Bilder vom Heiligen Martin: Brauchtum und Gebrauch seit dem 19. Jahrhundert* (Cologne: Böhlau, 2006).

Heinzelmann, Martin. *Bischofsherrschaft in Gallien: zur Kontinuität römischer Führungsschichte vom 4. zum 7. Jahrhundert: soziale, prosopographische und bildungsgeschichtliche Aspekte* (Zürich: Artemis, 1976).

———. *Gregor von Tours (538–594): "Zehn Bücher Geschichte." Historiographie und Gesellschaftskonzept im 6. Jahrhundert* (Darmstadt: Wissenschaftliche Buchgesellschaft, 1994); trans. Christopher Carroll, *Gregory of Tours: History and Society in the Sixth Century* (Cambridge and New York: Cambridge University Press, 2001).

Hermanowicz, Erika T. *Possidius of Calama: A Study of the North African Episcopate at the Time of Augustine* (Oxford and New York: Oxford University Press, 2008).

Hevelone-Harper, Jennifer L. *Disciples of the Desert: Monks, Laity, and Spiritual Authority in Sixth-Century Gaza* (Baltimore: Johns Hopkins University Press, 2005).

Hirschfeld, Yizhar. *The Judean Desert Monasteries in the Byzantine Period* (New Haven, CT, and London: Yale University Press, 1992).

Holze, Heinrich. *Erfahrung und Theologie im frühen Mönchtum: Untersuchungen zu einer Theologie des monastischen Lebens bei den ägyptischen Mönchsvätern, Johannes Cassian und Benedikt von Nursia* (Göttingen: Vandenhoeck & Ruprecht, 1992).

Honoré, Jean, Michel Laurencin, and Guy-Marie Oury, eds. *Saint Martin de Tours: XVIe centenaire* (Chambray: C. L. D., 1996).

Howard-Johnston, James, and Paul Antony Hayward, eds. *The Cult of Saints in Late Antiquity and the Early Middle Ages: Essays on the Contribution of Peter Brown* (Oxford: Oxford University Press, 1999).

Humphries, Mark. *Communities of the Blessed: Social Environment and Religious Change in Northern Italy, AD 200–400* (Oxford and New York: Oxford University Press, 1999).

Hunter, David G. *Marriage, Celibacy, and Heresy in Ancient Christianity: The Jovinianist Controversy* (Oxford and New York: Oxford University Press, 2007).

Kelly, J. N. D. *Golden Mouth: The Story of John Chrysostom—Ascetic, Preacher, Bishop* (London: Duckworth, 1995).

Klingshirn, William E. *Caesarius of Arles: The Making of a Christian Community in Late Antique Gaul* (Cambridge: Cambridge University Press, 1994).

Krawiec, Rebecca. *Shenoute and the Women of the White Monastery: Egyptian Monasticism in Late Antiquity* (Oxford and New York: Oxford University Press, 2002).

Krueger, Derek. *Writing and Holiness: The Practice of Authorship in the Early Christian East* (Philadelphia: University of Pennsylvania Press, 2004).

Leyser, Conrad. *Authority and Asceticism from Augustine to Gregory the Great* (Oxford: Clarendon Press; Oxford and New York: Oxford University Press, 2000).

Lizzi, Rita. "Ambrose's Contemporaries and the Christianization of Northern Italy," *Journal of Roman Studies* 80 (1990): 156–73.

———. "The Bishop, 'Vir Venerabilis': Fiscal Privileges and 'Status' Definition in Late Antiquity," *Studia Patristica* 34 (2001): 125–44.

———. *Il potere episcopale nell'Oriente romano: rappresentazione ideologica e realtà politica (IV–V secolo d. C.)* (Rome: Edizioni dell'Ateneo, 1987).

———. *Vescovi e strutture ecclesiastiche nell città tardoantica: l'Italia Annonaria nel IV–V secolo d. C.* (Como: New Press, 1989).

Lizzi Testa, Rita. *Senatori, popolo, papi: il governa di Roma al tempo dei Valentiniani* (Bari: Edipuglia, 2004).

———, ed. *Le Trasformazioni delle élites in età tardoantica* (Rome: Bretschneider, 2006).

Markus, Robert A. *The End of Ancient Christianity* (Cambridge and New York: Cambridge University Press, 1990).

———. *Gregory the Great and His World* (Cambridge and New York: Cambridge University Press, 1997).

Martin, Annik. *Athanase d'Alexandrie et l'église d'Égypte au IVe siècle* (Rome: École Française de Rome, 1996).

Martin, Dale B., and Patricia Cox Miller, eds. *The Cultural Turn in Late Ancient Studies: Gender, Asceticism, and Historiography* (Durham, NC: Duke University Press, 2006).

Mathisen, Ralph W. *Ecclesiastical Factionalism and Religious Controversy in Fifth-Century Gaul* (Washington, DC: Catholic University of America Press, 1989).

———. *Roman Aristocrats in Barbarian Gaul: Strategies for Survival in an Age of Transition* (Austin: University of Texas Press, 1993).

Mayer, Wendy. *The Homilies of St John Chrysostom, Provenance: Reshaping the Foundations* (Rome: Pontificio Istituto Orientale, 2005).

Mayer, Wendy, and Pauline Allen. *John Chrysostom* (London and New York: Routledge, 2000).

McGuckin, John Anthony. *St Gregory of Nazianzus: An Intellectual Biography* (Crestwood, NY: St Vladimir's Seminary Press, 2001).

McLynn, Neil. *Ambrose of Milan: Church and Court in a Christian Capital* (Berkeley and Los Angeles: University of California Press, 1994).

———. "Among the Hellenists: Gregory and the Sophists," in Børtnes and Hägg, eds., *Gregory of Nazianzus,* 213–38.

Millar, Fergus. *A Greek Roman Empire: Power and Belief under Theodosius II (408–450)* (Berkeley and Los Angeles: University of California Press, 2006).

Miller, Patricia Cox. "Desert Asceticism and 'The Body from Nowhere,'" *Journal of Early Christian Studies* 2 (1994): 137–53.

———. "Jerome's Centaur: A Hyper-Icon of the Desert," *Journal of Early Christian Studies* 4 (1996): 209–33.

Opelt, Ilona. *Hieronymus' Streitschriften* (Heidelberg: C. Winter, 1973).

———. *Die Polemik in der christlichen lateinischen Literatur von Tertullian bis Augustin* (Heidelberg: C. Winter, 1980).

Patlagean, Evelyne. "Ancienne hagiographie byzantine et histoire sociale," *Annales* 23 (1968): 106–26; trans. Jane Hodgkin in Stephen Wilson, ed., *Saints and Their Cults* (Cambridge and New York: Cambridge University Press, 1983), 101–21.

Patrich, Joseph. *Sabas, Leader of Palestinian Monasticism: A Comparative Study in Eastern Monasticism, Fourth to Seventh Centuries* (Washington, DC: Dumbarton Oaks Research Library and Collection, 1995).

Rapp, Claudia. *Holy Bishops in Late Antiquity: The Nature of Christian Leadership in an Age of Transition* (Berkeley and Los Angeles: University of California Press, 2005).

Rebenich, Stefan. *Hieronymus und sein Kreis: Prosopographische und sozialgeschichtliche Untersuchungen* (Stuttgart: Steiner, 1992).

Rebillard, Éric, and Claire Sotinel, eds. *L'Évêque dans la cité du IVe au Ve siècle: image et autorité* (Rome, 1998).

Rousseau, Philip. "Antony as Teacher in the Greek Life," in Tomas Hägg and Philip Rousseau, eds., *Greek Biography and Panegyric in Late Antiquity* (Berkeley and Los Angeles: University of California Press, 2000), 89–109.

———. "Ascetics as Mediators and as Teachers," in Howard-Johnston and Hayward, eds., *Cult of Saints,* 45–59.

———. "Augustine and Ambrose: The Loyalty and Single-Mindedness of a Disciple," *Augustiniana* 27 (1977): 151–65.

———. *Basil of Caesarea* (Berkeley and Los Angeles: University of California Press, 1994).

———. "Blood-Relationships among Early Eastern Ascetics," *Journal of Theological Studies* 23 (1972): 135–44.

———. "Cassian, Contemplation, and the Coenobitic Life," *Journal of Ecclesiastical History* 26 (1975): 113–26.

———. "Cassian: Monastery and World," in Miles Fairburn and W. H. Oliver, eds., *The Certainty of Doubt: Tributes to Peter Munz* (Wellington: University of Victoria Press, 1996), 68–89.

———. "Cassian's Apophthegmata," *Jahrbuch für Antike und Christentum* 48 (2005): 19–34.

———. "Christian Asceticism and the Early Monks," in Ian Hazlett, ed., *Early Christianity: Origins and Evolution to AD 600* (London: SPCK, 1990), 112–22.

———. "Christian Culture and the Swine's Husks: Jerome, Augustine, and Paulinus," in William E. Klingshirn and Mark Vessey, eds., *The Limits of Ancient Christianity: Essays on Late Antique Thought and Culture in Honor of R. A. Markus* (Ann Arbor: University of Michigan Press, 1999), 172–87.

———. "The Desert Fathers and Their Broader Audience," in Alberto Camplani and Giovanni Filoramo, eds., *Foundations of Power and Conflicts of Authority in Late-Antique Monasticism* (Louvain: Peeters, 2007), 89–107.

———. "The Desert Fathers: Antony and Pachomius," in Cheslyn Jones, Geoffrey Wainwright, and Edward Yarnold, eds., *The Study of Spirituality* (London: SPCK, 1986), 119–30.

———. "Eccentrics and Coenobites in the Late Roman East," in Lynda Garland, ed., *Conformity and Non-Conformity in Byzantium* = *Byzantinische Forschungen* 24 (1997): 35–50.

———. "The Exegete as Historian: Hilary of Poitiers' *Commentary on Matthew*," in Brian Croke and Alanna M. Emmett, eds., *History and Historians in Late Antiquity* (Sydney: Pergamon Press, 1983), 107–15.

———. "The Formation of Early Ascetic Communities: Some Further Reflections," *Journal of Theological Studies* 25 (1974): 113–17.

———. "The Historiography of Asceticism: Current Achievements and Future Opportunities," in Carole Straw and Richard Lim, eds., *The Past Before Us: The Challenge of Historiographies in Late Antiquity* (Turnhout: Brepols, 2004), 89–101.

———. "The Identity of the Ascetic Master in the *Historia Religiosa* of Theodoret of Cyrrhus: A New *Paideia*?" *Mediterranean Archaeology* 11 (1998): 229–44.

———. "In Search of Sidonius the Bishop," *Historia* 25 (1976): 356–77.

———. "Jerome: His Failures and Their Importance," in Gordon Harper and James Veitch, eds., *The Heritage of Christian Thought* (Wellington: Victoria University Press, 1979), 35–58.

———. "Jerome's Search for Self-Identity," in Pauline Allen, Raymond Canning, and Lawrence Cross, eds., *Prayer and Spirituality in the Early Church* (Everton Park, Queensland: Centre for Early Christian Studies, Australian Catholic University, 1998), 1:125–42.

———. "Knowing Theodoret: Text and Self," in Martin and Miller, eds., *The Cultural Turn in Late Ancient Studies,* 278–97.

———. "'Learned Women' and the Formation of a Christian Culture in Late Antiquity," *Symbolae Osloenses* 70 (1995): 116–47.

———. "Monasticism," in Averil Cameron, Bryan Ward-Perkins, and Michael Whitby, eds., *The Cambridge Ancient History,* vol. 14, new ed. (Cambridge: Cambridge University Press, 2000), 745–80.

———. "Moses, Monks, and Mountains in Theodoret's *Historia religiosa,*" in Maciej Bielawski and Daniël Hombergen, eds., *Il Monachesimo tra Eredità e Aperture* (Rome: Centro Studi S. Anselmo, 2004), 323–46.

———. "Orthodoxy and the Coenobite," *Studia Patristica* 30 (1997): 241–58.

———. *Pachomius: The Making of a Community in Fourth-Century Egypt* (Berkeley and Los Angeles: University of California Press, 1985). Paperback edition, with a new introduction, 1999.

———. "'The Preacher's Audience': A More Optimistic View," in T. W. Hillard, R. A. Kearsley, C. E. V. Nixon, and A. M. Nobbs, eds., *Ancient History in a Modern University*, vol. 2: *Early Christianity, Late Antiquity and Beyond* (Grand Rapids, MI: Eerdmans, 1998), 391–400.

———. "The Spiritual Authority of the 'Monk-Bishop': Eastern Elements in Some Western Hagiography of the Fourth and Fifth Centuries," *Journal of Theological Studies* 22 (1971): 380–419.

———. "The Successors of Pachomius and the Nag Hammadi Library: Exegetical Themes and Literary Interpretations," in James E. Goehring and Janet A. Timbie, eds., *The World of Early Egyptian Christianity: Language, Literature, and Social Context* (Washington, DC: Catholic University of America Press, 2007), 140–57.

Rousselle, Aline. *Croire et guérir: La Foi en Gaule dans l'antiquité tardive* (Paris: Fayard, 1990).

Rubenson, Samuel. *The Letters of St Antony: Monasticism and the Making of a Saint* (Minneapolis: Fortress Press, 1995).

Schroeder, Caroline T. *Monastic Bodies: Discipline and Salvation in Shenoute of Atripe* (Philadelphia: University of Pennsylvania Press, 2007).

Sotinel, Claire. "Les Évêques italiens dans la société de l'antiquité tardive: l'émergence d'une nouvelle élite?" in Lizzi Testa, ed., *Trasformazioni delle élites*, 377–404.

———. *Identité civique et christianisme: Aquilée du IIIe au Vie siècle* (Rome: École Française de Rome, 2005).

Stancliffe, Clare. *St Martin and His Hagiographer: History and Miracle in Sulpicius Severus* (Oxford: Clarendon Press; New York: Oxford University Press, 1983).

Sterk, Andrea. *Renouncing the World Yet Leading the Church: The Monk-Bishop in Late Antiquity* (Cambridge, MA: Harvard University Press, 2004).

Stewart, Columba. *Cassian the Monk* (New York: Oxford University Press, 1998).

———. *"Working the Earth of the Heart": The Messalian Controversy in History, Texts, and Language to A.D. 431* (Oxford: Clarendon Press; New York: Oxford University Press, 1991).

Straw, Carole. *Gregory the Great: Perfection in Imperfection* (Berkeley and Los Angeles: University of California Press, 1988).

Summa, Gerd. *Geistliche Unterscheidung bei Johannes Cassian* (Würzburg: Echter, 1992).

Timbie, Janet. "The State of Research on the Career of Shenoute of Atripe," in Birger A. Pearson and James E. Goehring, eds., *The Roots of Egyptian Christianity* (Philadelphia: Fortress Press, 1986), 258–70.

Trout, Dennis E. *Paulinus of Nola: Life, Letters, and Poems* (Berkeley and Los Angeles: University of California Press, 1999).

Utas, Bo. "Mānistān and Xānaqāh," in Jacques Duchesne-Guillemin and Pierre Lecoq, eds., *Papers in Honour of Professor Mary Boyce* (Leiden: Brill, 1985), 655–64.

Van Dam, Raymond. *Becoming Christian: The Conversion of Roman Cappadocia* (Philadelphia: University of Pennsylvania Press, 2003).

———. *Families and Friends in Late Roman Cappadocia* (Philadelphia: University of Pennsylvania Press, 2003).

———. *Kingdom of Snow: Roman Rule and Greek Culture in Cappadocia* (Philadelphia: University of Pennsylvania Press, 2002).

———. *Leadership and Community in Late Antique Gaul* (Berkeley and Los Angeles: University of California Press, 1985).

Vessey, Mark. *Christian Latin Writers in Late Antiquity and Their Texts* (Aldershot and Burlington, VT: Ashgate, 2005).

Von Campenhausen, Hans. *Kirchliches Amt und geistliche Vollmacht in den ersten drei Jahrhunderten* (Tübingen: Mohr, 1953).

Wessel, Susan. *Leo the Great and the Spiritual Rebuilding of a Universal Rome* (Leiden and Boston: Brill, 2008).

Williams, Megan H. *The Monk and the Book: Jerome and the Making of Christian Scholarship* (Chicago: University of Chicago Press, 2006).

Wipszycka, Ewa. *Études sur le christianisme dans l'Égypte de l'antiquité tardive* (Rome: Institutum Patristicum Augustinianum, 1996).

———. "The Institutional Church," in Bagnall, ed., *Egypt in the Byzantine World,* 331–49.

———. *Moines et communautés monastiques en Égypte, IVe–VIIIe siècles* (Warsaw: Journal of Juristic Papyrology, 2008).

———. "Le Monachisme égyptien et les villes," *Textes et Mémoires Byzantines* 12 (1994): 1–44.

ABBREVIATIONS

The titles of secondary sources, and some of the primary texts, are noted in full when first cited; and all are documented fully in the Bibliography. Here I note, for convenience, the more frequent or obscure abbreviations. Those used in Appendices II and III are explained *in situ.*

AB	*Analecta Bollandiana*
Ascet.	Esaias of Scetis, *Asceticon*, ed. Draguet
BLE	*Bulletin de Littérature Ecclésiastique*
BZ	*Byzantinische Zeitschrift*
Catech.	Either Pachomius, *Catéchèse à propos d'un moine rancunier*, or Theodore, *Catéchèses*; both trans. Lefort
CC	*Corpus Christianorum*
CIL	*Corpus Inscriptionum Latinarum*
Cod. Theod.	*Codex Theodosianus*
Con.	Cassian, *Conferences*, ed. Petschenig
CQ	*Classical Quarterly*
CR	*Académie des Inscriptions et Belles-Lettres, Comptes-Rendus*
CSCO	*Corpus Scriptorum Christianorum Orientalium*
CSEL	*Corpus Scriptorum Ecclesiasticorum Latinorum*
DAGL	*Dictionnaire d'Archéologie Chrétienne et de Liturgie*
De Inc.	Cassian, *De Incarnatione*, ed. Petschenig
DHGE	*Dictionnaire d'Histoire et de Géographie Ecclésiastique*
Dial.	Sulpicius, *Dialogues*, ed. Halm
EHR	*English Historical Review*
G	Greek *Apophthegmata Patrum* (*PG* lxv. 72-440), arranged in (Greek) alphabetical order of ascetics
HE	Various authors, *Historia Ecclesiastica*
HL	Palladius, *Lausiac History*, ed. Butler
HM	*Historia Monachorum in Aegypto.* Latin text (*PL* xxi. 387–462) referred to thus: ix, 422A. Greek text (ed. Festugière) referred to thus: x. 2.
Inst.	Cassian, *Institutes*, ed. Petschenig
JEH	*Journal of Ecclesiastical History*
JRS	*Journal of Roman Studies*
JTS	*Journal of Theological Studies*

MGH	*Monumenta Germaniae Historica*
Nau	Anonymous Greek apophthegmata, ed. Nau (*ROC*, 1908–13)
OCA	*Orientalia Christiana Analecta*
OCP	*Orientalia Christiana Periodica*
PG	*Patrologia Graeca*, ed. Migne
PL	*Patrologia Latina*, ed. Migne
RAM	*Revue d'Ascètique et de Mystique* (later *RHS*)
RB	*Revue Bénédictine*
REA	*Revue des Études Augustiniennes*
REL	*Revue des Études Latines*
RHE	*Revue d'Histoire Ecclésiastique*
RHEF	*Revue d'Histoire de l'Église de France*
RHR	*Revue d'Histoire des Religions*
RHS	*Revue d'Histoire de la Spiritualité* (formerly *RAM*)
RMAL	*Revue du Moyen Âge Latin*
ROC	*Revue de l'Orient Chrétien*
RSR	*Recherches de Science Religieuse*
RTAM	*Recherches de Théologie Ancienne et Médiévale*
V.	*Vita(e)*, as follows:
V. Amb.	Paulinus, *Vita Ambrosii*, ed. Pellegrino
V. Ant.	Athanasius, *Vita Antonii*, *PG* xxvi. 837–976
V. Aug.	Possidius, *Vita Augustini*, ed. Pellegrino
V. Hilar.	*Vita Hilarii*, ed. Cavallin
V. Mart.	Sulpicius, *Vita Martini*, ed. Fontaine
V. Pach.	*Vita(e) Pachomii*, as follows:
I, II, etc.	Greek lives (*Prima*, *Altera*, etc.), ed. Halkin
Bo	Bohairic life, trans. Lefort
S^1, S^2, etc.	Sahidic lives, trans. Lefort
Dion.	Dionysius Exiguus, Latin life, ed. van Cranenburgh
VC	*Vigiliae Christianae*
ZK	*Zeitschrift für Kirchengeschichte*

INTRODUCTION

This is a book that was in some ways written backwards: not as a search for roots, but as the exploration of a literary heritage, the ordered discovery of attitudes (above all on authority) gradually accumulated in the minds of Christians in the century after Constantine.

The book is about ascetics, but inquiry began with bishops, and Augustine in particular. What reputation could a man in his position acquire? What hold did he have over the imaginations of those who knew him, both living and after death? Hence an analysis of, among other things, hagiography: the life of Augustine by Possidius, but also, for comparison, those of other bishops—of Ambrose by Paulinus of Milan and, most important of all, the skilful and enduring biography of Martin of Tours by Sulpicius, his disciple.

Reading this last work, two features demanded attention, throwing light on the influence of bishops, but pointing the way also to what became the central concern of the book. First, there was a marked emphasis on Martin's ascetic aspirations, and on his specifically monastic endeavours (part of a forceful attempt, on the part of Sulpicius, to imply that an ascetic quality in Martin greatly influenced the development and success of his episcopal career). Second, the *Life*, coupled with Sulpicius's *Dialogues*, stood out as a literary masterpiece, not only destined but designed to impress upon a wider audience, both in his own and subsequent generations, the otherwise restricted influence of a relatively isolated churchman. Literary forms, in other words, (for the same observation applied to other *Vitae*, such as those by Athanasius and Jerome,) were being used to strengthen the effect of ascetic personality. The fruits of these reflections, as far as Martin and Sulpicius are concerned, will be found in Part Four.

So it became necessary to inquire further into the monastic life that had nurtured these men. Study of the *Life of Martin*, and some investigation into its later influence, pointed forward to the fact that many bishops in Gaul, during the fifth century, had been products of a monastic environment, not least that of Lérins and other communities in Marseille. This prompted a reading of Cassian, whose works (or at least ideas), it seemed just to suppose, would have provided an essential element in their formation. Impressions gained from Cassian's work are defended in Part Five. In spite of his praise of the eremitic life, in both *Institutes* and *Conferences*, he seemed to be at heart a coenobite: to advocate a spirituality and a monastic discipline that both reflected and encouraged the coenobitic life. Moreover, his comments on the non-monastic world, and on the clergy and episcopate, seemed to leave room for a link between the hopes and ideals of the monk—in particular, his conception of authority and discipline—and the pastoral opportunities offered by the church as a whole. Examples of monk-bishops in Cassian's lifetime, such as Rusticus of Narbonne and Honoratus of Lérins, did nothing to belie this impression (and linked the Gaul of Cassian, in some way, with that of Sulpicius), and it was supported further by his own readiness to enter a wider arena of controversy and pastoral concern—in his Thirteenth Conference on the issue of freedom and grace, and in the *De Incarnatione* against Nestorius. Finally, it became clear that, while he appeared to reproduce the intimate instruction of ascetic masters, delivered to a small circle of disciples, Cassian did so in a literary form, calculated to exert a more impersonal influence upon those who read his works, and in this respect he appeared as a link between the charismatic but transitory influence of the desert father and the greater rigidity of later monastic rules. Here was another species of literary enterprise to place beside that of Sulpicius.

Cassian emphasizes respect for tradition; and he points to his fidelity to the practice and principles of the first ascetics in support of his own opinion. Reading Cassian, therefore, one is inevitably led back to Egypt, where he had received much of his ascetic training. In the biographies of Antony and Pachomius, but above all in the *Apophthegmata Patrum*, features of the ascetic life were revealed similar to those already detected in the pages of Sulpicius and Cassian—

indeed, they suggested themselves as the explanation of much that followed. The sayings of the fathers showed a particular species of authority being exercised and obeyed; and eastern *Vitae* (together with more formal material, such as the rules of Pachomius) applied the same discipline to a wider audience and during a longer period, with more impersonal effect. There was a development, anticipating that in Cassian, away from the solitary towards the coenobitic life; increasing discussion about the authority of ascetic masters, and about the obedience and sense of tradition which that authority demanded; a growing involvement in the pastoral life of the church; and a flourishing literary tradition that soon began to acquire an authority of its own. The literature presented particular problems—problems of chronology in general, of reliability, and of the relations between the Greek and Coptic cultures represented by different texts. Judgement on this literary issue is included in an Appendix, and in the opening sections of Part One, which then goes on to study more fully the asceticism of the desert.

Although Cassian reflected this eastern world, and carried forward many of the developments initiated in Egypt, the link between them, between Egypt and Gaul, was neither direct nor immediate in time. Even Sulpicius, inspired by the *Life of Antony*, and acquainted (through the reports of pilgrims) with ascetic traditions in the East, had inherited many religious attitudes that were in some sense western. It was necessary to offer, therefore, a survey of asceticism in the West that covered the period between the first arrival of ascetic information from Egypt (perhaps during the exile of Athanasius in 339; certainly in the Latin translations of his *Life of Antony*, made about 370) and the death, in 397, of Martin of Tours. Such a survey would provide some explanation of the spread and popularity of ascetic literature in the West during the fourth century, and provide a background to the episcopal careers, not only of Martin himself, but also of Ambrose, Augustine, and other contemporaries. Hence Part Two.

This intervening period possessed, in addition, a dominating figure, Jerome, whose ascetic interest, clerical ambition, commanding capacity for criticism, and literary prowess seemed to reveal, again, the qualities discovered in Egypt and Gaul. But Jerome does more than sum up or exemplify ascetic developments in the second half of the fourth century: he had gained experience in both East and West. Converted at Trier, an admirer of Hilary, he lived with the monks of Syria and Palestine, and corresponded with contemporaries of Cassian. His career provides the material for Part Three.

Having worked backwards from Gaul to Egypt, a chronological presentation of the actual argument seemed possible: an exploration among desert ascetics (during the middle years of the fourth century in particular); a brief survey of asceticism in the western church until about 400; a selective study of Jerome; and then, moving into the fifth century, a reading of Sulpicius and Cassian. In this way the book offers comment on certain changes: the eventual triumph of the coenobitic movement, and its growing effect within the church, not least on the episcopate. But attention is focused chiefly on the development among ascetics of a certain concept of spiritual authority; on the attraction of that concept (as of asceticism generally) for a wider audience; and on its enduring formulation within a literary tradition of great influence.

The book had to remain, therefore, an essay in interpretation, rather than narrative history. The full story of events is not pursued in any one period or area. For example, the reader will part company with the history of asceticism in Egypt at the end of the fourth century, although its development continued, and its influence remained important. Several features of Jerome's life are referred to only in passing, and his influence after about 410, both as a monastic pioneer and as a scriptural commentator, is almost completely ignored. The cult of Martin is not examined, nor any documentation provided on the longterm influence of Sulpicius's *Life*. Even in the case of Cassian, with whom the book ends, his influence on the fifth-century monk-bishops of Gaul is described only in the briefest terms.

There were good reasons for adopting this structure in the argument; and they should provide a compensating unity and purpose. As far as logical sequence is concerned, and ease of comprehension, the 'steps sideways' from one line of historical development to the next—from the desert to Hilary and Jerome, from Jerome to Sulpicius, from Sulpicius to Cassian—are timed in such a way, it is hoped, that the suggested links are real in historical terms, while continuity is described and defended. The central theme demands nothing less: it concerns a development within ascetic society (and within the church) that does seem to have cut obliquely across the course of the century; and it was necessary to emphasize the real connection, established with remarkable speed, between ascetic authority in the desert and episcopal authority in Gaul. Once that central thread has been grasped, the examples that serve to plot its course can also point sideways, in a sense, to particular areas of historical investigation not pursued in detail here—especially in the individual careers of, say, Ambrose, Basil, or Chrysostom. The conclusions attempt, therefore, to offer the historian a perspective and a method of analysis that will enable him, in ways suggested in the Epilogue, to return over the same ground, studying in more circumscribed fashion the bishops and ascetics of the period.

When completing an enterprise of this nature, there are many debts one may gladly acknowledge. The book began as a doctoral thesis in the University of Oxford; and I owe a great deal, therefore, to my supervisor, Professor Peter Brown. His enthusiasm has always been infectious, his knowledge ground for admiration, but also for confidence, his patience humbling, and his criticism a constant safeguard and reward. He has continued to assist in the work of revision, seconded by the kindness of the Editors of the Oxford Historical Monographs, especially Miss Barbara Harvey.

I would like to record also the advice and encouragement of the Very Revd. Dr. Henry Chadwick, the Revd. Dr. John Halliburton, Miss E. A. Livingstone, Dr. J. F. Matthews, Mme Evelyne Patlagean, Dr. Geza Vermes, Professor J. M. Wallace-Hadrill, and the Revd. Dr. Kallistos Ware. The staff and resources of the Bodleian Library were an indispensable delight. I received much kindness and support also from my colleges, Campion Hall and Wolfson College; and to the last I am grateful for a graduate scholarship.

Finally, I must thank the University of Auckland for allowing me time in Oxford to complete the original thesis, and in particular my colleague Dr. Valerie Flint, who shouldered meanwhile my teaching commitments, and has remained a lasting source of encouragement and perception.

PART ONE

THE DESERT

I

DISCOVERING THE DESERT FATHERS

1. CONTEMPORARY JUDGEMENTS

Not a few men of the fourth and fifth centuries, balanced in their judgement, experienced either in government or in letters, viewed with anxiety, if not disgust, the public progress and effect of the monastic movement. To ignore it was impossible. Gibbon may exaggerate, but does not entirely falsify, the verdict of the age:

> The freedom of the mind, the source of every generous and rational sentiment, was destroyed by the habits of credulity and submission; and the monk, contracting the vices of a slave, devoutly followed the faith and passion of his ecclesiastical tyrant. The peace of the Eastern church was invaded by a swarm of fanatics, incapable of fear, or reason, or humanity; and the Imperial troops acknowledged, without shame, that they were much less apprehensive of an encounter with the fiercest Barbarian.[1]

An obedience based on faith, and an influence based on reputation: such were the chief characteristics, and (in the eyes of some) the dangers, of the ascetic life. Gibbon may have been indignant and disdainful: contemporaries like Eunapius of Sardis could be more harsh, and more precise:

> At that time they brought into the holy places so-called monks: men by all appearances, though they lived like pigs; and they openly tolerated, and indeed executed, evil deeds past number or description. Yet it was seen as a work of piety to despise the divine: for any man at that time dressed in black, and ready to demean himself in public, possessed a tyrannical power. Such was the depth to which human virtue had declined.[2]

'Tyrannical power', τυραννικὴ ἐξουσία: with this phrase, Eunapius identified a key element in the ascetic movement, perhaps in the more general triumph of Christianity itself—the growing reputation of the monk as a man of public

[1] Edward Gibbon, *Decline and Fall of the Roman Empire*, ch. XXXVII, ed. J. B. Bury, iv. 66.

[2] Eunapius, *Vitae Sophistarum*, vi (Aedesius). 11.

authority. Eunapius was making a specific comment on what he would have regarded as an illegal liberty, the liberty that enabled monks to destroy the temples of the pagans; but he could not have overlooked the common background of toleration, if not of admiring encouragement, that made such demonstrations possible. Nor was he alone. The great Libanius of Antioch displayed a more polished but no less deep hatred of Christian ascetics—not only because they attacked the practices and venues of pagan cult, but also because they appeared to reject that prized inheritance of the classical tradition, the culture, commerce, and government of cities.[3] For different reasons, Christian emperors betrayed anxieties of their own. Despite his undoubted approval of the destruction of the Serapaeum, probably the greatest pagan shrine in Egypt, and his comprehensive legislation against the pagan cult throughout that province,[4] the Emperor Theodosius felt it necessary to counteract the violent and often illegal activities of monks by banning them altogether from its town and cities.[5] His son, and successor in the East, Arcadius, attacked monks for harbouring criminals, and sought to bring them more closely under the control of their bishops.[6]

Neither pagan criticism nor Christian legislation achieved much success. Quite apart from their weakness in the face of anti-pagan riots, they offered no weapon against the pressure of ascetic mobs that forced the patriarch of Alexandria, Theophilus, to repudiate in 399 the theology of Origen, thus initiating a policy of persecution and exile that did much, as we shall see, to spread ascetic ideals to other parts of the empire. Nor, in the wider sphere of civil affairs, could they resist the tyranny of the Patriarch Cyril, his successor, who must bear greatest responsibility for the famous attack on the Prefect Orestes in 416, and the subsequent murder of the Neoplatonist philosopher and mathematician Hypatia—

[3] See especially Libanius, *Or.* xxx. 8 (*Pro Templis*). Both references and context are excellently described in Paul Petit, *Libanius et la vie municipale à Antioche* (Paris, 1955), 191–216. See also Ammianus Marcellinus, XXII. xi. 7 f.; xvi. 12, 23; Sozom. *Hist. eccl.* VI. xxvii. 10.

[4] *Cod. Theod.* XVI. x. 11.

[5] Ibid. XVI. iii. 1—quickly rescinded, it is true: XVI. iii. 2.

[6] Ibid. IX. xl. 16; xlv. 3; XVI. ii. 32.

events in which ascetic henchmen were undoubtedly involved.[7]

In the face of events like these, even limited to Egypt, one is drawn to repeat with more sympathy, or at least more curiosity, the words of Eunapius—*τυραννικὴ ἐξουσία.* 'Without approving the malice, it is natural enough to share the surprise, of the Sophist'.[8] A new interpretation of power, both social and religious, was beginning, it would seem, to gain acceptance, designed to enforce change and capture loyalty: and its roots and development demand investigation.

2. THE EVIDENCE TODAY

How is such investigation to proceed? While they appear to offer striking proof that monks were beginning to acquire a public role, a distinctive (in some eyes, alarming) authority in society at large, the sensational events recorded above were spasmodic, short-lived, and probably exceptional. They provide no more than a limited and possibly misleading account of the ascetic's desire to influence, and of his capacity to command, which reached, in fact, far beyond the seemingly anarchic power condemned by the contemporaries of Eunapius. The true home of ascetics was the desert still, above all the desert of Egypt: and it was within the desert communities of the Wadi Natrun and the Upper Nile that the full implications of spiritual authority in a much broader sense were first tested and expressed. After observing the flurry of mob violence or patriarchal favour, it is necessary to follow the monks, so to speak, on their journey home again, and to consult another body of evidence, more sympathetic and more detailed, which explains, in the context of their day-to-day lives, the enduring reputation for wisdom and leadership that many of them came to enjoy.

Here the historian has at his disposal a profusion of primary sources—of sayings, lives, and rules—that in themselves go far to explain the influence and popularity of the early monks. A striking feature of Egyptian asceticism in particular was the clear desire of ascetics themselves to communi-

[7] Socrates, *HE* vii. 13-15.

[8] Gibbon, *Decline and Fall*, ch. XXVIII, ed. Bury, iii. 208.

cate: to explain and defend their ideals, to praise their founders and heroes, and to prompt the admiring imitation of fellow Christians. Early ascetic literature has, as a consequence, an urgency of tone and seemingly immediate narrative quality that does much to account for its undoubted charm. Yet this same combination of personal reminiscence and religious propaganda presents the historian of the monastic movement with his chief difficulty and most pressing task. Ascetic writers recognized (and were often overcome by) the temptation to create an image, either of a person or of a pattern of life, that tended to be anachronistic or tendentious.[9] Less calculated in itself (but perhaps more dangerous to the historian, no matter how critical) was the ability of later editors and compilers to obscure, by alterations and additions, the different layers of source material built up during decades, if not centuries, of development within any one corpus of traditional teaching and narrative. The first, more conscious, distortion is found most in works of biography, while the second affected more the development of monastic rules, and of collections of apophthegmata; but both types of literature were exposed to either danger.

In spite of these pitfalls, there is little doubt that, if he could interpret them correctly, the historian would gain his most reliable insight into fourth-century Egyptian monasticism from the so-called *Apophthegmata Patrum*, the 'Sayings of the Fathers'—a collection of short anecdotes in Greek, many of them statements attributed by name to famous ascetics of the period.

These texts attempt, above all, to describe and resolve problems of human relationships. They concentrate on the wisdom and spiritual energy that attracted ascetics one to another, and on the sanctions that held them together. Each entry, therefore, in this fascinating series captures the attention of the reader like the flash of a signalling lamp—brief, arresting, and intense. The message as a whole, however, has been jumbled in the process of transmission. How is accurate interpretation to be guaranteed? Most important of all, how can the reader be sure that, in any particular passage, he has

[9] François Halkin, *Sancti Pachomii Vitae Graecae* (Brussels, 1932) 100 f.

touched upon more primitive and original layers of the collection?[10]

The persons named in one or another anecdote may provide initial guidance. Macarius the Egyptian, for example, is known to have lived in the fourth century; and stories referring to him may therefore reveal the ascetic life of the period.[11] There are dangers here. Stories in general, both oral and written, can undergo change with the passage of time. They may become attached in particular to the names of different persons. This is especially true of the Greek *Apophthegmata*, in which the items are distributed in groups under the names of various ascetics, arranged in alphabetical order. Sayings and anecdotes that are in themselves, therefore, anonymous (and there are many) may easily have been placed with time under the wrong names.[12] The reader may to some extent protect himself against this danger by concentrating on those apophthegmata in which something is told of a man by one who is known to have been his disciple. The 'disciple generation' does provide a link between the great figures of the fourth or early fifth centuries and the first written compilations.[13]

A second possible criterion is style. Apophthegmata that are simple in structure and straightforward in their concern are likely to date from the earlier period of the ascetic movement, while more prolix examples of catechesis, homily, and

[10] Once a MS. tradition emerges, in the fifth and sixth centuries, the matter becomes relatively more simple, thanks to the guidance of W. Bousset, *Apophthegmata* (Tübingen, 1923), and J.-C. Guy, *Recherches sur la tradition grecque des Apophthegmata Patrum* (Brussels, 1962). The difficulties raised in this chapter, as in the book as a whole, refer to the period before that MS. tradition was established, when oral accounts were beginning to acquire a written form.

[11] Bousset identified the various groups and generations in the early sections of the text, *Apophthegmata*, 61–4.

[12] e.g. *Apophthegmata Patrum*, Macarius Aegyptus 28 and 37: both give the account of one Paphnutius, the name given by Palladius to a disciple of Macarius of Alexandria (i.e. not Macarius the Egyptian), *HL* xviii. The many confusions possible become most clear when comparison is made between Greek and Latin collections of apophthegmata (about which more is said below). The Greek *Apophthegmata Patrum* (referred to henceforward as G) are in *PG* lxv. 72–440.

[13] Greater confidence may therefore be placed in stories about Arsenius, for example, told by his disciple Daniel: G Arsenius, 14, 17–19, 23, 26, 29, 33, 35, 39, 42–3, Agathon 28, Daniel 6–7, Poemen 138. For other important disciples who played this role, see Bousset, *Apophthegmata*, 65.

spiritual direction would seem to be the results of later development.[14] One immediate difficulty here is that literature associated with Pachomius and his followers, and perhaps also the work of Cassian, suggest that quite long discourses had their place in earlier times.[15]

There is a third and more reliable method of historical judgement: a comparison of the alphabetical collection of apophthegmata in Greek with the systematic compilation translated into Latin by the Roman clerics Pelagius and John towards the middle of the sixth century.[16] This comparison reveals what parts of the Greek collection were in existence at the time, and probably for a period before that date. To this relatively early corpus may be added a large part of the anonymous apophthegmata published at the beginning of this century,[17] and the even more certainly primitive collection attributed to Esaias of Scetis, or closely associated with the texts that bear his name.[18] Evidence acquired by this third method must command the greater respect; but a careful use can sometimes be made of the first or second.

The *Life of Antony*, attributed to the great patriarch of Alexandria, Athanasius, is known to have been written in the

[14] J.-C. Guy, 'Remarques sur le texte des Apophthegmata Patrum', *RSR* xliii (1955), 252-8. Bousset appealed to the same general criterion, *Apophthegmata*, 78-82.

[15] Guy suggests that the apophthegmata we possess would have become useful to a wider public, so to speak, only in the context of more lengthy teaching or discussion, 'Remarques', 254 f. The Greek apophthegma Nau 211 (see n. 17) shows that longer instruction was acceptable in semi-eremitic circles. There are references to longer conferences in *V. Pach.* I, 17, 25, 74, 77, 88. This general point is not undermined by instances where long texts appear to derive from (and therefore postdate) shorter apophthegmata – e.g. A. de Vogüé, 'L'anecdote pachômienne du "Vaticanus graecus" 2091. Son origine et ses sources', *RHS* xlix (1973), 407, 413.

[16] *Vitae Patrum*, V *in toto* and VI, i-iv, *PL* lxxiii. 855-1022. For the principles governing the choice of texts and the numbering, see Guy, *Recherches*, 124, 199 f.

[17] Especially Nau 133-369 (for full references, see Bibliography under 'Apophthegmata'). For the principles governing the choice of this 'noyau primitif', as he called it, see Guy, *Recherches*, 79-82, 106-11.

[18] *Les cinq recensions de l'Ascéticon syriaque d'abba Isaie*, ed. and trans. R. Draguet (Louvain, 1968), referred to henceforward as (Esaias) *Ascet.* Draguet summarized his dating principles, by which he hoped to identify the original collection compiled by Peter, Esaias's disciple, in 'Notre édition des recensions syriaques de l'"Ascéticon" d'abba Isaie', *RHE* lxiii (1968), 843-57. The dating has been modified (but still restricted to the fifth century) by D. Chitty, 'Abba Isaiah', *JTS*, n.s. xxii (1971), 47-72.

middle of the fourth century.[19] Even if this portrait of Antony lacked some historical accuracy,[20] the work would demand attention because of its undoubted later influence.[21] The *Life* does, however, bear more useful and immediate witness to the ascetic practice of Antony's day. By comparing the existing Greek text with fourth-century Latin translations, we can assure ourselves that this superb biography has retained for the most part its primitive form; and it is possible to distinguish history from propaganda partly by cross-reference to the *Apophthegmata Patrum*.[22]

Similar checks can be used to assess the value of the *Rule* of Pachomius and associated material,[23] and of the so-called

[19] *V. Ant., PG* xxvi. 837-976. The deciding events of importance, with their traditional dates, are the death of Antony (described in the text of the *Vita*), 356; the death of Athanasius, 373; the making of the first Latin translation, at an unknown date (but before the following); and the making of a translation by Jerome's friend, Evagrius of Antioch, *c.* 370. The full evidence is usefully rehearsed by L. W. Barnard, 'The Date of S. Athanasius' Vita Antonii', *VC* xxvii (1974), 169-75; but the response of B. R. Brennan is judicious and important, 'Dating Athanasius' Vita Antonii', *VC* xxx (1976), 52-4.

[20] Which need not necessarily be the case, even if the author of the work stood in a conscious literary tradition, part pagan, part Christian; and even if he had motives in writing that led him beyond mere narrative. The main points at issue can still be most usefully assessed by comparing K. Holl, 'Die schriftstellerische Form des griechischen Heiligenlebens', *Neuen Jahrbüchern für das klassische Altertum*, 1912, 406-27, and his critic R. Reitzenstein, 'Des Athanasius Werk über das Leben des Antonius., *Sitzungsberichte der Heidelberger Akademie der Wissenschaften*, phil.-hist. Klasse, V (1914), viii. Holl wished to safeguard the *Vita*'s Christian inspiration and effect: Reitzenstein was more impressed by the echoes of a classical and pagan past (and his argument is more detailed and compelling). Valuable additions to the debate have been made in more recent times by Hermann Dörries, 'Die Vita Antonii', *Nachrichten der Akademie der Wissenschaften in Göttingen*, phil.-hist. Klasse, 1949, 359-410; and A. Priessnig, 'Die biographische Form der Plotinvita des Porphyrios und das Antoniosleben des Athanasios', *BZ* lxiv (1971), 1-5.

[21] Discussed below, in Part Two.

[22] So Dörries, 'Die Vita Antonii'. Important variations will be discussed in the course of the chapters that follow. For the Latin translations, see (a) (for the earlier anonymous text) G. Garitte, *Un témoin important du texte de la vie de s. Antoine* (Brussels, 1939), whose text was taken into account by the more recent edition of H. Hoppenbrouwers, *La plus ancienne version latine de la vie de s. Antoine par s. Athanase* (Nijmegen, 1960); and (b) (for the translation by Evagrius) underneath the Greek text in *PG* (see n. 19).

[23] *Oeuvres de s. Pachôme et de ses disciples*, Coptic texts ed. and trans. L. Th. Lefort (Louvain, 1956); *Pachomiana Latina*, ed. A. Boon (Louvain, 1932), providing the various parts of the *Rule* of Pachomius, together with his letters, a letter of Theodore, and the *Liber* of Orsisius, all in the latin text of Jerome. H. Bacht,

Historia Monachorum in Aegypto.[24] There is no reason to suppose that Jerome's translation of the Pachomian corpus, made perhaps in 404,[25] is to any serious extent unfaithful or inaccurate.[26] In the same way, the fourth-century text of the *Historia Monachorum* can be laid bare with some confidence, if one refers to the translation made by Rufinus, the friend and later enemy of Jerome. The Greek version of this work has clearly undergone a development much more complex than that of the *Life of Antony*; and, while Greek may well have been the language of the original text, the Latin of Rufinus, easier to date, offers a more reliable witness to the fourth-century situation.[27]

The *Lausiac History*, written in about 420 by Palladius, then bishop of Helenopolis in Bithynia, needs to be handled with much greater care.[28] Palladius recounted events that

Das Vermächtnis des Ursprungs (Würzburg, 1972), offers a revised text of the *Liber*, with German trans. and commentary.

[24] Greek text ed. A.-J. Festugière, *Historia Monachorum in Aegypto* (Brussels, 1961); Latin text (the translation by Rufinus), *PL* xxi. 387–462. References henceforward will be to *HM* for both Latin (printed thus: ix, 422A) and Greek (printed thus: x. 2).

[25] Boon, *Pachomiana*, xlviii, following Cavallera.

[26] Attempts have been made to date, or at least to place in some chronological order, the various pieces collected by Jerome, particularly by A. Veilleux, *La liturgie dans le cénobitisme pachômien au quatrième siècle* (Rome, 1968), and in a series of articles by M. M. van Molle (see Bibliography). I have been swayed by the pessimism of A. de Vogüé, 'Les pièces latines du dossier pachômien. Remarques sur quelques publications récentes', *RHE* lxvii (1972), 26–67, and remain content to use the corpus as a whole as a witness to late fourth-century attitudes.

[27] Festugière has done most to argue for the priority of the Greek, not only in his edition, but also in 'Le problème littéraire de l'Historia Monachorum', *Hermes*, lxxxiii (1955), 257–84. The notes to his translation, *Les moines d'Orient*, iv, 1 (Paris, 1964), are also of interest. There are two particular difficulties about Festugière's analysis. Writing of those passages where Rufinus appears to have added to the Greek, he suggests that the Latin writer had before him a Greek text rather different from our own, 'Le problème', 267; but one needs to be sure that Rufinus did not compose these passages himself, thus meriting the statement of Jerome that he was the author of the work, *Ep.* cxxxiii. 3 (as mentioned by Festugière himself, 272). Second, the difference in the order of chapters between the Latin and Greek texts may point to the existence of Greek versions other than that known today; but are we sure that the existing Greek is in its original order? So the main point about priority may or may not be established; but Festugière's criticism of the Latin text, and his confidence in the existing Greek, are not always so acceptable. Further more detailed comments on the problem appear below.

[28] Cuthbert Butler, *The Lausiac History of Palladius* (2 vols., Cambridge, 1898, 1904). In my assessment of Palladius, I have almost always followed Butler, both in this work and in his *Palladiana* (Oxford, 1921), rather than E. Preuschen,

had occurred twenty years or more before.[29] A bishop since 400, he was placed as a writer in a new and entirely different setting: he drew up his account having lived through the condemnation of the works of Origen by Theophilus, patriarch of Alexandria, in 399, and having witnessed the trial and exile of John Chrysostom, patriarch of Constantinople, in 403-4—events that not only prompted bitter reflection but radically altered the pattern of his own life. Exactly the same considerations affect the interpretation of Cassian's work.[30] Both men represent, as we shall see, a more reflective stage in the development of ascetic literature, a more conscious attempt to capture allegiance and to influence the organization of the ascetic life; and, while it is possible to agree that the *Lausiac History* seems more balanced and more credible than the *Historia Monachorum*,[31] that is not to assume that the background of events and personalities were described by Palladius with greater accuracy.

It is the *Lives of Pachomius* that present the historian with his greatest problem in this field, especially the first two (in the order of their published form), the *Vita Prima* and the *Vita Altera*.[32] During the fourth and fifth centuries, the coenobitic life came to dominate all other forms of ascetic enterprise; and it is therefore vital, in a history of this development, that reference to more eremitic material (such as the *Apophthegmata Patrum* or the *Historia Monachorum*)

Palladius und Rufinus (Giessen, 1897), or R. Reitzenstein, *Historia Monachorum und Historia Lausiaca* (Göttingen, 1916). There is much valuable comment on the career of Palladius in E. D. Hunt, 'Palladius of Helenopolis', *JTS*, n.s. xxiv (1973), 456-80.

[29] Accepting Butler's approximate date of 420 for the composition of the work.

[30] Cassian also appears to have left Egypt after the condemnation of Origen in 399; and Palladius himself, in his *Dialogue on the Life of Saint John Chrysostom*, told of the role played by Cassian in the controversy over Chrysostom in 404. See further in Part Five.

[31] D. Chitty, *The Desert a City* (Oxford, 1966), 52.

[32] *Sancti Pachomii Vitae Graecae*, ed. Halkin. The Coptic lives were edited by L. Th. Lefort in 1925 (Bohairic) and 1933 (Sahidic)—full details are given in the Bibliography—; but, being unable to read Coptic, I have depended almost entirely on his French translations in *Les vies coptes de s. Pachôme et des premiers successeurs* (Louvain, 1943): it is these that are translated again, into English, throughout this book. Failure to make use of Coptic material was a grave shortcoming in my earlier essay, 'The Spiritual Authority of the "Monk-Bishop" ', *JTS*, n.s. xxii (1971), 380-419.

should be balanced by an appeal to these accounts of the founder of the coenobitic movement, and of his first disciples. As far as the Greek *Lives* are concerned, it is still possible to argue that the *Vita Prima* was the first.[33] But there is a Latin translation of a life of Pachomius, made by Dionysius Exiguus, which is closely associated with the Greek of the *Vita Altera*. This translation can be dated at least to the early sixth century (earlier, in other words, than the Latin apophthegmata of Pelagius and John), and, together with its Greek equivalent, it must be taken into account. Even if we suppose that the *Vita Prima* came first, traditional stories about Pachomius could have suffered more change between his death in 346 and the supposed compilation of the *Vita Prima* fifty years later than they need have done in the century or more that followed until the time of Dionysius.[34]

On the more vexed issue of which may lay claim to priority in time, Greek Lives or Coptic, criticism of those who supported the Coptic cause has often shown that they had yet to prove their case; but the Coptic documents seem to be winning the day, even if the matter is still in doubt.[35] The historian who ventures upon the field of battle when visibility is still a little poor must be content to find his bearings with the help of more obvious landmarks. It would be impossible to deny that some Coptic material reproduces early traditions, independent of the Greek corpus, and just as reliable as parts of the *Apophthegmata Patrum*. Certainly when Coptic, Greek, and Latin texts agree, we can with confidence suppose that we have stumbled upon reliable and primitive information.

[33] As did Chitty, 'Pachomian Sources Reconsidered', *JEH* v (1954), 38-77; and 'Pachomian Sources Once More', *Studia Patristica*, x (Berlin, 1970), 54-64. Chitty was responding to the arguments of Lefort; and Lefort made a reply (following Chitty's first article) in 'Les sources coptes pachômiennes', *Le Muséon*, lxvii (1954), 217-29.

[34] *La vie latine de s. Pachôme, traduite du grec par Denys le Petit,* ed. H. van Cranenburgh (Brussels, 1969). On the relation between Greek and Latin texts, see Appendix I.

[35] For further discussion, see Appendix I.

II

MASTERS AND DISCIPLES

1. THE DIALOGUE

What, then, do these sources tell us about the power of monks in fourth-century Egypt; about the growth and exercise of their authority and influence? To understand, indeed to sense, their power and attraction, one has only to observe the trust and reverence they were able to inspire. In the *Apophthegmata Patrum*, for example, men anxious to make progress in asceticism, or to become disciples in a more formal sense, ask acknowledged masters of the spiritual life questions of the greatest simplicity, reflecting their confidence that virtually anything their ἀββᾶς, or 'father', might say would be to their advantage. Εἰπέ μοι λόγον was their traditional request: 'Speak to me; some word, some phrase'. They refused to restrict the father's reply, either by the shortcomings of their own self-knowledge, or by the limits of any particular difficulty.[1] They asked questions that were also of considerable scope—'How may I be saved?'—trusting that the dialogue to follow would answer their deepest need.[2] By these general questions, they hoped to elicit an epitome of the master's teaching, to discover his favourite insight, summed up in a few words—'the personal resources of the spirit that each father had come to possess'.[3] They believed that, taken as a starting point, such brief statements

[1] G Arsenius 9, Macarius Aeg. 2, 34, Moses 6, Pistos, Sisoes 16; Esaias, *Ascet.* VI, 4Bh—this last, however, suggesting that questions of this type may have come at the end of a longer conversation, provoking a parting shot that would linger in the memory.

[2] G Euprepios 7; Nau 143. For less direct reference to salvation, see G Antony 3, Ammonas 1, 4, Biare 1, Cassian 5, Pambo 2; Nau 217, 223. For the wide significance of the question, 'How may I be saved?', see I. Hausherr, 'Spiritualité monacale et unité chrétienne', *OCA* cliii (1958), 18. *HM* ix, 423A, with its phrase, 'He begged to be given some commands, by the aid of which he might set out on the way of salvation', probably illustrates the type of situation in which such questions were asked.

[3] 'Das geistige Eigentum des Abbas', Bousset, *Apophthegmata*, 82.

(more often than not quotations from, or allusions to, the text of Scripture[4]) would inevitably lead them to further spiritual progress. Their attitude involved nothing less than a total surrender: 'Like sons bringing gifts to a loving father, each one offered his soul'.[5]

The same trust was shown in longer and more detailed conversation. Disciples asked for instruction, not only about the general principles of the spiritual life, but also about more particular courses of action.[6] They believed that their elders were men of insight, able to identify and describe their personal problems, and to propose for them suitable solutions. It was said of Paul, the disciple of Antony, that he saw the souls of his companions as clearly as their faces.[7] Far from inspiring fear, such formidable gifts encouraged candour. 'Each one asks about his *λογισμοί*, his secret thoughts, and the old men make their judgement'.[8] 'The man who will not reveal his thoughts finds them marshalled against him; but the man who speaks out with confidence before his fathers puts those thoughts to flight, and wins himself peace'.[9]

Finally, there was a widespread confidence in the worth of the father's own pattern of life. Men were curious, naturally, about the behaviour of well-known ascetics, and would travel great distances to admire it for themselves; but there was also a more serious-minded conviction that if one imitated others, if one modelled one's own life on theirs, one would arrive at a similar state of perfection: 'Just by remaining near him',

[4] Scripture as a source of authority: G Antony 3; Nau 217; *V. Pach.* I, 88; III, 42. The analysis of Scripture as a common method of instruction: G Arsenius 42, Zeno 4, Poemen 16, 50, 53, 60, 118, Hyperechius 1–2, 5; Esaias, *Ascet.* VI, 4Bf. On the availability of Scripture texts, G Gelasius 1 and most of the references given by Bousset, *Apophthegmata*, 82, n. 3, are of a late date; but earlier hints appear in G Serapion 2; Pachomius, *Praecepta*, 25, 82, 139–40; *Praecepta et Instituta*, 2; *Praecepta et Leges*, 7; Esaias, *Ascet.* X, 23, 54; XI, 68; *HL* xxi.

[5] *HM* vii, 411C.

[6] G Ares, Zacharias 3, John Colobos 19, Joseph of Panephysis 3–4, Motios 1, Poemen 8, 50, Pistamon; Nau 141, 202, 215, 324.

[7] G Paul the Simple 1; see also *HM* xiv, 433AB.

[8] Poemen S 2 (Guy, *Recherches*, 30). John of Lycopolis and Antony possessed this power of recognizing individual difficulties, *HM* i. 5; *V. Ant.* 88. See also G Ammonas 4, Cyrus, Nisteroos the Coenobite 2, Poemen 1; Nau 164, 195, 219; *HL* xviii, xix.

[9] Esaias, *Ascet.* XV, 76.

said one holy man of another, 'you will gain instruction'.[10] Their visible example was a lesson, in other words, as forceful as wisdom and spiritual insight.[11]

2. THE BASIS OF AUTHORITY

Such were the common attitudes displayed when ascetic masters were approached by their disciples. They persisted in Egypt throughout the fourth century, and were shared by men in a variety of situations. The earliest, more solitary heroes prompted precisely this trust and devotion. Antony, justly the most famous, flourished in the first decades of the century; born in about 251, his 'public life' as an ascetic began (after long preparation) in about 306; and he lived for another fifty years. During that period, although he never founded like Pachomius an extensive body of followers, many imitated his asceticism, and attracted their own disciples: Amoun of Nitria, for example, who died in 352, and Macarius the Egyptian, who settled in Scetis (the Wadi-el-Natrun) in about 330, although he lived through many more developments in the ascetic life, dying only in about 390. Scetis and Nitria (the latter with its attendant community of Kellia, the Cells, founded by Amoun in 338) grew throughout the century. Rufinus says 3,000 ascetics lived in Nitria in the 370s;[12] Palladius mentions 5,000 as the figure two decades later.[13] When Cassian was in Scetis, about this time, there were four separate congregations of ascetics.[14] Yet, in spite of this expansion, these communities never lost their eremitic quality, but continued to foster the traditional bond between men of wisdom and outstanding selfdenial and those eager to learn and imitate; and the *Apophthegmata Patrum* and the *Historia Monachorum* describe many of their leading figures—Isidore, for example, Paphnutius, John Colobos and Pambo—in terms that Amoun would have understood well.

[10] G Poemen 65. See also Motios 1, Pistos, and (more generally) Epiphanius 4, Eulogius, Poemen 53; Nau 339; *HM* vii, 419C.

[11] This was particularly true in the case of Pachomius, *V. Pach.* I, 25, 50. See also Esaias, *Ascet.* XII, 11.

[12] Rufinus, *HE* ii. 3.

[13] *HL* vii. See also *HM* Greek xx, Latin xxi.

[14] Cassian, *Con.* x. 2.

The same is true of Pachomius and his followers. Pachomius began his experiment in more ordered asceticism in about 320. His first community at Tabennesis (built in the cultivated land of the Nile valley, in contrast to Antony's retreat, and the later settlements of Nitria and Scetis) soon grew beyond 100 in number; and another monastery was founded at Faou, where Pachomius moved his headquarters in 337. Other major monasteries were later built at Panopolis (Akhmim), downstream from Faou, in 340, and upstream at Latopolis (Esneh) a few years later. Pachomius died in 346. By that time, if we may trust Palladius, 3,000 monks acknowledged Pachomius as their leader;[15] and the number had probably more than doubled by the end of the century.[16] Yet, once again, in spite of increasing numbers, and (more important in this case) in spite of the ordered regime of more coenobitic communities, the authority of Pachomius, as of his successors Theodore (d. 368) and Orsisius (d. *c.* 395), and the relationship between them and their monks, are portrayed by the sources in terms very similar to those employed in descriptions of Antony and of leaders in Scetis.

Although there was variety, therefore, and growth in Egyptian asceticism (and this we shall examine further in the chapter that follows), there was a common attitude to spiritual authority, a common response to masters of the ascetic life. But no one took power for granted. A claim to the title of ἀββᾶς, spiritual father, depended on a wide range of qualifications, recognized throughout the desert. Ascetics of all types were convinced, first of all, that their leaders belonged to an historical tradition, to a religious group whose place could be clearly identified, not only in the history of the church, but also in the longer and more general history of God's dealings with mankind. Antony saw the drama of contemporary asceticism as one more stage in the lasting intervention of God's mercy; a feature of human affairs highlighted by the life of Moses, the giving of the Law, the teaching and example of the prophets, and the coming of Christ.[17]

[15] *HL* vii. [16] Ibid. xxxii.

[17] Antony, *Letters*, ii. 9-15; iii. 4, 17-28; iv. 8-14; vi. 8-25: all from the Latin trans. of a Georgian MS. by G. Garitte, *Les lettres de s. Antoine* (2 vols., Lou-

It was a vision that inspired his own achievement: 'The ascetic must observe most closely', he said, 'the life and practice of the great Elijah'.[18] Pachomius shared his conviction. 'Do you wish to live among men? Imitate Abraham, Lot, Moses, and Samuel. Do you wish to live in the desert? Ah, there you will have all the prophets as your forbears'.[19] So Pachomius, and all those who followed his pattern of life, were seen by a later generation as descendants of patriarchs, of prophets, and of the apostles themselves.[20]

Such emphasis reflected, to some extent, a fear that tradition was threatened, that continuity was no longer guaranteed. Pachomius once dreamed of followers trapped by fire; and he interpreted the dream publicly in this sense, that after his death no suitable leader would emerge powerful enough to comfort the brethren in their various trials.[21] Pachomius himself appears to have lived with a lasting sense of doom. 'Fight, my dear friends, for the time is near, the days are cut short. Fathers no longer teach their children: no child obeys his father. . . . Hearts become harder: those with understanding hold their tongues . . . and each man is his own master'.[22] It was in the interest of his successors to strike a more optimistic note, not least as a safeguard of their own authority. Thus a clearer line of descent was marked upon the historical chart of uncertain development and varying personal fortune; a line that passed from the Bible and the early church, through Pachomius, and on to the following generations.[23] Yet we shall see that both the pessimism of Pachomius and the urgent assertions of his successors hinted

vain, 1955). The MS. is defended by Garitte as 'the most ancient known witness to the seven letters of Antony', i. p. vi. See also *V. Ant.* 89.

[18] *V. Ant.* 7. See B. Steidle, *Antonius Magnus Eremita* (Rome, 1956), 162–5.

[19] *Catech.*, trans. Lefort, 6. See also *Praecepta et Instituta*, introd.

[20] *V. Pach.* I, 98; Bo, 108; perhaps also Orsisius, *Liber*, 21. Compare the invocation in Inscriptions 27 and 203 at the monastery of Jeremias, in J. E. Quibell, *Excavations ai Saqqara*, iii, 1907–8 (Cairo, 1909), 36; iv, 1908–9, 1909–10, *The Monastery of Apa Jeremias* (Cairo, 1912), 59–60.

[21] *V. Pach.* I, 71. II, 69, possibly referring back to this incident, recounts a similar experience, focusing this time on the danger of future authority being falsely based; compare Dion. 45. A third version, I, 102, contains kindred elements. For anxiety expressed as the inability to overcome fire, see Nau 361.

[22] *Catech.* trans. Lefort, 21, 25; see H. Bacht, 'Pakhôme et ses disciples', *Théologie de la vie monastique* (Paris, 1961), 46.

[23] Theodore, *Catech.* iii, trans. Lefort, 41; *V. Pach.* Bo, 194, 198.

at a need very soon to be acknowledged; a need for some alternative to the traditional authority of the charismatic ἀββᾶς.

A sense of tradition affected equally the more personal and day-to-day encounters of the ascetic life. Each ἀββᾶς would appeal to his own humble but essential pedigree. Masters had to be themselves the disciples of holy men; and the links between one generation and another were traced with care.[24] Only in this way, it was felt, could they preserve their 'heritage of power', ἡ κληρονομία τῶν χαρισμάτων.[25] 'Brothers', said Esaias of Scetis, 'whatever I heard and saw in the company of those old men I have handed on to you; adding nothing, taking nothing away'; and he continued, according to one version (which may be the earliest), 'so that, walking in their footsteps, we may be judged worthy to share their inheritance'.[26]

This determination of the fathers to maintain contact with the past (not only cultural, as it were, but also personal) brings to mind another basis for the confidence that they inspired—their own experience. Questioners and disciples believed that their elders had undertaken the same programme of self-improvement as themselves, and had encountered and solved similar problems. Conversely, the fathers were reluctant to preach what they had not practised. 'I never followed inclinations of my own', said John the Coenobite, 'nor did I ever teach others to do what I had not first done myself' (combining again, with remarkable precision, personal experience and historical continuity).[27] A relationship could develop of almost mutual advantage, in which only the experience bestowed by greater age marked off master from his fellows: 'You must conduct yourselves like children', Antony said, 'telling your father what you know;

[24] Chitty, *Desert*, 67 f. See above, pp. 13 f., and n. 13.

[25] *HM* xv. 2. Here Pityrion inherits the *virtutes* of both Antony and Ammonas (an ambiguous word). Contrast the opinion of Serapion of Thmuis, that the *potentia* of Antony was shared among his followers—R. Draguet, 'Une lettre de Sérapion de Thmuis aux disciples d'Antoine (A.D. 356) en version syriaque et arménienne', *Le Muséon*, lxiv (1951), 18—but the same point is made. *HM* xxviii, 450A portrays Macarius as the heir of Antony.

[26] *Ascet.* VI, i.

[27] G Cassian 5. Pachomius, according to one tradition, warned masters to adopt the same standards as their disciples, *V. Pach.* Bo, 79.

and I will share with you what I know in return, and the struggles I have lived through'.[28]

Such attitudes imposed an important and useful discipline upon ascetics of all ages. No one could set himself up as a mere oracle of wisdom, but was expected to reflect in his own life the fruits of a vigorous and enduring regime of self-perfection. The ideal ascetic was 'a man of words and deeds';[29] but deeds had to come before words. 'You need to labour in the spirit to reach this level of perfection; for it is otherwise a heavy task to teach by word of mouth what your own body never worked at'.[30] Not surprisingly, therefore, labour was contrasted with learning as the mark and mould of the teacher.

This conviction in favour of labour is clearly betrayed in a famous dialogue between Evagrius and Arsenius.[31] Evagrius of Pontus—a cultivated man with great speculative powers, once protégé of Basil and Gregory Nazianzene, and later ordained a deacon—had embraced the ascetic life on the Mount of Olives at the instigation of Jerome's friend Melania. In 383 he had come to Egypt, and eventually settled in the Cells, where he gained great influence as a teacher in the tradition of Origen, counting among his pupils Palladius and Cassian. Arsenius, who made his home in Scetis, was another 'foreigner', arriving in Egypt in 394; and, according to Cyril of Scythopolis, writing more than a century later, he was a man of letters also, having been tutor to the sons of Theodosius the Great.[32] Evagrius is portrayed, in the dialogue referred to, as a man very conscious of his education; and anxiously, almost guiltily, he contrasts his own meagre achievements in the spiritual life with the greater virtues of his unlettered fellow ascetics. Arsenius admits, more humbly, to the same misgivings. Although he virtually echoes, in doing so, the words of his companion, he manages to imply very forcibly that, whatever he and Evagrius may possess in the way of learning, they acquired in a world quite alien to that

[28] Antony to his monks, *V. Ant.* 16; see also 22.

[29] *V. Pach.* Bo, 60; see Pachomius, *Catech.*, trans. Lefort, 23.

[30] Nau 240. See also G Theodore of Pherme 9, Poemen 25; Nau 252; *HM* vii, 411C, 412D.

[31] G Arsenius 5; see also 6, and Euprepius 7.

[32] *Vita Euthymii*, 21.

of the monk. The virtues of the *ἀγροίκοι*, as they call them, these 'peasant' ascetics, spring from personal initiative and their own hard labour. There was little to one's credit, Arsenius believed, in learning by rote at the feet of other men: the monk must concern himself with a fresh creation that was truly his own. The argument is expressed with subtlety and tact; but it was an indictment, nevertheless, of secular learning in the rhetorical schools—precisely the system Arsenius had represented (if we may believe tradition) as a tutor at court. It was also an indictment of Evagrius himself (always suspect to many in Egypt, as an 'intellectual', and an Origenist to boot), and a criticism to be levelled at any ascetic who tried to form a school of disciples on the basis of ideas or doctrine, rather than on practical discipline in imitation of the master's model.[33]

This belief that sheer hard work could be joined with the development of an inner life was one of the most remarkable characteristics of ascetic theory in Egypt. *Σωματικὸς κόπος*, in the sense of physical exertion, was taken for granted; but so was interior watchfulness. Ascetics were praised for being 'bodily untiring', but also for being 'wise-minded'; above all for being *αὐτάρχης ἐν πᾶσιν*, masters of themselves, independent of all others 'in the labour of their hands, in their food, and in their clothing'.[34] Such a combination of virtues, such a breadth of personality, was vital. However vigorous and socially involved his pattern of life might be, it was still from his inner purity of heart that a teacher's words would have to flow. For Poemen, the guiding principle was, 'Teach your lips to speak what lies in your heart'.[35] It was the principle of a whole generation. When Amoun of Rhaithou admitted to Sisoes a secret desire 'to acquire some taste and skill in words, so that I may reply more readily to those who

[33] We shall see more of this dispute, and of the teaching and influence of Evagrius. He and his followers were to suffer from the eventual condemnation of Origenist ideas in 399; but he always tried to balance in his own writings speculation on the theological basis of the ascetic life with more practical instruction on the day-to-day demands of that theology.

[34] G Agathon 8, 10. The same emphases are combined in Nau 269.

[35] G Poemen 63. The difference in the Latin version, in *Vitae Patrum*, V, viii. 14 (*PL* lxxiii. 908), is certainly interesting, and may be important: 'Teach your heart to observe what your tongue has taught others'. The sixth-century West was more ready to redeem the hasty assumption of a teaching role!

question me', the old man replied, with the wisdom of an earlier age, 'There is no need for that: the gift of speech, and indeed of silence, you may gain for yourself by purity of mind and heart'.[36]

This purity of heart enabled the ascetic to speak with authority, to acquire the spiritual perception that prompted the trust of disciples, and to receive in addition visions of a more literal kind. Pachomius was described by a biographer as 'one who saw the invisible God in the purity of his heart':[37] and Arsenius made a similar link between the vision of God and the inner life, declaring that, 'if we seek God, he will reveal himself to us; and if we hold him fast, he will remain close to us'.[38] The most forceful example, however, was Antony himself: 'He sat upon his mountain with heart unstirred, and the Lord showed him even distant things'.[39] (To have lived as a monk in Egypt at that time would have involved a constant sense of being watched and known: of Antony again it was said, 'And often when something was afoot in Egypt, there on his mountain he saw it all'.)[40] Such power was not gained without effort. A lady writing to Paphnutius expressed confidence in his prayers, 'because, through your ascetic labour and your dedication, a world that for us lies hidden is open before you'.[41] Antony himself regarded foreknowledge and insight as weapons against evil, rather than ends in themselves;[42] but they were, nevertheless, features of the ascetic life that one might with confidence anticipate.[43]

[36] G Sisoes 17. Amoun of Nitria 2 may also refer to Amoun of Rhaithou (Chitty, *Desert*, 79, n. 83), and comments on the same misguided anxiety. For another example, probably late, see the interpolation into *HL* (ch. cxvi), *PG* xxxiv. 1219.

[37] *V. Pach.* I, 22. Festugière, in his trans., *Les moines d'Orient*, iv, 2 (Paris, 1965), 117 f., points to a similar phrase in *V. Pach.* S[3]; and he suggests that the sentiment in both texts must spring from a primitive tradition.

[38] G Arsenius 10.

[39] *V. Ant.* 59.

[40] Ibid. 82; see also 60, 64.

[41] Quoted by W. Seston, 'Remarque sur le rôle de la pensée d'Origène dans les origines du monachisme', *RHR* cviii (1933), 212.

[42] *V. Ant.* 34.

[43] Ibid. Seston, op. cit. 206, 212, *contrasted* Antony's opinion with that of Valeria, the lady writing to Paphnutius: there may be a contrast of motive, or explanation, but not of effect.

Leading ascetics of the earlier generations could certainly be reticent about visionary experience, especially when more was involved than foreknowledge or sound judgement;[44] but this was because of their caution and humility, rather than because of any scepticism or disapproval. Pachomius discouraged curious and exaggerated interest in visions, suggesting that normal human experience provided sufficient revelations of divine power;[45] but in the same breath he asserted that God could indeed reveal hidden things, and even his own person, to those he might choose.[46]

Reticence was, in any case, under pressure; convictions of individual disciples, the needs of a developing ascetic society, and indeed the temper of the age, demanded such experience, and called for its interpretation. The important consideration was to safeguard humility, and to keep knowledge of these matters within the ascetic group. The life and teaching of Pachomius himself provide many examples. He would limit the account of his own visions to 'those which lead to faith and self-improvement'; and he spoke of them only to the elders.[47] 'Apa Cornelius said to him, "Tell us about the time you were carried up to heaven" '; and, when Pachomius demurred, 'Apa Cornelius said to him, "Tell us as much as concerns ourselves" '.[48] Antony suffered from the same pressure, and displayed the same measured candour: 'Like a father, he could not hide things from his children'; and he spoke of his visions 'in order to be of help'.[49]

As a result, stories of visions became as much a feature of ascetic conversation as the sayings of the fathers, and were handed on in the same way to future generations.[50] Some of these accounts had a clearly social function, guaranteeing, for

[44] e.g. G Antony 2, Arsenius 27, Zacharias 5, Tithoes 1.

[45] A point heavily emphasized by Chitty, *Desert*, 28. Certainly some ascetics expressed less sophisticated desires: G Antony 12, Silvanus 3; Nau 173, 190—this last particularly striking: after a week of rigorous fasting, the master asks his disciple, 'Have you seen anything yet?' For the background to such occasions, see R. Arbesmann, 'Fasting and Prophecy in Pagan and Christian Antiquity', *Traditio*, vii (1949-51), 1-71.

[46] *V. Pach.* I, 48. Dionysius either did not know, or chose to omit, this chapter; II, 92 mentions only the possibility of seeing God.

[47] *V. Pach.* I, 88; see also 99, and Bo, 73.

[48] *V. Pach.* S^{1a}, trans. Lefort, 376.

[49] *V. Ant.* 66.

[50] G Arsenius 33, Theodore of Pherme 25; *V. Pach.* I, 125.

example, and impressing upon others, the right of some ascetic to recognition as a teacher and guide of the community.[51] Palladius gives a remarkable instance of the potential link between visionary power and the exercise of authority. Pambo had been asked for his opinion on the relative merits of two brothers; and he concluded a provisional reply with the command, 'But wait for a while, and give me time to receive some revelation from God'. After a few days, he felt able to make a more definite statement: 'I have seen', he said; 'I have seen them both standing in Paradise'; and he spoke ὡς ἐπὶ Θεοῦ, like one in the presence of, or under the inspiration of, God himself.[52]

This supposed inspiration by God was the essential basis of trust in the teaching of the fathers. An apparently intimate relationship with God, a complete dependence upon him, did more than anything else to give experienced ascetics a permanent standing in the eyes of other men. So Pambo, travelling with colleagues and disciples, could demand of laymen by the roadside that they greet his companions with reverence; 'For they have spoken face to face with God, and their lips are holy'.[53] Some texts harped upon this awesome privilege, but with a nostalgic exaggeration that suggests it may have been already a thing of the past.[54] For others, inspiration seemed more arbitrary and unpredictable. Pachomius, rebuking one man, found that his remarks aroused compunction in the heart of another. 'See now', he said, 'it is not merely when we wish it that we see the hidden truths of salvation, but when God in his foreknowledge decides that it shall be so'.[55] Other elders, faced with a question, found

[51] G Ephraim 1-2. In the latter, one of the elders dreams that Ephraim is given a book by angels (an interesting comment on the background to Pachomius's supposed vision in *HL* xxxii): 'And rising early, he heard as it were a spring, welling from Ephraim's mouth; and he knew that whatever came from Ephraim's lips was of the Holy Spirit'. Nau 177, 179-80 provide other examples of the social use to which the visionary charism might have been put.

[52] *HL* xiv. The same phrases occur in x, also referring to Pambo; and G confirms the story, saying of Pambo, 'He was not quick to speak, unless God inspired him', Pambo 2.

[53] G Pambo 7.

[54] See particularly *V. Pach.* Bo, 55, 72—more insistent but less subtle than the corresponding I, 82, 97: here Chitty may well have been right, that I represented an original sentiment, 'Pachomian Sources Once More', 59 f.

[55] *V. Pach.* I, 97.

themselves deprived of inspiration. They could only say, 'God has taken from the old men their gift of speech',[56] thus fulfilling the prediction of Pachomius, 'When the Lord ceases to reveal himself, we are but men, like every other man'.[57] With time, however, the unpredictable became more closely interwoven with everyday asceticism. The inspiration of God was no more easy to explain; but it gave rise to situations which both masters and disciples felt able to handle with greater confidence. One knew, in short, how to behave. 'If you receive a revelation concerning sacred Scripture, speak out; but take care for yourself as well, that you do not rob the words of their effect'.[58] So disciples prayed that their masters might receive this inspiration;[59] and masters in their turn acknowledged that inspiration could depend on the faith and application of their disciples.[60] Like visions, belief in inspiration had come to acquire a social and public significance, binding communities together. Pachomius once saw Christ, in a vision, seated on a high throne, teaching the monks: so later he sat in the same place himself, to instruct his brethren.[61] Just such a throne, a stone seat placed at the head of a flight of steps, was found in the ruins of the monastery of Jeremias as Ras el-Gisr.[62] It reflects a forceful attempt to harness charismatic inspiration to the regular pattern of the coenobitic life.

Such developments began to have effect, or at least to arouse interest, suspicion, perhaps even resentment, beyond the boundaries of the ascetic world. One of the most forceful declarations of this belief in God's inspiration came, in fact, from Pachomius; and it is significant that he should have made it while defending himself publicly before a synod of bishops at Latopolis, in 345.[63] The point at issue there was

[56] G Felix; see also Macarius Aeg. 25. For the link between these two texts, see Bousset, *Apophthegmata*, 80, n. 3. G Bessarion 4 and *V. Pach.* I, 66 make the same point. Some of these passages may reflect a later period of more general decline: see below, pp. 37 f.

[57] *V. Pach.* I, 48.

[58] Esaias, *Ascet.* XI, 65.

[59] Ibid. XII, 33.

[60] G Isaac of the Cells 7, Felix; *V. Pach.* Bo, 102.

[61] *V. Pach.* Bo, 102.

[62] Quibell, *Excavations*, iii. 7 f., and Plates XIII, XIV.

[63] *V. Pach.* I, 112.

precisely his spiritual discernment; and he laid claim to it without fear as *το χάρισμα τοῦ θεοῦ*, a gift from God. It had, he admitted, a human basis, namely man's understandable familiarity with those among whom he lived. That such a natural gift should be intensified in some, and raised to a spiritual level, did no more than reflect the providence of God, and his desire to save all men. Some he would choose as his special instruments, singled out not so much by quality of character as by their accidental association with those most in need of their help. To these chosen men he gave exceptional gifts of judgement and insight. Anyone who strove to do God's will, Pachomius asserted, and to help his fellow men, had after all the scriptural promise of God himself that he would dwell within him.[64]

This is to anticipate; but we do possess a series of literary portraits that show how all these qualities of leadership—tradition, experience, insight, and inspiration—were readily adapted to the coenobitic life: the portraits of Theodore, successor of Pachomius. Theodore was a model disciple. He followed the example of the whole community, but of Pachomius in particular, whom he obeyed as a representative of God.[65] He strove to achieve personal sanctity far beyond the norm.[66] Thus he merited the title, 'son and heir'.[67] Pachomius himself foresaw that he would make a worthy successor;[68] and eventually he gave Theodore a formal share in his own authority: 'Theodore and I offer to God the very same service; and he is possessed of an authority that makes

[64] Lefort believed that *V. Pach.* S[1a] might refer to this event (*Vies coptes*, lxxxiii): 'If I go there, they will kill me; but if they have some quarrel with me, in the light of the canons of the church, then let them come here', trans. Lefort, 375 f. This introduces a surprisingly harsh and dramatic note; and it must be read in conjunction with the argued assertion of Veilleux, 'One can find not the slightest sign of a desire to displace the hierarchy based on law by a hierarchy based on charismatic gifts', *Liturgie*, 233.

[65] *V. Pach.* I, 36, 50; Bo, 30, 32; but not II or Dion.

[66] *V. Pach.* I, 36. Bo, 32 stresses the social effect of Theodore's charisma.

[67] *V. Pach.* I, 107–8. Bo, 95, another version of the parable, stresses more the importance of *blind* obedience, and quotes I Cor. ii. 18, 'If anyone among you thinks that he is wise in this age, let him become a fool that he may become wise'. I cannot agree with Festugière that the variations are 'of no consequence', *Moines d'Orient*, iv, 2, 55.

[68] *V. Pach.* I, 36; omitted by II and Dion.

him worthy of the title "father" '.[69] Theodore was thus a man of experience in the fullest sense; and, in spite of an intervening period of disfavour and controversy, that experience did gain him recognition as leader of the Pachomian communities. Several years after the death of Pachomius, his successor Orsisius was forced to resign; and Theodore took his place. Those who had supported Theodore's claim, 'those who acknowledged him from the beginning', rejoiced at this vindication of their longstanding conviction that, because of his filial devotion to Pachomius his master, he was rightful heir to the position he had now acquired. He represented, in other words, an orthodox tradition.[70] While Pachomius was alive, Theodore had travelled every day from Tabennesis to Faou, to hear his master's catechesis: and he would travel back to repeat it to his own community.[71] Now that Pachomius was dead, Theodore continued to repeat his teaching.[72] Yet again, while Pachomius was alive, Theodore had been invited to interpret the Scriptures publicly; 'and he began to speak as the Lord inspired him'.[73] The old charism still remained in later years, another ground for the joy and confidence of his subjects: 'His words were full of grace, and brought healing to souls in affliction'.[74]

[69] *V. Pach.* I, 91. Bo places these events at the end of 74, equivalent to I, 89. This displacement may represent subsequent praise of Theodore at the expense of Pachomius: Festugière, op. cit., 47.

[70] For the full significance of this 'comeback', see Chitty, 'A Note on the Chronology of the Pachomian Foundations', *Studia Patristica*, ii (Berlin, 1957), 384, Bacht, *Vermächtnis*, 18 f.

[71] *V. Pach.* I, 88.

[72] *V. Pach.* Bo, 190.

[73] *V. Pach.* I, 77.

[74] Ibid. 130.

III

THE GROWTH OF ASCETIC SOCIETY

1. FROM HERMIT TO COENOBITE

Masters and disciples have been observed thus far in a series of poses—of anxiety and guidance, of submission and authority. Some of their motives and convictions have been laid bare—factors, in other words, that might have made for change—; but this kind of account, dependent on isolated anecdotes, is in danger of providing little more than disjointed images. The reader of the *Apophthegmata* wanders, as it were, in a gallery of monastic icons: their colours are often brilliant, their effect (for many) of great spiritual worth; but they can remain, nevertheless, static in one's imagination, even when seen against the changing and familiar background of their age. It is the task of the historian (in contrast, perhaps, to that of the devotee, or the disciple) to set these figures in motion: to identify and explain, within ascetic society itself, the process of historical development. Hints about the possible direction of that development have emerged already: their belief in visions and in inspiration could create or maintain among these men a growing sense of social dependence and corporate responsibility; and the resulting coenobitic institutions could absorb and adapt the charismatic wisdom and insight of more solitary masters. The fuller story is now called for, a story more detailed and complex.

An essential contributing factor to the historical process—to the increasing adoption of more communal patterns of life—was precisely the current understanding of authority in Egypt, the charism of ascetic pioneers. Their commanding presence had prompted the formation of various groups. Now other factors—their own ambition, perhaps; but much more their very patterns of instruction, and the stability and habits of dependence that instruction encouraged—all led them first to demand, then to organize, and eventually to rely upon, an arena, or audience, of ever greater social complexity, within which to achieve their effect.

In the early stages of ascetic history, those who appear 'eremitic' or 'semi-eremitic' and those regarded as 'coenobitic' had many characteristics and customs in common. Even the most primitive group—master and disciple—could involve the concept of community.[1] Antony, traditionally the proto-hermit, wished to distinguish (according to the *Life*) between community and mere association. He enjoyed the company of other ascetics, and gave them advice; but he would not eat with them.[2] Nevertheless, having conquered the demons at the beginning of his own ascetic life, he deliberately sought out the company of an older man; and only when meeting refusal did he withdraw alone to the inner desert.[3] Later, he himself provided the focus for a new ascetic group, calming fears, healing enmities, and gathering disciples.[4] Pachomius, on the other hand, the coenobitic pioneer, displayed in the early stages of his ascetic career exactly the same hesitation. Having formed his first community, 'he gave them a rule: each man was to fend for himself, and manage matters on his own'. He was able to impose communal meals and a centralized economy: but 'he saw that they were not ready yet to bind themselves together in a true community'. Certainly he was unable to command their obedience.[5]

It is unrealistic to suggest, therefore, that Antony represented an earlier eremitic tradition, doomed to fail, handing on the torch in the nick of time to younger coenobitic pioneers. Antony and Pachomius had many common roots. There is, it is true, a famous passage in the *Vita Prima* of Pachomius, in which Antony supposedly praises the coenobitic life: 'In the early days, when I became a monk, there was no community for the nourishment of other souls: following the persecution, each of the early monks practised

[1] 'A certain old man, together with another brother, set up a community [*κοινόβιον*]', Nau 281; see also 340: both texts emphasize the economic element, especially communal food.

[2] *V. Ant.* 45.

[3] *V. Ant.* 11.

[4] Ibid. 14 f.

[5] All in *V. Pach.* S[1], 2, trans. Lefort, 3. On this last point, see below, pp. 51 f.

asceticism on his own. But afterwards your father embarked upon this enterprise, with good effect, helped by the Lord'.[6] Some of this was wisdom after the event;[7] but, even as it stands, the passage does not merely reflect the judgement of one generation on the achievements of another. Κοινόβιον, 'community', was not a term exclusive to the world of Pachomius. The important phrase in the passage above is 'for the nourishment of other souls'; and it is with this broader concern that the words 'on his own' are contrasted. Moreover, Antony's statement is made in reply to the assertions of his Pachomian visitors. Even in the *Vita Prima* they say, 'No, it is you, father, who are the light of all this world';[8] and later (and otherwise more exaggerated) texts maintain this emphasis: 'You are far more worthy of honour than we, for you are the last of the prophets'.[9] So it was not a question of who was first, but of who most accurately interpreted and expressed the aims and traditions of the ascetic life. Apart from a note, in Antony's reply, of disappointment at opportunities lost, and apart from the approval expressed in his words 'the nourishment of other souls', there is another clue to Antony's humility in this passage. He recognized that Pachomius had secured the continuity of his experiment; and this may reflect a corresponding sense of failure in his own life: 'You are all become like Abba Pachomius'.[10] Authority still depended on a man's ability to capture allegiance: 'Bring many to salvation while in this life, and you shall rule as many in the next'.[11]

It seems just to suppose, therefore, that the small group of ascetic master with one or more disciples ('those who sat about him')[12] represents a primitive stage in the history of

[6] *V. Pach.* I, 120.

[7] This applies to all the biographies, of whatever date, Greek and Coptic; but I agree with Chitty that *V. Pach.* I is the least tendentious, and therefore (on this point) least misleading as an historical witness, 'Pachomian Sources Reconsidered', 44 f. Bacht was nevertheless right to suggest that Antony's ability to make some such statement rested in part on the proto-coenobitic quality of his own life, 'Antonius und Pachomius', *Antonius Magnus Eremita*, ed. Steidle, 103 f.

[8] *V. Pach.* I, 120.

[9] *V. Pach.* S⁶, trans. Lefort, 323.

[10] *V. Pach.* I, 120. S⁶ is much more developed, but in the same tradition.

[11] *HM* ii, 405C.

[12] G Poemen 3; see also 4; *HM* iv, 408A; *HL* xxxv.

monasticism. The biographies of Pachomius, as well as that of Antony, offer due warning that development beyond this stage, in either a coenobitic or a semi-eremitic direction, was neither predictable nor inevitable. Nevertheless, the three types of encounter between master and disciples, described in Chapter II, may reflect a subsequent social development, not only in the Pachomian communities, but among Egyptian ascetics as a whole. In the first instance, and especially during the early decades of the century, questioners may have come on isolated occasions, to appeal in general terms to the father's spiritual wisdom. Such an approach would not have demanded more permanent relationships between them.[13] Later, for example during the period when communities were expanding in Nitria and Scetis, questioners may have sought for more detailed advice, which would have required a more lengthy revelation of their state of soul, and longer acquaintance and deeper knowledge on the part of the father.[14] Finally, once a young man had found a mentor suited to his taste,[15], he would stay in his company, and in that of his fellow disciples, for a considerable time, even until death.[16] In this way loyalty, coupled with an increasing dependence on the example, rather than the word, of the holy man, could have led to the develop-

[13]That such questions arose most at the beginning of the individual ascetic's career, if not exclusively in the earlier period of monasticism, is suggested by G Antony 1, Arsenius 1, where they are addressed to God, implying that a human director was unavailable. Antony's first letter reveals his sense of isolation, as he brings his understanding to bear for the first time on the waywardness of his body, *Letters*, i. 77 f. Exactly the same atmosphere pervades the corresponding passages in *V. Ant.*, especially 10.

[14]Some elders, following the older customs, would first outline general principles, but then apply them at a more particular level: G Joseph of Panephysis 3, Joseph of Thebes, Cyrus, Macarius Aeg. 3, Poemen 62. The elder's knowledge of the individual before him is sometimes mentioned specifically: G Ares, Poemen 22, 27, Pambo 3 (although here Pambo depended on the report of others), Paphnutius 2, Serapion 2; *HM* i. 5. For such consultation involving closer ties: G Ammoes 1, John Colobos 8. Poemen 183 says that the word of God needs to be applied to the soul again and again. For a particularly beautiful example of patience and availability, Nau 164. The theoretical insight behind such patience is revealed in G John Colobos 18: the ἀββᾶς is a lamp undiminished by giving light to others.

[15]Many were critical, and travelled from one ἀββᾶς to another: G Agathon 28, Poemen 4, 88-9, 97-8; Nau 216-17, 245.

[16]G Arsenius 32, Gelasius 1; Nau 190.

ment of more stable religious communities.

We can suppose with some confidence that this was indeed what happened, because it is possible to identify (as we shall see in more detail later) changes in the understanding of authority that appear to keep pace with the development of a corporate asceticism. There are signs that the 'charism of the word', which played so prominent a part in more primitive encounters, suffered a decline as the century proceeded; and that the example of the elders acquired increasing importance in later stages of the ascetic movement.

One must not oversimplify. It is true that an emphasis on example would have seemed strange to many of an earlier generation: Macarius the Egyptian, for instance, was seriously perturbed, when visitors showed more interest in his pattern of life than in revealing to him their problems and temptations.[17] But change, when it came, did not entirely override former attitudes and customs. Taken by itself, a growing unwillingness or inability to make oracular statements could have maintained, perhaps even enhanced, the social function of the holy man: for he then took upon himself the equally impressive role of intercessor before God. Unable to offer inquirers the traditional word of wisdom, fathers were more and more frequently faced with the request, 'Pray for us'.[18] John of Lycopolis (who began his ascetic career when Pachomius died, and reached the peak of his fame in the 380s and 390s) expressed this new attitude very clearly. 'Am I a prophet, or in a position to play the judge? . . . Even so, I have prayed for you, and for your household and your husband, so that what you have hoped for so trustfully may come to pass'.[19] There is an element of continuity here, which suggests that the old convictions were only slowly modified; and it seems still to have been accepted in the time of Evagrius of Pontus (at the end of the century) that more could be gained from the words of a holy man, even when recounted at second hand, than from direct acquaintance

[17] G Macarius Aeg. 31.

[18] This became, with time, almost a formal feature of monastic life: *HM* i. 13 (also in the Latin, i, 394B); Esaias, *Ascet.* X, 46.

[19] *HM* i. 8. Such a role had been rejected in an earlier age, e.g. G Antony 16; but see Pambo 2, The Roman 1, Felix; Nau 170.

with his visible pattern of life.[20]

Nevertheless, even the earliest ascetic literature shows that imitation was gaining ground as a common method of instruction. Antony says, in the *Life*, 'As for ourselves, we have those holy men as masters; and our duty is to act as they did, and imitate their vigour'.[21] Theodore urged his monks to avoid giving scandal to their companions: 'Let us keep the law, and let each one edify his neighbour'. For Theodore, this was the charism *par excellence*, 'a gain far beyond what our labours deserve'.[22] One can detect in the *Lives* of Pachomius similar suggestions at the expense of traditional charismatic teaching. Theodore himself was much influenced by the example of Pachomius, proof that even when silent his master was impressive.[23] Others who had gathered around the great pioneer, attracted by his virtue, are described in the *Vita Prima* as 'those who heard—or, rather, who observed him'.[24] In the thirty-second chapter of the *Lausiac History*, where he recounts the famous story of Pachomius's vision of an angel dictating the *Rule*, Palladius may have drawn upon a well established historical tradition, accurate not in details of fact but in the attitudes it reflected.[25] The words of the angel

[20] *HL* xxxv. Here Evagrius was warning Palladius himself not to visit John of Lycopolis; and this recalls John's own command, 'Do not long for the bodily features of the servants of God, but meditate in the spirit on their deeds and achievements', *HM* i, 393A. John was making an Origenist, or at least an anti-anthropomorphite, point (hence the importance of his agreement with Evagrius): he did not want to be divinized—compare his assertion, 'I am a man, sinful, and subject to passion like yourselves', *HM* i. 8 (not in the Latin; but note his later warning about seeing God 'mentally, not bodily; with the understanding that knowledge brings, not in the appearance of the flesh', i, 397C). Palladius, however, came from an even younger generation, and made his visit even so.

[21] *V. Ant.* 27; but other passages show that Antony had already diverged from the mainstream of ascetic development: imitation must be guided by personal judgement, 38; and the pressure of other men's opinion, as a spur to one's own development, may be not so much an actual experience as a salutary skill of the imagination, 55. Dörries considered that such passages betrayed the increasing isolation of the hermit, 'Die Vita Antonii', 383. See also Appendix II below.

[22] Theodore, *Catech.*, trans. Lefort, 41 f. *V. Pach.* Bo, 105 makes the same point.

[23] See above, pp. 31 f.

[24] *V. Pach.* 1, 14; and Bo, 21 (the corresponding chapter) maintains the emphasis: Pachomius was tempted 'with God's leave and for his own schooling, as also for the benefit of others'.

[25] This is not to call into question the opinion of Halkin about the relation between *HL* on the one hand and *V. Pach.* III, IV and VI on the other: 'L'histoire

suggest that among the Pachomian communities a link had been made between example and a regulated pattern of life: 'And in accordance with the model I have given you [κατὰ τὸν τύπον], draw up now laws for your followers'.[26] It may have been no accident, therefore, that in the *Vita Prima* itself the *Rule* is described as τύπος.[27] Perhaps no less revealing is a point made in the Prologue to the *Apophthegmata Patrum*, in a passage that may well reflect attitudes of the early fifth century: praise is bestowed first on what the text calls 'valiant asceticism—a wondrous way of life'; and only then is reference made to 'the words of those blessed and saintly fathers'.[28]

There are signs, therefore, of a change from word to example, a change linked in some way to a process of social development. This change is clearest when one compares features of the ascetic life as practised at the beginning and end of the century. It is much more important, however, to capture intermediate developments; and there does seem to have been a transitional stage in the lives of some ascetics that was not merely 'semi-eremitic' but part of a movement from the solitary life to the coenobitic. Ascetics were blessed with both the opportunity and the incentive to change their pattern of life, not least because of the immense variety of practice. The *Historia Monachorum* speaks of 'some in the outskirts of towns, others in the country, but most (indeed, the best) scattered through the desert';[29] and even of the latter it says, later, 'some lived together in large groups, others with a few companions, others again on their own.'[30] Variety gave rise to rivalry, and prompted comparisons. Palladius wrote of two brothers, Paesius and Esaias, who wished to embrace the ascetic life, but could not agree on the method.

lausiaque et les vies grecques de s. Pachôme', *AB* xlviii (1930), 257-301. Draguet, who agreed with Halkin, thought nevertheless that Palladius may have drawn upon *some* written sources of Pachomian origin: 'Le chapitre de l'*Histoire Lausiaque* sur les Tabennésiotes, dérive-t-il d'une source copte', *Le Muséon*, lvii (1944), 53-145; lviii (1945), 15-95. The whole controversy over *HL* xxxii has been usefully summarized by Veilleux, *Liturgie*, 139 ff.

[26] *HL* xxxii.

[27] *V. Pach.* I, 25.

[28] *PG* lxv, 72A.

[29] *HM* (Latin) Prologue, 390.

[30] Ibid. xxi, 443B.

One chose the strict life of the desert; the other built a hospice for pilgrims. Faced with anxious questions about this apparent inconsistency, Pambo passed favourable judgement on both men, in terms already quoted.[31] Even for ascetics already accustomed to one way of life, the question of possible change could cause anxiety. One old man from the Cells asked Ammonas whether he should withdraw to the desert, travel as a pilgrim to a country where he was not known, or enclose himself completely within his cell.[32] The *Historia Monachorum* contains an interesting story about Paphnutius and three virtuous laymen. Paphnutius kept receiving revelations that this or that layman was as virtuous as he was. The story concludes with an obvious moral (emphasizing variety): 'In every walk of life, there are men pleasing to God, prompting God's love by deeds that are hidden to others'.[33] But the actual development of the story reveals an enormous anxiety in Paphnutius. He always strove, with some success, to draw these laymen into the desert, and to teach them more formal principles of asceticism. This may have sprung partly from a desire for a disciple; but most of all from a need to prove that his own way of life *was* better,[34] and from a feeling that virtue had no business flourishing in secular surroundings.[35]

Impelled in part by such anxieties, ascetics did adapt themselves to changing circumstance. Copres, a 'presbyter',[36] is described as 'having a monastery';[37] and it is specifically mentioned that he had changed from the solitary state to the coenobitic.[38] Hor is portrayed in like terms. Having lived in the 'uttermost desert', he subsequently founded

[31] See above, p. 29.

[32] G Ammonas 4. For a full discussion of this passage, see Bousset, 'Das Mönchtum der sketischen Wüste', *ZK* xlii (1923), 27 f.

[33] *HM* xvi, 439B. [34] *HM* xiv. 16.

[35] Ibid. 21. The Latin contains both elements, but in a weaker form; and clearly the Greek finds more motive here for the story as a whole.

[36] Which may or may not mean 'priest': see below, pp. 62 f.

[37] *HM* ix, 422. The Greek (x. 1) has ἡγούμενος ἀδελφῶν. Bousset asserted that the title ἡγούμενος marked off the coenobite from the hermit, 'Das Mönchtum', 8. His corresponding assertion that ἀββᾶς never occurs in coenobitic contexts is contradicted by G Poemen 6 (he overlooks its coenobitic implications, 26), and Nau 328.

[38] In the Greek only.

a monastery 'near a town', and was now 'the father of many monasteries'.[39] The story of Hor introduces a new element in this type of transition. His decision to found a monastery was coupled with a vision of an angel saying, 'You shall become a great nation, and many shall believe in you, and through you shall thousands find salvation'.[40] This was precisely the path followed by Pachomius;[41] and he and Hor were not alone: Apollonius, while still a solitary, heard the voice of God himself assuring him that he would be father to a vigorous people, and so founded a community.[42] These stories of visions and voices demonstrate clearly that the changes involved were deliberate and fully understood. They show that one is dealing not merely with contrasting types of asceticism, but with moments of change in the lives of individuals.[43]

The wide range of ascetic practice, and the opportunity or readiness to change from one style of life to another, made continuity, and even confusion, inevitable. Master and disciple in their cell would sit together in the evening, while the master taught; the disciple would unfold his problems, and the master tender his advice; they would pray together, and rise in the night to pray again.[44] From this it was no far cry to the more coenobitic groups of the *Historia Monachorum*. After communion, at about the ninth hour, the brethren gathered for instruction, followed by a common meal. Some would then withdraw to the desert, to learn or recite the Scriptures throughout the night, while others remained together, singing psalms.[45] Many hermits seem to have been monks in the making. Visitors would apologize for interrupting their *κανών*, their rule of life—and receive the most sociable reply: 'My rule of life is to set you at rest, and send

[39] *HM* ii, 405B.

[40] *HM* ii, 405C (note the persistent allusion to Gen. xii).

[41] *V. Pach.* I, 12, 23.

[42] *HM* vii, 411A.

[43] Both contrast and change were real: so, while I agree with Reitzenstein that the solitary and the coenobitic life were not merely two forms of one institution, 'Des Athanasius Werk', 45 f., mutual influences must be allowed. Other points connected with these anecdotes I have discussed in 'The Formation of Early Ascetic Communities', *JTS*, n.s. xxv (1974), 116.

[44] Nau-211.

[45] *HM* vii, 418AB.

you away in peace'.[46] Hermits could betray that fear of their own will, which underlay the coenobitic ideal of obedience.[47] Those, on the other hand, already engaged in more communal asceticism would bring the problems raised by their new surroundings to be solved by more solitary masters in the traditional manner: 'If I were living in the company of brethren, and I saw something done that was not fitting [the vaguest of criteria], would you wish me to make some comment?'–and the masters could now advocate a silent conformity![48] Men were drawing together. One text tells how the fathers used to travel from cell to cell, keeping an eye on the younger brethren who wished to practise asceticism on their own; and, when they found one who was tempted, they would take him to the 'ecclesia' (perhaps a church, perhaps some assembly of monks), and bathe him with water in which all the others, having prayed, had washed their hands.[49] An archaeology of this development, revealing huddled groups of cells that preserve solitude while allowing a sense of community, has now begun to emerge.[50]

Many of the historical threads are usefully brought together by the story of John in the *Historia Monachorum*. After three years as a solitary, he sees in a vision an angel, and becomes 'filled with the gifts of knowledge, and the powers of a teacher'. The angel commands him to travel around other parts of the desert, visiting ascetics, and instructing them 'in the word and teaching of the Lord'.[51] Only later is there talk of monasteries. When these have been founded, John is able to discover by revelation each monk's state of soul; but he remains to some extent aloof, communicating with the monasteries by letter.[52] The story

[46] Nau 283.

[47] Nau 284.

[48] Nau 318.

[49] Nau 351.

[50] F. Daumas, 'L'activité de l'Institut Français d'Archéologie Orientale durant l'année 1965-6', *CR* 1966, 298-309, and 'Les travaux de l'Institut Français d'Archéologie Orientale pendant l'année 1966-67', *CR* 1967, 436-51; A. Guillaumont, 'Le site des "Cellia" (Basse-Egypte)', *Revue Archéologique*, 1964, ii. 43-50; R. Kasser (ed.), *Kellia 1965* (Geneva, 1967); S. Sauneron, 'Fouilles d'Esn d'Esna (Haute-Egypte): monastères et ermitages', *CR* 1967, 411-18.

[51] Compare *HM* xi, 430D-431C.

[52] Ibid. xv, 434 f. For a parallel development, see ix, 423C-424A.

moves, therefore, from a solitary through an intermediate to a coenobitic stage. It culminates in the use of writing, but shows that more charismatic authority was to some extent maintained.

This impression of an intermediate or 'proto-coenobitic' stage in the history of the ascetic movement prompts fresh inquiry into other features of the ascetic life that seem at first sight to be typical only of an eremitic *milieu*. Ascetic texts are full, for example, of movement. The *Apophthegmata Patrum* speak frequently of travellers;[53] the *Asceticon* of Esaias debates in passage after passage the proper behaviour for monks on journeys.[54] In the time of Agathon, a 'third generation' man,[55] when the grouping of disciples around a master was a normal feature of ascetic life, monks were still regarded as ἀκάθιστοι, rootless men. Rootlessness was defended at a theoretical level: 'Such men are happy, because, with God's help, they have changed, and despise all things'.[56] This or that particular setting might suit only one type of ascesis: any change in one's programme, any step forward in the spiritual life, might demand a literal move to some other place.[57] Boredom, lethargy, a lack of challenge: such were the dangers that only mobility could counter.[58] In the eyes of some ascetics, therefore, the ξένος μοναχός, the wanderer, possessed greater virtue than those more settled, the ἐντόπιοι.[59]

Yet, here again, traces of development can be detected, and a sense of community. Mobility, coupled with an increase in numbers, led to greater communication, and to a feeling that the ascetic movement embraced more than one man's horizon. The fear of the devil himself, as betrayed in a vision to Antony, had been fulfilled: 'the desert is filled with monks'.[60] The wandering master was drawn into the

[53] G Arsenius 25, John Colobos 17, Milesius 2, Nisteroos 1, Poemen 26. Even demons might call a monk 'wanderer', G Macarius Aeg. 13.

[54] Especially XI.

[55] In Bousset's terms, well into the fifth century: *Apophthegmata*, 64. Chitty placed his death after 434, 'Abba Isaiah', 56 f.

[56] G Agathon 6.

[57] Nau 247.

[58] Nau 251.

[59] Nau 250. For similar distinctions, see Nau 367, *HM* xx. 5.

[60] *V. Ant.* 41.

narrower orbit of small and stable groups.[61] Scattered cells were no obstacle to a growing sense of unity: 'Their dwellings were divided one from another, but in spirit and faith and love they were bound together, and remained inseparable'.[62] So readers of the life of Pachomius could later be warned that monks who travelled from hermit to hermit, and set them at odds with one another by gossip and slander, deserved to burn in hell.[63] A later generation would assume that the ἀρχᾶιοι, the pioneers, had encouraged mobility for three reasons only: if they were gaining too much praise in any place, too great a reputation; if their neighbours had something against them that could not be resolved; and if they were tempted to impurity.[64] All three reasons concern social relationships, and betray the assumptions of men who had begun to feel the burdens of stability.

Perhaps the most famous advice in early ascetic literature is the simple command, 'Sit in your cell'.[65] It has an air of stability about it; and it is therefore instructive to note how early it may have been used. Macarius the Egyptian, tempted (as the text puts it) at an early stage of his ascetic career to investigate the remoter parts of the desert, found two naked men living a life of great simplicity and rigour. When he confessed that such valour was beyond him, they advised him, 'Sit in your cell, and weep for your sins'. The event, if based on fact, would date from the 330s; and the phraseology may also belong to the earlier stages of oral and written tradition: if so, the solitude of the cell was soon being contrasted with the solitude of the desert.[66] Antony himself is said, in the

[61] *HM* i, 403A. P. Nagel forcefully denied any continuity between 'wandering prophets' and ascetics who stayed in their cells, *Die Motivierung der Askese in der alten Kirche und der Ursprung des Mönchtums* (Berlin, 1966), 70–4. Certainly, there were some men in each category who never met or influenced each other, and it is equally certain that 'wandering prophets' persisted in a later period, in contrast to the (by then) well established coenobitic and semi-eremitic groups; but it is the less clearly defined examples that provide a key to change, and must be taken into account.

[62] *HM* xxi, 443B. See also the Prologue, 389 f.

[63] *V. Pach.* Bo, 88.

[64] Nau 194. For other examples, supporting this interpretation, see Poemen S 2 (Guy, *Recherches*, 29 f.); Esaias, *Ascet.* XI, 38; XII, 34; XV, 78 f.

[65] G Ammonas 4, Biare 1, Macarius Aeg. 2, Moses 6, Paphnutius 5, Poemen 2; Nau 147. 195, 202. Some of these texts are examined in what follows.

[66] G Macarius Aeg. 2. What is clearly the same story appears in *HM* xxix (under the name of Macarius of Alexandria); xxi in the Greek.

Apophthegmata Patrum, to have given the advice, 'Wherever you happen to be, do not move quickly'.[67] Another of Antony's statements, this time in the *Life*, may help to explain the phrase, 'Fish that are stranded for any time on land will die. So also monks who loiter in your company [he is addressing secular visitors], and fritter away their time among you, become dissipated and enfeebled. And therefore, like fish to the sea, we must be off to the mountain: delay will make us forget the inner life'.[68] This statement found its way into the *Apophthegmata Patrum*, but with interesting changes:[69] instead of 'in your company', the *Apophthegmata* have 'outside their cells'; and instead of 'to the mountain', they have 'to our cells'. In other words, the *Apophthegmata* have harnessed the reputation of Antony to a new emphasis on staying in one's cell, although the exact date of the text is as obscure as in the case of Macarius.[70]

These texts, therefore, with roots reaching back into the fourth century, suggest yet another change. The literal privacy of the desert gave place to privacy more fragile and intense within the group. 'They maintain the greatest silence, even when eating their food, so that you would hardly think there was anyone there at the tables where they sit; and although they are gathered together in great numbers, each one conducts himself as if he were alone'.[71] Pachomius imposed this very discipline by rule.[72] More was involved than outward formality. He wished to safeguard, amidst increasing pressure, the atmosphere of tranquillity and perception that every ascetic, whatever his style of life, would need. 'Set yourself apart', he said, 'like the wise commander

[67] G Antony 3.

[68] *V. Ant.* 85.

[69] G Antony 10.

[70] Dörries seems almost indignant that *V. Ant.* should have failed to agree with G (which is almost certainly later), 'Die Vita Antonii', 365 f. On some other points: the absence, in *V. Ant.*, of G's phrase, 'with a consequent strain upon their practice of solitude' (coming before the words, 'became dissipated and enfeebled') could be due to failure in the MS. tradition of *V. Ant.*; and the difference, 'the inner life' (*V. Ant.*)/'the safeguarding of the inner life' (G) hardly seems important. What *is* interesting is that Evagrius, translating μεθ'ὑμῶν, 'in your company', wrote *cum saecularibus*, 'in the company of seculars': G at this point reads 'outside their cells, or in the company of seculars'.

[71] *HM* iii, 407C–408A.

[72] Pachomius, *Praecepta*, 7.

of an army: weigh every thought, whether you live alone, or in the company of others'.[73] Esaias of Scetis, in a world less closely knit, made the same point: 'Let each man fear God, and keep watch upon himself in secret—upon his work, his prayer, his very soul'.[74] The air of reticence, of a hidden asceticism, enforced by the proximity of others, was essential to this new situation. Eulogius, a disciple of John Chrysostom, had been accustomed to wander in the desert with a band of companions; but then he visited Joseph of Panephysis and his more settled group, and became an *οἰκονομικός*, a 'community man': 'and even he learned to work in hidden ways'.[75]

By the end of the fourth century, therefore, it was no longer enough even to sit in one's cell. This, for Poemen for example, was no more than *τὸ φανερόν*, a superficial thing, external: he was more concerned that monks should 'make hidden progress in their cells'.[76] 'It is easy to keep silence in one's cell, but a man must never cease to ask of God the strength to combat his evil thoughts'.[77] The human heart itself had now become the cell in the most proper sense (what Augustine, in the West, would later call 'the royal cell of wisdom').[78] Ammonas, disciple of Antony, could say (as it were in one breath), 'Up, then, sit in your cell, and reckon in your heart that you are already a year in your tomb'.[79] 'The cell of a monk', says another remarkable text, 'is like the furnace in Babylon, where the three young men saw the son of God; and like the pillar of cloud, in which God spoke to Moses'.[80] It was within this enclosed arena of self-awareness that the ascetic battle was now fought.[81]

A certain emphasis on the inner man had long been a feature of the ascetic life; but it sprang from a sense that each ascetic had carved out around himself a spiritual, a mental,

[73] Pachomius, *Catech.*, trans. Lefort, 23.
[74] *Ascet.* VIII, 15; see also X, 4.
[75] G Eulogius.
[76] G Poemen 168.
[77] Esaias, *Ascet.* XIV, 13.
[78] Augustine, *Enarrationes in Psalmos*, xlvi. 10; see also Chromatius of Aquileia, *Sermo* xl. 1; Cassian, *Con.* ix. 35.
[79] G Poemen 2.
[80] Nau 206.
[81] Esaias, *Ascet.* XI, 104.

perhaps even a physical, area of self-possession and mastery that demons could not penetrate. 'When we recall', said Macarius, 'the evils that men inflict upon us, we rob ourselves of the power that comes from recollecting God; but when we recall the evils wrought by demons, nothing can harm us'.[82] These are the words of the hermit, conscious of literal withdrawal: intercourse with men means distraction from God; but one may face the demons bravely. The ascetic's imagination, in particular, stood as a no-man's-land of disputed territory, where demons might taunt him, sporting themselves between a hostile world and the stronghold of his own sanctity. He remained hidden, nevertheless, as Antony said, behind closed doors, and beyond their power.[83] This attitude reflected the lonely and exposed world of early ascetics. 'Unless a man says in his heart, "I am alone in this world with God", he will gain no rest'.[84] Demons were often the only other tenants of this empty landscape. Some were tied to one place,–in ruined temples, for example,–disillusioned or dangerously angry heirs to vanquished paganism; but early ascetics, many of them committed to lives of literal detachment, felt the whole air about them filled with wandering spirits.[85]

The inner awareness of a later generation was quite different. Even the *Life of Antony* heralds the change. The attainment of virtue, Antony says, is a task initiated and completed within the ascetic himself, and a life of restless wandering

[82] G Macarius Aeg. 36.

[83] *V. Ant.* 28, see G Phocas 1 (a late example); *V. Pach.* I, 87 (which I shall compare with the experience of Martin of Tours, below, p. 156 and n. 25); Cassian, *Con.* vii. 12–15.

[84] G Alonius 1; compare Cassian, *Con.* i. 10; iv. 3.

[85] *V. Ant.* 21. For other examples of local demons, see G Anoub 1, Macarius Aeg. 13; perhaps *HM* xxix, 453A. See also Festugière, *Moines d'Orient*, i, *Culture ou sainteté* (Paris, 1961), 31; but in his subsequent analysis, 33–9, he is too ready to describe as naïve and uncultured the struggle against demons seen as symbols of inner or personal weakness. Such struggle represented the gaining of a power base of rationality and self-control. It is nevertheless very difficult to know what to make of the conflict with demons regarded as forces outside the self. Dörries felt that the vivid conflicts of *V. Ant.* were suspiciously at odds with the portrait of Antony in G, 'Die Vita Antonii', 383 f. G may reflect a later world, where such self-expression would have been a dangerous and disruptive luxury; but even in *V. Ant.* itself, this type of conflict has a studied, almost ritual, air, particularly in 22.

is no condition of success.[86] Younger men articulated even more clearly the mechanics of this self-discipline. God created man, Esaias said, with the capacity to stand in judgement over his passions. Sin deflected this force away from the self, and turned it upon other men in the form of anger. Asceticism stifled anger, inhibited disruption, enmity, unkindness, and focused man's disapproval on his own imperfections.[87] Here was another effect of corporate asceticism. The self, instead of forming an oasis of security and refreshment, from which one could move outwards, to contend with elemental demonic powers, had now become more an intractable garden to be tilled.[88] The difficulties and strain caused by closer involvement with others, especially when combined with a discipline of silence, became interior problems, afflicting the mind, examined and resolved in private. Even dying to others, one of the basic requirements of a solitary ascetic, became more an inner disposition, quite compatible with proximity to other men. 'Unless a man tells himself in his heart that he lies already three days dead in his tomb, he will come nowhere near the perfection I speak of'.[89]

Many of these changes are illustrated by a shift in the meaning of *ξενιτεία*, exile, or pilgrimage. Taken literally, the word suggests mobility, and an isolation from that which is familiar. Hence among ascetics the word implied withdrawal from society, and from family ties.[90] With time, the notion became joined to that of stability: 'Retain the spirit of a stranger [*φρόνημα παροίκου*] in whatever place you live'.[91] It was combined with emphasis on the inner life. Agathon, for example, who had been a wanderer in his time, warned questioners later not to move from place to place, seeking the locality they considered best suited to their virtue. They should develop, he said, an interior strength that could survive anywhere.[92] Restlessness brought no respite:

[86] *V. Ant.* 20.

[87] *Ascet.* IX, 7-10; see also XIV, 56, and compare the statement of Jerome, 'Men show anger: Christians hurt no one', *Ep.* xii. 1.

[88] Compare Augustine, *Confessions*, x. 16: 'I have become to myself a soil laborious and of heavy sweat', trans. F. Sheed (London, 1948), 180.

[89] G Moses 12.

[90] Pachomius, *Catech.*, trans. Lefort, 4; Esaias, *Ascet.* XI, 21.

[91] Poemen S 4 (Guy, *Recherches*, 30).

[92] G Agathon 13.

'Wherever you may go, you will find that what you flee from goes before you'.[93] Ξενιτεία also became associated with a gradual disengagement from other ascetics; a gradual increase in the value placed on privacy. Esaias of Scetis, asked for the meaning of the word, replied, 'Wherever you live, keep silent, and say, "What is there to disturb me?" '.[94] Agathon went so far as to include it among those virtues demanded precisely by the coenobitic life.[95] The sense of mobility implied could achieve, in these new circumstances, a radically different effect: in reply to the question, 'What task is demanded of the pilgrim?', one old man said that one should come when summoned, and withdraw when dismissed—a very coenobitic emphasis![96] By the middle of the fifth century, the change in meaning was complete. Longinus expressed the desire to 'go on pilgrimage'; and Lucius replied with the warning, 'If you do not master your tongue, you will be no pilgrim, wherever you may go'. He went on to make a similar point about fasting; and then, in reply to Longinus's final request—'I wish to flee the company of men'—he connected this whole process of interiorization with an emphasis on the value of community life: 'If you do not first set yourself to rights in the company of men, you will never be able to do so on your own'.[97]

2. POWER WITHIN THE COMMUNITY

What effect did these changes have on the interpretation and exercise of ascetic authority—this stress on example, the increasing stability, the interior isolation of the coenobite? The first result was an increase in formality, reflecting the growing complexity of relationships among ascetics, and a growing sense that they had to define the extent to which they could encroach upon each other. Antony questioned God, in the place of an ἀββᾶς, and heard that some things

[93] Nau 200.

[94] *Ascet.* VI, 6Bb. This version is more reliable than G Pistos, which I used in 'Spiritual Authority', 393. The attribution in G is misplaced, Draguet, *Cinq Recensions,* iii. 73. See also Chitty, 'Abba Isaiah', 58 f.

[95] G Agathon 1; but, once again, Esaias, *Ascet.* VI, 5Aa (another version of the same) may be more reliable.

[96] Nau 306.

[97] G Longinus 1.

must remain 'matters for God to judge . . . it is not fitting that you should learn of them'.[98] In this way were the limits of discipleship marked out.[99] It was often taken for granted that a holy man's disciples would also be in some sense his servants.[100] This could sometimes create a relationship of tenderness and humanity rather than of hardship:[101] even Ammoes, who had been a difficult master to John of Thebes for many years, paid him, while dying, the memorable compliment, 'He is an angel, not a man'.[102] But these loosely defined groups of master and disciples soon acquired a more rigid framework, sometimes enforced by solemn promises;[103] a framework in which every individual had his appointed place.[104] Any attempt to reverse or undermine appointed roles within the group, even when done through the humility of older men, caused great consternation.[105] During the lifetime of Pachomius, members of his community found it hard to accept the authority of the younger Theodore.[106] Conversely, Poemen's willingness to call the young Agathon ἀββᾶ ('His words have gained for him the title') was noted with surprise as an exception, and recounted only at second hand, for the admiration of a later generation.[107] Even among equals, outspoken-

[98] G Antony 2; see also Nau 326.

[99] This was an enduring problem: compare the care of Sulpicius Severus, in his relationship with Martin of Tours, below, pp. 145 f.

[100] Especially in the case of Arsenius: G Arsenius 3, 17, 20-1; but also Silvanus 4; Nau 149, 151, 341; *V. Ant.* 51, 91; Esaias, *Ascet.* XI, 23.

[101] G Arsenius 32, Macarius Aeg. 1, 9. Macarius Aeg. 1 and *HM* xvi may provide clues as to how these relationships began.

[102] G John of Thebes. Implications of this and of the following texts I have discussed more fully in 'Blood-relationships among Early Eastern Ascetics', *JTS*, n.s. xxiii (1972), 135-44.

[103] See, e.g., the use of the word 'covenant' in *V. Pach.* I, 12, 20, at moments when association was being suggested formally.

[104] G Poemen 167. The groups themselves were not allowed to encroach upon one another, to sow dissension, or to entice away another man's disciples: a striking example, G Poemen 4; theoretical condemnation, Esaias, *Ascet.* XI, 38.

[105] When Moses asked young Zacharias the traditional question, 'Tell me, what shall I do?', 'Hearing this, he threw himself on the ground at his feet', G Zacharias 3; see also The Roman 2, Zacharias 1; *V. Pach.* I, 24.

[106] *V. Pach.* I, 77. Nevertheless, age was not always an inevitable requirement: 'Do not take it for granted that the Kingdom of Heaven is for old men alone', ibid. 119; see also G Zacharias 1, Carion 1; Nau 246, 340.

[107] G Poemen 61.

ness was to be avoided.[108] Reticence was demanded by association with others, the very first rule for the observance of men who wished to live together.[109] The only openness allowed was the admission of guilt, the request for forgiveness.[110]

In this atmosphere of formality, authority became more institutional. This does not mean that the ascetic world of Egypt presented, in later decades of the fourth century, a static contrast between *Freiheit* and *Zwange*;[111] between, on the one hand, a world where disciples chose their masters, and wandered at will, and, on the other, blind obedience that dared not question commands, however outrageous. These attitudes, in more modified form, in fact converged, to match the increasing complexity of ascetic society. Continuity in this development was maintained by the value attached to humility, a virtue prized by ascetics of whatever type. Change, on the other hand, was achieved, not by the mere restriction of freedom, but by the fact that the supervision of disciples could be prolonged—thanks precisely to growing emphasis on stability, loyalty, and imitation.[112]

This change was not sudden. Early misgivings about obedience, the typical virtue of the coenobite, can be found even in Pachomian literature. Pachomius himself had to face great opposition from his first disciples: 'Seeing his humility . . . they treated him with scorn, and very little respect. If he ever gave them an order about the course of action to be followed in some matter where their needs were concerned, they argued to his face, insulted him, and said, "We shall not obey" '.[113] His own fears about the future of his community[114] may have centred on what he regarded as the danger of more institutional authority; and he felt compelled to prophesy, with evident disapproval and foreboding,

[108] This was the obverse of Agathon's enforcement of *ξενιτεία* in community life, G Agathon 1: see above, p. 48.

[109] Esaias, *Ascet.* VI, 5Ab; X, 28.

[110] Pachomius, *Catech.*, trans. Lefort, 25.

[111] Bousset, 'Das Mönchtum', 9.

[112] Bacht, 'Antonius und Pachomius', 94.

[113] *V. Pach.* S[1], 3, trans. Lefort, 4. For comment, and a criticism of M. M. van Molle, see F. Ruppert, *Das Pachomianische Mönchtum und die Anfänge klösterlichen Gehorsams* (Münsterschwarzacher Studien, xx; 1971), 46–57.

[114] See above, p. 23.

'Jealousy and conflict are inevitable. Self-interest will govern every hotly debated contest as to who should be in charge, or thought the greater. Good men will be slandered, and the evil chosen; and, in his desire to be preferred above others, each will appeal, not to his virtuous conduct, but to his years and rank'.[115]

Even when obedience was accepted on more definite terms, 'virtuous conduct', and the admiration that it might inspire, were still regarded as important qualities. Readiness to conform remained at root the willing response to a charismatic master, and therefore took place in the context of traditional relationships. Pachomius wished those who governed his communities to be 'men of spiritual power';[116] and he described dependence upon them in traditional terms: 'If you cannot manage on your own, seek the company of some other man who labours in accordance with the Gospel of Christ, and with him you will make progress. Either listen well yourself, or submit yourself wholly to one who listens'.[117] It was still faith that prompted obedience; the belief that, by submitting to the guidance of the father, one could guarantee fulfilment of God's will.[118] Fathers, for their part, recognized this link between obedience and trusting admiration. A command must be given with care, 'in the fear of God, and with humility': then 'the word, uttered with God's help, will make the brother submissive, and lead him to do his duty'. If, on the other hand, commands were given 'as if with authority', then 'God . . . will not inspire him either to listen or to carry out the command'.[119] The continuity is clear. Advising one man, who had already gathered a group of disciples about him, Poemen vigorously argued against rigid authority: 'You must be an example to them, not a legislator'.[120] When Anoub set up a new community

[115] *V. Pach.* Dion. 45.

[116] *V. Pach.* I, 54. When Palladius came to write *HL*, he could still explain the title 'abbess', even in the ordered context of a Pachomian monastery, with the words, 'for this is what they call those endowed with the Spirit', *HL* xxxiv.

[117] Pachomius, *Catech.*, trans. Lefort, 6. When he says earlier, 'My son, obey me' (Lefort, 3), the context makes it clear that he means, 'Follow my advice, based on experience'; compare the phrase, 'Listen to me', *V. Pach.* I, 42.

[118] Nau 290. [119] Nau 315.

[120] G Poemen 174.

with his brothers, after the devastation of Scetis by barbarians in 407, he demanded obedience, and imposed on them a common life; but it was the charismatic quality of his example and teaching that had bound them together in the first place.[121]

One can detect, however, a gradual hardening of attitudes. Macarius was faced with a man accused of murder, yet pleading innocence. Practical as ever, he raised the murdered man to life, and revealed by questions that the other had indeed been wrongfully accused. The bystanders involved, no less alive to their opportunity, demanded that Macarius discover the true culprit; but the holy man replied, 'Enough for me that an innocent man has been set free: it is no task of mine to bring to light the guilty'.[122] Such was the judgement of the pioneers. Later attitudes are reflected in a story about Theodore. He was counselling a group of monks, among them one who had eaten some food against his better judgement—'He had not obeyed the inner promptings of the Lord'. The monks asked Theodore to tell them their faults; and while speaking to another, he aroused the compunction of the glutton. 'Pray for me,' the monk cried, 'for I set my conscience at nought, knowing what duty demanded. Because I disobeyed the worthy suggestions of my heart, the Lord has rebuked me publicly'.[123] Here, individual judgement and charismatic insight begin to play a part in the development of more social sanctions. A further step of some importance was the insistence of superiors that they be consulted in advance, as it were, and not merely informed of problems which disciples had recognized, analysed, and grappled with for some time alone.[124] At a final stage, wrongdoers had to be expelled, for the protection of the group. 'When evil men

[121] Esaias, *Ascet.* VI, 2. This version must replace, as more reliable, that used in my 'Blood-relationships', where the incident is discussed more fully, 141 f. The story appears also, without naming Anoub, in *Vita Melaniae*, 44.

[122] *HM* xxviii, 450D–451A.

[123] *V. Pach.* Bo, 87.

[124] Esaias, *Ascet.* XII, 30. Questions in G in the form 'What shall I do?' may mark the beginning of this process: Antony 1, Ares 1, Biare 1, Zacharias 3, John Colobos 19, Joseph of Panephysis 4, Poemen 50, 62, 64, Pistamon 1; see also Nau 195, 202, 215; and (less directly stated) G Ammoes 1, John Colobos 8, Cyrus 1, Nisteroos the Coenobite 2, Poemen 1; Nau 219.

increase in number alongside others, the anger of God comes down no less upon those others who are good, and all are subject to his curse'.[125]

The teaching of Peter, disciple of Esaias, (flourishing, therefore, in the late fifth century,) illustrates these developments. First, he demanded an honest candour: 'Every thought, every affliction, every wish, and every burden–hide none of them, but make them known readily to your father–; and whatever you hear him say, set yourself to carry out with confidence'.[126] But more formal obedience to his precepts was a condition of remaining in his company; and there was an element of *quid pro quo* in this assertion, together with a hint of more theoretical sanctions: 'If you keep my commands, both secretly and openly, then I shall speak to God on your behalf. If you do not keep them, God will demand to speak with you about your neglect–and indeed with me about my carelessness'.[127] The need to cooperate with others, to become involved in larger groups, was therefore making its mark. Humility and love continued, for a long time, to stand in place of regulations, and even then to override them; but more stable asceticism, in a relatively crowded setting, called for great self-control, and submission to others.[128] Where numbers were even greater, discipline was more obvious. Readers of the *Liber*, the last gift of Orsisius to his Pachomian subjects,–'living in community, and bound to us in love',–were nevertheless conscious of a new emphasis: 'The cross, basis of our life, is also the basis of our teaching'.[129] Pachomius, in his *Praecepta atque Iudicia*, legislated almost entirely for problems concerning relationships with others, and gave the warning, 'Anyone who despises the commands of the elders, and the rules of the monastery, which have been laid down in accordance with God's command, or anyone who attaches little weight to the advice of older men, shall be punished in the manner laid down, until he mends

[125] *V. Pach.* Bo, 107. [126] Esaias, *Ascet.* VIII, 27.
[127] Ibid. 28 f.
[128] Esaias, *Ascet.* XII, 26-7, and especially 48, sum up the point very forcefully.
[129] Orsisius, *Liber*, 50 (following the text and trans. of Bacht, *Vermächtnis*, 174-7, and n. 229).

his ways'.[130] Superiors were becoming more impersonal and remote; and the awareness was growing that outward conformity might be achieved without an interior submission.[131] Attention became focused, therefore, here as elsewhere, upon private, hidden difficulties, and upon sanctions that had their chief effect in secret. Ascetics must obey willingly, but 'full of virtue, and the fear of God': 'Anyone who wishes to live without stain . . . must carry out, in the sight of God, all things commanded'.[132] Monks in the later monastery of Jeremias would rarely have escaped from this more absolute authority, but would be compelled to turn over frequently in their minds the silent but insistent admonitions inscribed on their walls: 'Examine thyself, be contented, control thyself alone, obey, be humble, judge not, condemn not, forgive that you may be forgiven and that you may live in God'.[133]

[130] Pachomius, *Praecepta atque Iudicia*, 8.
[131] Theodore, *Catech.*, trans. Lefort, 45 f.
[132] Pachomius, *Praecepta ac Leges*, 3, 8; Orsisius, *Liber*, 19.
[133] Quibell, *Excavations*, iii. 37 f.

IV

ASCETICS IN THE CHURCH

At this point, we can allow ourselves to emerge again upon a wider stage of events in the Eastern Church and Empire—'to go up to Egypt', as the monks of Scetis used to say—: the history of asceticism had by this time reached the threshold of a more public forum for the exercise of spiritual authority. We have seen how the power of the holy man could startle and transform his closer associates; and how his authority sometimes encouraged, sometimes responded to, the development of corporate asceticism. But that power, as Eunapius bore witness, asserted itself beyond the confines of the desert, especially towards the end of the century; and the urge to share his experience with others not only compelled the ascetic to form or join groups of like-minded men but allowed him to respond to, or even to anticipate, the invitation to affect a wider audience.

This response took the form, in part, of a desire to convert men, and to share in the priestly ministry of the church. Pachomius, in particular, is credited in some sources with apostolic motives that seem to point beyond the organization of his disciples. He was supposedly praised by Antony, as we have seen, precisely because his new community experiment represented a concern 'for the nourishment of other souls'.[1] His first experience of Christianity, according to the *Vita Prima*, had been of a selfless regard for the welfare of others. Its followers were described to him as 'doing good in every way to all men'; and in his first prayer to the God of the Christians, Pachomius responded in similar terms: 'Loving all men, I shall serve them in accordance with your commandment'.[2] Palamon, his first instructor in asceticism, gave him a similar example, praying habitually that God

[1] See above, pp. 34 f.

[2] *V. Pach.* I, 4 f.

might rescue both himself and all men from the tyranny of evil.[3] Pachomius's own enterprises were marked by a similar spirit, impelled by divine revelation: 'It is God's wish that you should minister to the human race [a wide-ranging ambition], reconciling men to himself'.[4] Much of this may represent, of course, the personal feelings of the writer of the *Vita Prima*, for whom the change of life that properly marked the beginning of an ascetic career was closely linked with conversion to the church.[5] Yet the same note is sounded in the *Historia Monachorum*, for example, which says of monks in general, 'There should be no doubt: it is by their merits that the world still stands'.[6]

Some of these statements may reflect wisdom after the event; the attempt by a later generation to justify or explain developments. Words in the *Vita Prima* attributed to Pachomius—'The community itself is the model for all those who wish to bring souls together as God desires; to give them aid, until they reach perfection'—are in fact recounted there by Theodore.[7] Similarly, in the Bohairic life, it is Theodore who emphasizes this interpretation of the past: 'God made with Pachomius a solemn promise that he would save, through this his minister, a multitude of souls'.[8] The *Liber* of Orsisius recalls the work of Pachomius in much the same terms.[9]

More to the point is the fact that such 'apostolic' sentiments can be flatly contradicted in closely associated texts. The first Christian prayer of Pachomius, with its phrase,

[3] Ibid. 11.

[4] Ibid. 23. Coptic sources make the same point. *V. Pach.* S[1], 1: 'It was revealed to him that he must labour *for the souls of men*, so that he might present them as a pure offering to God', trans. Lefort, 1. Bo, 52 (= S[5], 52): 'You must also set up a monastery at Tkahšmîn, so that you can restore to unity for me *one people in that district*', trans. Lefort, 247. On this last point, one may anticipate some of the problems discussed below by pointing out that the later phrase in Bo, 88, 'to the brethren, *and to the whole word*', trans. Lefort, 149, is *not* reproduced in S[5].

[5] *V. Pach.* I, 2.

[6] *HM* Prologue, 390, later echoed in one of the most striking inscriptions from the monastery of Jeremias: 'This is the spot on which our lord and father Apa Jeremias bowed himself, until he removed the sins of the people of the whole world', no. 188, Quibell, *Excavations*, iv. 55.

[7] *V. Pach.* I, 136.

[8] *V. Pach.* Bo, 194.

[9] Orsisius, *Liber*, 47.

'I shall serve them', is reproduced in the corresponding chapter of Dionysius by the words, 'I commit myself to serve you [referring to God]'.[10] The revelation to Pachomius, with the phrase, 'that you should minister to the human race', appears in Dionysius as 'that you should serve him with a pure mind [referring again to God]', and in the *Vita Altera* as, 'that you should minister to him'.[11] Variations within the Greek tradition are difficult to interpret, not least because of doubts about dating. Dionysius and the *Vita Altera* must either reflect an earlier, 'pre-ecclesial', world, coming before a reinterpretation of events in the *Vita Prima*,[12] or else they attempt to support later reaction against involvement with the church.[13] In either case, they offer warning that some statements in the *Vita Prima* may be partisan; and they show that controversy soon arose over the closer association of ascetics with the broader pastoral ambitions of the church as a whole.

One is not surprised to find, therefore, other signs of reluctance in this matter, although, by the time they came to be expressed, in the texts we now possess, attitudes had been compromised, if not confused, by long-standing debate. Pachomius felt, for example, that to seek office in the church was to run the risk of pride.[14] His anxiety on this score was, however, more for the community than for the individual. He did not wish to see his subjects afflicted by divisions and enmity, so widespread a feature of the church in his day; divisions and enmity fomented most, it seemed to him, by clerical interest. It was, nevertheless, the *seeking* of office that he prohibited: he foresaw without dismay that individual monks might soon be called upon by bishops and

[10] *V. Pach.* I, 5; Dion. 4.

[11] *V. Pach.* I, 23, Dion. 21; II, 21. I, 24 contains the phrase 'serving God and yourselves'; and strangely enough Dion. alters this as well (22), applying it to the disciples: 'thus serving [plural, *servientes*] the Lord, and loving one another according to his command'.

[12] *V. Pach.* Dion. 26 (= II, 25) makes this the less likely suggestion.

[13] The textual divergences are fully discussed by Ruppert, *Pachomianische Mönchtum*, 13–18, with conclusions analogous to my own. He emphasizes the theologizing tendency of *V. Pach.* I, and suggests that this text may mark the moment of change between an emphasis on serving men and serving God. See also his discussion of other events in Pachomius's life, 18–41.

[14] A point much emphasized by Chitty, *Desert*, 23.

superiors to undertake priestly duties within the community. Provided that they fulfilled their ministry worthily, and restricted themselves to those sacred functions, they deserved the honour traditionally offered to ascetics of senior rank and outstanding sanctity.[15] Pachomius himself avoided ordination,[16] but he was aware of a common bond between the clergy and professional ascetics. He prayed for them with special affection, and commanded that they should be entertained in the community with great respect.[17]

A less moderate attitude appears in later texts. The Bohairic life describes the care of the sick in nearby villages, for example, as a task suitable for clerics, but forbidden to monks.[18] They should concentrate, rather, on ceaseless prayer, vigils, readings from God's law, and manual labour. On this last, a more hopeful note is struck—with reference to manual labour, Scripture gives us certain commands, allowing us to extend a hand to those in need—; but this is shown to be a secondary effect, albeit fortunate, the main purpose being to render monks, through their resulting self-sufficiency, 'free from any human obligation'.[19]

This air of two separate spheres of activity, the ascetic and the secular, can be detected in some earlier passages also, particularly (as one might, perhaps, expect) in the *Apophthegmata Patrum*. The attitude of desert fathers to the secular world in general seems accurately summed up in Arsenius's retort to a rich lady from Rome: 'I have prayed God to wipe away from my heart all memory of you'.[20] It must be noted, however, that this abrupt manner was a reaction against what the fathers regarded as appeals for the wrong kind of help or advice; appeals that did not reflect, in other words, the docile faith of the true disciple.[21] It explains why Arsenius could reject so brusquely even the

[15] So, on the whole issue, *V. Pach.* I, 27; but Bo omits the last concession.

[16] *V. Pach.* I, 29 f., but with great tact: compare the exaggerated emphasis of Bo, 28.

[17] *V. Pach.* Bo, 101; Pachomius, *Praecepta*, 51. In this last, 'clerics . . . or monks' are treated together, distinct from the 'seculars' of 52; and they are allowed to eat and pray with the monks of Pachomius's own monastery.

[18] *V. Pach.* Bo, 9.

[19] Ibid. 35—omitted in I.

[20] G Arsenius 28; see also 31; *HL* x, lviii.

[21] G Daniel 3, Poemen 3, 7, Sisoes 18.

Patriarch Theophilus.[22] Pambo was supposed to have done the same, maintaining a stoney silence during the churchman's visit, and justifying himself afterwards with the famous remark, 'If he gained no assistance from my silence, then nothing I could say would have been of help to him'.[23] Both men were making the point that Theophilus had not come with the attitudes and aims of a disciple.

There are several such examples of fathers who rejected mere curiosity in those who came to see them.[24] Other anecdotes, however, reveal that, when a visitor was already a member of the ascetic group, and when he had already identified himself with those who truly sought perfection, then such a desire simply to see the holy man, and to appeal to his intercessory powers, was perfectly acceptable.[25] It is in this light that one should read Antony's statement, 'When we gain a brother, we gain God'.[26] The word 'brother', ἀδελφός, was consistently used to refer to ascetics; and all the other examples of Antony's concern for his fellows in the *Apophthegmata Patrum* refer to the ascetic world.[27]

This unwillingness on the part of some to take note of a wider audience shows only how keenly they were aware of forming a definite group, with its own aims, its own problems, and, not least of all, its own standards. They were anxious to maintain, in the face of outside pressure, the identity of that group. The moderation of Pachomius, on the other hand, and the signs of debate in the literary sources, point to changes in this group mentality, and to the weakening of this reluctance to exercise spiritual influence further afield.

Change was not abrupt, but kept pace with a widening definition of discipleship. Some ascetic communities absorbed new members only with difficulty; and these were

[22] G Arsenius 7. Theophilus 5 shows that the Patriarch continued, even so, to hold Arsenius in high esteem.

[23] G Theophilus 2. It could not have been Pambo, in fact, Chitty, *Desert*, 56; and, since Pambo shows a quite different attitude in G Pambo 4, Theophilus 2 may reflect rather later opinion on the matter.

[24] G Moses 8, Poemen 5, Simon 1 f.

[25] G Macarius Aeg. 4, 33–4, Poemen 6.

[26] G Antony 9.

[27] G Antony 15, 21, 23.

even more reluctant to establish contact with a non-monastic world. Others were embarking upon programmes of confident expansion, and more readily welcomed the interest and demands of outsiders. In other words, involvement with the affairs of the church as a whole was furthered precisely by those pressures that were prompting the growth of the coenobitic movement. The very images used by ascetics to describe, interpret, and encourage that movement reveal at its centre a principle of vitality too powerful, too universal and ambitious, to be contained within the movement itself. Ascetics are 'firebrands to light the world', 'the seed blessed by God'.[28] Describing the brotherhood of his followers, Pachomius piles up theological terms that embrace the salvation of all men: 'What dangers we run, when we hate others—those who are our brothers, bound to us like members in one body, the sons of God, branches of the true vine, that spiritual flock gathered together by the true shepherd, God's only begotten son, who offered himself in sacrifice for us'.[29] The letters of Antony are equally wideranging: 'The creator of all things . . . has built for us a house of truth, the Catholic Church, which is the source of unity; for God wished us to be converted to himself, the very origin of all things'.[30] Orsisius, advising superiors, quotes the words of Christ, 'The good shepherd lays down his life for his sheep', and his command to Peter, 'Feed my lambs'; and then, in case the point is not startlingly clear, he urges upon the 'leaders of the monasteries' the same sense of responsibility, 'For you know that you will have to give an account for the whole flock over which the Holy Spirit appointed you as watchmen, and as pastors of that church of God which he gained by his own blood'.[31] With similar confidence, the *Historia Monachorum* (quoting Isaiah, 'The wilderness and the dry land shall be glad, the desert shall rejoice and blossom like the crocus') adds by way of explanation, 'Although these things were said of the church, they have been historically fulfilled even in the desert of Egypt'.[32] Reading these passages, all from the fourth

[28] Pachomius, *Catech.*, trans. Lefort, 17; Theodore, *Catech.*, trans. Lefort, 43.
[29] Pachomius, *Catech.*, trans. Lefort, 15.
[30] *Letters*, ii. 9 f.; see also ii. 22 f., iii. 27 f., iv. 91, v. 30, vi. 24 f.
[31] Orsisius, *Liber*, 17, 40. [32] *HM* vii, 413B.

century, one can more readily understand how, within a generation, men who claimed the desert fathers as their patrons would embrace without hesitation the duties of the episcopate.

So much for the attitude, the cast of mind: what was its practical effect? The first hint of later development comes with a proliferation of 'presbyters' among the ascetic communities.[33] It is hard to decide what was their precise function. Antony calls himself a presbyter, but with the clear implication that it does not mean priest.[34] Such men may have ministered, like Macarius, or indeed like Pachomius himself, to the purely material needs of their colleagues;[35] but there were those who did exercise liturgical duties in no way dependent upon their personal sanctity, or capacity for leadership.[36] Dorotheus, presbyter at Antinoe, probably represents the norm: he combined these sacred and material duties in the service of the solitaries who lived nearby.[37] Macarius of Alexandria, described by Palladius as a presbyter in the Cells, certainly celebrated the eucharist, and at the same time possessed sufficient authority and self-confidence to rebuke a fellow priest for impurity, and a misplaced love of learning, forcing him in the end to revert to the status of layman.[38] In Nitria there were (again, according to Palladius) eight priests, whose duty is was, not only to celebrate the eucharist, but also to instruct the monks, and even to pass judgement upon them.[39]

More important than the function of this monastic priesthood was the effect it had, in ascetic society, on the understanding of authority. It became, at first, a support for that authority, and then a substitute. Events in the life of Isidore of Scetis show what could happen at intermediate stages of

[33] In addition to the examples discussed below, see G Benjamin 2, Eulogius, Esaias 4, John Colobos 7, Isidore 1, Isaac of the Cells 1, 8, Carion 2, Matoes 9, Poemen 11, 44, Pambo 11 (but see Bousset, *Apophthegmata*, 61), Timothy 1; *HM* ix, 422A; xiii. 10.

[34] *V. Ant.* 16

[35] *HL* xxv; *V. Pach.* S[1], 2; Nau 259.

[36] Nau 254. Ascetic priests, ministering to colleagues, may be implied by *HM* xi, 430B; xv, 434A.

[37] *HL* lviii.

[38] Ibid. xviii.

[39] Ibid. vii.

this process. Priesthood enabled him to criticize with greater confidence the conduct of his colleagues, and to stand apart, to some extent, from their various patterns of association and discipleship.[40] In the end, however, functions traditionally reserved for spiritual leaders endowed with charismatic power were gradually taken over by men whose qualifications were almost entirely clerical. It was clerics, now, who gave spiritual assurance, when famous holy men were no longer able to 'speak the word'; it was clerics who possessed visionary power; and the peace of soul that had previously come from hearing the words of the fathers could now be brought about by formal penance, performed in company perhaps more numerous and less familiar than the group of disciples around their spiritual master.[41] A man's priesthood could play an important part in the attraction of disciples, and in the preservation of the group.[42] Macarius the Egyptian, one of the pioneers of asceticism, and a typical charismatic leader in the old style,[43] experienced many of these changes in his own career. Not only did he become a priest, but he tried to establish during his lifetime what amounted to a priestly dynasty, handing on his ministry to his disciple John.[44] The manner in which authority had been passed down traditionally, from one generation to the next within the ascetic group, was now becoming confused with the continuity of a clerical system. The process was no less marked in Pachomian circles. By the time he felt able to found a community of women, Pachomius thought it best to place them under

[40] He gave shelter and hospitality to ascetics rejected by their communities, G Isidore 1; and Poemen 44 shows him leaving a community whose standards had declined; but *HL* xix suggests that he continued to exercise more traditional duties. Compare G Isaac of the Cells 7, where a similar withdrawal was threatened: Isaac, in charge of the 'ecclesia' there (Isaac of the Cells 8), felt that the more traditional basis of his leadership had become weakened: 'I have no commands to give you, for you do not keep them'.

[41] G Pambo 2, Esaias 4; Nau 165. G Bessarion 7 shows that other ascetics still rejected this tendency; and see Bessarion 5, where the traditional holy man is called in to rescue clerics from their own incompetence. But Moses, caught cooking on a fast day, was reported to, and publicly rebuked by, the local clergy, Moses 5. Compare the role of the presbyter in Nau 242.

[42] *HL* xlvii, xlix.

[43] G Macarius Aeg. 25, 27–8, 41.

[44] *HL* xvii. Cassian told how Paphnutius attempted to do the same with his disciple Daniel, *Con.* iv. 1.

the sole authority of a presbyter and a deacon. These were the only men allowed across the river to the women's monastery, and that only on Sundays. Their function extended well beyond the sphere of liturgy. When a dispute arose within the community, the presbyter excommunicated the offender, barring her from the eucharist, and cutting her off for a long time from the companionship of her sisters.[45]

Acquiring its own clergy in this way could have made the monastic movement even more independent of the church as a whole, particularly in the administration of the sacraments; but, in the event, ascetic groups seem to have been drawn more within the orbit of episcopal control. A number of ascetics seem to have placed their charismatic power at the disposal of the hierarchy;[46] others found themselves more often under pressure from local priests.[47] This was still a far cry from promptly accepting ecclesiastical office outside ascetic circles, a move against which there was much more resistance.[48] Even those who allowed themselves to become bishops, like Netras of Pharan, (a late example, in any case,) did so with considerable misgivings, and with the determination that they would continue, as far as possible, to put into practice in their new surroundings the ideals of their former state.[49] Events in general moved more slowly. Bishops tried, with varying success, to engage ascetics in long-term projects. As early as 330, Serapion of Tentyra had expressed a wish to organize the monks of his diocese under the general supervision of Pachomius, whom he had hoped to ordain a priest. Nothing came of this.[50] About ten years later, Arius of

[45] *HL* xxxiii.

[46] A striking example, of uncertain date, concerns Macarius: Preuschen, *Palladius und Rufinus*, 124-30. On the relation of this text to *HL* (open to suspicion) and to G (much more likely), see Butler, *Lausiac History*, ii. 194, n. 28. The caution betrayed, not only by the Greek text in Preuschen, but also by the variety in the tradition of the story, shows how long misgivings persisted. For a fuller discussion, with reference to Rufinus and Cassian, see below, pp. 214 f.

[47] G Bessarion 5, Moses 2, Simon 2. In these cases, the role of the clergy in summoning their help is important. Ascetics who interfered on their own initiative could expect a sharp rebuke, Agathon 14.

[48] G Theodore of Pherme 25, Macarius Aeg. 1, Matoes 9, Moses 4.

[49] G Apphy, Netras.

[50] *V. Pach.* I, 29. Bo omits the incident. Dion. 26 (= II, 25) emphasizes even more strongly that Pachomius had not been completely unwilling to cooperate; but no doubt the threat of ordination deterred him. Chitty suggested that the

Panopolis was able to persuade the community at Tabennesis to found another monastery nearer his city, 'so that, thanks to you, the blessing of the Lord might be bestowed upon our district'. He may have won their co-operation more easily by being himself 'an ascetic, and a servant of Christ'.[51]

Cooperation could be dangerous. It was no doubt flattering, and an excitement, to be invited to Alexandria by the Patriarch himself, 'to offer up prayers, and destroy the temples';[52] but could one anticipate and counter the duplicity of the man? Initially, Theophilus approved the teaching of Origen; but later, under pressure from the desert, he condemned those ascetics who applied his ideas. Isidore, 'the hostelier', he finally disowned—a monk in Nitria, once; later his own close servant (as of Athanasius before him); and almost Patriarch of Constantinople. And then, in 399, he hounded from Egypt the so-called 'Tall Brothers', together with hundreds of other Origenist monks (among them Palladius and Cassian). Such events were a grim reminder that the favour of the great was an unpredictable and risky privilege.[53] Other bishops had already displayed what would have seemed to many ascetics an unhealthy anxiety about the authority of their leaders.[54] We have seen how they summoned Pachomius to a synod at Latopolis, in 345;[55] and when Arians in Alexandria claimed the support of Antony (probably in 330 or 337), both bishops and monks called him to the city, and heard his denial with very evident relief.[56]

foundation of Faou at this time, in a neighbouring diocese, may have been a move to escape Serapion's jurisdiction, 'A Note on the Chronology', 381.

[51] *V. Pach.* I, 81 f.; S[5], trans. Lefort, 248; see also Dion. 39, 42; II, 66; Bo, 55.

[52] Nau 162; but the text illustrates well (and amusingly) how out of place ascetics could be in the city.

[53] This is not the place for a full account of events, although they will be discussed further with reference to Jerome and Cassian, who were both involved. One of the best surveys, and certainly the most exciting, is that of N. H. Baynes, 'Alexandria and Constantinople: a Study in Ecclesiastical Diplomacy', *Byzantine Studies and Other Essays* (repr. London, 1960), 97-115.

[54] In addition to obvious references, such as those discussed here, there are some more obscure hints. In Nau 161, a 'presbyter of Scetis' goes to Alexandria to visit Theophilus: to report? The 'deacon' who visits a community in Nau 177 looks suspiciously like an episcopal agent. See also above, p. 63, n. 41.

[55] *V. Pach.* I, 112; see above, pp. 30 f.

[56] *V. Ant.* 69 f.

Interference of this sort continued to provoke a reaction. Nathanael stated, politely but firmly, 'I have died to my lords the bishops, as indeed to the whole world'; and Arsenius, we have seen, rejected Theophilus himself.[57] Pachomius, more cautious, did not underestimate the importance or the rights of bishops;[58] but he would attempt, in a subtle way, to restrict them to activity on a spiritual plane.[59] He tried, without complete success, to avoid identifying authority and office, and appealed more to an underlying power (again, ἐξουσία), such as Theodore possessed, which he saw as the basis of all true authority. He admitted that some men in the church appeared to be shepherds, others sheep; but all men in reality were sheep, under Christ the one shepherd. Christ had given his apostles the command to feed his flock, and bishops certainly inherited that fatherly responsibility; but there were others, lacking official status in the church, who could nevertheless lay claim to the same inheritance, and exercise the same function: those who heard the voice of Christ within them.[60]

Yet it was Pachomian communities that seem, in the end, to have shown the most submission. Such at least is the impression given in the *Vita Prima*. It tells how Athanasius, making a triumphant return to Alexandria (after yet another exile) in 363, and meeting Theodore (at that time leader of the communities), insisted that the title of 'father' belonged not to bishops but to monks and their superiors; to Theodore in particular, in whom the Patriarch professed to see Christ himself. But Theodore was quick to return the compliment—'When we look at you, it is as if we looked upon Christ'—; and that was the opinion that prevailed.[61] In the closing

[57] *HL* xvi; see above, pp. 59 f.

[58] *V. Pach.* I, 2.

[59] Ibid. 37: a mother had come with episcopal letters, demanding to see her son (a monk in the community); but Pachomius confidently suggested that the bishops would value more highly the woman's obedient acceptance of Pachomius's prohibition than they would Pachomius's acceptance of their original command.

[60] *V. Pach.* I, 135.

[61] Ibid. 144; and even more strongly in Bo, 202, although a motive is there expressed that is entirely monastic: 'because of our great faith in you, for you are our father', trans. Lefort, 223. See also I, 94. One cannot help recalling the later cry of the Patriarch Theophilus, faced with the monks who objected to his

pages of the *Vita Prima*, after the death of Theodore himself, Athanasius is seen taking more and more control. He virtually confirms Orsisius in his position as leader for the second time, and claims a partnership in his authority; he requests to be kept in touch with community affairs; and he directs the prayers of the monks to intercession for the peace of the church.[62]

Festal Letter against anthropomorphism: 'When I see you, it is like seeing the face of God', Socrates, *HE* vi. 7.

[62] *V. Pach.* I, 150.

V

THE WRITTEN WORD

This account of links in the East between ascetics and the church is necessarily inconclusive. By 400 events and personalities in the West are demanding our attention; and at that time the *entente* in Egypt was scarcely under way. In the condemnation of Origen, the exile of the Tall Brothers and their companions, the death of Evagrius, and the departure of Palladius and Cassian, the century ended with a drastic demonstration of misunderstanding and bitterness between bishops and monks. Beside this upheaval, the unholy alliance of Theophilus and the 'anthropomorphites' opposed to Origen carries less weight, offering no proof that the ascetic movement was yet successfully harnessed to the purposes of the church.

The justice in taking, at this particular moment, the first of our 'sideways steps'—in this case, from Egypt to the world of Jerome—depends on the fact that, by the end of the century, asceticism in Egypt had reached a new level, as well as a new stage, in its development. Attitudes in the *Vita Prima*, for example, analysed at the end of the last chapter, bring an historian to his senses: the text is clearly a weapon, defending one interpretation of how monks should regard their patriarch. In describing the social framework, therefore, within which spiritual authority was exercised, we are victims of the sources; the fascinated, if reluctant, disciples of ascetic masters. So, of course, were many before us. The *Apophthegmata Patrum*, the *Lives* and *Rule* of Pachomius, helped to create the world they revealed; and the authors regarded not only their interpretation of events but also the literary forms in which it was expressed as the natural culmination of ascetic history. Once again, the pace and pattern of change had encouraged, indeed compelled, those in authority to exercise power and protect their leadership in new ways—in this case by writing.

The change must be examined: the *Life of Antony* inspired the literary style, if not the ascetic ideals, of Jerome and Sulpicius Severus; the *Rule* of Pachomius, in its written form, represented a new desire to codify ascetic practice, not only in the East; and the emergence of the *Apophthegmata* provided an essential background to the writings of Palladius and Cassian.

Decline in charismatic power, growth in numbers, and an increasing emphasis on example brought about important changes in the relationships of ascetics one with another. Many of the rank and file, particularly within large coenobitic communities, could no longer hope for the eventual position of ἀββᾶς, and may have found Pachomius, Theodore, or Orsisius, amidst the crowd, remote.[1] They turned more often to each other, so that colleagues and companions now had at least as great an effect as spiritual masters on personal development. In the company of his own brethren, a monk would discuss the teaching of the elders, before retiring for the night.[2] Together, they exercised control over more immediate superiors.[3] When those in authority were absent, they regulated their own affairs, teaching each other, and passing judgement on their equals.[4] Orsisius, having stressed that superiors were answerable to Christ, continued, 'And this is to be understood, not only of those in charge of the various houses, but also of each of the brethren in the common body: all must carry one another's burden, in order to fulfil the law of Christ'.[5]

The source of these illustrations, for the most part the *Rule* of Pachomius, hints at the sequel. The impact of monk upon monk, now beyond the immediate reach of ascetic masters, had still to be regulated by a lasting and universal sanction; and written texts met such a need. The preservation of authority itself was at stake.

In communities less strictly organized, such as those in Scetis, the danger that accompanied this growth in numbers,

[1] Bacht, 'Antonius und Pachomius', 95; but see *V. Pach.* Bo, 80, 107, 195.
[2] Pachomius, *Praecepta*, 19, 122.
[3] *Praecepta et Instituta*, 17.
[4] *Praecepta ac Leges*, 13 f.
[5] Orsisius, *Liber*, 11.

this expansion of a community of equals, was clearly recognized. Ascetics were urged to discuss their problems only with their elders.[6] When talking to brethren, they should recount no more than they had seen themselves; and, in such conversations, no one should attempt to dominate his fellows, or claim greater authority for his own words.[7] John of Lycopolis warned of those who renounced the world, 'in order to go and see some holy father, hear a few words from his lips, pass them on to others, and boast of having learned from this man or this: they want to teach others instantly–not the things that they themselves have done, but things they have heard and seen'.[8] It was probably in just these ways that the sayings of the fathers had been preserved; but one can see why example and imitation came to be regarded as better safeguards of tradition. Emphasis lay on preserving immediate relationships with the fathers themselves, hinting at a world where such contact was becoming harder to maintain.

As with the *Rule* of Pachomius, therefore, so with other sources: the written word was seized on as a more accessible alternative to the charismatic authority of the holy man. Certainly, the compiler of the *Apophthegmata Patrum* saw his work in this light. The collection was designed 'to encourage an eager envy, a discipline, a willingness to imitate among those who wished to follow aright a heavenly way of life'.[9] Envy, discipline, and imitation had been precisely the effects formerly produced by the epigrammatic wisdom, the detailed advice, and the vivid example of the fathers.[10] Palladius regarded his writings in the same way. They marked the beginning of a new tradition, a new pattern of discipleship and spiritual formation. By presenting as examples the lives of holy men, he hoped that his readers would become examples in their turn.[11]

New bonds and new sanctions were accompanied by new and sometimes lower standards. Pachomius in particular was

[6] Esaias, *Ascet.* V, 11; XIII, 2. [7] Ibid. X, 55; XXIII, 6s.
[8] *HM* i. 397AB. [9] *PG* lxv. 72A.
[10] The three types of encounter described above, pp. 19 ff., 35 ff.
[11] *HL*, Preface.

anxious to provide an environment for men of moderate goodwill, as well as heroes,[12] 'those brethren of lesser note in the common life, who do not devote themselves to labours of great moment, or an exaggerated asceticism, but proceed in a simple way, obedient to the rules set down, ready to serve, their bodies pure'.[13] It was for such as these that order was demanded, and rules written; safeguards which the perfect would not need.[14]

The move from an oral culture to a written culture was made easier by the sense among ascetics that their true masters were now dead. By the end of the century, leadership had passed to a new generation of men, who always thought of themselves as disciples, dependent for their teaching on the insights of the past. They appealed to the words, counsel, or example of their predecessors, 'memory of whom must remain forever fresh'.[15] Their attitude is summed up in a remark attributed to Arsenius: 'Judge by what the fathers said to you: I have no words for you, beyond their own'.[16] In a world where each ascetic group, growing in numbers, looked beyond itself for instruction, the resulting demand for continuity, for an authentic voice from the past, prompted the creation of works like the *Paralipomena* of Pachomius, the *Asceticon* of Esaias, and the *Apophthegmata Patrum* themselves.[17] They replaced the precarious and sometimes remote memories of loyal disciples.

[12] Bacht, 'Antonius und Pachomius', pp. 100 f. Note also the desire expressed in G 'to offer aid to many', *PG* lxv. 73A.

[13] *V. Pach.* Bo, 105.

[14] *V. Pach.* I, 25, 54. Note the phrase in the latter passage, 'The perfect man does not stumble, even in a situation of freedom or disorder'. Palladius, writing of the *Rule* of Pachomius, uses similar terms: 'Perfect men have no need of rules', *HL* xxxii. Draguet, in his attempt to show that much of *HL* xxxii is out of touch with the thought of Pachomius, picks on the word 'perfect' as an example, 'Le chapitre', *Le Muséon*, lviii, 19 f. (excerpt vii, n. 51). There is clearly a problem here; but the important point, with such a clear distinction (between the perfect and those less advanced), is that someone was making an issue of the matter. To suggest, as does Festugière, that these sentences in *V. Pach.* I (omitted by Bo) are 'commonplace' is not convincing, *Moines d'Orient*, iv, 2, 32.

[15] G Theodore of the Ennaton 2. In addition to the references given above, p. 13, n. 13, see G Dioscorus 2, Evagrius 6, Isaac of the Cells 7, Nisteroos 2, Poemen 31, Pistos, Pistamon, Peter Pionita 2; Nau 141, 264; *V. Pach.* Bo, 190; *HL* iv.

[16] G Paphnutius 5.

[17] Chitty, *Desert*, 67.

The *Life of Antony* illustrates the process in miniature. After the death of Antony, it says of his followers, 'Like orphans robbed of their father, they had only his memory with which to comfort one another, holding fast at the same time to his warnings and his exhortations'.[18] This represents the period of a flourishing oral tradition. Quickly it was felt that this was not enough. His most intimate disciples claimed his clothing; and of this event the *Life* says, 'Indeed, to look on them is like seeing Antony; and wearing them is like pondering his warnings with joy'.[19] Here was an attempt to set up an ascetic dynasty, within which teaching could be protected; a group of disciples, who not only preserved the memory of the holy man, but had his spirit living in them. (The same conviction appears in Pachomian literature: the founder himself lived on in Theodore,[20] and Theodore in Orsisius.)[21] Finally comes the purpose of the written *Life* itself: the desire to spread the fame of Antony, 'for the sake of . . . helping others'.[22] He is presented as a timeless ideal, to be imitated by men who never knew him.[23]

Another facet of this exaltation of the dead appears in even more startling form in Pachomian sources. Orsisius warned his monks that, if they wished to arrive at the 'place of victory', shared by dead fathers and brethren, they must follow in their footsteps. Then, as an added incentive, he pictured Pachomius in that heavenly company, cast in the role of a patron: 'Rejoicing on our account, he will say to the Lord, "As I taught them, so have they lived" '.[24] The *Life of Antony* appeared very soon after the death of its hero, perhaps because its author felt that only by means of a written account could he protect the memory and guarantee the influence of such a man, whose immediate circle of disciples had been small and isolated. Pachomius, on the other hand, like many of the characters in the *Apophthegmata Patrum*, had time to grow in the imagination of a great body of

[18] *V. Ant.* 88. [19] Ibid. 92.
[20] *V. Pach.* I, 144; Bo, 204.
[21] *V. Pach.* Bo, 210. I, 150 is a little less explicit.
[22] *V. Ant.* 94.
[23] Ibid., Preface; see Holl, 'Die schriftstellerische Form', 412, 424.
[24] Orsisius, *Liber*, 3, 12; see also 46.

followers, before the details of his life were committed to writing. 'We glorify and bless even more the Spirit of God dwelling in that man. Indeed, even if we bless his very flesh, it is truly deserved, for his flesh was a temple of the Lord'.[25]

Faith in the presence of this immortal spirit symbolized a desire for continuity; and to some extent it guaranteed its achievement. There was a tangible basis on which such confidence could build: 'I too [said Theodore] was nourished by our father in the commandments of God for eighteen years; and now, for another eighteen, I in my turn have taken up my post in the midst of you, to the best of my ability, by the command of God, and of our father Orsisius'.[26] But the reality was more fragile than the image. 'Give your close attention to what I have to tell you: for certainly a time is coming when you will find no one able to tell you the same'.[27] A more forceful invitation to take up the pen could scarcely have been tendered.

Genuine continuity *was* involved, even so—within the change, rather than in spite of it. Hor, the solitary turned coenobite,[28] had been unlettered in his youth. When he founded a monastery, however, 'grace was given him from God': he began to recite the Scriptures by heart; 'and, when the brethren offered him a scroll, like a man for a long time learned in letters, he began to read'. How skilfully these men staged their adaptation to changing circumstance![29] John of Lycopolis was another who recognized and welcomed this new pattern of instruction: why should one travel, he said, to seek out ascetics, when one could stay at home and read the prophets?[30]

So Hor and John, traditional ascetics, could yet look forward with confidence to the opportunities of a more literate, as well as a more settled, generation—although *their* text was still the Bible. Younger men looked back, to ascetics now dead, whose lives and principles were preserved for them as much in codices as on the lips of those who knew them.

[25] *V. Pach.* Bo, 194.
[26] Ibid. 199.
[27] Ibid. 196.
[28] See above, pp. 40 f.
[29] *HM* ii, 406A.
[30] *HM* i, 395BC.

But they responded to their virtue in terms that John and Hor would still have recognized, 'Let us imitate the fathers who, to the day they died, refused to give themselves up to sin, but followed their holy inspirations, as God would have wished'.[31] Theodore exhorted his monks to put into practice the teaching of Pachomius 'with a confidence born of faith, knowing that, in listening to him, we make ourselves servants of Jesus'; and, when he quoted the words of God,–'This is my beloved Son, with whom I am well pleased; listen to him',–it was Pachomius he wished them to hear, as well as Christ.[32]

Nor was it only the dead masters who retained their charism, their capacity to inspire this faith: the new literary tradition was mediated by men who had inherited many of the gifts and techniques of their predecessors. The *Rule* of Pachomius, for example, was not handed to each monk as a complete text, but developed over a long period, and designed in different parts for different persons. This meant that, for most of the monks, commands and advice would still be given orally. They attended the community assembly 'to hear the word of God'.[33] The superiors taught the brethren in each house 'how to live a holy life'.[34] Orsísius commanded them, 'Never cease to offer warning, and to teach what is holy, and be in yourself an example of good works'.[35] Even in his day, therefore, and even in the Pachomian context, one concept of authority enlivened two patterns of instruction, oral and written. He exhorted his readers, 'Let us take care to read and learn the Scriptures'; and then, to support his demand, he quoted from Proverbs, 'From the fruit of his mouth a good man eats good'; and from Deuteronomy, 'You shall therefore lay up these words of mine, which I have commanded you this day, in your heart and in your soul; and you shall teach them to your children, talking of them when you are sitting in your house, and when you are walking by the way, and when you lie

[31] Esaias, *Ascet.* XI, 102.
[32] Theodore, *Catech.*, trans. Lefort, 51.
[33] Pachomius, *Praecepta et Instituta*, Introduction.
[34] *Praecepta ac Leges*, 12.
[35] Orsisius, *Liber*, 9.

down, and when you rise'.[36] All these quotations evoked situations long traditional in ascetic society.

But note what follows, still quoted in the *Liber*: 'You shall write them as a sign upon your hand, and they shall be unmoving before your eyes'. The new corpus of ascetic wisdom was to be permanent, and accessible at will, 'too hard for the teeth of time'. It was the inscription on the wall of the cell writ large;[37] a silent, almost watchful and unmoving censor of monastic discipline. Beside the painted warnings and exhortations in the monastery of Jeremias, the monk could contemplate the colourful figures of dead saints and patrons–Makare, for example, or Phib–and each one held a book, the ultimate source of those few admonitions, and of many more.[38] John of Nikiou understood the true significance of *graffiti*. When Jeremias gave advice, he said, to the exiled Emperor Anastasius, 'he engraved it on the walls of his heart, just as Moses the prophet had received from God the tables of the covenant, on which were engraved the commandments of the law'.[39] Such was the atmosphere in which the monk would read his inscriptions–and contemplate his portraits. It was said of Pambo, in the *Apophthegmata Patrum*, 'Just as Moses, when his face was glorified, took on the likeness of the glory of Adam, so the face of the Abba Pambo shone like lightning, and he was like a king sitting on his throne'.[40] This was where the encounter between master and disciple was preserved. The λόγος, the word of the father, was patiently copied, and carefully lodged in the niches of the cell; and the master himself, the patron now dead but still admired, and lovingly portrayed upon the wall, stood watchful guard over the reading and meditation. When Theodore set in motion the compilation of the lives of Pachomius, he did more than initiate a hagiographical tradition. His anxious warning, 'a time is coming when you will find no one able to tell

[36] Orsisius, *Liber*, 51.
[37] See above, p. 55.
[38] Quibell, *Excavations*, ii, 1906-7 (Cairo, 1908), 64, and Plate XLIV.
[39] Quibell, iii, p. iii.
[40] G Pambo 12.

you the same',[41] awakens a distant but recognizable echo in the heart of a monk many centuries later, painting the wall of his cell:

> Woe is me!
> For a time will be when I shall not be:
> The writing shall endure;
> The hands shall perish in the tombs.[42]

[41] See above, p. 73.

[42] W. E. Crum, 'Inscriptions from Shenoute's Monastery', *JTS* v (1903–4), 562.

PART TWO

WESTERN BEGINNINGS

I

EXILES AND PILGRIMS

The monks of Egypt were not allowed to remain in obscurity; they were, before the end of the fourth century, 'discovered'–indeed, they became something of a tourist attraction; not only for the East generally, but for travellers from the West, like Rufinus and Jerome. This far-reaching fame, and the fact that men returning to Italy and Gaul could carry or compose an increasing amount of ascetic literature, explains the importance of Egyptian fathers in a western context. Sulpicius Severus and John Cassian, to whom we must turn later, were in many senses products of that eastern desert culture. Sulpicius had read the *Life of Antony* (as his own work betrays), and had spoken with travellers from Egypt; Cassian had lived there, and wrote of eastern heroes.

But the links between Egypt and Gaul (the world of Sulpicius and Cassian) were not direct, nor simply forged. Both men were western figures. The style and structure of their works were almost wholly Latin in their inspiration. Their themes pointed forwards, gaining effect, and arousing admiration in the European middle ages: Martin of Tours, the wonder-working bishop; Cassian's portrait of monasticism, which stood, in the mind of Benedict, second in rank to nothing but the Bible.

To understand these men, to savour to the full Sulpicius's *Life of Martin*, or the *Institutes* and *Conferences* of Cassian, some knowledge of Egypt is essential, which the chapters above have attempted to provide; but fuller justice depends on explaining the western roots of these two writers. While remaining aware of ascetic developments in the East, Christians of the West in the fourth century developed a particular style of religious enthusiasm, and a much greater readiness to link a life of dedication, more or less monastic, to the needs and anxieties of the church as a whole; and these were features without which the work of Sulpicius and Cassian would not have been possible. Here, then, is the 'sideways step', bringing into heavier relief a series of background events and personalities in the West that help to explain the opportunities and motives of later writers, and even anticipate much of their concern and interest.

To trace in detail the progress of asceticism in the West during the first decades of its development would be to attempt scarcely less than the religious history of the age. We must content ourselves with a more limited but important task: to explain and interpret the disruption and mobility that characterize the period. We must retain the sense of a church perpetually restless; not yet assured, either of its identity, or of its destiny. It cast about, therefore, this side and that, with fortunate privilege in an age when stable conformity, and involvement in local affairs, were imposed upon many as a legal ideal.[1] The forceful (even rebellious) character of its leaders, many of them exiles or pilgrims for much of their lives,–almost, one might say, professionally restless,–with constantly shifting careers and ambitions, created just the circumstances in which a more charismatic type of authority could be brought to bear on the embryonic institutions of the newly tolerated church. The resulting picture can appear bewildering; but the eye of the historian will find, even so, a place of rest and focus: Christians in the West have left us their own specifically ascetic literature to study, much of it translated from the Greek; and they possessed, as a worthy and fascinating hero, Jerome–at once the chronicler and victim of events.

Long before ascetics in the East had lived through all the changes and developments already described, men and women in the West were awakening to similar aspirations, and responding to the influence of eastern pioneers. There

[1] Ordination could provide an escape from the restrictions of the law; and with escape came greater opportunities. The demands, and failures, of *Cod. Theod.* are fully discussed by A. H. M. Jones, *The Later Roman Empire* (Oxford, 1964), 739–57 (on the enforced stability of the *curiales*), 795–803 (on the lot of the *coloni*), 920–9 (on the social roots and contrasting fortunes of the Christian clergy). See also M. K. Hopkins, 'Social Mobility in the Later Roman Empire: the Evidence of Ausonius', *CQ*, n.s. xi (1961), 239–49; R. MacMullen, 'Social Mobility in the Theodosian Code', *JRS* liv (1964), 49–53.

had been some form of western asceticism, certainly in Rome, before the beginning of the fourth century. Individuals, or loosely ordered groups, had dedicated themselves to lives of chastity and prayer; but they remained within the city, and more often than not within their family homes.[2]

During the fourth century itself, on at least four outstanding occasions, persons either leaving or returning from the East greatly modified this Italian asceticism, and inspired it with new fervour. First, in 339, the Patriarch Athanasius was banished, for the second time, from his see of Alexandria; and he spent most of the following seven years in Rome, travelling also to other parts of Italy, notably Milan and Aquileia.[3] He and his companions, according to Jerome, greatly impressed the leading families of Rome, and encouraged some among them to imitate more closely the asceticism of the East.[4] Then, second, in 373, (Athanasius having died,) his successor Peter also came to Rome, and probably brought with him more detailed information about the ascetic movement in Egypt, which had reached by this time, as we have seen, a more advanced stage of its development. Third, in 382, Jerome himself arrived in the city, and, during the next three years, found time to inspire a number of well born ladies to embrace the ascetic life. His influence, thanks most of all to his letters, was maintained for some years after his departure in 385. Finally, in 397, Rufinus returned, after many years in Egypt and Syria; and he very soon set about translating (among other works) the *Historia Monachorum*, and the ascetic writings of Basil of Caesarea.[5]

[2] For this early period, see G. D. Gordini, 'Origine e Sviluppo del Monachesimo a Roma', *Gregorianum*, xxxvii (1956), 221 f.

[3] During his previous exile, spent partly in Trier, he may have inspired the ascetics described by Ponticianus in Augustine's *Confessions*: see below, pp. 92 f.

[4] Jerome, *Ep.* cxxvii. 5; but see Gordini, 'Origine', 227 f. for comment on the chronology of Jerome's recollections. *HL* ii and Socrates, *HE* iv. 23 provide supporting evidence.

[5] With more than twenty years of eastern asceticism behind him, the enterprise is no puzzle—compare F. X. Murphy, *Rufinus of Aquileia* (Washington, 1945), 82; but see also 119. *HM* is particularly hard to date. A reference in his *HE* to a 'specific work' on ascetic history (xi. 4) is taken by M. Villain to refer to *V. Ant.*, 'Rufin d'Aquilée et l'*Histoire Ecclésiastique*', *RSR* xxxiii (1946), 201; but by Festugière to refer to *HM*, 'Le problème *littéraire*', 257. *HM* xxix makes a reference to the *HE*; but, since the words come at the end of the chapter, they could easily have been added later.

In other words, a wealth of varied information and encouragement had poured into the city over a period of sixty years. Athanasius gave added substance to whatever stories about the followers and colleagues of Antony and Pachomius may have reached the West already;[6] and the effect of this personal report was soon strengthened by Latin translations of his *Life of Antony.*[7] Peter may have been able to say more about the success and orderly expansion of Pachomian foundations.[8] Jerome brought with him personal experience of asceticism in Syria and Constantinople. Rufinus introduced into the West, or made more widely known, the urban and pastoral emphasis of Basil's monasticism.[9]

The enduring fame (or notoriety) of Jerome and his circle—the wealth of his surviving work, his importance as a writer, and his obvious influence on the ascetic movement—inclines the religious historian to focus attention on Rome and its ascetics. Yet the events described above—the arrival of Athanasius and Peter, of Jerome himself, and of Rufinus—were not merely incidents in the history of the ascetic movement. They were the moments when that movement became more closely involved in wider issues; and the career of Jerome (as of all ascetics) must be placed in the context of those issues, the ecclesiastical politics of the age. Monks in the East had rejected the world, and were only slowly reabsorbed. Many of their western counterparts, on the other hand, embraced asceticism in mid-career. Certainly, it afforded them new insight and greater confidence; but enduring

[6] Gordini, 'Origine', 224 f., and R. Lorenz, 'Die Anfänge des abendländisches Mönchtums im 4. Jahrhundert', *ZK* lxxvii (1966), 8. It would be hard to date the arrival in Rome of Serapion, *HL* xxxvii; but its effect was precisely to coax a Roman virgin from her household retreat, where she had stayed for twenty-five years.

[7] Paula, once she had been persuaded to leave Rome, thought immediately of going to visit the places described in the *Life*, Jerome, *Ep.* cviii. 6.

[8] Jerome, *Ep.* cxxvii. 5. Lorenz suggested that the Roman monasteries seen by Augustine, during his stay there, and described by him in *De Moribus Ecclesiae Catholicae*, i. 70, showed the influence of Pachomius, 'Anfänge', 8.

[9] A study of Basil and Chrysostom would provide a natural eastern counterpart to developments traced here in the West. On Basil, initial reference may be made to W. Lowther Clarke, *St Basil the Great* (London, 1913); E. Amand de Mendieta, *L'ascèse monastique de saint Basile* (Maredsous, 1949); J. Gribomont, 'Saint Basile', *Théologie de la vie monastique*, 99-113. Chrysostom has been much less well served; but see, in addition to D. Attwater's biography (London, 1959), L. Meyer, *Saint Jean Chrysostome, maître de perfection chrétienne* (Paris, 1933).

ambition, and the controversies that had already claimed their attention, impelled them to preserve a more lively and public framework for their ascetic dedication. In order to appreciate the characteristic development of asceticism in the West, it is necessary to keep in mind this wider arena within which ascetics moved, and by which they were greatly influenced.

Even Jerome, whose career will be treated in more detail below, ranged far beyond Rome.[10] He gained direct experience of new styles of Christian life, and of church affairs and controversy, in both Antioch and Constantinople. His stay in Rome was concerned, not merely with the development of the ascetic life among the aristocrats of the city, but also with his own ambitions as a churchman. He became involved, in later life, in controversy over the study and translation of Origen (a matter to be touched upon later). His opposition to Pelagius, and his influence on early monasticism in Palestine, (aspects of his career on which there will be less room for comment within the limits of this survey,) also show the extent to which he engaged in public affairs to the end of his life.

Athanasius, among his other claims to fame, was also an ascetic writer; one of the first in that particular period during which ascetic literature came to play so vital a role. It was as a writer that western ascetics eventually remembered him most; and the popularity of his biography of Antony ensured that, from its very beginning, organized asceticism in the West was armed with a highly polished literary model. He was also, of course, throughout his public life, (from the time of the Council of Nicaea, in 325, until his death in 373,) the dominant figure in the Arian controversy; and his arrival in Rome marked the beginning of a specifically western Arian conflict, a conflict of immense importance to ascetics.[11]

The debate in the West centred not only on doctrine but also on the structure and organization of the church.[12] The chief supporter of the orthodox cause was Hilary of Poitiers—

[10] See below, pp. 99 ff.

[11] I have depended a great deal on the general account given by M. Meslin, *Les Ariens d'Occident* (Paris, 1967).

[12] Meslin, 29 f.

another who 'returned from the East' (after an exile), although in his case to Gaul. His early career, before his exile, was marked by a note of surprise at the opportunities open to churchmen, following the conversion and legislation of Constantine; surprise, in particular, at the use to which such opportunities could be put by ambitious bishops such as Saturninus of Arles and Paternus of Périgueux (his chief opponents in the early stages of the conflict, who had allied themselves, for various ends, to secular and imperial authority).[13] Hilary had already, some years before, made a forceful plea to the Emperor Constantius II against secular interference in the affairs of the church.[14]

Exiled himself to the East in 360, ('not because of any offence on my part, but through the plotting of my enemies',)[15] Hilary arrived in Phrygia, not only indignant at the triumph of doctrinal error, but with an increasing sense that the new-found influence and freedom of the church had all too soon been turned against its legitimate leaders. With some bewilderment, he longed for the simpler issues of the pre-Constantinian era: 'There was never any doubt that you were dealing with persecutors: they pressed you to deny your faith with punishment, sword, and fire'.[16] Now he was able to identify what he regarded as new forces of destruction in the church: the ability of the emperor to play the patron; the willingness of bishops to succumb to the flattery of his guidance and protection. Of Constantius and his Arian bishops, Hilary now wrote, 'They fawn upon him, to gain mastery over him', and 'He does not bring you liberty by casting you in prison, but treats you with respect within his palace, and thus makes you his slave'.[17] He saw all too clearly how both secular and religious leaders were compromising themselves, through their calculated attempts to gain superior advantage.

[13] Hence Hilary's pained and hopeful allusion to Julian, Caesar in Gaul at the time, as 'deceived' (by the expectant flattery of heretics), *Ad Constantium*, ii. 2; see Meslin, 35.

[14] *Ad Constantium*, i *passim*.

[15] Ibid. ii. 2.

[16] *Contra Constantium*, 4.

[17] Ibid. 5. The seriousness of his complaint must be assessed within the context of Ammianus's judgement, that Constantius was 'an easy target for the devious', XX, ii. 2.

Like Jerome, he was beginning to think of the church as 'greater in power, but diminished in virtue':[18] 'She is delighted to find herself honoured by the world, even though she cannot have part with Christ unless the world hates her'.[19] So he was forced (like Athanasius) to consider afresh the proper relationship between himself as a bishop and the civil power.

It is difficult to discover how much Hilary was influenced during his exile by the lifestyles of the eastern church; but it is hard to believe that he could have remained unmoved by the example of ascetics. The effect of their reputation for sanctity and power, combined with their well defended freedom, would have presented him with new ideals and a new model of authority immediately relevant to the solution of his own difficulties in the West. (The same would be true of his fellow exile, Eusebius of Vercelli.)

There were two very particular reasons for this. First, to one so full of admiration for those who had resisted Diocletian, and so keenly aware of what resistance had involved, his exile might look dangerously like flight. Fortunately, the feeling had grown in this period that truth was something to be defended, not so much by the heroic witness of the martyr as by the protracted debate of the living and secure. Athanasius, the most respected champion of orthodoxy, had used just such an argument to make flight respectable—not only with reference to his own exile, but even to flight during the persecutions themselves.[20] (Hilary was to devote the rest of his life, therefore, to literary polemic.) The second reason was closely related: ascetics in the desert had also engaged in a certain flight—in their case, from the world—; indeed, there was the suggestion that some of the earliest, faced with persecution, had helped to pioneer this new form of witness to the truth.[21] It was Athanasius, again, who pointed out this link

[18] See below, p. 135.

[19] *Contra Auxentium*, 4.

[20] Athanasius, *Apologia de Fuga Sua*, 22; see also *Apologia contra Constantium*, 32.

[21] As an introduction to some of the problems involved, see E. Malone, *The Monk and the Martyr* (Washington, 1950).

between asceticism and the defeat of error, in his later biography of Antony.[22]

So there was every reason why a persecuted exile like Hilary should feel affinity with ascetics. Writing from Phrygia, he continued to compare the ambition of worldly Arians with the fervour of a former age; but he did so in terms that not only recalled the heroism of martyrs but also placed in equally longstanding historical perspective the experience, and the terminology, of the desert hermit:

May I ask you, bishops, (for such you believe yourselves to be,) with what credentials did the apostles claim a right to preach the gospel? . . . They supported themselves by hard work, the work of their own hands. They met together in hidden garrets. They wandered about villages and country forts, over land and sea, amongst almost every nation—all in the face of senate legislation, and the edicts of kings. Yet was it not they who held (so I firmly believe) the keys of the Kingdom of Heaven?[23]

Let me warn you of one thing: beware of Antichrist. What an evil it is, this love of building that possesses you: you think that roofs and walls make a church of God worthy of your reverence, and a setting fit enough in which to call down upon yourselves the blessings of peace. Can you doubt that in these very buildings Antichrist will find refuge? Safer by far, to my mind, are the mountains, the woods, the lakes—indeed, dungeons and pits—: these are the places where, inspired by God's Spirit, the prophets spoke—some of them to survive, others to be overwhelmed.[24]

On his return to Gaul, Hilary certainly seems to have harnessed asceticism to the politics of the church, producing a new programme of pastoral organization and government. By this emphasis on the coming of Antichrist, and on the possibility of preserving a more 'disestablished' church, he paved the way for Martin of Tours.[25] But he also had his influence on Jerome. His attack on Auxentius (an Arian, appointed bishop of Milan by Constantius II) may have supplied Jerome with a model for his own attack on John of Jerusalem.[26] This later and more personal squabble included

[22] *V. Ant.* 46, 69, 89, 94. [23] *Contra Auxentium*, 3.

[24] Ibid. 12. Easterners would also make such links: compare the terminology of Basil, *Ep.* xc.

[25] This link will be treated further in Part Four.

[26] Y.-M. Duval, 'Sur les insinuations de Jérôme contre Jean de Jérusalem: de l'Arianisme à l'Origénisme', *RHE* lxv (1970), especially 366-70. Jerome passed some less complimentary judgements on Hilary, *Epp.* xxxiv. 3; lviii. 10; see P.

doctrinal differences, but it was also concerned with the issue of authority—the authority of a bishop *vis-à-vis* his clergy and neighbouring ascetics.[27] The incident is a reminder of the extent to which the Arian controversy dominated the minds of that generation.

Gaul will be central to the later stages of our inquiry—and hence the need to say something of Hilary—; but, for the time being, it was in Italy that events of importance were taking place. In the Italy of the Arian Constantius II, Jerome reached his early manhood; and it was there that the political aspects of the Arian controversy were most clear.[28] Of immediate importance for Jerome was the exile of Eusebius of Vercelli, in 355. Eusebius had taken a vow of virginity, and may have begun to live a quasi-monastic life with his clergy, before his departure for the East.[29] Certainly, his experiences there strengthened in him a determination to embrace a more ascetic, indeed a more monastic, life on his return. The example of this experiment had a considerable influence on the monasteries and ascetic groups of Aquileia, with which Jerome was later intimately connected. 'O blessed house . . . O happy roof', Jerome would later exclaim (referring to the household of Bishop Valerian): 'every day, of course, you bear witness to Christ, keeping his commandments; but now this personal glory is added to by a public

Antin, 'Hilarius Gallicano cothurno attolitur', *RB* lvii (1947), 82–8. But, while a young man at Trier, Jerome had copied out the works of Hilary, and had wished to read them again while in the desert of Chalcis, *Ep.* v. 2; and he always maintained a balanced regard for the Gallic doctor, *Epp.* xx. 1; lxxxii. 7; cvii. 12.

[27] A central issue was the ordination, by Epiphanius of Salamis, in another bishop's diocese, of Jerome's brother, Paulinianus; see below, pp. 130 f. Oddly enough, the monks of Bethlehem would echo the sentiments of Hilary, 'I am at one time an exile, at another time a priest', *Ad Constantium*, ii. 8; but, while Hilary longed to return to the pastoral fray, as it were, they felt entitled to remain outside that orbit of concern. The links between Arianism and later controversy are traced with particular usefulness by Hunt, 'Palladius of Helenopolis', especially 463 f.

[28] Meslin, 36.

[29] So Chitty interprets Ambrose, *Ep.* lxiii. 66, *Desert*, 61, n. 8 (this must be the passage to which Chitty refers, even though the reference is different). Lorenz is less certain. The argument must rest merely on the fact that Ambrose refers to the exile of Eusebius (in *Ep.* lxiii. 68) *after* mentioning the monastic household. Greater confidence in the implication may be supplied by the fact that the same sequence is observed in Ambrose, *Sermo de Natali Sancti Eusebii* (= *Sermo* lvi), 3.

and undisguised declaration'.[30]

In Rome, the course of the Arian conflict also affected the later career of Jerome, and of his patron, Pope Damasus. When Constantius exiled their bishop, Liberius, also in 355, the clergy of the city were quick to rally to the cause of the Arian Felix (in order to avoid, perhaps, the fate of Milan and Naples, which had been forced to accept new bishops from elsewhere).[31] Certain groups among the aristocracy of Rome expressed hesitant opposition.[32] Other sections of the populace were more forthright, voicing their support for Liberius with unambiguous slogans—'one God, one Christ, one Bishop'.[33] Liberius returned, and was reconciled with his clergy; but this did not prevent a schism in the city, following his death, and the disputed election of Damasus himself, in 366.[34]

More famous, and perhaps ultimately more important, passions were aroused in Milan. Auxentius, the Arian candidate of the emperor, had the good fortune to outlive his predecessor, Dionysius, and did not have to deal with a 'government in exile'. He also outlived his patron Constantius, and enjoyed under Valentinian I the imperial policy of maintaining, for the sake of peace, the *status quo*. Against entrenched *de facto* power, the efforts of Hilary and Eusebius were useless. The policy of peaceful toleration was applied not least by Ambrose, at that time Governor of Aemilia-Liguria, with his seat in the city. When Auxentius died, in 374, Ambrose, the unbaptized civil servant, was accepted as a compromise candidate—by the Catholics because of their weakness as an independent pressure group; by the supporters of Auxentius because they thought that he would continue to maintain as bishop the policies he had enforced as governor.[35]

The subsequent career of Ambrose—his conflict with pagan

[30] Jerome, *Ep.* vii. 6. [31] Meslin, 40.

[32] Hesitant, in that only the wives had the courage to brave the anger of the emperor, Theodoret, *HE* ii. 14.

[33] Ibid. This was no doubt a reaction to the 'two bishop' compromise evolved at the Council of Sirmium, in 357.

[34] See also the useful account in A. Chastagnol, *La préfecture urbaine à Rome sous le Bas-Empire* (Paris, 1960), 151 ff.

[35] Meslin, 45.

senators, his opposition to an Arianizing court, his successful domination of a Catholic emperor—is too well known to need elaboration; but it formed another vital element in the background to the ascetic movement in the West. It provided an example of how powerful the church could become when its bishops repudiated the stifling patronage of secular authority. Nor should one forget that Ambrose was himself an ascetic, the patron of virgins and monks. This commitment added a special tone to many of his public acts as a bishop.[36]

So much for Athanasius, his enemies and allies. The patriarch died in 373, too soon to see the triumph of his cause at the Council of Constantinople in 381. This virtually brought to an end, within the empire at least, the controversy over the teachings of Arius. Ambrose lived on, to fight other battles, until 397. During that intervening period, as we shall see, Jerome made his mark in Rome; but it was not until the same year, 397, almost a generation after the death of Athanasius, that Rufinus, our fourth 'arrival', reached Italy from the East.

He had been away for more than twenty years, had gained a thorough knowledge of the desert ascetics, and had established himself as a theologian of some consequence. Studied (as he often is) in the context of Jerome's life, or even of ascetic history more generally, he can appear as a mere adversary—the local champion of Origen, the writer of ascetic works, the protégé of pious ladies. His numerous translations, of course, and his familiarity with the western aristocracy, should make him more than a foil to the study of Jerome; but, even when examined more broadly, the familiar aspects of his career can suggest an air of domesticity; and it is quite misleading. Rufinus was not just a well read confidant: he wrote the *Ecclesiastical History*.

This was a consciously 'popular' work, little concerned with the anxieties of an ascetic coterie.[37] Undertaken at the instigation of Chromatius, bishop of Aquileia, it demonstrated the influence and interest of the 'Aquileia circle', with its complex emphasis on preaching, asceticism, and the

[36] Some examples will be given in Part Four; for a fuller review, see my 'Spiritual Authority', 407-19.

[37] Villain, 'Rufin d'Aquilée', 167.

organization of the clergy. But more than that, the terms of Chromatius's request raised the work to the level of political treatise. Following the disastrous success of the Goths in 401, (Alaric's invasion of Italy, and the siege of Aquileia itself,) Rufinus was to restore the faith of his readers in the strength and enduring mission, protected by providence, of a truly Christian empire. His image of the emperor, for instance,–*religiosus princeps*,–contrasted (in those sections of the work composed by Rufinus himself) with the *εὐσεβὴς βασιλέυς* of Eusebius of Caesarea (whose history Rufinus was extending to his own day). For Eusebius, the religious element in the personality of the emperor had been represented by his supposed contact with God. For Rufinus, it was reflected more in his generosity to the church. Like Theodosius, face to face with John of Lycopolis, the emperor was to seek God through holy men; and the imperial power sanctioned by God was bestowed upon him through the mediation of the church.[38]

The world of Rufinus, in other words, was post-Ambrosian: it had (or hoped it had) consolidated the achievements of the Milanese bishop, in his opposition to Valentinian I and his successors (even Thodosius himself), and attempted to transform them into ecclesiological principle. The work of Rufinus reflected also the experience of ascetics. The saint was now seen as a mediator, the guarantee that one heard the voice of God, and that God in his turn would hear one's prayers. Sanctity had a social, indeed a political, role to play. This emphasis on holy man, bishop, and emperor as intercessors before God reflected a confidence that Christian (and, more important, ascetic) values and aspirations could acquire status and effect within the structures of the empire.

This survey of events has been brief; but it is designed only to show how varied and complex were the careers of early western ascetics, and in particular how much their asceticism was bound up with more public affairs. The historian needs to explain how it was that, while they

[38] Y.-M. Duval, 'L'éloge de Théodose dans le *Cité de Dieu* (V, 26, 1): sa place, son sens et ses sources', *Recherches Augustinennes*, iv (1966), 173; F. Thélamon, 'L'empereur idéal d'après l'*Histoire Ecclésiastique* de Rufin d'Aquilée', *Studia Patristica*, x (Berlin, 1970), 311–13.

appeared to strip away the accepted apparatus of ambition and power,—the self-conscious and flamboyant style of life, the skill in attracting patronage, the careful control of marriage and inheritance, the landed wealth,—they were able to retain their hold over persons, their control of events; and were able also to nourish in themselves a desire for power of a different sort, and so to sharpen their understanding of authority.

II

ASCETIC LITERATURE

In order to explain these developments, a survey of events, no matter how essential or revealing, is obviously not enough: as in the East, an understanding of inner history is required; an understanding of concept and motive. We have touched upon this somewhat in the case of Hilary; but he remains, for the most part, hidden behind the arguments of his theological treatises. Fortunately, we do possess a very famous piece of inner history, referring precisely to the years, and to the province, that concern us, albeit written some time later: the *Confessions* of Augustine. In the eighth book, Augustine describes a moment, in 386, that may be central to the history of asceticism in the West—a moment of conversion. It was central in this sense: it was made possible, in part at least, by the character of western Christian life described above, with all its involvement and diversity; at the same time it explains, in its own turn, how men could take advantage of events, and steer them further, in directions we shall discover in the chapters that follow.

In the passage concerned, their friend Ponticianus has just revealed to Augustine and Alypius events in the marvellous life of Antony. He goes on to recount how he and three friends once walked in the country near Trier; how two of them came upon a small community of ascetics; and how there they found a copy of the *Life of Antony*. (The party could have included Jerome himself.)[1] As one of them read the text, he turned to his friend and said,

> What is the goal of our ambition in all these labours of ours? What are we aiming at? What is our motive in being in the public service? Have we any higher hope at court than to be friends of the emperor? And

[1] So P. Courcelle, *Recherches sur les Confessions de saint Augustin* (Paris, 1950), 181–6. This is no more than a possibility; but Jerome's conversion could easily have followed upon such an experience: F. Cavallera, *Saint Jérôme, sa vie et son oeuvre* (Louvain, 1922), i, 1, 18.

at that level, is not everything uncertain and full of perils? And how many perils must we meet on the way to this greater peril? And how long before we are there? But if I should choose to be a friend of God, I can become one now. He said this [Augustine continues], and all troubled with the pain of the new life coming to birth in him, he turned back his eyes to the book.[2]

Amicus Dei, the friend of God, is certainly a vital concept; but the key word of the statement is *nunc*, without a doubt; 'amicus autem Dei, si voluero, ecce nunc fio'. The speaker was reaching out to embrace a new career, a new opportunity of instant success; and in this description of conversion, Augustine invited his readers to witness the birth of entirely new concepts of ambition and power.[3]

Neither the friends of Ponticianus nor Augustine himself thought it necessary to embrace, in literal terms, the life of the desert. This short passage from the *Confessions* takes in a much broader sweep of ascetic history. The hero of the piece, Antony, was certainly a hermit, remote in his own lifetime; but his memory and example were preserved by a skilful biographer for a wider body of disciples (many of them quite differently placed from the rougher heroes of the desert). The figures in the passage itself were like any other young rhetors of the day—urbane, ambitious, yet curious and susceptible—: Ambrose and Augustine, Jerome and Rufinus; all had known such chances and anxieties. The writer, Augustine, was by 397 (when the book was begun) both bishop and monk; a man reared to a life of influence and ease, transformed by intense devotion, and now endowed with all the spiritual power that a Christian empire could bestow upon its bishops.

Augustine's account helps to make two things clear, therefore: first, the call to an ascetic life was heard, in the West, by those already shaped for careers of opportunity, conflict, and power; and second, their response was heavily dependent on the availability of a religious literature. Augustine's phraseology points in particular to the way in which a reading of the *Life of Antony* had its first effect within: 'all troubled with the pain of the new life coming to birth in him . . . he was changed within, where you can see; and his

[2] Augustine, *Confessions*, viii. 15, trans. Sheed, 159.

[3] Compare Jerome's use of the word *statim*, *Ep.* xiv. 6.

mind was divested of the world, as soon became clear'.[4] Having experienced this inner change, the would-be ascetic was then faced with a need to find some different setting, some equivalent to the desert of Egypt, in which to put his new ideals into practice. This was not always easy. He remained dependent on texts, and on the associated stirring of the imagination; and this explains why, in the middle of the century, much of the asceticism of Italy, and of Gaul, was restricted, at a visible level, to rigorous fasting, to a certain manner of prayer, and to a rough simplicity of clothing—all adopted by men still tied to former friends and responsibilities, and still in pursuit of influence and power. The leopard may have changed his spots, but hunted in familiar habitat his former prey.

So visitors from Syria and Egypt could reinforce in some an existing inclination to piety and rigour; and the course of religious controversy could eventually give many ascetics a new sense of purpose. But dedication to more precise forms of the religious life gathered momentum at precisely that period (the last thirty years of the century) when a corpus of ascetic literature became available to western readers. Works like the *Life of Antony* and the *Historia Monachorum* provided above all a model—not so much for servile imitation, (although that can be found,) but more of a hero and spiritual father: a pioneer, whose life would guarantee that renunciation of the world was possible, and likely to bear fruit; a master, whose teaching bore the stamp of authority. It was only when such models were to hand that the correspondence of a Jerome or Paulinus could encourage the curiosity of a reading public, and that later translations of Basil and Pachomius, or the work of Cassian *par excellence*, could suggest more concrete means of putting admiration into practice.

What must be stressed is that both the need for models, and the literature in which the models were displayed, were features of the ascetic life proper to the West. Evagrius of Antioch, Rufinus, and Jerome were dependent on eastern texts; but they undertook their translations at the invitation of Latin-speaking devotees; and, at least in the case of

[4] Augustine, loc. cit.

Evagrius and Rufinus, they modified the sources from which they worked, making a conscious adaptation to a different ascetic *milieu*. In this sense the text of Evagrius in particular represents a step forward in the development of western ascetic literature.[5] The *Lives* written by Jerome and Sulpicius mark a further stage, at which (inspired, it is true, by an Athanasian model) the careers of rather different and (in the case of Sulpicius) specifically western holy men were made more widely known. Paulinus of Milan, the biographer of Ambrose, and Possidius, who wrote a life of Augustine, followed in what was by then a well-established western tradition. Meanwhile, at a further stage, the entirely original (although not necessarily fictitious) dialogues of Cassian applied the principles of eastern asceticism (grasped now at a more theoretical level) to a western situation.[6]

[5] It would be misleading to reproach him with charges of falsification and inaccuracy, or to suppose that the seeming fidelity of the earlier anonymous trans. of the *V. Ant.* was merely a contrasting sign of ignorance and servility. Many of Evagrius's variations and paraphrases display nothing more than a desire for clarity and elegance; and it may be that the earlier translator remained more 'faithful' to his original simply because he did not have particular readers in view. His style was nevertheless calculated in its own way: see Christine Mohrmann, 'Note sur la version latine la plus ancienne de la vie de saint Antoine par saint Athanase', *Antonius Magnus Eremita*, ed. Steidle, 35-44; 'Le rôle des moines dans la transmission du patrimonie latin', *Mémorial de l'Année Martinienne*, ed. G. Le Bras (Paris, 1962), 189. Some particular examples of variation between translations are examined in Appendix II, below.

[6] These interpretations will be defended more fully in Parts Four and Five.

PART THREE

JEROME

I

ANTIOCH, CONSTANTINOPLE, AND ROME

We have seen how the western church of the fourth century was blessed, or afflicted, with public controversy, with energetic leadership, (fired by ambitions both devious and saintly,) and with a new ascetic fervour that sought out, or created, texts with which to nourish its curiosity and devotion. Sulpicius and Cassian were to reap the fruits of this volatile enthusiasm. They also provided for many of its failings.

The earlier period of relative turmoil was dominated, however, by another figure, Jerome, whose life and career take on their full meaning only when placed within this framework of events.[1] His letters and *Lives* offer the most significant corpus of ascetic literature in the West during this intermediate period, as well as the best introduction to his own biography. To depend on them in this way is no mere matter of convenience. His correspondence lays bare the chronology of a varying ambition; and both Jerome himself and readers of a later age rightly regarded the letters as a self-sufficient fund of experience and instruction: 'the book remains, even though men have passed away'.[2] In any case, particularly after his departure from Rome for Bethlehem in 385, written contact with others was the only yardstick of progress or achievement in his life:

Every day we are dying, every day we change; and yet we think ourselves eternal. This very letter that I dictate—written down, read over, corrected—is something stolen from my life. For every mark the scribe makes, a moment of time is lost to me. We write letters, and reply to letters, back and forth across the sea; and, as the boat cuts through

[1] It is a matter of some regret that J. N. D. Kelly, *Jerome* (London, 1975), appeared too late to be taken into full account here, although references will occur.

[2] *Ep.* cxxx. 19. See, for example, J. Leclercq, 'Saint Jérôme docteur de l'ascèse, d'après un centon monastique', *RAM* xxv (1949), 140–5: the MS. discussed there is little more than a collection of excerpts from Jerome's letters.

the waves, with every splash of water on the prow, the span of our lives is lessened.[3]

It is as a voyager that Jerome first appears in his letters, riding at anchor in the harbour of a foreign land. He looks towards the shore, teeming with strange life, and longs to acquaint himself with it more fully. Some fearful reluctance, and a sense of nostalgia, for the past and for his homeland, draws him back. The harbour was Maronia, the estate of Evagrius, near Antioch; the distant shore, the desert of Chalcis; the date, 374.[4] Jerome was in transit, as it were: thrust out of Aquileia by some obscure quarrel that is still not fully understood; and yet not wholly committed to any new style of life.

From the temporary safety of his rural retreat, Jerome wrote two letters that reflect his attitude at this time towards the ascetic life.[5] He was excited (although apprehensive) to find himself so close to real asceticism, to the 'wonderful fellowship' of anchorites, living in a desert that Jerome described as 'a city delightful above all others'. He was not afraid to admit his admiration: 'I was seized by the greatest possible desire to share in that enterprise'. Yet plunged, as it were, into a new environment, and breathless with shock, he confessed to some hesitation: 'I did not wish to go back, but I could not go forward'. The desert hermits had, he thought, the power to release him from this bondage of self. Their prayers would lead him 'out of the shadows of this world', and carry him 'to a harbour on that shore that I long for'.[6]

Meanwhile, he continued to cherish the memory of ascetic companions left behind in Italy. His longstanding friend Bonosus, having embraced a way of life inspired entirely by the exemplars of Scripture, was living now alone on an island—'but not alone, for Christ is your companion.' Jerome was entirely confident about the fruits of this enterprise: 'He is safe. He fears nothing. He takes upon himself all the

[3] *Ep.* lx. 19.

[4] For the dating of Jerome's career, I have relied on Cavallera, *Jérôme*, as modified by Kelly, *Jerome*, in the light of P. Nautin, 'Études de chronologie hiéronymienne', *REA* xviii (1972), 209-18; xix (1973), 69-86, 213-39; xx (1974), 251-84.

[5] *Epp.* ii (to the hermit Theodosius), iii (to Rufinus).

[6] *Ep.* ii.

armour the Apostle speaks of. Now, when he reads once more the divine words of Scripture, he hears God. When he prays to the Lord, he speaks with God. Perhaps, like John, he has visions, there on his island'. Bonosus was 'newly settled in Paradise'; he had 'enrolled himself in a new city'.[7] In the face of such radical dedication, Jerome admitted again to reluctance and compromise—'While I sit here wishing for it, he has achieved it'—; but Bonosus, like the anchorites of Chalcis, would also be an advocate: 'I thank you, Lord Jesus, that on the last day I have someone who can plead with you on my behalf'.[8]

These two letters are invaluable. They reveal the mind of Jerome before the better known events of his life—his retirement to the desert, the hectic years in Rome, the long period of study, controversy, and self-discipline in Bethlehem. They show what understanding of asceticism he had acquired, before enjoying direct experience in the East. They bear witness to a surprising degree of indecision, in a man who appears to have toyed with the ascetic life for several years already. They suggest that his interpretation of that life involved many features typical of Egypt—the variety of association, the growing sense of an organized institution, the role of the ascetic as an intercessor, the certainty that, by embracing this vocation, a man could live in the presence of God. Jerome felt attracted to the company of others, to 'the heavenly family here on earth';[9] but to a life in other ways withdrawn from men, a life of prayer.

Quite why, and in what circumstances, Jerome eventually decided to go out into the desert of Chalcis is not certain. Perhaps his famous dream, described to his disciple Eustochium nearly ten years later, impressed on him the need to make some final decision in his life: Christ reproached him, in the dream, with the words, 'You are no Christian, but a Ciceronian'.[10] Eloquence, at least, was to be left behind, with its vast apparatus of classical pagan scholarship. It was a brave

[7] *Ep.* iii. 4. The image recurred, *Ep.* lii. 5.

[8] *Ep.* iii. 5.

[9] *Ep.* iii. 1.

[10] *Ep.* xxii. 30. The memory of this event certainly endured: see *Comm. in Ep. ad Galatas*, iii (introd.); *Apologia*, i. 30.

decision; but, for a man of Jerome's temperament and background, doomed to fail.

His letters from Chalcis reveal a man at odds with both self and circumstance. In spite of nightmares, he still demanded books—books on religious topics, it is true; but heavily weighted towards controversy.[11] He built up something of a library, and had at his disposal copyists, 'who support me in my study of the past'.[12] The Ciceronian, in other words, was still alive and well; and ready with sharp comments about the 'simple minded', and the barbarous language of the desert.[13] But he was also very lonely, and began to see, at an early stage in this period of retirement, the possible conflict between dedication to the eremitic life and his love for friends in Palestine and Italy.[14] Several letters to Aquileia survive; and these became charged in time with a further sense of dissatisfaction. More than lonely, Jerome felt abandoned and betrayed. He reproached his old friend Niceas, by that time subdeacon at Aquileia, for reestablishing himself 'amidst the pleasures of the fatherland'; and he hoped that such pleasures would be seasoned with the memory of arduous pilgrimage.[15]

This inability to understand or tolerate the motives of those who returned to the West came to a head in a letter to Heliodorus. This was a last ditch attempt to justify his own ambitious repudiation of the world, and to recall to the East a man who had already foreseen the folly of so completely rejecting the past. Jerome was forced to take a stand against courses of action that he was very soon to imitate; and he later rejected both the tone and the teaching of the letter.[16] It bears important witness, nevertheless, to several of his

[11] Hilary's *De Synodis*, certainly; perhaps also the *Commentaries* of Fortunatianus (bishop of Aquileia before Valerian, and slightly inclined to Arianism), some Aurelius Victor, 'because of what he says about the persecutions', and some letters of Novatian: *Epp*. v. 2; x. 3. However, *Ep*. x may not date from the Chalcis period: see J. Labourt, *Saint Jérôme, Lettres* (8 vols., Paris, 1949-63), i. 163; Kelly, *Jerome*, 60 f.

[12] *Ep*. v. 2.

[13] *Epp*. vii. 2; x. 3.

[14] *Epp*. v. 1; vii. 1.

[15] *Ep*. viii.

[16] *Ep*. lii. Even so, *Ep*. xiv continued to find readers: Fabiola knew it by heart, *Ep*. lxxvii. 9.

convictions in this period, and also to the painful process of development through which his ascetic life was passing.

The true ascetic, he suggested, must break completely with his family, renounce all his possessions, and above all live in solitude.[17] He will be committed, by implication, to a life of exile. (Jerome's argument proceeds from the statement in Scripture, 'A prophet has no honour in his own country', to his own conclusion, 'The perfect monk cannot live in his fatherland'.)[18]

So much for his desire to defend, in effect, his own position. The second half of the letter is perhaps even more important. Heliodorus aspired to the priesthood (and was later to become bishop of Altinum). Jerome was therefore led to discuss the feasibility of combining the clerical with the ascetic life. He was careful to give the clergy their due:

> Far be it from me to say anything about them detrimental. Heirs to the dignity of the Apostles themselves, they bring to perfection, by their own holy words, the Body of Christ. It is through them that we, too, become Christians. Possessing the keys of the Kingdom of Heaven, they judge, as it were, before the Day of Judgement. By their chastity and tempered life, they safeguard the Spouse of the Lord.[19]

The clergy could lay claim, in other words, to a specific function—teaching, nourishing, even judging the church. But they also laid claim to a public forum, and the power that went with it: to a system of relationships, and of rights and obligations (not to mention ritual and buildings), within which their power could be exercised. Jerome felt forced to continue, therefore, 'Monks, as I say, have one type of business to attend to, the clergy another entirely';[20] and, in so doing, he seems to have made three points. First, the priesthood is a dangerous vocation: 'I am delighted to see men elevated to the priesthood, but dread to see them fall. . . . When a monk falls, the priest will intercede for him; but who will intercede

[17] *Ep.* xiv. 3–6. [18] Ibid. 7.

[19] Ibid. 8. The phrase 'Christi corpus sacro ore conficiunt' is difficult. I would like it to mean that the *teaching* of the clergy builds up the church, thus perfecting the mission of the Apostles. Labourt is ambiguous, but sacramental in his allusions—'consacrent le corps du Christ', *Lettres*, i. 41. I cannot follow Mierow, 'partake of Christ's body with holy lips', *The Letters of St. Jerome*, i (Westminster, Md., 1963), 65: *conficere* in that sense seems too harsh and destructive for the sacramental context.

[20] *Ep.* xiv. 8.

for a priest, when he falls too?'[21] Second, the clergy are tied to a city life; and this means that the monk, as Jerome understood the word, cannot identify himself with the clerical order.[22] The third point was the most important, summed up in Jerome's famous phrase, 'Not all bishops are bishops'.[23] Office itself, in other words, was no guarantee, either of perfection or of God's approval. Even more important, men not formally chosen for public office could be seized upon by the Spirit, and endowed with the cunning of Daniel, the vision of Amos, the authority of David himself.[24]

As far as reproaches were concerned, events in the East were soon to make Jerome eat his words. His last three surviving letters from Chalcis show that he had become deeply involved in conflict over the schism that had arisen in the church of Antioch, and that he was being forced to think again about the relationship between ascetics and the church at large. Dispute concerned the orthodoxy of Melitius, bishop of Antioch since 360. The Arian Constantius had banished him almost immediately; but he nevertheless failed (largely perhaps, through his own lack of tact) to gain the support of the orthodox Athanasius. Basil of Caesarea, who was to become the leading opponent of Arianism in the East, after the death of Athanasius himself, was, by contrast, Melitius's firm supporter. The chief party among his local opponents (for the situation became very fragmented) appealed to the teaching of a former bishop, Eustathius, also an exile in the cause of orthodoxy (during the reign of Constantine); and they acknowledged a rival bishop, Paulinus, consecrated to the same see in 362, thanks to the meddlesome concern of the notorious Lucifer of Cagliari.[25]

Jerome now wrote to Damasus, bishop of Rome, outlining

[21] *Ep.* xiv. 8, 9.

[22] Ibid. 6, 8.

[23] Ibid. 9.

[24] Ibid. Compare the statements of Pachomius, at the Synod of Latopolis, above, pp. 30 f.

[25] See F. Cavallera, *Le schisme d'Antioche* (Paris, 1905); R. Devréese, *Le Patriarchat d'Antioche* (Paris, 1945), 17–44. A useful summary, with full bibliographical reference, is provided by M. Spanneut, 'Evagre d'Antioche', *DHGE* xvi (Paris, 1964–7), 102–7. See also J. Taylor, 'St Basil the Great and Pope St Damasus I', *Downside Review*, xci (1973), 186–203; 262–74; W. de Vries, 'Die Ostkirche und die Cathedra Petri im IV. Jahrhundert', *OCP* xi (1974), 114–44.

his own theological convictions, seeking the Pope's advice, and asking in particular which of the two bishops he should support.[26] This was not merely a private anxiety, as the sequel disclosed (for Basil had been trying to interest the West in the whole affair). Damasus was slow in replying; and Jerome wrote again. He was clearly under pressure from ascetic colleagues: 'The monks who live around me are voicing their opposition, based on longstanding authority'.[27] (The phrase reveals, not only that the monks of Chalcis involved themselves in the affairs of the church at Antioch, but also that Jerome retained for them some of the respect that men in their state of life, he thought, deserved.)

His final letter from the desert was addressed to a local priest, who had been pressing him to make an open declaration. Jerome now made an attempt to plead some right to silence, defending in the process his conception of the ascetic life:

> What is this judgement (I blush to speak of it) that we pass upon the world from the caves where we build our cells? Why should we bandy opinions about bishops, while clothed in sackcloth and ashes? What is so lordly a mind doing beneath a penitent's garb? Chains, dirt, disordered hair: these are not the symbols of a ruler, but of one who weeps. Let them allow me my silence, I beg you.[28]

Jerome was fighting, not only the external pressures of ecclesiastical controversy, but also the habits of the monks themselves. 'Clearly, you are afraid that I, a man most skilful with my tongue, in both Syriac and Greek, will wander around the churches, leading people astray, and causing a schism'.[29] Such fear was unlikely to have been aroused, unless there had been monks who were happy to do just that. It is not surprising, therefore, that Jerome's protestations that he wished for no more than a life of pious solitude were not enough to convince his neighbours of his good intentions!

Jerome's stay in Chalcis was a bitter lesson. He had summoned up the courage to embrace completely the life of the desert portrayed in the *Life of Antony*. He had attempted to abandon country, friends, even culture itself. Yet he

[26] *Ep.* xv.
[27] *Ep.* xvi. 2.
[28] *Ep.* xvii. 2.
[29] Ibid.

had found himself burdened by the memories and habits of an educated youth and a lively mind; and he was drawn, like his friends, into the public affairs of the church. A change was called for; and Jerome adapted himself with a characteristic and thoroughgoing fervour.

There now began one of the most fascinating, important, and obscure periods of Jerome's life. He set out, in effect, upon a further voyage of discovery, during which, like Palladius a generation later, he was able to savour and reflect upon various ways of living the Christian life. After the disillusionment of the desert, (again like Palladius,) it was the cities that attracted him most, where the toleration of Christianity was allowing more and more predominantly wealthy people to preserve their virginity or widowhood, to study the Bible, to support the poor with alms, and (not least) to entertain the wandering ascetic.[30]

Returning first to Antioch, and to the estate of Evagrius, Jerome either wrote or revised his *Life of Paul*—essentially a call to poverty and faith, addressed to men of wealth and relatively undisciplined piety.[31] He took up a more public position in the church of Antioch by identifying himself wholeheartedly with the party of Paulinus (probably acting as much on the advice of Evagrius himself as of the Pope in Rome),[32] and he even accepted ordination to the priesthood at the hands of the Eustathian bishop. In view of his letter to Heliodorus, this seems an odd step to have taken; but it

[30] Many of the later chapters of *HL* portray the well born in their private houses, unobtrusively attending to their own spiritual welfare, and to that of their relatives and servants, engaging in good works, and maintaining the most correct relationships with priests and bishops: lvi, lvii, lxi, lxvii. See A. Momigliano, 'Popular Religious Beliefs and the Late Roman Historians', *Popular Belief and Practice*, ed. G. J. Cuming and D. Baker (Cambridge, 1972), 12-16. Some idea of what Jerome may have found among the religious families of the cities of the East may be obtained from E. Amand de Mendieta, 'La virginité chez Eusèbe d'Emèse et l'ascétisme familial dans la première moitié du IVe siècle', *RHE* l (1955), 777-820.

[31] This and Jerome's other *Lives* will be discussed more fully below, pp. 133-9.

[32] After returning from Italy to the East in 373, Evagrius had abandoned his role of mediator in the schism, and moved more closely into league with Paulinus. Damasus finally recognized the claims of Paulinus in 375, in his letter *Per Filium* (*Ep.* iii). See Spanneut, 'Evagre', 103 f. For Jerome's part in these events, see Cavallera, *Jérôme*, i, 1, 50 f., and Taylor, 'St Basil the Great', 262 f.

may not have been entirely his own idea,[33] and he certainly did not allow ordination to tie him to this one city, or to undermine his new role as an inquiring exile.[34]

He tried his hand at controversial writing,[35] and began to take a keen interest in the study and interpretation of Scripture. But these were hesitant experiments, rather than true alternatives to a desert life; and his dominating urge was to explore, to move again, this time to Constantinople.[36] Under the influence of Gregory Nazianzene, he continued and improved his essays in translation and exegesis.[37] But the opportunity of friendship with the Cappadocian, and his experience of the Oecumenical Council of 381, would have involved Jerome even more deeply in the public affairs of the church, and also (more important) would have introduced him to yet another circle of urban devotees, inspired by the personal fervour of Gregory, and by his ascetic teaching. So Gregory's conception of the priesthood, with its emphasis on the roles of peacemaker, father, healer, teacher, and mediator, may have encouraged Jerome in his own attempt to link priesthood and asceticism.[38] Certainly, he helped to develop Jerome's understanding of virginity, the characteristic *par excellence* of the urban ascetic.[39]

Finally, Jerome maintained his connection with Rome. He continued to write to Damasus, mainly on matters of

[33] If we may believe his later protests: 'You will hear him say exactly what Bishop Paulinus, of holy memory, heard from my lips, wretch that I am: "Did I ask you that I should be ordained?" ', *Contra Iohannem Hierosolymitanum*, 41. The person alluded to here was Jerome's own brother, Paulinianus; see below, pp. 130 f.

[34] 'If you make us priests in such a way as not to rob us of our monkhood, then decide on the matter as seems best to you. But if, under the pretext of priesthood, you rob me of that for which I left the world, then I hold fast, as always, to what is mine: ordaining me cost you nothing', loc. cit.

[35] The *Altercatio Luciferiani et Orthodoxi*.

[36] Cavallera suggested that Jerome merely sought to improve his mind in the capital, *Jérôme*, i, 1, 58. Duval, 'Sur les insinuations de Jérôme', 357 f., suspected that affairs in connection with the schism at Antioch may have played their part—a more welcome hypothesis, corroborated cautiously by Kelly, *Jerome*, 66 f., without allusion to Duval.

[37] e.g. *Ep.* xviii; see Cavallera, *Jérôme*, i, 1, 62-72. For his meeting with Gregory, see *Epp.* l. 1; lii. 8.

[38] On Gregory and the priesthood, see M. Serra, 'La carità pastorale in S. Gregorio Nazianzeno', *OCP* xxi (1955), 337-74.

[39] *Adversus Iovinianum*, i. 13.

exegesis, but also with ascetic reflections—as, for example, in a long commentary on the parable of the prodigal son, with extensive reference to human freedom and the value of repentance.[40] He thus acquired another powerful and admiring urban patron, who would have been able to see in Jerome not only a man of experience, learning, and style, loyal to the see of Rome, but also a fervent ascetic of wideranging curiosity.

Jerome arrived in Rome itself in 382, in the company of Epiphanius of Salamis and Paulinus of Antioch. His visit was not merely an 'interlude' in a life otherwise withdrawn,[41] but followed naturally upon involvement in eastern controversy, and upon his more personal quest for a fitting way of life. He arrived with patrons ready to hand: Damasus the bishop was at first the more important;[42] but there were also domestic *potentes*, Paula and Marcella, hostesses to the bishops in whose company he came.[43]

The three years that followed were probably the most important of his life. He established himself as a knowledgeable and ambitious churchman; and he developed to the full his interpretation of the ascetic life. Although he lived for more than thirty years after his enforced departure from the city in 385, many of his subsequent decisions and judgements either reinforced, adapted, or consciously reacted against the experience and convictions of those years in Rome.

Most of Jerome's surviving letters from this period are addressed either to Damasus or to Marcella and Paula; and a great many of these are works of exegesis. The most famous, however, is almost certainly his letter to Eustochium, a complete account of his opinions on asceticism at that stage of his life.

He still saw the ascetic as in some sense an exile: 'God tells the human soul to go from country and kindred, to leave Ur of the Chaldaeans (which means "demon-like"), and dwell

[40] *Ep.* xxi. 6, 22, 38. Jerome remembered this commentary in later years, when attacking Iovinianus; and he used the same arguments to make his point, namely that without variety of motive and achievement asceticism could not survive as an independent vocation in the church: *Adversus Iovinianum*, ii. 31; see below, pp. 128 f.

[41] R. Syme, *Ammianus and the Historia Augusta* (Oxford, 1968), 82.

[42] *Ep.* xlv. 3 reveals the order of events.

[43] *Ep.* cviii. 6.

in the land of the living'.[44] But the experiments of Chalcis were behind him, and his own exile in Bethlehem still unforeseen. Eustochium was tied, by youth and unavoidable dependence, to a world of more populous danger. She was threatened by more than her own pride and weakness: a worldly and outraged aunt would spirit her away from prayer and penance, deck her in fine clothes, and try to launch her again on the social scene;[45] she might have to run the gauntlet of accusing fingers, and the taunt of heresy;[46] false ascetics and insinuating priests, so Jerome (ascetic and priest himself) had thought, would try to gain her patronage, and mislead her virtue.[47] Rather than advocate, therefore, in one so young, a literal withdrawal to the desert, Jerome wished more to redefine the bonds between Eustochium and her family and class. Only in this way could she consummate her spiritual marriage, and call herself the bride of Christ.[48] In a society for which *pietas* was a keystone,—loyalty to the family, both living and dead,—Jerome preached a startling message: 'it is a kind of family loyalty to be disloyal for the sake of the Lord', and 'Too great a loyalty to one's own is a betrayal of God'.[49] His favourable description of coenobitic monks in Egypt was also directed against an important social value—property: 'I put their example before you, so that you will despise, not simply gold and silver and other riches, but the very earth and sky. Bound to Christ, your song shall be, "The Lord is my chosen portion"'.[50] So there was more going on beneath the surface of Jerome's spiritual direction than advocacy of exile, emphasis on virginity as an alternative to marriage, or praise of the coenobitic life.

Eustochium was, in any case, no repentant widow, with a past to live down: rather, one of those 'who have no need of remorse'.[51] The asceticism of Chalcis—'weeping in open,

[44] *Ep.* xxii. 1.
[45] *Ep.* cvii. 5.
[46] *Ep.* xxii. 13, 27; see *Epp.* xxxviii. 5; liv. 5.
[47] *Ep.* xxii. 27 f. Jerome was not alone in this anxiety: see *Cod. Theod.* XVI, ii. 20.
[48] *Ep.* xxii. 1.
[49] *Epp.* xxxviii. 5; xxxix. 6—both echoed in the later cix. 3.
[50] *Ep.* xxii. 36.
[51] *Ep.* xxi. 3.

desert places over the sins of our youth, we call down upon ourselves the mercy of Christ'[52]—would have little relevance in her own case. 'The first of Rome's noble virgins',[53] she presented both Jerome and the church with more than a nostalgic counterfeit of repentance: pure and unspoiled, she offered the chance of sanctity without regret. It was safe enough, therefore, to allow her some literary refinement, and even a certain 'holy pride'; a sense of privilege proper to a person of her class.[54] She must remain, however, in the safety of her home, avoiding ostentation, submissive to the guidance of an older man of sanctity, and surrounded by a pious household, in whose life and daily tasks she shared completely.[55] Like Asella before her, ('the pattern of the perfect life',) 'let her find in the busy city the desert of the monks'.[56]

This willingness to tolerate a city life was later modified, but only slowly abandoned. Perhaps after the death of Damasus his patron, and after the even more dramatic death of his disciple Blesilla, which aroused so much resentment against him,[57] the city itself may have seemed a less welcome setting for asceticism. Jerome wrote to Marcella, 'As soon as we may, let us seek out the haven of a secluded countryside'. He wished to avoid the decadent distractions of a pagan city, and the misguided visits of Christian neighbours.[58] It was in this light that, more than twenty years later, he would remember the period: 'The fields and gardens beyond the city were your monastery: you chose the country for its loneliness'.[59] Yet in the following letter to Marcella he reverted to previous emphases: the consecrated virgin prepares herself for martyrdom, waiting for the coming of her Lord, spending her time in fasting and prayer, and all in a very closed environment.[60] It is probably unwise to suggest too soon (if

[52] *Contra Iohannem Hierosolymitanum*, 41.
[53] *Ep.* xxii. 15.
[54] *Ep.* xxii. 16f., balanced by warnings in 27.
[55] *Ep.* xxii. 25, 27, 29.
[56] *Ep.* xxiv. 4.
[57] *Ep.* xxxix. 6: Jerome was blamed for imposing upon her too rigorous an asceticism.
[58] *Ep.* xliii. 3.
[59] *Ep.* cxxvii. 8.
[60] *Ep.* xliv.

ever) a distinction in Jerome's mind between 'fields and gardens' and the spacious peace of a wealthy city household; and, conversely, experience at Antioch would have assured him that a country estate need not involve the sacrifice of urban refinement.[61]

Jerome was concerned, not merely to theorize about the ascetic life, but to give practical advice about the protection of virtue.[62] He also wrote as a priest; and one of the striking features of this letter to Eustochium is the extent to which his conception of the ascetic life had now become completely identified with, or absorbed into, the public life of the church. It is so easy to forget that Jerome did not pen his famous criticisms of the Roman clergy as an outsider. His remarks to Damasus, for example, about the taste of the clergy for pagan learning (still a sore topic with Jerome) show him as a reformer, working, to some extent, from within the system;[63] and, while refusing to shelter the clergy with false privilege, he was careful to define the proper ways in which they might be criticized.[64] This is not to overlook the fact that Jerome could appreciate the qualities of charismatic leadership valued in the East. He wrote later of Lea as a superior who taught her companions 'more by her example . . . than by what she said'.[65] Long afterwards, he was to say of his ascetic colleagues,–'sad, pale, dirty; pilgrims in the world, as it were',–'Although they say nothing, their clothing and behaviour speak volumes'.[66] So the old man who was to guide Eustochium must lead a life fit to be her example; must be of an age to command respect; and must possess a reputation that would allow others to consider her well advised. But he also had a quasi-ecclesial role, since he (like Paul) must be able to say, 'I betrothed you to Christ to present you as a pure bride to her one husband'.[67] Eustochium

[61] Petit gives a full and vivid description of the *villae* around Antioch, 'built like city houses' by rich citizens who were 'affected more by the delights of city life than by any inclination to the measured manner expected of religious simplicity', *Libanius*, 380 f. Maronia may not have been very different.

[62] *Ep.* xxii. 23.

[63] *Ep.* xxi. 13. He was anxious specifically about their neglect of Scripture.

[64] *Ep.* xxvii. 3.

[65] *Ep.* xxiii. 2.

[66] *Adversus Iovinianum*, ii. 36.

[67] *Ep.* xxii. 29.

must therefore read the works of Cyprian, Damasus, and Ambrose: men whose interpretation of virginity would be stamped with the authority of the episcopate.[68] The ascetic household Jerome described elsewhere as a 'domestic church':[69] Eustochium must always remember that her vocation to virginity had value only because it was fulfilled within the church.[70]

Jerome left Rome with a flourish.[71] The generous-hearted Asella had the doubtful privilege of receiving his parting comments: 'It will come, the Day of Judgement, it will come; and you will weep with me to see that not a few are burning'.[72] Yet the very implication of an unvanquished and virtuous minority explains this reversal of fortune. Whatever antagonism he may have aroused among the clergy,–'an assembly of Pharisees',[73]–Jerome's 'disloyalty' had certainly driven an unforgiveable wedge into the aristocratic society of Christian Rome; a wedge between the advantages of birth–the opportunity for leisured devotion and a bookish curiosity–and the corresponding obligations of heredity. The smooth path of public duty and family pride, even the most orthodox and moral, had been ploughed up and obscured by Jerome's industry and fervour–or rather, roughly deflected into less familiar thickets: penury, sterility, and the friendship of God. Few were yet ready to follow the friends of Ponticianus, in ways that Augustine would later describe; and in the vortex of conflicting ambitions that followed on the death of Damasus, Jerome was thrown clear. Power would always depend on patronage, and spiritual power on the ability to persuade a patron that some continuous thread of *potentia* still lay across the chasm between an able governor like Ambrose, for example, and a saintly bishop. Jerome had failed, left with nothing but misleading rhetoric: 'What a fool I was, wishing to sing the Lord's song in a foreign land,

[68] *Ep.* xxii. 22. [69] *Ep.* xxx. 14.

[70] *Ep.* xxii. 38.

[71] On the circumstances of his virtual expulsion from the city, see Kelly, *Jerome*, 110 ff. The well documented speculations of Cavallera, *Jérôme*, are also useful, i, 1, 86 ff.

[72] *Ep.* xlv. 1, 7.

[73] Jerome, *De Spiritu Sancto*, Preface.

leaving Mount Zion to seek the aid of Egypt'.[74] But Bethlehem, as an alternative, had little more at first than symbolic value: it was to be a disappointing compromise between the complete and real dedication of Chalcis and the now lost golden opportunities of the papal household.

[74] *Ep.* xlv. 6. The allusion (confusing in the context) is, of course, biblical rather than geographical; see also *De Spiritu Sancto*, Preface.

II

LETTERS FROM BETHLEHEM

Once established in Bethlehem, Jerome never left the region; but his life was in no way monotonous. An enormous literary output bears witness to intense activity; and his letters reveal a wide network of acquaintance, an undying interest in other people, and developing convictions of his own. Most important of all, his more settled life did not dull that anxious curiosity that had driven him from city to city, seeking 'the pattern of the perfect life'.[1] The greater proportion of his letters, during the rest of his life, show him answering questions forming in his own mind, as well as in the minds of correspondents, about the best way to live as a Christian.

One immediate reaction to his failure in the West, reflected in several letters, was to persuade others to follow him into exile.[2] His friends should seek more the quiet and simplicity of the countryside; a land filled with the biblical songs of the ploughman and gardener.[3] No doubt the Kingdom of God was within (perhaps Marcella had urged this very objection,—the letter was addressed to her,—reflecting a Roman sense that an outward show of fervour was uncalled for, if not dangerous); but in Palestine, according to Jerome, standards were better protected, and ascetics found a welcome freedom from the judgement (and the control) of others: 'We may speak different languages, but our religion is one'.[4] To Desiderius and Serenilla, he suggested that pilgrimage to the holy places would be a natural sequel to their religious conversion. He did admit that they need not remain there, if they found that customs and people were not to their taste—espousing a concept of pilgrimage, in other words, not

[1] *Ep.* xxiv. 1.

[2] I say 'he' because although *Ep.* xlvi came from Paula and Eustochium, there is every reason to suppose that it reflected the opinions of Jerome himself.

[3] *Ep.* xlvi. 12.

[4] *Ep.* xlvi. 10—a reminder of the 'international' flavour of the ascetic communities in the holy land.

quite the same as dedication to an exiled asceticism.[5] But even in the 390s, he could still praise the youthful desire of Nepotianus to go to Egypt, to Mesopotamia, or perhaps to some island nearer home.[6]

Nevertheless, this willingness to encourage exile weakened with time. Letters to Paulinus of Nola illustrate the change.[7] Paulinus, freshly converted, must leave the West; such was Jerome's first response to news of his change of heart. He must embrace a life of religious exile in the holy places—not least since death might come upon him when he least expected it.[8] But in his second letter, literal exile was not insisted on: 'I would not dare to confine within narrow bounds the almighty power of God, nor restrict within a little stretch of earth him whom the heavens cannot contain'; and, echoing Marcella, 'the Kingdom of God is within us'.[9] He merely pointed out that monks should not live in cities, and that bishops and priests who did were seeking their salvation by saving others, rather than by a direct attack on their own shortcomings. They had their own inspiring models, the apostles—different from Elias and Elisaeus, 'the authoritative pioneers of our enterprise'.[10]

This modification, accepting in effect the quasi-monastic community set up by Paulinus at Nola (not unlike those that Jerome had known in Aquileia), may explain in part why he did not cease to praise the household asceticism he had done so much to encourage in Rome. He now saw more clearly (as he had warned Marcella)[11] that the demands of a great household or estate could militate against ascetic standards—

[5] *Ep.* xlvii. 2.

[6] *Ep.* lx. 10. The last course Bonosus had chosen,—see above, p. 100—as also Martin—see below, p. 148. The custom continued to gain in popularity: Fabiola visited or cared for ascetics living on islands, and in other remote regions, *Ep.* lxxvii. 6; and there are the famous references made by Rutilius Namatianus, *De Reditu Suo*, i. 439 ff., 515 ff.

[7] On the dating and order of these letters, see Kelly, *Jerome*, 192–4, with its documented appeal to the arguments of Nautin. At issue are the opinions of Cavallera, *Jérôme*, i. 2, 89–91, and of Courcelle, 'Paulin de Nole et saint Jérôme', *REL* xxv (1947), 250–80 (an article that retains, nevertheless, its usefulness).

[8] *Ep.* liii. 1, 11; compare liv. 18.

[9] *Ep.* lviii. 3.

[10] Ibid. 4, 5. He was thinking not least of Jerusalem—occupied, of course, by his opponents, John and Rufinus.

[11] *Ep.* xliii. 3.

'With modesty and holiness comes frugality; and frugality is frowned upon by servants'[12]–; but he could still detect, and place some faith in, the survival of what one might call a Christian family culture: 'Imitate, rather, your holy mother–I say it again most forcefully. Let the promise of your father's name be fulfilled (I mention him with respect: not because he was consular or patrician, but because he is a Christian); and allow him the joy of having conceived a daughter for Christ, and not for the world'.[13] In this letter to Furia, he still portrayed asceticism in terms of exile, or at least as separation from home and family; but he did not press the image in literal terms: she was to practise perfection at home.[14] This was not an isolated message to one person: Jerome knew well, and assumed for some time to come, that the letter would be widely read.[15]

For a brief period, in fact, at the end of the fourth and beginning of the fifth centuries, Jerome's hopes for Roman asceticism were given new strength. The wife of Pammachius, daughter of Paula, had died (in 395, or early the following year); and this, in Jerome's eyes, heralded a new era in the religious history of the city: 'Paulina sleeps, so that [Pammachius] might keep watch: she has gone before her husband, to leave behind a servant for Christ'.[16] The women of the family had summed up for Jerome every grade of religious perfection: 'In these three women, joined both by blood and by virtue, I see three gifts bestowed by Christ: Eustochium has plucked the flowers of virginity; Paula has ground in weariness the wheatgrain of her widowhood; and Paulina has kept pure her marriage bed'.[17] Pammachius himself was now a free man, a born leader in a Christian empire, who might inject into public life the principles of Christian perfection. He willingly took his seat in the Senate dressed in the humble garb of a monk–'Rome has gained in our time what the world has never known before'–: he was a second

[12] *Ep.* liv. 5.
[13] Ibid. 6.
[14] Ibid. 3, 13.
[15] *Epp.* cxx. 3; cxxiii. 17.
[16] *Ep.* lxxvii. 10.
[17] *Ep.* lxvi. 2. The reference is to Jerome's interpretation of the parable of the sower, with its hundredfold, sixtyfold, and thirtyfold; see *Ep.* xlix. 2 (also addressed to Pammachius).

Aeneas, and the follower of Abraham.[18] This last accolade had signified, in former letters, at least withdrawal from public life and family commitment, if not from the fatherland itself; but Pammachius modelled himself on the patriarch in different ways: he built hostels for the poor, the sick, and homeless.

Jerome's enthusiasm did not indicate a feckless reversal of former principle: it was accompanied by renewed appreciation on his part of the importance of inner asceticism. Mere virginity, the mere uprooting from a cultural bed, the mere dispensing of wealth, were no longer enough.[19] It was the surrender of self that mattered: 'It is a much greater thing to lay aside habits of mind than of manner'.[20] But externals had taken on a new degree of importance, as the symbols of a supposed transformation in Roman society:

There are many monks who are wise, powerful, well born; but my Pammachius is wiser, more powerful, and more noble than all of them: he is great, even among great men; he leads, even among leaders—a veritable Field Marshal among monks. Paulina has left to us, by her death, children no less glorious than she could have wished for while living. Sing, o barren one, who did not bear; break forth into singing and cry aloud, you who have not been in travail! For as many poor as there are in Rome, you have gained yourself sons.[21]

The note of euphoria was, for a while, maintained. Fabiola, who died in 399, was seen by Jerome as another example and another proof of this Christian optimism. She too was a follower of Abraham—and for the same reason: she built a hostel for the sick.[22] But it is in Jerome's description of her funeral that one sees a Roman Christian drawing the universal attention and public grief reserved for leading citizens: 'I have heard the report. Crowds went before her, a sea of people pressed around her bier: neither squares, nor arcades, nor the overhanging roofs themselves could carry the spectators. At that moment Rome saw her people drawn together as one: all rejoiced to give glory to the penitent'.[23]

[18] *Ep.* lxvi. 4, 6, 11.

[19] *Ep.* lxvi. 8; compare *Ep.* lxxi. 3: 'To cast aside one's gold is the mark of a beginner only, not of the perfect'.

[20] *Ep.* lxxvii. 2.

[21] *Ep.* lxvi. 4. These 'sons', of course, were the fortunate occupants of Pammachius's hostels.

[22] *Ep.* lxxvii. 6, 10. [23] Ibid. 11.

There is no trace of satire here, but rather of confident triumph. Jerome was not always the carping outsider. He had hopes for Rome; he worked for their achievement; and, at this period at least, he felt they were near success.

The air of confidence, however, was fragile and misleading. Even Jerome did not place all his eggs in the Roman basket. He wrote at almost the same time to Salvina, widow of a former friend Nebridius, daughter-in-law of a *Comes Orientis*, and still resident in Constantinople. Although he averred that he was not seeking patronage[24] (as he had with Pammachius, many years before[25]), he was writing at a time when, beset by supporters of Origen, patrons were just what he needed. He was willing, in his own cause, to write to Salvina (as he had to Furia) encouraging no more than the preservation of piety in a domestic setting. He praised in her dead husband precisely the compromise he had deprecated in Paulinus of Nola: 'To a man on active service, there is no harm in cloak, or belt, or a party of retainers: beneath the uniform of one king, he serves another'.[26] This letter, again, was no mere piece of opportunism, but a carefully calculated treatise that would later find readers in Gaul.[27]

Comparison of Jerome's letters to Furia, Pammachius, and Salvina reveals an insecurity in Jerome, at least on the level of the question, 'How should one live?';[28] an insecurity made even more distressing, of course, by the threat of the Origenist controversy. At one moment Jerome harked back to the memories of his stay in Rome; at another he encouraged in himself the vision of a new Jerusalem on the ruins of the Capitol; at another again he reached out to fresh opportunities among a less familiar audience. Such disjointed expectations bred despair; and Jerome's correspondence at this time takes on a new note, of unwillingness to become involved at all. This may have been due partly to what he

[24] *Ep.* lxxix. 1.

[25] *Ep.* xlviii. 1.

[26] *Ep.* lxxix. 2; compare *Ep.* cxlv: 'Who can help but love the man who, wearing his cloak, and the clothing of this world's service, takes upon himself the labour of the prophets?'

[27] *Epp.* cxx. 3; cxxiii. 17.

[28] *Ep.* liv. 1.

regarded as approaching old age, and to a feeling of peaceful achievement. He had already written to Nepotianus, in 394: 'Let me warn you again: they show more learning in their old age,—more skill in proportion to their efforts; more wisdom in proportion to the time passed by,—who school themselves in youth by worthy endeavours, and contemplate day and night the law of the Lord: they are the ones who gain the surest fruit from the labour of their years'.[29] There may have been a feeling, too, that Palestine was only one place among many, no longer the focus of the ascetic world: 'Each province is blessed with its own insight'.[30] But the bitter experiences of the conflict with John of Jerusalem, and later with Rufinus, were obviously leaving their mark. In the early stages of Jerome's misunderstanding with Augustine, for example, the old Chalcis theme recurs: 'We deserve our rest'.[31] Jerome was particularly reluctant to become involved with bishops—a feeling that endured.[32] He even suggested, with an ominous note of detachment, 'But if you want to show off and test your learning, why don't you seek out younger men, educated and of good family? I hear Rome is full of them'.[33] By 403, of course, Rome—or Italy more generally—had become the home of Rufinus and his allies.

In spite of his sarcasm, Jerome was still able to conjure up a picture of pagan defeat and Christian triumph in the capital: 'The gilded Capitol falls into disrepair; dust and cobwebs cover all Rome's temples. The city shakes on its foundations, and a stream of people hurries, past half-fallen shrines, to the tombs of the martyrs'.[34] But this image of extravagant destruction (merely echoing the exaggerations of the *Adversus Iovinianum*)[35] does not suggest a man any longer eager to inherit the ruins of the past. The same letter contained a command: the young Paula must be sent out to

[29] *Ep.* lii. 3. But I still find it hard to believe, with Kelly, that Jerome was born in 331; see his *Jerome*, 337–9.

[30] *Ep.* lxxi. 6.

[31] *Ep.* cii. 2; see also cv. 3, and p. 105, above.

[32] *Ep.* cv. 4; see cxvii. 1.

[33] *Ep.* cv. 3.

[34] *Ep.* cvii. 1.

[35] *Adversus Iovinianum*, ii. 38: 'The Capitol falls into disrepair; the rites of Jupiter have crumbled with his temples'.

Bethlehem for her ascetic training.[36] Paula was a child, of course; a special case: she offered Jerome the opportunity of another Eustochium, and demanded ruthless protection.[37] Yet, by 407, (before the sack of Rome, in other words,) even Pammachius, the hostel-building 'Abraham' of Jerome's earlier vision, had become no more than the example of what a man should do when his wife had died; and Jerome concluded his advice to this later widower, Julianus, with the exhortation to a life, once again, of religious exile.[38]

Clearly, a change had taken place. 'I am content with a few people's approval; comfort enough, the praise of friends: they query my work, but swayed by love for me, and concern for the Scriptures'.[39] This was the period of the *Contra Vigilantium*, which, in spite of Jerome's attempt to link it with earlier controversy, looked away from Rome,—away from the Rome of Iovinianus, with its concern for virginity and hierarchy,[40]—and more towards Gaul, its martyr cults, its interest in miracles, its anxiety about how to dispose of wealth immediately threatened by barbarian incursion. The *Contra Vigilantium* itself bears the stamp of a confident interest in a new field of debate. An earlier but connected letter, *To a Mother and Daughter in Gaul*, reveals the doubt, the puzzlement, the insecurity that accompanied this change. Jerome made a defence of *pietas* between this mother and her daughter, which (after his letter to Laeta about the young Paula) scarcely rings true.[41] He criticized local clergy, who tried to come between them;[42] and yet he seems to have been doing precisely that himself. The mother was perhaps beyond redemption,[43] and her peculiar domestic arrangements made asceticism difficult: she employed a monk as major-domo, 'and all the servants snapped at him; whatever their mistress would not give, they complained it was he who had acquired

[36] *Ep.* cvii. 13.

[37] Ibid. 8.

[38] *Ep.* cxviii. 5, 7. Jerome even mentions Abraham again; but this time as a man who was willing to sacrifice his son.

[39] *Comm. in Isaiam*, xii, Introduction (the work begun in 408).

[40] See below, pp. 128 f.

[41] *Ep.* cxvii. 2; compare cvii. 4.

[42] *Ep.* cxvii. 1, 5.

[43] Ibid. 3.

it in their stead'.[44] The daughter, on the other hand, (and this, again, recalls his letter to Laeta,) needed protection, and should be made to join, he thought, some separate community of virgins like herself.[45]

This was a muddled letter. Jerome more or less admitted that it was not entirely sincere (by which he may have meant no more than that it seemed unsuited to the public eye); and he insisted that it should be kept a secret.[46] By the time he wrote the *Contra Vigilantium*, he was more sure of himself. Part of the reason was increasing familiarity with Gaul. Already, in 406, large numbers of people from the area around Toulouse, for example, had visited Jerome in the holy places, (precisely during the period, of course, when Sulpicius was writing his *Dialogues*,) a movement that increased with the years.[47] Familiarity led Jerome to treat the Gauls with great respect. He saw himself no longer as an oracle of wisdom, but as one voice among many; a man whose thoughts on the interpretation of Scripture, based on personal experience, might be of additional interest to those already versed in exegesis.[48] At the same time, he felt that the holy places provided in a new sense some focus of loyalty, some promise of relief, to men and women whose lives had been disrupted by barbarian invasion. His advice to Rusticus (not of Narbonne), that he should follow his wife Artemia (now his spiritual sister) to the holy land, was based precisely on the knowledge that their world had been overturned in this way.[49] He wrote to Geruchia with the well worn phrases he had used in letters to ladies in Rome, praising her Christian family and household, and urging her to remain a widow, in spite of the pressure of domestic obligation, and the social and economic complexity of her household.[50] But, in the face of the barbarian threat, such advice, he now added, was almost academic.[51] This letter, too, was carefully constructed,

[44] *Ep*. cxvii. 8. [45] Ibid. 4, 6.
[46] Ibid. 1, 12.
[47] See *Ep*. cxix. 1, and the refs. in cxxx. 4.
[48] *Epp*. cxix. 1; cxx, Preface; cxxi, Preface.
[49] *Ep*. cxxii. 4. [50] *Ep*. cxxiii. 1, 13.
[51] Ibid. 15.

and designed for a wider audience.[52]

Because of what follows below, concerning the Gaul of Sulpicius and Cassian, Jerome's letter to Rusticus of Narbonne is of special interest. His censure of a gullible taste for wonderworking (a strange echo of Vigilantius)[53] may have been a passing judgement on Sulpicius himself;[54] and, at the end of the same letter, he recommended the guidance and example of Proculus of Marseille, father of his clergy, patron of monasticism, and friend of Cassian.[55] Like Cassian, Jerome sought inspiration from the example of Egypt.[56] Like Cassian, he recommended the coenobitic life, at least in the case of Rusticus himself, as the only guarantee of experienced instruction; a school of humility that would offer worthy preparation for both the eremitic life and ordination to the priesthood and episcopate.[57] Jerome also reproduced his own longstanding convictions. The essence of the monastic life, he wrote, was poverty and solitude, away from the city.[58] But the radical disruption of life by barbarian incursion had introduced into Jerome's thought a new note of urgency; a feeling that asceticism was a matter of all or nothing, now or never: 'It is a slippery path you have set out on; and, if great glory follows on success, much greater shame results from failure'.[59]

Jerome had begun to sense, perhaps, the fragility of his own achievement. So many of the landmarks by which he had plotted his own ascetic course had now gone—not least, both friends and enemies in Rome. The well born patrons and the luckless butts of Jerome's pen had all been bound up

[52] *Ep.* cxxiii. 17.

[53] 'He speaks out against the miracles and other demonstrations of power that take place in the basilicas of the martyrs. They may benefit the gullible, he says, but not true believers', *Contra Vigilantium*, 10.

[54] *Ep.* cxxv. 9; particularly Jerome's criticism of the judgement that, 'according to certain people (scarcely qualified to speak), [the finest ascetics] are unaware that demons, mounting attacks upon them, are able to stage false miracles'. Martin's disciples, on several occasions, at least *heard* him demonstrating his perception in the face of such illusions: *V. Mart.* xxii; Sulpicius, *Dial.* ii. 13; iii. 6.

[55] *Ep.* cxxv. 20; see below, p. 175.

[56] *Ep.* cxxv. 11.

[57] Ibid. 9, 17; see below, pp. 217 ff.

[58] *Ep.* cxxv. 7 f.

[59] Ibid. 1.

with the institutional fabric of Roman Christianity, which was now, for a moment at least, cast into disarray. Jerome had always been an urban guerilla at heart, sniping in the built up areas of late classical culture. Now it was as if he had been thrust out onto an exposed and darkening plain, filled with figures hurrying from their homeland, 'ignorant of the past, fearful of the present, longing for the future'.[60]

Jerome allowed himself one more appeal to Rome in the old style: his letter to Demetrias. Much of what he said was repetition of old themes; but the Rome of Demetrias had witnessed changes that called for some new spiritual direction. Jerome advised her, as he had Eustochium, to seek perfection within her household.[61] Like Eustochium again, she was no penitent–'the ship is saved: she is a virgin unsullied'–; and Jerome desired to protect (as he had in the cases of Paula and Pacatula) the purity of youth.[62] He maintained the conviction of an earlier letter: 'Soft and tender years can be bent one way or the other: they follow wherever you lead'; and, (with a more sensible note of protective discipline,) 'Let everyone remain true to his first calling'.[63] But his anxiety was tempered now by admiration for spontaneous choice: the decision of Demetrias to remain a virgin had been entirely personal and free.[64] Jerome had recommended Eustochium to read Cyprian; but Cyprian had been exhorting his readers to embrace a state of life not yet achieved: Jerome's concern now was to safeguard a decision already made.[65]

There were other changes that compelled a different approach on Jerome's part. These events had taken place in the aftermath of the fall of Rome and barbarian invasion. Demetrias would live in her own household; but this was seen now as a monastery in the stricter sense; a coenobitic community that would discipline her against fantasy, self-

[60] This, his description of Pacatula, (written in 413,) could well have been applied to himself: *Ep.* cxxviii. 5.

[61] *Ep.* cxxx. 12.

[62] Ibid. 7, 9.

[63] *Ep.* cxxviii. 3 f.

[64] *Ep.* cxxx. 4.

[65] Ibid. 19; compare xxii. 22.

will, and bad temper.[66] Her wealth was not to be spent on building churches, but dispensed to the poor and the servants of God.[67] There was no need, in Jerome's mind at least, for elaborate stage-setting as a background to Christian triumph: 'That city of yours, once the capital of the world, is now a tomb for Romans'.[68] The whole atmosphere of the letter makes a vivid contrast with his counsel to Eustochium. The serious-minded determination of Demetrias, and the visible destruction of city and empire, made her ascetic regime at once more lonely and more independent.

[66] Jerome's terminology, referring to the company in which Demetrias was to practise asceticism, would have won the approval of Pachomius: 'So it is well to obey those older than yourself; to show a docile respect for those who are perfect; to learn from others–in the light of what Scripture commands–the path your life should take. Have nothing to do with that counsellor worse than all others–your own rash confidence', *Ep.* cxxx. 17. The conversion of Demetrias, or at least its successful fruition, presupposed (in Jerome's eyes) an ascetic society within which it might be encouraged.

[67] *Ep.* cxxx. 14.

[68] *Ep.* cxxx. 5. Demetrias herself did, in the end, revert to a more confident and public form of urban asceticism. For the significance of this later development, see Peter Brown, 'Aspects of the Christianization of the Roman Aristocracy', *JRS* li (1960), 10; 'Pelagius and his Supporters', *JTS*, n.s. xix (1968), 98-100–both repr. in his *Religion and Society in the Age of St Augustine* (London, 1972), 179 f., 189-92.

III

JEROME ON THE PRIESTHOOD AND EPISCOPATE

By the time Alaric had sacked Rome in 410, Martin of Tours was more than ten years dead, and Sulpicius Severus had completed both *Life* and *Dialogues*. As far as chronology is concerned, it is time for us to take another 'sideways step', and turn to Gaul. But first we must go back, and examine, in the light of his career to date, Jerome's attitudes on the two basic themes of our inquiry—authority and literature.

For an understanding of Jerome's life and conviction does not depend on plotting the rise and fall of his fortunes in Rome, nor indeed on the rise and fall of the fortunes of Rome itself. His willingness to identify himself with the public affairs of the church points to another influential interest, (indeed, to a sense of duty,) which was to persist throughout his life. His conception of the link between monk and church emerges very clearly in letters and documents written during the years just before and during the Origenist controversy (often, in other words, discussed in the context of wide, or at least different, issues). In his commentary on Paul's epistle to Titus, for example, written between 387 and 389, Jerome the priest affected the air of *noblesse oblige.* He declared that the clergy had a duty to be better than anyone else, and arranged them in a neat hierarchy of ascending excellence; and he couched this exhortation to virtue in terms that recall more ascetic concerns: 'What can we hope for from the formation of a disciple who thinks himself greater than his master? Therefore bishops, priests, and deacons need to take special care that they outstrip, in their speech and behaviour, all those over whom they are set'.[1]

This certainly betrayed, with a vengeance, 'the cautious *esprit de corps* of the Latin clergyman'.[2] More important,

[1] *Comm. in Ep. ad Titum*, ii. 15.
[2] Brown, 'Patrons of Pelagius', 71; repr. *Religion and Society*, 225.

perhaps, it echoed the harsher strictures of his earlier letter to Heliodorus: leave family and homeland, where your true worth is so little appreciated; and yet remember, therefore, that nothing short of perfection is good enough.[3] But, by the 390s, Jerome knew better how to combine both points of view, and how to fit the ascetic into an ecclesiastical hierarchy. In his letter to Nepotianus, written in 394, he agreed that monks could become members of the clergy (which was what his correspondent wanted to do) without sacrificing personal standards. The statement involved (as he himself admitted) a specific retractation of what he had said to Heliodorus.[4] It was not necessary to suppose that men would be either monks or clergy: Jerome's distinction now was between clergy who were monks and clergy who were not. To become a priest might mean, for some, a new and exciting (not to say tempting) *cursus honorum*—a life of opportunity and fame, made respectable by the legislation of a Christian empire—; but the man of better motive would acknowledge ascetic precepts that applied to anyone with a sense of religious vocation, whether he intended to become a cleric or not.[5] It is interesting that Jerome felt able to give Nepotianus the specifically clerical advice, leaving his guidance in the principles of monasticism (by word and example) in the hands of his bishop (no less a person than Heliodorus himself!).[6] Not surprisingly, his portrayal of the ideal episcopal household not only pointed back to his own experience under Valerian in Aquileia, but also forward to the conception of office propagated by, and recognized in, Proculus of Marseille: the bishop must be the father of his clergy; and they in turn must obey him with filial devotion.[7]

There was another retractation involved in this letter (and in other writings of the period)—not so explicit; but contrasting, again, with that letter to Heliodorus. Jerome had ended then, in 376, with a portrait of the exiled ascetic, (as he hoped his friend would be,) laughing on the last day, 'rusticanus et

[3] *Ep.* xiv. 2, 7; see above, pp. 102 ff.
[4] *Ep.* lii. 1.
[5] *Ep.* lii. 1, 5 f.
[6] Ibid. 4.
[7] Ibid. 7; see below, p. 175.

pauper', while the figures of ancient wisdom stood condemned: 'That simpleton Plato will be led forward with his followers; Aristotle will find no refuge in his arguments'.[8] But, by 394, a contrast between holiness and learning could not be so forcibly asserted, not least because holiness was now seen by Jerome as more compatible with–indeed, a necessary adjunct of–the clerical office; an office that called, in its turn, for learning of a kind. Jerome was careful: the preacher seeks compunction in his hearers, not applause; he is 'mysterii peritus', not a demagogue.[9] The mystery here, of course, is that of Scripture, from which the priest can draw sound teaching for the faithful, and arguments against opponents of the church.[10] Scripture, therefore, is like the young maiden Abishag, warming the limbs of the ageing David–a new wisdom, to revive an old culture (the 'gentilis litteratura').[11] There was a certain indecision in Jerome's mind: 'No brother, relying on his straightforward nature and lack of urbanity, should think himself holy merely because he knows nothing; but nor should the man of learning and polished language consider holiness a question of how one speaks. Neither condition is perfect–although a saintly lack of sophistication is much better than sinful eloquence'.[12] Nevertheless, writing to Paulinus of Nola at about the same time, Jerome described Plato–that Plato whom he had condemned twenty years before–as 'peregrinus atque discipulus . . . preferring to learn with modesty from others, rather than lay before them without shame his own ideas'.[13] The rest of the letter–emphasizing the status of Scripture as *the* Christian literature, the importance of instructed exegesis, the need for a *magister*, and the value of Scripture in its appeal to different levels of understanding–anticipates the effort of Augustine to safeguard the habits of reflection and literary expertise in a post-pagan society.[14] It was an effort

[8] *Ep.* xiv. 11.

[9] *Ep.* lii. 8.

[10] Ibid. 7.

[11] Ibid. 2 f. The allusion is to I Kings, i. 1-4; Kelly misses the point of this, 'one of Jerome's most audacious feats of exegesis', *Jerome*, 191.

[12] *Ep.* lii. 9.

[13] *Ep.* liii. 1.

[14] Especially in his *De Doctrina Christiana*; see Peter Brown, *Augustine of Hippo* (London, 1967), 259-69.

linked—for Jerome, certainly—with the task of introducing the professional ascetic into the clerical body. It enabled him to say to Oceanus, only a few years later, 'People look for learning in a priest: the Old Testament demands as much; and Paul to Titus develops the theme. A man innocent in his behaviour, but with nothing to say, may profit others by his example, but does them equal harm by his silence. The fury of wolves is frightened off by the way the dog barks, and by the shepherd's rod'.[15]

Jerome concluded the letter to Nepotianus with a Virgilian plea for diversity—'We cannot all do everything'—; and this, too, had its implications for authority and order in the church.[16] The religious devotee could not attempt to sum up in himself all the canons of Christian excellence, nor meet all the needs of the church: each individual formed part of the whole. This belief had found even clearer expression in Jerome's recent tract, *Adversus Iovinianum*: 'We know that, in a great household, not only are there vessels of gold and silver, but also of wood and clay; and on the foundation of Christ, which the architect Paul laid down, some build in gold, silver, and precious stones, others with straw, wood, and stubble'.[17] Yet this was not a static picture. He wished to plead against Iovinian the value of freedom, and the real possibility of relapse; and therefore also the need for incentive, and for a scale of rewards: 'When [the devil] sees us building on the foundation of Christ with straw, wood, and stubble, he sets those ablaze. So let us build in gold, silver, and precious stones, and he will not dare to tempt us'.[18] Jerome would also say, it is true, that 'bishop, priest, and deacon are not the names of virtues, but of duties'. This was not to depict, however, a church of impersonal structures: he was a realist, and allowed for human imperfection. The decision to allow married men, for example, to become bishops—in part, a surrender to the weakness of the Gentiles—was also recognition that there were not enough virgins

[15] *Ep.* lxix. 8.
[16] *Ep.* lii. 9.
[17] *Adversus Iovinianum*, i. 3.
[18] Ibid. ii. 3.

available, and that not all virgins automatically possessed the virtues necessary for episcopal office: ascetic simplicity and a shrewd mind (especially when combined in one man) were not always popular with those responsible for the election of bishops. Nevertheless, realism was not to obscure or stifle the ideal: Jerome continued to address himself to an *élite* with higher principles, not only of ascetic conduct, but also of ecclesiastical discipline. 'I shall say what may cause offence to many, although good men will show me no anger, because no sense of sin afflicts them with remorse'.[19]

It is instructive to place these statements alongside the writings of Siricius, successor to Damasus as bishop of Rome, and remembered for his opposition to the ascetic movement.[20] Jerome by now considered that as many clerics as possible should be consecrated virgins; and, in this marriage of two disciplines, he had come to see an improvement of standards in the church, rather than the threatened compromise of ascetics. What of the bishop of Rome? In his letter *Directa* of 385, to Himerius of Tarragona, Siricius attacked certain classes of ascetic who repudiated their former dedication to a life of chastity (whether in monasteries, or in less clearly defined groups); but he agreed that monks could, under certain conditions, be admitted to the ranks of the clergy. With regard to these monastic candidates, 'recommended by their sober bearing, and the saintly character of their habits and beliefs', he added an important warning: 'They should not be raised in one leap to the lofty status of a bishopric'.[21] Here was a foretaste of the emphasis for which Siricius would indeed become renowned: all clerics, whether or not their background was monastic, must rise through the ranks.

Siricius shared Jerome's feeling that the clergy should not think of their office as a path to honour; and this conviction may have lain behind his command that no man should be ordained who had been involved in 'the service of this world'.[22]

[19] *Adversus Iovinianum*, i. 34.

[20] See, for example, with specific reference to Jerome and Martin, J. Fontaine, 'Vérité et fiction dans la chronologie de la *Vita Martini*', *Saint Martin et son temps* (Rome, 1961), 210 f.

[21] Siricius, *Ep.* I, vi (7), xiii (17).

[22] Siricius, *Ep.* V, ii (canon 3); see also VI, i (3).

Writing to the bishops of Gaul, after the Synod of Rome in 386, Siricius was even more explicit on this matter:

The same applies to anyone engaged in the service of this world, even though he be one of the faithful. It is well known that he will enjoy a certain liberty that comes with official status. Who will be able to restrain him? Who can deny that he will attend the games; that he will resort to violence and injustice, because of his involvement with money? Those who acquire power in this world fall under the sway of this world's law; and it is clear that they cannot remain free from sin.[23]

Jerome may have been rather less enthusiastic about the pope's continuing determination to maintain a professional spirit among the clergy, and to encourage the supposition that all priests and bishops should be gradually promoted from within the clerical order: 'There is one thing, certainly, that must not be allowed. No one newly received into the church, nor any lay person who has not yet exercised some ecclesiastical office, shall be ordained priest or deacon without due thought. In the matter of ordinations, the strictest care is to be taken that only clerics become bishops'.[24] The reason for this prohibition—'Those not yet taught are suddenly compelled to teach'[25]—was to be echoed with pessimistic insistence in later papal pronouncements.[26]

Jerome's attitude to his own priesthood is revealing. The documents in which he is most candid date from the moment of balance in his career as a priest. When he was first ordained by Paulinus at Antioch, Jerome made it clear that he had no wish to allow his priesthood to restrict his freedom as an ascetic; and the memory of that demand was much in his mind at the time of his conflict with John of Jerusalem. This arose over the ordination of Paulinianus (Jerome's brother, and a monk at Bethlehem) by Epiphanius of Salamis (bishop, in other words, of another diocese). (Jerome had refused to exercise his own priesthood, even within the Bethlehem community, 'through shame and humility'.)[27]

[23] Siricius, *Ep.* X, ii (7), v (13). This was only a partial ban—on the promotion of such men to the episcopate—: provided they did penance for their past, such converts could aspire to the priesthood.

[24] Siricius, *Epp.* VI, iii (5); X, v (15).

[25] Siricius, *Ep.* VI, iii (5).

[26] See below, p. 217, n. 88; 219, n. 96.

[27] According to Epiphanius himself, if we can trust Jerome's translation of his letter, *Ep.* li. 1. (Jerome admitted that his version had been hurried, and subjected to much subsequent criticism, *Ep.* lvii. 2.)

Epiphanius thought that John, in whose diocese Bethlehem lay, should not concern himself with the government of priests who exercised their ministry solely within the orbit of a monastic community (as Paulinianus intended).[28] This was a line of argument that Jerome was to take up himself, against Theophilus of Alexandria, in 396–7. He voiced the hopeful and flattering assumption that Theophilus would not forcibly subject monks to this authority, but gain their voluntary submission. He repeated that the ordination of Paulinianus had been an entirely monastic affair. Then, speaking of the danger that he and his followers ran, from being expelled from Palestine, (as John had threatened,) he made the important assertion that those who had already exiled themselves for the sake of Christ naturally escaped any such sanction. His concluding remarks sum up many themes: 'Our hearts are not so puffed up that we forget what is owing to Christ's priests. Anyone who receives them receives, not them alone, but him whose bishops they are. But be content with that distinction. Remember you are fathers, not masters—especially among those who, casting aside the honours of this world, value peace and retirement above all things'.[29] No doubt such sentiments were to some extent *ad hominem*; but they do tally with other signs mentioned above, of a new element of withdrawal and disillusionment in Jerome's life.[30]

One later statement of importance on the matter of the priesthood, already touched upon, came in his letter to Rusticus of Narbonne.[31] The ascetic life is deliberately portrayed as a preparation for the priesthood; and the priesthood in its turn can help to humble—an interpretation that must be seen against the background of Jerome's growing respect for the independence, the vitality, and the particular qualities of the church in Gaul.[32] Although he concluded with a personal invitation to exile,[33] the general theme of the letter involved a recognition of developments in that province, both monastic and ecclesiastical, that will be

[28] *Ep.* li. 1 f. See Cavellera, *Jérôme*, i, 1, 212.
[29] *Ep.* lxxxii. 3, 8, 11.
[30] See above, p. 119.
[31] See above, p. 122.
[32] *Ep.* cxxv. 8 f.
[33] Ibid. 20.

illustrated more fully in chapters below, dealing with the life and writings of John Cassian. Jerome also joined again, as in his earlier letter to Nepotianus, these remarks on priesthood and monasticism with other reflections about Scripture and learning. Scripture was to be the basis of priestly teaching, and a means of self-improvement.[34] The true Christian was one who was not afraid, in matters of culture also, to start afresh–and to discipline himself thereby, as well as learn:

> When I was a young man, barricaded behind empty stretches of desert, I was unable to endure the promptings of vice and fiery nature; yet, when I had broken them with persistent fasting, my mind remained aflame with thoughts. To tame them, therefore, I submitted to the teaching of a certain brother, a convert from Judaism. After having mastered the precision of Quintilian, the copious eloquence of Cicero, the dignity of Fronto, and the gentleness of Pliny, I learned my alphabet, turning over in my mind words harsh and breathy.[35]

And yet the most striking image of the letter betrays a telling ambiguity.[36] Rusticus is already on the path of virtue, because he has seen (with Peter the apostle) the 'great sheet, let down by four corners upon the earth' (what Jerome called the 'vas evangeliorum quadrangulum');[37] and he knows that 'all men can be saved'. The point in the Acts of the Apostles, of course, (to which Jerome alludes,) is the voice commanding, 'Rise, Peter; kill and eat'; and the assurance, 'What God has cleansed, you must not call common'. Religious purity could not remain aloof from the good things of this world; and they could include, as well as priesthood, the 'gravitas Romana' that Rusticus had gained in Italy, (at his mother's behest, and to Jerome's delight,) a balance against 'the abundance and brilliance of your Gallic speech'. That same mother was to be cherished, therefore: 'loved for the nourishment she gave you; revered as a saint'.[38] Rusticus (in Jerome's eyes) knew, in other words, 'the kinds of animal that one may hunt for, as food in the desert of this world'.[39]

[34] *Ep.* cxxv. 8, 11.
[35] Ibid. 12.
[36] Ibid. 2.
[37] Referring to Acts, x. 9-16.
[38] *Ep.* cxxv. 6.
[39] Ibid. 2.

IV

JEROME'S *LIVES*

Jerome, priest and spiritual master, was also hagiographer. The letters reveal as much, many of them threnodies and panegyrics: designed for wide readership, they presented their subjects as models for imitation, exactly in the style of Athanasius or Sulpicius. The three specific *Lives* that Jerome wrote are no less intriguing. It could be that, in his case as well, 'the idiosyncrasy of an author is best penetrated through his inventions'.[1] Certainly, he allowed these careful portraits to reveal something of his own experience and anxiety, and to underline in more vivid terms many of the principles expressed in his formal tracts, and in his letters. This quasi-autobiographical contrivance is an important comment on the work of Sulpicius and Cassian, where so much that is personal has been disguised as narrative and reminiscence.

Jerome wrote his life of Paul the first hermit either in the desert of Chalcis, or during his second stay in Antioch.[2] Since the work seems to have been designed in part to prove that Antony had not been the first ascetic in Egypt, Jerome may have wished to rival the achievement of Athanasius. His acquaintance with Evagrius of Antioch (and perhaps his personal experience) would have proved to him how influential the *Life of Antony* and similar works could be; and he may have sought a comparable reputation, and a kindred effect.

The *Life of Paul* was not pure fiction. Jerome's account of Antony's dream, for example,–that someone more perfect than himself lived further within the desert,–rings absolutely true: it may not have reproduced a specific event in the life of Antony himself; but it was typical of many anxieties

[1] Syme, *Ammianus*, 4. Kelly's discussion is detailed and perceptive, *Jerome*, 60-1, 170-4.

[2] See Cavallera, *Jérôme*, i, 2, 16 f.

expressed in other sources by Egyptian ascetics.[3] It is striking, too, that in the aftermath of the reigns of Constantius and Julian Jerome should have taken up the old debate about flight from persecution (with the phrase so typical of himself, 'What was inevitable became, in his hands, something wished for').[4] The mark of authenticity also appears in the dispute between Antony and Paul about discipleship. Antony, visiting the hermit, had already insisted that Paul should break bread first, on the grounds of his greater age: Paul, on the other hand, revealed with some humility, 'God once promised me that you would be my fellow servant'.[5]

What was the purpose behind this short and muddled collection of anecdotes—bizarre stories of visions in particular? Two passages seem to provide a key. First, Paul's prophecy with regard to Antony: ' "You must not seek", he said, "for what is yours, but for what belongs to another. Having cast aside the burdensome demands of the flesh, you must follow the Lamb. But the rest of your brethren—they must model themselves on you" '.[6] The age of the pioneers, or of experiment, Jerome suggested, was over: ascetics now had an example they could follow. His second point is contained in the phrase, 'What did this destitute man ever lack for?'; and he concluded with a plea to his readers, 'At least use sparingly, I entreat you, the wealth that claims your love'.[7]

This was not a measured work, nor particularly perceptive. It preserved the reactions of an exiled *littérateur*, who was at once intrigued by, and uncritically enthusiastic about, the ascetic culture he had experienced in Chalcis. His main emphasis was on the need for poverty and withdrawal: the opening of the later *Life of Hilarion* shows that these were precisely the emphases attacked by critics of the earlier work. Jerome was inviting western readers, in a somewhat guileless

[3] *V. Pauli*, 7. Compare the supposed rivalry between Antony and Pachomius, discussed above, pp. 34 f., and, for another rival of Antony, see G Amoun of Nitria 1.

[4] *V. Pauli*, 5. Either in Chalcis or soon after, Jerome wrote to the West for copies of Aurelius Victor, 'because of what he says about the persecutions', *Ep.* x. 3. He (and many contemporaries) might have felt justified in supposing that, in the Arian controversy, the age of persecutions had endured.

[5] *V. Pauli*, 10 f. Compare the arguments discussed above, pp. 49 ff.

[6] *V. Pauli*, 12.

[7] Ibid. 17.

way, to join what amounted to a new society; to feel no longer at a loss about their ascetic aspirations, but to follow whole-heartedly the firm example set by ascetic pioneers. These were emphases that fit in well with what has already been told of Jerome in this period.[8] They also suggest a great confidence in the value of ascetic models as such, displayed in literary texts. Jerome no doubt expected to inspire his readers with Paul, as he had been inspired, perhaps, by Antony. His own attempt in Chalcis, to identify himself with a literary hero, was already proving unsatisfactory. This literary product of the same period (and the same experience) made a further appeal to the imagination that would probably have had its most immediate effect, therefore, among a more refined and urbanized society.[9]

Jerome's other two lives were written after his stay in Rome—after his admission that some less radical way of life was called for. The *Life of Malchus* looks like a trial run for some bigger work; an opportunity to get his hand in at real writing, after so much office work and spiritual direction![10] He already had in mind this greater task—'to write . . . of how the church of Christ was born, and with whose help; how it matured; how it grew under persecution, to be crowned by the martyrs; how then, with the advent of Christian emperors, it became greater in power and wealth, but diminished in virtue'.[11] A reflection on his feelings about Rome!

The trial run was no lighthearted essay in romantic biography: a clear and serious point was made. Malchus, threatened by marriage, rejected first all ties with his family, and the prospect of a good career.[12] Apparently, the discipline of the ascetic life—'I gave myself up to instruction by monks, earning my bread by the labour of my hands, and taming with fasts the desires of my flesh'—did not agree with him either; and, rejecting the pleas of his abbot, he succumbed to temptation, and returned to the arms of his mother.[13]

[8] See above, pp. 102 ff.

[9] See above, pp. 93 ff. Certainly Paul of Concordia, to whom Jerome spoke of the *V. Pauli*, would have seemed more at home in the later pages of the *HL* than in G: *Ep.* x. 3.

[10] Cavallera, *Jérôme*, i, 1, 130.

[11] *V. Malchi*, 1; see above, p. 85.

[12] *V. Malchi*, 3.

[13] Ibid. 3, 5.

En route for home, however, he was captured as a slave, and forced to tend sheep; and this prompted him to the revealing reflection, 'Thank God for his judgement: in my own land I lost my monkhood; but here in the desert I have found it'.[14] Following a long series of adventures and intrigues, Malchus managed to make his way back to freedom, and ended by returning to the estate of Evagrius at Maronia.[15]

It was a simple and charming story, a gentle tribute to an old man whom Jerome himself had known, and notably more measured than his previous effort. The story had a very pointed moral: 'I have told you about this old man, giving an account of chastity to those who are chaste. Virgins, guard your chastity. Tell those who come after you that threats of the sword, the desert and its wild beats, can never hold modesty captive. The man who is dedicated to Christ may die; but he can never be defeated.'[16] This was the triumphant cry of the persecuted exile. Whereas the *Life of Paul* had emphasized a need for poverty and withdrawal, the *Life of Malchus* (as one might expect, in the light of Jerome's experience in Rome) placed much greater weight on the value of virginity. This was a virtue, Jerome was assured, that could not be tied down, either by such traditional Roman values as wealth or dynastic continuity, or by the common fear of exile: it represented the freedom of a new culture.[17]

The *Life of Hilarion* is the longest and most impressive of the three. In it, Jerome went far towards defining a distinction between the panegyric in some of his letters and the hagiography on which he was now embarking. He referred to a letter already written by Epiphanius of Salamis about Hilarion, 'which has been widely read'; but he added, 'it is one thing to praise the dead with conventional phrases, another to describe in due order the virtues that were truly his'.[18] In this he anticipated the motives of Sulpicius: 'I think it would be wrong to keep hidden the virtues of so great a man'.[19] He also had some sharp words for the critics of his

[14] *V. Malchi*, 5.
[15] Ibid. 6–10.
[16] Ibid. 10.
[17] See above, pp. 112 f.
[18] *V. Hilar.* 1.
[19] *V. Mart.*, Dedication, 5.

Life of Paul: 'I despise the judgements of those who speak ill of me. Having criticized my Paul, they will probably criticize Hilarion even more. They blame the former for his life of solitude; and the latter, no doubt, for mixing so with others. The man who remained hidden they say never existed: the one seen by many they will hold in little honour'.[20] In spite of this avowed contempt, Jerome was in fact responding to the criticism. Hilarion was very different from Paul, at least as portrayed in the *Life*; and, by writing as he did, Jerome was attempting to defend the change he had effected in his own ambition and style of life.

He began by stating more clearly his earlier assertions about the discipleship of Antony, and about following in the footsteps of the pioneers, instead of embarking upon fresh enterprises of one's own. Hilarion went to see Antony, studied his way of life, and stayed in his company; but then, faced with the crowds attracted by Antony's power and virtue, Hilarion felt it would be better to begin at the beginning, to follow through from start to finish the whole pattern, the *ordo*, of Antony's life. So he returned to Palestine, sold all, and retired to the desert. Jerome was still able to regard the life of Antony, in other words, as a rule that could be followed from stage to stage.[21]

The next period of Hilarion's life had equal affinity with the life of Antony. He remained in the desert for twenty-two years before anyone dared go near him; but, once he had been 'discovered', and his reputation spread abroad, 'they came to him in streams from Syria and Egypt, so that many believed in Christ, and professed themselves monks'.[22]

There followed a successful career in wonderworking; and Jerome took the opportunity to record a series of anecdotes that served to illustrate themes he regarded as important. One man whom Hilarion had cured offered him a gift; but the ascetic replied, 'You are better able to distribute your property, for you move about the cities, and know who are poor. I have left all my goods behind: why should I seek

[20] *V. Hilar.* 1. [21] *V. Hilar.* 3.
[22] Ibid. 13 f. Compare *V. Ant.* 14.

those of others?'[23] Hilarion refused, in other words, to act as an economic mediator, collecting wealth from some to dispense to others; [24] and he regarded almsgiving as a worldly activity, distinct from the pursuit of the ascetic life.[25] Yet Hilarion saw his wonderworking as a gift for the service of the church. Asked to assist, by spiritual power, the successful outcome of a horserace, he refused to stoop to so secular a cause; but he changed his mind when it was suggested that the reputation of the church itself might be at stake. Pagan adversaries, not surprisingly, brought against him an accusation of sorcery, although Hilarion was in general careful to avoid providing the opportunity for such charges.[26] The hard-headed Jerome comes through these popular idioms: the cherished integrity of the professional pauper, mindful that with the protective reputation of the church his own eccentric and alarming freedom stands or falls.

The saint now became dissatisfied with his new reputation as a thaumaturge; and he embarked upon a third stage in his career, which was not so much another withdrawal into the desert as a prolonged pilgrimage, a lifetime of escape from reputation, and from the danger of becoming rooted in one place. He retired to the site of Antony's retreat. He moved again, with two disciples, to the oasis of Aphroditon. He thought then of hiding on an island. He went to Sicily; and, still dogged by popular acclaim and the loyalty of old disciples, he finally considered exile among the barbarians.[27] This deliberate dedication to a life of pilgrimage is a vivid comment on Jerome's own enforced situation, following his expulsion from Rome; and the terms in which it is recounted may reflect in Jerome himself a mixture of dissatisfaction and guilt at the stability and relative ease of his own life in

[23] *V. Hilar.* 18. Here was another glimpse of Jerome's renewed antagonism to the city life, following his departure from Rome: see refs. to *Ep.* xlvi above, p. 114.

[24] Compare this with the opinions of Cassian and his contemporaries in Gaul, discussed below, pp. 205–12.

[25] This, again, was an anti-urban emphasis. Palladius, who created many vivid portraits of the 'urban ascetic' (see above, p. 106), certainly regarded almsgiving as a vocation quite distinct from the various patterns of desert dedication: e.g. *HL* xiv, discussed above, pp. 29, 39 f.

[26] *V. Hilar.* 20 f.

[27] *V. Hilar.* 29–38.

Bethlehem. It was not much later, after all, in 395, that he made his famous remark to Paulinus of Nola, 'It is not being in Jerusalem that we must praise, but living in Jerusalem well'.[28]

[28] *Ep.* lviii. 2.

PART FOUR

MARTIN OF TOURS

I

A BISHOP AND HIS BIOGRAPHER

1. SULPICIUS THE DISCIPLE

The narrative of Jerome's life (or rather of some, at least, of his successive hopes and convictions) links the asceticism of Egypt with the monasticism of Gaul. Jerome himself may not have been the chief mediator of ideas and practices between the two, nor even a major influence on western monks of the fifth century; but his career was like the first curling of a wave, carried forward by deeper and more varied currents; and its spectacular release on the shores of early western monasticism echoed chiefly in the writings of Sulpicius and Cassian.

Jerome provided exemplary proof that many of the changes taking place among Egyptian ascetics could be reflected, and even carried further, in a different setting. His own ascetic life in Palestine was at once more coenobitic and less remote than that of Egypt.[1] In Antioch, Constantinople, and Rome, he encountered and encouraged a style of religious life more urban, more closely linked with secular society. As an ascetic priest, he faced the problem (both for himself and for others) of how to combine personal dedication to an ascetic life with a sense of pastoral responsibility. Above all he showed, in his letters and *Lives*, how the written word could encourage, and even regulate, the practice of the ascetic life, and how many kinds of treatise could acquire a lasting influence and authority in distant and diverse parts of the empire.

Jerome's biography can also be used to provide a more specific bridgehead between Egypt and Gaul. His own conversion took place at Trier, where memories of Athanasius may well have lingered (to influence Sulpicius, not less than

[1] For a treatment of Palestinian monasticism during the early fifth century, see Chitty, *Desert*, 82–97.

himself);[2] he must surely have known the biography of Antony; and he tasted the life of the desert. At the same time, he admired the works of Hilary, and praised the later exegetes of Gaul; he set himself to direct the religious life in wealthy households and estates (not unlike that which Sulpicius had tried to form at Primuliacum); and he acknowledged without regret (in Provence, as well as Aquileia) the increasing links between ascetic discipline and preparation for the priesthood and episcopate.

But it was as a hagiographer, as 'the first Christian writer in Latin to show a taste for stories about miracles',[3] that Jerome represented a tradition passing from Athanasius to Sulpicius. Paulinus of Milan, the biographer of Ambrose, certainly read his *Life of Paul*;[4] and, although Sulpicius made no direct reference to his biographies, it is equally likely that he knew of them.[5] Where Sulpicius followed Jerome most was in reacting *against* the *Life of Antony*: against the notion that Antony was the sole exemplar or pioneer of the ascetic life.[6] This wish to rival Athanasius was probably more important than the inevitable dependence of subsequent biography on the patriarch's account of Antony.[7] Sulpicius seems to have felt, not only that in Martin he possessed an acceptable alternative hero, but also that he and his fellow admirers had access to a truly alternative tradition. Not only were they no longer dependent on Antony as a model;[8] they were no longer totally dependent on the appeal to the imagination inherent in a literary account.[9]

[2] J. Fontaine, *Vie de saint Martin*, i (Paris 1967), 150; ii (Paris, 1968), 593 f.

[3] An unusual, but nevertheless accurate, description of Jerome: H. Delehaye, 'Saint Martin et Sulpice Sévère', *AB* xxxviii (1920), 79.

[4] Paulinus, *V. Amb.* 1. [5] Fontaine, *Vie*, i. 119. [6] Ibid. 79.

[7] On the relation between the two *Vitae*, the scepticism of Delehaye is still the most convincing reaction: 'Everyone who has read them agrees that there is a marked distinction between the personalities concerned–the way they are described, the way they behave, the impression one gains from the work as a whole', 'Saint Martin et Sulpice Sévère', 47; see also, for detailed comparisons, 40 ff. In this, Delehaye is followed by Fontaine, *Vie*, i. 60, n. 2; 71, 131. But it is just to remember that E.-Ch. Babut also admitted that particular parallels were not always easy to substantiate: *Saint Martin de Tours* (Paris, n.d.), 73–83.

[8] Fontaine, *Vie*, ii. 416.

[9] In this sense the circle that produced the *Life of Martin* and the *Dialogues* had progressed beyond (or perhaps had never known) the situation described above, pp. 93 ff.

Hence the emphasis in the *Life of Martin* on the value of oral evidence.[10] These western ascetics had, in a sense, created their own desert, where teaching could be handed on from one generation to another. Some passages in Sulpicius, especially those concerned with dreams and visions, point to the existence of a well defined group of disciples, who had preserved among themselves, and wished to hand on to others, a particular interpretation of Martin's ideals and work.[11] The *Dialogues* point more explicitly to the habits of an oral culture—'It is well worth the effort to recall even his intimate and informal conversation, seasoned as it was with qualities of the spirit'[12]—; and they insist, even more than the *Life*, on the need for oral witnesses, and for care that their tradition should be faithfully preserved.[13] (Possidius, in his life of Augustine, recounted sayings of Ambrose; and these were, in effect, further examples of western apophthegmata. Since they were subjected to yet more interpretation by Augustine himself, they reveal in miniature a similar long-standing oral tradition translated into literary form.)[14]

Yet Sulpicius was a man of letters, as well as a disciple. When he went to visit Martin, he may have been seeking the advice of a spiritual master, after the example of the East;[15] but he admitted himself that on the very same occasion, 'I was aflame with the thought of writing his life'.[16] It was, in part at least, the curiosity of a biographer that impelled him to make such a journey.[17] This self-appointed role involved a new conception of discipleship. Sulpicius did not live for long periods, like an eastern ascetic, in the company of

[10] *V. Mart.* v. 6; vii. 7; xxiv. 8; see Fontaine, *Vie*, i. 50.

[11] Martin told some of his associates about his visions, *V. Mart.* xxi. 3; and others had witnessed his struggles with demons, xxii. 3. The dream recounted after Martin had shared his cloak (iii. 3-5) offers a theological reflection on an act of simple moral worth, and may represent a subsequent attempt by others (not necessarily Sulpicius) to give the event a wider significance. The same may be true of Martin's vision of the devil, xxiv. 4-8. Visions now represent a dialogue, not only with God, but with a reading public: compare above, pp. 27 ff.

[12] Sulpicius, *Dial.* ii. 10; see also iii. 5.

[13] *Dial.* i. 15, 27; ii. 5. See Babut, *Saint Martin*, 108; Delehaye, 'Saint Martin et Sulpice Sévère', 33-9.

[14] Possidius, *V. Aug.* xxvii. 6-10.

[15] Fontaine, *Vie*, iii (Paris, 1969), 1046.

[16] *V. Mart.* xxv. 1.

[17] H. Leclerq, 'Primuliac', *DACL* xiv, 2 (1948), 1782.

Martin his master.[18] He was content to admire from a distance; to think of Martin as a patron of whom one had visions, as a master who was closer to disciples after death than when he was alive.[19] He was ready to hold in his mind a series of anecdotes and isolated incidents, and to unfold them in due time in a carefully constructed literary portrait.[20]

The finished product involved, in addition, a new conception of authority. In one of his opening remarks,—'The Kingdom of God is not a matter of fine words, but of faith',—Sulpicius betrayed the fear that his book might stand between the reader and Martin himself, as an object of quite independent worth and beauty; might disrupt, in other words, the traditional relationship of trust and admiration between master and disciple.[21] Nevertheless there was, he thought, a need for such a biography, 'because, even if *we* do not live in such a way as to be an example for others, we can at least strive to make sure that a man who *should* be imitated does not remain in obscurity'.[22] Sulpicius was willing, in other words, to take upon himself the traditional duties of an ascetic teacher: he felt, indeed, that he lacked the 'charism of the word'; that, like Postumianus, he was 'much more the admirer of another man's virtue: I could not myself attempt so heavy and difficult an enterprise'.[23] These shortcomings on his part were to be compensated, therefore, by the book itself, regarded as a new and alternative source of authority.

It is possible that Sulpicius, a biographer at once calculating and somewhat remote from his subject, tried (like Palladius and Cassian) to engage the attention of a new audience, different from that which had been formed by the

[18] A point emphasized by Delehaye, 'Saint Martin et Sulpice Sévère', 34 f. Sulpicius himself hinted at the limits of discipleship (see above, p. 50): *V. Mart.* i. 7; xxvi. 2.

[19] Sulpicius, *Ep.* ii. 3–4, 8, 16, 18. The parallel with eastern attitudes described above, pp. 74 ff., is striking enough, both with regard to the icon-like brilliance of Sulpicius's vision, and to the link between literary enterprise and admiration for dead masters.

[20] He was also, in the canny judgement of Babut, 'highly sensitive about his literary success, and very much alive to the need to please, by his writings, a world the end of which he believed to be imminent', *Saint Martin*, 53.

[21] *V. Mart.*, Dedication, 3; see also xxvii. 6 f., and *Dial.* iii. 5.

[22] *V. Mart.* i. 6.

[23] *Dial.* i. 16.

direct teaching and example of Martin himself. It has been suggested in particular that in the *Life of Martin* Sulpicius wished to make an unlettered and eccentric Martin more acceptable as a hero to some highly educated clientele.[24] Certainly, there is a striking scene in the *Dialogues*, when a large crowd of people, having heard that anecdotes of Martin were to be recounted, gathered at the door, and asked to be admitted. Aper, one of the ascetics present, insisted with some force, 'By no means should such people mix with us: they come here to listen, not in the name of religion, but through sheer inquisitiveness'. Sulpicius professed to be embarrassed at this outburst; but he admitted later, 'It was quite right, Aper's forcefulness: he cast out unbelievers, judging that only men of faith should be allowed to hear'.[25] The same point was made in the *Life*: 'A reward has been prepared by God, I hope, not for those who read, but for those who believe'.[26] The disciples of Martin did, therefore, form an *élite*; but admission could be gained by faith, the traditional eastern response of disciple to master.[27] It is significant that the earlier praises of Martin in the *Dialogues* are expressed by the symbolic figure of Gallus, who is made to declare, 'I know that I am a mere Gaul, holding conversation with men from Aquitaine; and I am afraid that the speech of a countryman will too much offend your polished ears'.[28] There is a gentle reproach in the phrase; and both Sulpicius and his readers may have wished to escape from sophistication. Certainly, Sulpicius appears to have approved of the lesser importance attached to writing in Martin's monastery at Marmoutier, and of the nobility's willing abasement there—'Reared to an entirely different life, they forced themselves to this degree of humility and patience'.[29]

[24] Fontaine, *Vie*, i. 137 ff.
[25] *Dial.* iii. 1, 5.
[26] *V. Mart.* xxvii. 7.
[27] See above, pp. 59 f.
[28] *Dial.* i. 27.
[29] *V. Mart.* x. 6, 8.

2. MARTIN THE MASTER

Here, then, was another ascetic *littérateur*: Sulpicius had identifiable roots in the tradition of Athanasius and Jerome; he understood something of discipleship and spiritual authority; and he wished to make better known, by means of a text, a certain ideal of virtue and power. Not surprisingly, therefore, Martin is portrayed in the *Life* as an ascetic also, and as a man involved in the organization and government of monastic communities. There are his first efforts at Milan, and afterwards on the island of Gallinaria; and then, with Hilary's return from exile, come the new communities at Poitiers and (later) at Tours.[30] Against this background of organization, Sulpicius gives many more detailed indications of Martin's enduring monastic character. Even as a soldier, he is described as 'monk'; and his inspiration is very much that of an ascetic—'He was not anxious about tomorrow'.[31] His journey to convert his parents, undertaken after a vision, is described as a 'peregrinatio', a pilgrimage (like that of Sulpicius to Martin).[32] He would leave his monastery only with great reluctance; he fearlessly presented himself as a candidate for episcopacy with unkempt hair and dress; and, during his subsequent career, his personal manner of life was still that of a monk—a round of fasting, prayer, hard work, and frugal sustenance.[33] Sulpicius gives a fairly full picture of Martin's monastery at Marmoutier, emphasizing its seclusion, its regulated poverty, its alternation of communal meals and solitary prayer; and the *Dialogues* reveal his admiration for the characteristic obedience of the coenobite, which he hoped his readers would imitate.[34]

Those readers are not allowed to forget for long, therefore, that Martin was an ascetic. Yet this was not, of course, the whole story. Probably the most important thing about the *Life of Martin* is that it portrays its subject as a bishop also, throwing himself wholeheartedly into a round of pastoral duties—exemplified in a particular way by his

[30] Milan, *V. Mart.* vi. 4; Gallinaria, vi. 5; Ligugé, vii. 1; Marmoutier, x *passim*.
[31] *V. Mart.* ii. 7 f. Compare Cassian, *Inst.* iv. 5; *Con.* xix. 8.
[32] *V. Mart.* v. 5; xxv. 1.
[33] *V. Mart.* ix. 1, 3; xxvi. 2; Sulpicius, *Ep.* i. 10.
[34] *V. Mart.* x. 4–8; *Dial.* i. 10, 18.

confrontation with pagans and heretics, and by scenes of his involvement in the official government of the church.[35] There is no suggestion here that Martin was leading a double life, trying to fulfil two separate functions at once. From the very beginning of his ecclesiastical career, Martin had shown (according to Sulpicius) this ability to combine the pastoral and the ascetic life. He had sought out Hilary, before the latter's exile, partly as a patron and spiritual master, perhaps, but most of all as a pillar of orthodoxy against the Arians of Italy and Gaul; and it was on this account that he had agreed to accept ordination at Hilary's hands, at least as an exorcist.[36]

Further cooperation was interrupted by Hilary's exile; and, when he returned from the East, Martin's relationship with him seems to have become more personal in quality, inspiring him to endeavours that were at first predominantly monastic.[37] There was a great difference, however, between the caution and obscurity of his settlements at Milan or on Gallinaria, and the confidence and positive development now displayed at Ligugé.[38] The precise degree of Hilary's influence here is hard to assess. Martin could have learned from him something of Eustathius of Sebaste, of Basil, or of Epiphanius of Salamis—of eastern ascetics, in others words, anxious to channel their fervour into more social activity.[39] In this case, Ligugé would represent Hilary's first attempt to inject ascetic standards into

[35] *V. Mart.* xii–xiv (but see also the earlier enterprises of v and vi); xvi; xx. 1.

[36] 'He sought out Saint Hilary, whose faith in matters pertaining to God had been widely demonstrated and recognized', ibid. v. 1.

[37] 'When he had been received by him most favourably, he set up a monastery for himself, not far from the town', ibid. vii. 1. Almost the first thing Augustine did, according to Possidius, following his ordination as a preaching priest by Valerius, his Greek-speaking bishop, was to found a monastery, *V. Aug.* v. 4; see Brown, *Augustine*, 140.

[38] 'He was, for the first time in his life, free, confident, master of his vocation', C. Jullian, 'La jeunesse de saint Martin', *REA* xii (1912), 277.

[39] Fontaine, *Vie*, i. 157–9, and 'Une clé littéraire de la *Vita Martini* de Sulpice Sévère: la typologie prophétique', *Mélanges offerts à Mlle Christine Mohrmann* (Utrecht-Anvers, 1963), 93. But J. Gribomont (who would certainly have been able to detect the influence of Basil, at least) asserted that 'oriental influence did no more than colour an ascetic ideal that was basically original', 'L'influence du monachisme oriental sur Sulpice Sévère', *Saint Martin et son temps*, 147.

controversy and pastoral expansion.[40] This is not to deny that Ligugé was very much a monastic institution: Martin's first disciple there is described as a 'catechumen'; but he came with the motives of an ascetic, 'wishing to be formed in new ways by the holy man's instruction'.[41] The point to note, however, is that whatever pastoral effect Ligugé may have had is presented by Sulpicius as the result of a unified pattern of life. Pastoral activity was not an *alternative* to ascetic discipline, either at Ligugé, or during any later stage of Martin's life.[42]

Sulpicius was clearly convinced that exact correspondence could be achieved between the demands of spirituality and an ecclesiastical career. His terminology vividly recalls the ideals of Egypt, and attempts to show that Martin's inner life was consistently ascetic in character: 'He concentrated rigorously on maintaining his former character and attitude. His heart was blessed with the same humility, his clothing with the same coarseness. In this way, with a totally commanding but generous bearing, he did justice to his rank as bishop, without abandoning the tasks and virtues of a monk'.[43] Sulpicius was particularly struck by Martin's ability to combine in his own life the varying achievements of ascetic predecessors.[44] Yet he did not regard his success as a bishop as anything new or different, but rather as the

[40] So J. Mulders, 'Victricius van Rouaan, leven en leer', *Bijdragen, Tijdschrift voor Philosophie en Theologie*, xvii (1956), 10 f. Mulders was anxious to suggest that Victricius might also have lived for a time at Ligugé, and that this would explain the later development in Rouen of a similar combination of Trinitarian orthodoxy and ascetic enterprise.

[41] *V. Mart.* vii. 1. Jullian overlooked this element, attaching too literal a meaning, in a rather modern sense, to the phrase in this chapter, 'vere apostolicus' (vii. 7): 'La jeunesse de saint Martin', 277 f.

[42] To this extent Mulders was justified in referring to Poitiers as 'one centre for two great movements', which he described as 'doctrinal' and 'ascetic'; but then he misleadingly appealed to the thesis of J. Lecoy de la Marche, and to his phrase, 'Each chose for themselves, like Martha and Mary, a different part', 'Victricius van Rouaan', 10 f. Jullian made the same mistake about Marmoutier,–'The younger men were engaged in the task of writing: those more advanced accompanied the bishop on his visitations', 'Remarques critiques sur la vie et l'oeuvre de saint Martin', *REA* xxiv (1922), 309,–completely overlooking the clear statement in *V. Mart.* x. 6: 'This task, however, [writing,] was assigned to younger men: their elders occupied themselves in prayer'.

[43] *V. Mart.* x. 1 f.

[44] *Dial.* i. 25.

manifestation of a longstanding virtue previously hidden.[45] It is necessary to take very seriously this clear expression of Martin's desire to safeguard as a bishop his original commitment to the ascetic life. It need not have been a mere literary conceit on the part of his biographer, designed to emphasize his hero's consistency, or strength of character.[46] A stress on *constantia*, a pagan ideal traditional in classical biography, can be detected in the pages of Sulpicius; but he was also aware how much that ideal remained at odds with what was, for him, a more Christian and a more important concept, that of conversion.[47] Those who had become bishops in the East feared that their virtue might thereby suffer, precisely because they knew well that virtue was no birthright.[48] So Sulpicius tells openly how Martin upheld against the devil himself the reality, the gratuitous and unpredictable quality, of religious conversion.[49] It was because of this drastic break in their former lives that such men refused to allow their ordination to effect a similar discontinuity.

[45] Ibid. ii. 4.

[46] So Fontaine, who is skilful in detecting these classical elements, *Vie*, i. 63.

[47] Certain followers of Pachomius had admitted to a belief in *constantia*, but later repudiated it as a pagan error: 'We thought that all holy men were made such by God . . . and that sinners were not able to live religious lives . . . But now we can see the goodness of God more clearly, working in this your father [sc. Pachomius]: having been born a pagan, he has become to such a degree the servant of God', G Psenthaisius: compare *V. Pach.* Bo 107.

[48] G Apphy: 'God's gift has not deserted me, just because I am a bishop'; G Netras: 'So that I do not destroy the monk in me'. Compare Cassian on Archebius below, p. 216.

[49] *V. Mart.* xxii. 3-5.

II

AN APOSTLE IN GAUL

One of the most important clues to this continuing balance in Martin's personality, and to his consistent sense of purpose, lies in the spiritual authority that he felt himself to possess. Although there appear to be two types of activity in the *Life* and the *Dialogues*, pastoral and ascetic, the same kind of authority is described in either situation. Martin possessed 'the charism of the word', closely associated (as in he East) with an understanding of Scripture; and he used biblical quotations as a powerful weapon against evil spirits, as well as a basis for the conversion and guidance of men.[1] This virtuosity was based on more than familiarity with the text: 'How sharp, how skilful he was', wrote Sulpicius; 'with what speed and grace he unravelled the problems of Scripture'.[2] Martin also possessed that spiritual insight typical of ascetic leaders in Egypt: the devil could never escape his all-seeing eye.[3] He used this gift in the monastic sphere—protecting his monks, for example, against the pretended authority of pseudo-prophets, such as Anatolius: 'So who can doubt that this was another of Martin's virtues; that, when the devil appeared before him in some illusory vision, he was not able to maintain the pretence for long, or keep hidden his true identity?'[4] But the same skill was turned to pastoral use. It was with the aid of such insight that Martin was able to control, by questioning a demoniac, the demoralizing panic that had seized a city at the rumour of imminent barbarian attack.[5] He was able to perceive, in the same way, that the

[1] With men (in his conversion of the robber), *V. Mart.* v. 6; with demons, vi. 2; compare Nau 184: 'Even if we ourselves cannot see the power which our own words have, the demons, when they hear them, scatter in terror'.

[2] *V. Mart.* xxv. 6.

[3] Ibid. xxi. 1.

[4] *V. Mart.* xxiii. 11.

[5] Ibid. xviii. 2.

pagan gods who claimed so great a hold over the hearts of his people (a hold he never dismissed as either fanciful or unimportant) were no more than manifestations of his constant enemy, the devil.[6] The physical penance, fasting, and prayer that properly marked the ascetic could achieve (in Gaul as well as Alexandria!) such useful pastoral ends as the destruction of pagan temples.[7] Finally, in his capacity as administrator and judge, Martin displayed a great gentleness of manner, 'judging no one, condemning no one', and he never appealed merely to his rank in order to gain the respect and obedience of his clergy.[8] (It was in this regard, where his official status as a bishop was involved, that he most resembled Ambrose and Augustine: 'A loyal and saintly man, who bore with patience the waywardness of his brethren',[9] Augustine regretted the need [according to Possidius] to stand in judgement on his fellows;[10] and Ambrose would weep in such a situation, seeking thereby to inspire the sinner to repentance, 'leaving a sound example to the priests who followed him, that they should rather intercede with God than bring charges against men'.[11] Neither the description nor the moral would have seemed out of place in the pages of the *Apophthegmata.*[12])

Such parallels with the ascetic authority of the East appear, not only in the types of activity described, but also in the response that this activity provoked in others. Martin restored a catechumen to life (his first disciple); and onlookers immediately acknowledged in him qualities over and

[6] Ibid. xxii. 1 f., and *Dial.* ii. 13; iii. 6. 'Wherever you go, whatever you try to do, the devil will oppose you', *V. Mart.* vi. 2.

[7] 'And so he withdrew to a nearby place. There, for three days, covered in sackcloth and ashes, fasting all the time, and praying, he besought the Lord to destroy that temple with his own divine power, since human hands had not been able to overthrow it', *V. Mart.* xiv. 4.

[8] Ibid. xxvi. 5; compare the judgement of Postumianus on Theophilus of Alexandria, *Dial.* i. 7–particularly in the light of Jerome's comments in his *Ep.* lxxxii: see above, p. 131.

[9] *V. Aug.* xviii. 8; see also xxv. 3. Augustine's *Sermo* ccclv strongly supports this judgement.

[10] *V. Aug.* xix. 2–5; see Augustine's own comments in *De civitate Dei*, XIX, vi, with its final cry, 'Bring me out of my distresses'.

[11] *V. Amb.* 39.

[12] Compare G Ammonas 9, Poemen 22 f., and Nau 180; see also the story about Macarius above, p. 53.

above his sanctity: he was accepted as 'a man of power, a true successor of the Apostles'; and this 'apostolica auctoritas' was understood to colour all his actions, pastoral as well as private.[13] Pagans were so impressed by Martin's preaching that they willingly destroyed their temples; willingly repudiated their past, in other words, and changed the whole pattern of their lives, undergoing conversion in the fullest sense.[14] Even in cases where temples were destroyed by more drastic means, Sulpicius reveals in realistic terms a lack of confidence among the pagan onlookers; an inevitable readiness to submit to this personality—so convinced in mind, so strong in faith, that he must be divinely guided and inspired.[15] Much of this does little more than repeat an emphasis made in the earlier parts of the *Life*. Martin's military companions revered him as 'a monk'—'with remarkable affection'—; when he shared his cloak with the beggar, onlookers blessed with 'a more balanced mind [than his critics, that is] ' were driven to compunction; and a robber in the Alps responded to Martin's words with an admiration familiar to us now, 'praying that he would entreat the Lord on his behalf'.[16] The *Dialogues* continue to dwell on this theme of response, and in similar terms. Eastern ascetics, Postumianus reports, master wild animals, not least because the beasts themselves can recognize virtue when they see it; and he continues, with half an eye on Gaul, and Martin's reputation, 'What cause this is for grief: wild animals sense your supreme authority; but men do not hold you in fear'.[17] Demons were more perceptive; and the clergy of Tours were conveniently warned, when their bishop

[13] *V. Mart.* vii. 7; xx. 1. On the meaning of 'apostolicus', see Fontaine, *Vie*, ii. 731 f. I agree that the term has a long history, and means more than reference to 'the gift of miraculous power in the fullest sense' (Babut, *Saint Martin*, 234); but there is also an ascetic connotation, the implication of a certain degree of sanctity: Delehaye, 'Saint Martin et Sulpice Sévère', 51–3.

[14] *V. Mart.* xv. 4.

[15] Ibid. xiv. 7; see also, for a similar impression, xii. 4. Babut detected parallels between these accounts and the apocryphal *Acts of John*, *Saint Martin*, 236. Both Delehaye and Fontaine suspected this suggestion: 'Saint Martin et Sulpice Sévère', 54–6; *Vie*, ii. 632. But the element of doubt and surprise among observers does recall features of a Gnostic understanding of conversion: see (with specific reference to the *Acts of John*) P. Aubin, *Le problème de la conversion* (Paris, 1963), 93 ff.

[16] *V. Mart.* ii. 7; iii. 2; v. 6.

[17] *Dial.* i. 14.

approached, by the cries and groans of evil spirits sensing impending exorcism.[18] Even pagans, seeking the cure of their sons, knew how to address the passing bishop as 'Friend of God'; and Martin realized that his reputation as an ascetic was one of the keys to his support among the people: 'The church will feed us and clothe us', he said, 'so long as it is seen that we seek nothing for our own use alone'.[19]

When called upon to assess the validity of another man's claim to authority, Martin was not concerned with the circumstances in which it was exercised, as if different types of authority were to be looked for in different situations; and in this sense he embraced 'an asceticism that was, again, very charismatic, and but slightly involved with hierarchy'.[20] The true authority of a commanding and saintly personality seemed to him the same, wherever it was found. His inquiry centred more upon interior, or at least less tangible, factors: on the theological basis for exercising authority, and for accepting it in others. Even the conduct of such an inquiry was more an exercise in discernment than an attempt to preserve discipline or church structure. The case of Anatolius provides a clear instance of this interior and personal emphasis. His supposed authority was not related to any role within an institution, either monastic or hierarchical. He simply claimed that God had spoken to him, and that God would prove it by giving him a white garment: 'This will be a sign for you that, as God has clothed me, so is my power the power of God'. Martin, for his part, quite literally saw through the falsity of the man's claim.[21] It was a confrontation of equals, in a sense; of the true and false ascetic: neither party claiming the advantages of status; each making a bid for spiritual leadership. All that distinguished them was insight and inspiration.

Sulpicius deliberately contrasted this ascetic image of authority with the pretensions of the Gallic clergy, for whom

[18] Ibid. iii. 6. For the link with Hilary, *Contra Constantium*, 8, see Delehaye, 'Saint Martin et Suplice Sévère', 49.

[19] *Dial.* ii. 4; iii. 14.

[20] Fontaine, *Vie*, i. 153; but this need not stand as a *contrast* with the East, where asceticism was not yet restricted to the patterns of Pachomius, or of Jerome's descriptions in his *Ep.* xxii to Eustochium.

[21] *V. Mart.* xxiii. 5, 10 f.

success in office called for an impressive rise in their standard of living: 'Those who previously were happy to travel on foot, or on a donkey, must now be carried haughty on their snorting steeds'.[22] But having rejected, on the one side, a hollow appeal to status, wealth, or legal right, he (and probably Martin as well) was faced with equally dangerous exaggerations on the part of men who made more informal and arbitrary claims to leadership. Sulpicius regarded what he saw as an increase in the number of pseudo-prophets as a sign that the coming of Antichrist was imminent.[23] This was the fear that lay behind Martin's vision of the devil. His arch enemy appeared to him in the guise of Christ himself, presenting a radiant picture of authoritative majesty.[24] Martin refused, however, to believe that this exalted image could be reconciled with the suffering and humility of the crucified Christ, who represented for him the most genuine example of a man to be heard and obeyed. Rejecting the vision in this way, Martin was undoubtedly pointing to the humility and abnegation of true religious authority; and it is significant that the whole incident should have passed in such vivid terms into the oral tradition of his followers.[25]

There is a heavy emphasis on miracle in both the *Life* and *Dialogues*, and Sulpicius saw this as an essential element in Martin's power, and in his claim to other men's allegiance.[26] This may contrast with the reticence displayed in some eastern texts (although Martin could show reluctance: his excuse, 'That is beyond my capacity', echoes exactly the

[22] *Dial.* i. 21.

[23] *V. Mart.* xxiv. 3; *Dial.* ii. 14; Sulpicius, *Ep.* ii. 1. Such concern gives a slightly different flavour to accounts of Martin's foresight, compared with similar passages in *V. Ant.*, Fontaine, *Vie*, iii. 942.

[24] *V. Mart.* xxiv. 5; compare the terminology—'clothed in a royal robe, resplendent in a diadem of gold studded with jewels'—with Sulpicius's vision of Martin, *Ep.* ii. 3.

[25] Compare this with Pachomius's vision of the devil, *V. Pach.* I, 87. Martin assesses the situation by reference to that-which-is-seen: it just does not *look* right. Pachomius is guided more by the effect of the vision upon *himself*. Compare *V. Ant.* 42.

[26] The miracles are certainly integral parts of the literary structure itself, G. Luck, 'Die Form der Suetonischen Biographie und die frühen Heiligenviten', *Mullus, Festschrift Theodor Klauser*, ed. A. Stuiber and A. Hermann (Munster, Westf., 1964), 237. Whether Sulpicius felt that miraculous power was essential to a genuine episcopate is less certain than Babut suggested, *Saint Martin*, 259 f.

assertion of Poemen, 'That is no task for me'[27]); but it also reveals a willingness on Martin's part to employ his charismatic gifts outside the ascetic group.[28] There is a very public air about much of Martin's wonderworking; and it is interesting to find that, in the *Life*, many of these marvellous events appear to have been carefully restricted to what one might call 'ecclesiastical' places or occasions. Martin was actually in church when asked to heal a young girl at Trier: he was urged to respond to the appeal of her father by bishops who happened to be present; and, avoiding the spectacular gestures of which he was certainly capable, he cured the girl by anointing her with blessed oil.[29] In the case of the slave of Taetradius, the cure was effected by the laying on of hands. As a result, Taetradius himself was converted; but this did not involve any commitment to the ascetic life: he simply accepted the institutional status of a catechumen, and was eventually baptized.[30] It is true that, when Martin cured the daughter of Arborius, the father responded to this demonstration of spiritual power with rather more drama, promising that his daughter would be consecrated to a life of virginity; but this generous impulse was put into effect in a formal church ceremony, in which Martin solemnly clothed the girl with the monastic habit.[31] Even when he interrogated the demoniac, whose evil spirit had spread disturbing

[27] *V. Mart.* xvi. 5; G Poemen 3, 33.

[28] Hence the suggestion of Fontaine that in *V. Mart.* the miraculous is always 'functional, and bound up with the proclamation of the word', *Vie*, i. 163. But, again, this need not have been in contrast with the East, at least in the later stages of ascetic development. Theodoret discerned in miraculous power what A. Adnès and P. Canivet describe as a 'rapport with Scripture': 'Monks were the instruments of God's action in nature--making use of gestures that were always directed towards piety, charity, or justice', 'Guérisons miraculeuses et exorcismes dans l'"Histoire Philothée" de Théodoret de Cyr', *RHR* clxxi (1967), 66.

[29] *V. Mart.* xvi. 2-7 (to be linked with *Dial.* iii. 2). Compare the 'healing style' of Augustine, *V. Aug.* xxvii. 2; and what J.-R. Palanque called 'the normality, so to speak, of equipment made use of in miraculous cures' in *V. Amb.*, 'La *Vita Ambrosii* de Paulin', *RSR* iv (1924), 406. The use of such restrained and formal gestures is important. Compare the judgement of Adnès and Canivet on Theodoret: 'No monk, in the *Religious History*, makes secret preparations, or utters magic formulae: it is a question, rather, of blessed oil or water, of the sign of the cross, of a prayer that is often silent', 'Guérisons miraculeuses', 151.

[30] *V. Mart.* xvii. 1-4.

[31] Ibid. xix. 1 f.

rumours about a barbarian attack, the impressive scene took place in a church.[32]

Now these examples of Martin's 'gratia curationum' are all linked together by Sulpicius in one section of the *Life*; and his continual reference to their taking place in church, or at a time when Martin was carrying out specifically episcopal duties, seems more than likely to have been deliberate.[33] Isolating them in this way also sets them apart from certain other miracle stories, particularly those concerned with Martin's less organized forays against pagan gods and temples. Individual in style, these latter not only contrast with more formal incidents, but are themselves linked by certain common themes. They were of less immediate benefit to individuals; and they proved that Martin possessed a power over nature that eastern ascetics, even in earlier periods, would readily have recognized as a charismatic gift associated with authoritative sanctity. The power over nature is mentioned specifically. Martin defies the force of gravity by deflecting in its fall a tree about to crush him.[34] He leaps upon a rooftop to fight a fire; and 'you could see the flames turning back, in a remarkable manner, against the force of the wind, so that there seemed to be some kind of struggle taking place, as if the elements fought among themselves'.[35] Then there is the strange account of Martin's attack upon some kingfishers. This not only involves an intervention in nature, but is also used by Martin as an opportunity to instruct the monks who accompany him. Sulpicius explains, too, that in scattering the birds Martin made use of the very same power with which he subdued the demons themselves.[36]

It is difficult to deny that there is in the *Life of Martin* an

[32] *V. Mart.* xviii. 1 f. There is one passage in the *Dialogues* where Martin employs, 'in the midst of the church', his characteristic methods as an ascetic wonderworker: 'clothed in sackcloth, sprinkled with ash, he lay flat on the ground and prayed', iii. 6; compare *V. Mart.* xiv. 4, quoted above, p. 153, n. 7.

[33] There are four other miracles recounted in this section of *V. Mart.* that are not specifically 'ecclesiastical'; but two of them are 'urban' (xvii. 5–7; xviii. 3–5), while the other two refer to cures of Paulinus of Nola, and of Martin himself (xix. 3 f.).

[34] *V. Mart.* xiii. 3–8.

[35] Ibid. xiv. 2.

[36] 'And then he commanded, with words of great power, that they should seek out the dry and empty regions of the world', Sulpicius, *Ep.* iii. 8.

element of 'res, non verba' typical of the Roman tradition;[37] but his remarkable vigour and impressive power would not have seemed strange to eastern ascetics, depending as they did on more than their words to maintain their influence and prove their authority. Moreover, this distinction between the formal and the spectacular in Martin's miracles recalls, again, the pattern of development in the East, where men were gradually being drawn out of their ascetic groups, to display their spiritual powers in a wider, pastoral sphere.

The *Dialogues* suggest that Sulpicius was forced to come to terms with similar changes in what might be called the status of the miracle. In spite of its content, the work is careful to condemn exaggerated attitudes: 'They should learn to serve God with humility, rather than congratulate themselves on their miracles and virtues. An awareness of weakness is better than a strong man's vanity'.[38] Sulpicius may have been facing here the criticisms of such as Vigilantius.[39] Certainly, he made no attempt to suppress the opinion of Brictius (who succeeded Martin as bishop of Tours): 'Martin has now grown old in his mindless superstition, what he imagines to be visions, a madness that invites our laughter'.[40] It may be no accident, therefore, that by far the most startling marvels in the *Dialogues* spring from the obedience of coenobites. Obedience is their 'prima virtus'–a loaded word: 'This is your virtue, O Christ; this, Christ, your miracle'[41]–; and, faced with its often bizarre results, Sulpicius responds with exalted acclamations: 'Well deserved, your happiness; well deserved, your glory; proven by obedience, you are glorious in your suffering'.[42] The contrast is with Gaul, and may involve the admission that miraculous power had been channelled into more 'social' situations, (both for

[37] Fontaine, *Vie*, i. 65.

[38] *Dial.* i. 10; see also 18.

[39] Babut, *Saint Martin*, 48 f. See above, p. 120. Sulpicius's remarks on ascetic women, particularly on their need for silence and seclusion, recall Jerome's advice to the mother and daughter of his *Ep.* cxvii; and he gives the impression of very widespread opposition to such rigorous advice, *Dial.* ii. 6–8, 11 f.

[40] *Dial.* iii. 15.

[41] *Dial.* i. 14; see also 10, 18.

[42] Ibid. i. 18.

monks and for churchmen,) and perhaps in the process subdued.[43] Wonderworking, Sulpicius admits, can lead to flattery and pride, which in themselves may break a man, and lay him open to possession; and the 'false justice' that can accompany such power—'We in Gaul suffer from no evil more destructive'—encourages the added danger of 'incerta mobilitas', the rootlessness and indiscipline of wandering ascetics.[44] Both observations hint at a crowded and stable environment. Martin's 'ecclesiastical' miracles, therefore, may have represented the more successful, or at least the more inevitable, results of ascetic virtue in a western churchman of the time.

[43] G. Penco suggested that the *Dialogues* in particular represented a movement away from eastern models, under the pressure of more social demands, 'Il concetto di monacho e di vita monastica in Occidente nel secolo VI', *Studia Monastica*, i (1959), 43 f., and n. 266. For the relative inability of the coenobite to rise to the heights of the miraculous, see Adnès and Canivet, 'Guérisons miraculeuses', 60.

[44] *Dial.* i. 20-2.

III

MARTIN'S AUDIENCE

The *Life of Martin* reveals, therefore, a consistent pattern of behaviour, springing always from the same singleness of purpose, the same charismatic personality. So it is not in these terms (of aim or character) that one can define any fragmentation in Martin's life. Yet there is an element of variety that cannot be ignored. The least misleading way of describing it would be to suggest that there was in his career a continual movement towards, or away from, some focus of concern, some natural resting place. He and the group that had formed itself around him seem at times to draw inwards upon themselves, and then, on other occasions, to turn their attention outwards, in response to wider opportunities, and the needs of other people.[1]

The inward movement is represented by the formation, instruction, and preservation of an intimate group of followers and disciples, attracted by the holy man's charismatic power, and recognizing his authority. It is in this context that references to personality and human relationships have their place. Mention has already been made of Martin's impact at Poitiers, where the catechumen he cured accepted his leadership, 'wishing to be formed in new ways by the holy man's instruction'.[2] Where one man took the initiative, others followed; and Sulpicius could refer soon after to the presence

[1] Sulpicius describes, for example, how Martin went out to settle some ecclesiastical dispute, and then returned to his monastery, *Ep.* iii. 6-9. This is not a banal alternation: note phrases such as, 'aut circa monasteria aut circa ecclesiam', *V. Mart.* ii. 4; 'aut ecclesiis frequentissimis aut monasteriis', and 'aut ecclesias aut monasteria', xiii. 9. Compare the phrase in *V. Aug.* vii. 1:, 'in private and in public, in his home and in the church'; and K.-H. Lütcke makes a relevant distinction between '*auctoritas* for the perfect' and '*auctoritas* for the less perfect', *'Auctoritas' bei Augustin* (Stuttgart, 1968), 78-109. See also the reference of Fontaine to a *rythme évangélique*, 'a necessary alternation between the active life and the contemplative life', *Vie*, i. 149.

[2] *V. Mart.* vii. 1.

of a band of *fratres*.[3] The same acceptance of Martin's authority by a clearly defined group of disciples, permanently gathered about him, appears at Tours: 'There were almost eighty disciples', Sulpicius wrote, 'who formed themselves after the example of their blessed master'.[4] It was a pattern that others reproduced, arousing no jealousy in Martin himself. Of Clarus, one of Martin's most loyal and cherished disciples, Sulpicius wrote, 'Many of the brethren stayed in his company'.[5] This more intimate activity was in no way restricted to the years before ordination or episcopal consecration. Martin the bishop founded Marmoutier in part as an escape from crowds; and, even in the midst of his pastoral duties, he was able to withdraw to an inner sanctum of ascetic peace: 'He had a cell close by the church'.[6] There, no doubt, he prayed, while his priests were 'either chatting to visitors, or attending to business'.[7]

The suggestion that such an intimate, inward-looking, and domestic emphasis could be reconciled with the circumstance and anxiety of a bishop is made not only in the *Life of Martin* but also in the later biographies of Ambrose and Augustine. Augustine, whose monastery was 'in the grounds of the church', found in the company of his monks precisely the refuge and comfort that episcopal duty demanded.[8] One striking example reveals the style of life that Possidius wished to portray. An extempore digression in one of Augustine's sermons had unexpectedly touched the heart of the Manichee Firmus. When Augustine hears of this, he is seated in his monastery, surrounded by his monks; and it is in their presence that he acknowledges, in traditional ascetic terms, the inspiration of God involved in the event: 'Both we and our words are in his hands'.[9] Paulinus of Milan, for his part, recounts the visit of certain Persians, 'men of great influence

[3] *V. Mart.* vii. 2.
[4] Ibid. x. 5.
[5] Ibid. xxiii. 2.
[6] Ibid. x. 3.
[7] *Dial.* ii. 1; see Delehaye, 'Saint Martin et Sulpice Sévère', 107.
[8] *V. Aug.* v. 1; xix. 6; xxv.
[9] Ibid. xv. 3-5; compare *V. Pach.* I, 97, where Pachomius's words by chance arouse compunction in a bystander for whom they were not intended: he takes the opportunity to make the same point—that it is God who guides one's speech.

and wisdom', as proof of the splendour and effect that Ambrose created in his capacity as bishop.[10] These Persians had been attracted some distance by Ambrose's personal reputation; and they brought with them 'a large number of problems, with which to test the wisdom of the man'. They were inspired, in other words, by precisely the motives of curiosity that had moved some of those visiting the fathers of the desert. Ambrose showed less anger than Pambo or Arsenius[11]–a sign of his greater willingness to make himself available to a wider public–; and he held the visitors in conversation for a whole day, and much of the night. Palladius tells how Antony did the same, faced with a similar type of guest.[12] Egyptians who visited him at Pispir were entertained in a manner familiar from the pages of the *Apophthegmata*: they were given a little food, and, after joining Antony in a short prayer, departed. Visitors from Palestine, however, whose asceticism was more intellectual or subdued, would sit with Antony the whole night through, talking of matters pertaining to salvation. Ambrose is presented, therefore, like Antony, not only as a man of wisdom and reputation, but also as one who possessed the insight and skill much prized among ascetics of the East: the ability to tailor one's method and message exactly to the requirements of one's questioner.[13]

The complementary outward-going movement is represented by an awareness in the holy man that a wider public has need of his gifts. It is within this framework that the miracles of Martin acquire their fullest meaning: they show him 'amidst the crowd, moving among the people'[14]–not so much a teacher, now, as an intercessor. This was a movement made by the ascetic group as a whole. When engaged in activity that appears to be predominantly pastoral, Martin does not act alone. Exposing the fraudulent martyr shrine, for example, (almost his first 'official' act as bishop,) he was at one and the same time exercising his power of spiritual perception and taking a stand on issues of church discipline and

[10] *V. Amb.* 25.
[11] See above, p. 59.
[12] *HL* xxi.
[13] See above, pp. 19 ff.
[14] *Dial.* i. 24.

episcopal authority. Yet the act itself, although inspired in part by the advice of his clergy, was not performed in their presence, nor with their immediate help: at the moment of truth, Martin's only companions were his fellow monks.[15] They were present, too, when he escaped death at the hands of pagans beneath the falling tree.[16] A 'milling crowd of brothers' habitually accompanied him on all his journeys and episcopal visitations; and he took the opportunity, while travelling, to instruct them in the traditional manner.[17] It is this outward movement that gives full meaning, also, to the statement by Sulpicius that Martin's monastic foundations produced an increasing number of recruits for the priesthood and episcopate.[18]

After describing in these terms the apparent variety of endeavour in Martin's life, it is easier to identify the motives of his biographer. Sulpicius was taking up a position on the question of spiritual authority. Martin's life is presented as a continuous debate about the use to which he should put his spiritual gifts. Sulpicius demonstrates how Martin's personal charism, with its ascetic quality and its eastern roots, achieved its effect in different situations, involving different responsibilities or opportunities. Then, with the deliberation of the propagandist, he points to the precise framework within which he felt that such a charism might most profitably be employed.

The heaviest emphasis, therefore, is on Martin's pastoral success; and thus ascetic power is transferred to the context of the episcopate. On only one occasion does Sulpicius admit that Martin felt a need to retire now and again from his round of episcopal duties;[19] and he gives little further evidence that the opportunity was regularly taken. Martin associated closely with monks; but the *Life* shows both himself

[15] The event would have taken place before Marmoutier could have flooded the clerical market with monastic candidates; and an important distinction is made in the text between 'those who were his seniors, both priests and clerics', and 'the few brethren whom he took with him', *V. Mart.* xi. 1-5.

[16] Ibid. xiii. 7, 9.

[17] Sulpicius, *Epp.* i. 13; iii. 7; *Dial.* ii. 4, 11; compare G Antony 14, Arsenius 25, Poemen 72.

[18] *V. Mart.* x. 9; compare *V. Aug.* xi. 1-5.

[19] *V. Mart.* x. 3.

and his ascetic companions always on the move. At the end of his life, the monastic framework seems to have closed in on Martin a little; but other clergy attended him at his death, and his willingness, even then, to continue his pastoral labours is strongly emphasized.[20]

The skilful construction of the portrait in the *Life of Martin* must overshadow in importance the question of how historically accurate an impression of Martin is given thereby. The motivation of the writer himself had, in the long run, a greater effect. Sulpicius showed clearly his awareness that he had at his disposal, in the opportunities provided by a new tradition of religious literature, a powerful weapon capable of bringing about considerable change in future patterns of church organization and apostolic enterprise. His own work represents a further stage in the process whereby sanctity was harnessed to the purposes of the church; a process that could be modified later, to match a number of different situations. Inspired by eastern example, he had proposed a new definition of spiritual power; decided how it was to operate, in this or that circumstance; and set up an influential pattern of admiration, discipleship, and obedience for the next generation of western churchmen.

[20] Sulpicius, *Ep.* iii. 10–16; especially the phrase, 'Lord, if I am still needed by your people, I do not refuse the task'.

PART FIVE

CASSIAN

I

AN EXILE IN REVERSE

One of the chief inheritors of the traditions described above was John Cassian. Hilary and Martin had encouraged an organized monastic movement in certain parts of Gaul. The writings of Sulpicius had attempted to make their achievements more widely known, and to inspire with monastic ideals the pastoral life of the church. It remained for someone to give more detailed and lasting guidance on the daily conduct of asceticism, and to ensure adherence in Gaul to concepts of authority—of obedience and tradition in particular—that would maintain an ordered development within monasticism itself, yet still allow scope for ascetics within the pastoral sphere. Such was the effect, if not the intention, of Cassian's literary work.

Unfortunately, little is known of Cassian's life before his arrival in Gaul, in 415.[1] He was a native of the Dobrudja, in what is now Romania and Bulgaria, on the shores of the Black Sea;[2] and, after a period in Bethlehem, he lived as an ascetic in Egypt for two years at least, if not longer.[3] Apart from hints in his own writings, the only direct evidence concerning him after his departure from Egypt, in 399, comes from Palladius and Pope Innocent I, and refers to the role he played in a delegation from Constantinople to Rome, in 404, pleading the cause of Chrysostom.[4] A reference in Gennadius states that Cassian then became a priest, settled in Marseille, and founded two

[1] The commonly accepted date for Cassian's arrival in Marseille. The most clearly marshalled chronology of his life, with the fullest reference to the opinions of modern scholars, is given by H.-O. Weber, *Die Stellung des Johannes Cassianus zur ausserpachomianischen Mönchstradition* (Münster, Westf., 1960), 1-5.

[2] I follow, with O. Chadwick, the judgement of H.-I. Marrou, 'La patrie de Jean Cassien', *OCP* xiii (1947), 588-96.

[3] See O. Chadwick, *John Cassian*, 2nd edn. (Cambridge, 1968), 15-18. Unless otherwise stated, future references will be to this edition.

[4] Palladius, *Dialogue*, iii; Innocent, *Ep.* vii.

monasteries there.[5] All that can be said of the years between is that he seems to have retained his devotion to the ascetic movement.

This obscurity has led some to despair of ever establishing any chronology of Cassian's life. Of his career in Egypt there is no record, apart from his own formalized account, written after his arrival in Gaul. The only event mentioned there that can be linked with other sources is the publication, in 399, of a *Paschal Letter* of Theophilus.[6] When Palladius wrote of Cassian's departure from Constantinople for Rome, in 404, he gave no real indication of when or why Cassian had come to the eastern capital, nor of what he did when the delegation had achieved its task. Even after 415, his career is marked out and dated merely by his literary products, which tell us virtually nothing about his other activities. Modern commentators often feel reduced on this account to ignore chronology altogether. They content themselves with an analysis of Cassian's writings under various headings, and with the problems of his intellectual roots, traced largely at a literary level by a comparison of texts.[7]

This is not only a counsel of despair, but bad history. To discover that a problem is impossible to solve is no justification for saying that it is unimportant.[8] It is clearly significant, for example, that Cassian became involved with John Chrysostom, regardless of whether it is possible to discover the details of that involvement. It may well be true that Chrysostom had no direct literary influence on Cassian's

[5] Gennadius, *De Scriptoribus Ecclesiasticis*, lxii (conveniently printed with Cassian, *Inst.*, *CSEL* xvii, pp. cxv–cxvi). His phrase, 'a priest of Marseille' leaves open the question of where Cassian received the priesthood. For a description of Cassian's monasteries, see E. Mâle, *La fin du paganisme en Gaule et les plus anciennes basiliques chrétiennes* (Paris, 1950), 155 ff., and F. Bénoit, 'Le *Martyrium* rupestre de l'abbaye Saint-Victor', *CR*, 1966, 110–25.

[6] Cassian, *Con.* x. 2–5.

[7] So, almost entirely, S. Marsili, *Giovanni Cassiano ed Evagrio Pontico* (Rome, 1936), and P. Munz, 'John Cassian', *JEH* xi (1960), 1–22; Chadwick, *Cassian*, to a lesser extent, although the events of Cassian's life are still, for him, largely literary events. Weber, *Stellung*, does not link his chronology with the literary analysis that is his chief concern.

[8] J.-C. Guy, *Jean Cassien, vie et doctrine spirituelle* (Paris, 1961), outlines the two main suggestions about Cassian's career between 404 and 415, and then makes the remarkable suggestion that 'between these two hypotheses . . . it is neither easy *nor necessary* to choose', 27 (italics mine).

works.[9] Yet, in the *De Incarnatione*, Cassian described himself as the disciple of Chrysostom; and part of his argument against Nestorius was based on a feeling that, just as the monasteries of Egypt and Gaul were haunted by the enduring presence of dead heroes, so Constantinople should maintain its awareness of, and loyalty to, the influence of Chrysostom.[10] It may have been admiration for the patriarch that had drawn Cassian away from Egypt in the first place.[11] About Chrysostom himself a great deal is known. During his stay in Constantinople, Cassian would have found in the patriarch a man who had tried the strict life of a hermit, and who had decided to become a priest instead, maintaining his ascetic fervour in a more pastoral setting.[12] When one finds that Cassian himself was later emphasizing less the solitary and more the coenobitic life, involving himself in public controversy, and retaining for more than twenty-five years some sense of dependence upon Chrysostom, it is clearly important to recall that he came under his influence for several years, even if little else of it can be traced.

Yet a careful analysis of what evidence there is opens up many other possibilities. The fact that certainty is impossible does not mean that these should not be investigated.[13] First, it is not stated in any source that Cassian left Egypt simply because of the condemnation of Origenism by Theophilus of Alexandria.[14] He was undoubtedly a supporter of the Origenist cause; and his own ascetic teaching was influenced by Evagrius of Pontus, at that time chief exponent in Egypt of Origen's theology. When he wrote the *Conferences*, Cassian appears to have sympathized with Paphnutius, who supported Theophilus against the anti-Origenist ascetics

[9] Chadwick, *Cassian*, 31.

[10] Cassian, *De Inc*. vii. 30 f. Nestorius, patriarch of Constantinople since 428, was now facing, in both East and West, accusations of heresy that led to his condemnation at the Council of Ephesus in 431. The full implications of Cassian's statements will be examined below, pp. 227 f.

[11] H.-I. Marrou, 'Jean Cassien à Marseille, *RMAL* i (1945), 17, n. 89.

[12] Palladius, *Dialogue*, v.

[13] Two excellent examples of what can be done are provided by Marrou, 'Jean Cassien à Marseille', and by E. Griffe, 'Cassien a-t-il été prêtre d'Antioche?', *BLE* lv (1954), 240–4.

[14] Chadwick justly restricts himself to saying that it is a 'fair inference', *Cassian*, 30.

of the desert, before the patriarch's volte-face in 399.[15] But Cassian was a young man at the time of the events themselves; and he appears to have been influenced more by forceful personality and ascetic formation than by the abstract speculations on cosmology and salvation for which Origen was ultimately condemned. There is reason to suspect, moreover, that Cassian was not altogether happy in Egypt, and that he may have wanted (as is hinted at the end of the *Conferences*) to return to his native country.[16] If this was in the Dobrudja, Constantinople would have lain *en route*. There is also the possibility, mentioned above, that he had been attracted by the reputation of Chrysostom. In other words, Cassian may not have left Egypt merely as a persecuted intellectual: there may have been a restlessness about him, an uncertainty, that laid him open to the influence of persons and events, and augured a career of great involvement and mobility.

It is certain that from Constantinople Cassian went to Rome. He went as a supporter of Chrysostom; but in what capacity? Cassian had been ordained a deacon by Chrysostom; and he carried to Rome 'the letters and documents of all John's clergy'.[17] Palladius described Cassian and his companion Germanus simply as 'pious men'; and he mentioned as an entirely separate group such professional ascetics as had also made the journey. Cassian travelled, therefore, as a cleric—a fact of some significance. Constantinople may have been a disillusionment (and Cassian was not the first ascetic to leave there for Rome!). In Egypt, Origenist monks had seemed men of learning, and refinement, marked off from the more simple and literal-minded; their confidence bolstered for a long time by the apparently secure support of the patriarch of Alexandria. Transferred by circumstance to Constantinople, they may have seemed rough, less cultured men, alarming in their asceticism; a cause for resentment among the clergy of the city. Perhaps Cassian had attempted to throw off such an image (to follow Jerome, in a sense, by taking on the new role of cleric and ecclesiastical

[15] *Con.* x. 2–5.

[16] *Con.* xxiv. 1, as interpreted by Griffe, 'Cassien . . . prêtre d'Antioche?', 240.

[17] Palladius, *Dialogue*, iii. On his ordination by John, see *Inst.* xi. 18; Gennadius, lxii.

diplomat). In view of his later monastic endeavours, it would be foolish to exaggerate; but the seeds of moderation and compromise may well have been sown in the company of Chrysostom.

It seems likely that Cassian returned to Constantinople with Pope Innocent's reply.[18] Authors who suggest that he stayed in Rome point to his supposed friendship with Leo, the future pope, evidence of which is restricted to Cassian's words in the Preface to his *De Incarnatione*.[19] It is hardly necessary to begin in 404 a friendship for which the evidence occurs only in 431; but the text itself does not suggest so longstanding or intimate an association.[20]

But, having returned perhaps to Constantinople, Cassian could hardly have stayed there after the fall of Chrysostom: he would have been swept up in the diaspora of Chrysostom's supporters described by Palladius.[21] It is unlikely that he returned to Bethlehem.[22] He continued to have a low opinion of his earlier associates there, suggesting that the community had been rather primitive in its inspiration and achievement.[23] Moreover, he made little later reference to Jerome, who would have been his neighbour (nor did Jerome mention him).[24] This is not to say that Jerome need have appeared in the writings of Cassian, even if he had lived nearby—their

[18] Marrou, 'Jean Cassien à Marseille', 18; accepted by Griffe, 'Cassien . . . prêtre d'Antioche?', 241. The letter concerned (Innocent, *Ep.* vii) opens with the words, 'From the letters of Your Charity, which you sent through the priest Germanus and Cassian'; but it ends with a reference to the *bishops* who had come from Constantinople, and whom Innocent had consulted on events in the eastern capital (*PL* xx. 501-7). Palladius reveals that a large number of people of varying rank had made the journey, *Dialogue*, iii; and, taken together, the texts must serve as a small warning that Cassian may not have been so prominent a figure in the affair as Marrou appears to suggest.

[19] e.g. Chadwick, *Cassian*, 32; Guy, *Cassien*, 27; E. Pichery, *Jean Cassien, Conférences*, i (Paris, 1955), 18 f. (although, to be just, he is clearly not at ease with the implications of the traditional thesis).

[20] 'Sed vicisti propositum ac sententiam meam laudabili studio et imperiosissimo affectu tuo, mi Leo, veneranda ac suscipienda caritas mea, Romanae ecclesiae ac divini ministerii decus'.

[21] Palladius, *Dialogue*, xx.

[22] See Marrou, 'Jean Cassien à Marseille', 18.

[23] Particularly *Con.* xvii. 5-7.

[24] Cassian would have left Bethlehem before Jerome's arrival there: Chadwick, *Cassian*, 12. Had he met Jerome subsequently, it would have been after the central years of the Origenist controversy.

dramatis personae were deliberately restricted to Egypt—; but, when Cassian does mention him, it is as a writer, rather than as one whom he had known on more immediate terms.[25]

Some other place of settlement in the East seems possible, therefore: Antioch, perhaps.[26] It was at Antioch that Alexander, elected bishop in 413, restored to the diptychs the name of Chrysostom.[27] References in the *De Incarnatione* corroborate the possibility. Cassian appealed to the faith of the church at Antioch, in his attempt to shame Nestorius into adherence to the teaching he had received as a young man.[28] Once the possibility is accepted, it is reasonable to ask whether Cassian should be identified with the person of that name mentioned by Pope Innocent, in connection with the healing of the schism within Antioch itself, and between Antioch and Rome.[29] This Cassian, referred to by the pope as 'our fellow presbyter', had come to Rome as a person of influence (perhaps as the leader of a delegation; certainly as one who was intimately acquainted with the situation in Antioch itself). If this Cassian and the author of the *Institutes* and *Conferences* were one and the same, it would be easy to understand why he should have been chosen for the role: he was known in Rome, and was experienced (after the affair of 404) in the handling of ecclesiastical diplomacy.[30]

An enduring link with the East might also suggest why Cassian went to Marseille: he could have returned there with Lazarus of Aix, the one-time disciple of Martin of Tours, who had played such a prominent role in opposing Pelagius at the Council of Diospolis.[31] Bishop of Aix from

[25] *De Inc.* vii. 26.

[26] Griffe, 'Cassien . . . prêtre d'Antioche?', *passim.*

[27] For Alexander, see Theodoret, *HE* v. 35. Before becoming bishop, Alexander had lived as a monk; here, perhaps, was another example for Cassian.

[28] *De Inc.* vi. 5 f. Nestorius had been a monk at Antioch, and probably a pupil of Theodore of Mopsuestia, the close friend of Chrysostom. For further discussion, see below, p. 229.

[29] Innocent, *Epp.* xix, xx.

[30] Griffe, 'Cassien . . . prêtre d'Antioche?', wants to suggest also that Cassian was ordained priest at Antioch. The Cassian of Innocent's letters was a priest—a priest of Antioch, as likely as not—; and the words of Gennadius do not exclude the possibility.

[31] Marrou links Cassian with these events, 'Jean Cassien à Marseille', 22. Certainly, *De Inc.* shows a detailed knowledge of the Pelagian issues and the course of the controversy.

408, and exiled in 412, he had suffered from association with the usurper Constantine III; but, as a former monk, he had also won the patronage of Proculus of Marseille, who became his metropolitan. It was Proculus who encouraged Cassian to settle in his city, and to found a monastery; and he would have strengthened the impressions possibly made by Chrysostom or Alexander. Almost twenty years before,[32] the Council of Turin had been forced to give canonical recognition to his particular conception of episcopal authority, which depended on the personal loyalty so much praised by Jerome,[33] and which ran counter to the Council's attempt to bring ecclesiastical jurisdiction into line with the areas of civil administration: 'The Primate is to be received with honour in those churches of the Province of Narbonensis II in which, it is agreed, he set up parishes, or ordained his disciples. . . . The holy Proculus himself, like a dutiful father, must respect his fellow priests as sons; and the priests of that Province, like good sons themselves, must accept him as their father'.[34] These arrangements had been made 'only so long as he lives'—no doubt the Council expected him to die before too long—; but his support for the followers of Martin, and for Cassian himself, provided a striking link between the world of Hilary and those who read the *Institutes* and *Conferences*.[35]

There is little that can be proved about Cassian's life, given the available evidence; but everything suggested here conforms to that evidence, and is often provoked by positive hints in Palladius, in papal letters, or in the *De Incarnatione*. The resulting picture has the merit of providing a framework for Cassian's life in these years. It reveals a man who had become involved (like Jerome) in the clerical life of two, if not three, of the empire's greatest cities, and in controversies that touched upon theological and ascetic

[32] I take 398 as the date of the Council of Turin, following J.-R. Palanque, 'Les dissensions des églises des Gaules à la fin du IVe siècle et la date du concile de Turin', *RHEF* xxi (1935), 481-501. Whatever date is taken, the point made here is only partially affected.

[33] Jerome to Nepotianus, *Ep.* lii. 7; see above, pp. 126 f.

[34] *Concilia Galliae, 314-506*, ed. C. Munier, *CC*, ser. lat. cxlviii (Turnhout, 1963), 55.

[35] See Chadwick, *Cassian*, 35. Proculus did not die until about 428.

principle, and upon the rights of bishops and their relations with other sees. This could have been, therefore, the background to Cassian's later career in Gaul, which was so much concerned with the links between monk and church, and which produced the Thirteenth Conference and the *De Incarnatione*.

II

HERMITS OR COENOBITES?

Established in Gaul, Cassian was called upon to share his experience of eastern asceticism with a new audience, many of them successors, so to speak, of Martin and Sulpicius. He did so, not as a mere *raconteur*, but as a teacher sensitive to the needs and expectations of his readers. He was compelled to recognize and accept, and indeed to cater for, an ascetic movement that was becoming increasingly coenobitic in character.

To say this may seem surprising. Cassian is regarded as a 'contemplative' writer, in the theological tradition of Origen and Evagrius; and many of his statements about the contemplative life appear to imply also a distinction between coenobite and hermit, and (more important) the superiority and ultimate importance of the latter.[1] It might seem unlikely, therefore, that he would seek extensive involvement in the community life of Gallic monasteries, let alone help to direct their development. His writings recall much more, after all, the eremitic heroes of Egypt in an earlier period.

It is possible to show, however, that Cassian did not regard a contemplative life as foreign to the capacities or normal experiences of the coenobite—nor even dependent on an ultimate 'graduation' to more solitary asceticism. Distinctions in his work—between contemplative and active; between community and solitude—are by no means as clear as one may imagine. This means that several spiritual qualities proper, at first sight, to hermits have their place also in community life.[2] What matters more, for our purpose at the moment, the relationship between the two ways of life—or rather, their separation—is not as sharply defined as Cassian's

[1] Many depend on Marsili, *Giovanni Cassiano*; but see also M. Olphe-Galliard, 'Vie contemplative et vie active d'après Cassien', *RAM* xvi (1935), 252-88.

[2] See my 'Cassian, Contemplation and the Coenobitic Life', *JEH* xxvi (1975), 113-26.

reputation might suggest. In the second book of the *Institutes*, he does appear to segregate them markedly. 'These books', he says, 'are designed more for the observance of the outer man, and the formation of coenobites'; but then, (looking ahead to the *Conferences*, which he had yet to write,) 'those following will relate more to inner discipline, the perfection of the heart, and the life and teaching of anchorites'.[3] He makes it clear, however, later in the same book, that at least the terms 'outer' and 'inner' (*exterior* and *interior*) do not necessarily refer to two distinct groups of people—this is the crucial point—: 'Developing side by side the virtues of body and soul, they account of equal value the gains of the outer man and inner enrichment: they hold down the errant liberty of the heart, the shifting changes of thought, with the heavy weight of their labour—a firm, unmoving anchor'. These two activities, 'thought' and 'labour', (*cogitatio* and *opus*,) form a real unity, 'so much so that it is almost impossible for anyone to decide which depends on which'.[4]

Cassian discussed the issue again in the Preface to the first set of *Conferences*. He had set out to recount the teaching of anchorites, the anchorites of Scetis; and he dedicated the work to Helladius, who had decided to follow their 'instituta sublimia'. It was here that Cassian made his most categorical assertion that the eremitic life was in some way superior: 'We make a distinction between the coenobitic life and that of hermits; between the active life developed in community and the contemplation of God: this last is greater, involving a higher level of activity'.[5] As he developed the theme, however, Cassian softened the edge of his argument: 'We make a transition now from the monk's outer, visible way of life, which we discussed in those earlier books, and turn to the unseen cast of mind of the inner man'.[6] The important distinction here is not that between 'outer' and 'inner', but between 'way of life' and 'cast of mind' (*cultus* and *habitus*). Cassian could certainly separate a serious-

[3] *Inst.* ii. 9.
[4] *Inst.* ii. 14.
[5] *Con.*, First Preface, 4.
[6] Ibid.

minded and carefully regulated adherence to a pattern of life on the one hand, and the intense cultivation of new attitudes, the increasing strength of will that might go with it, on the other; but—again, the crucial point—he made no direct suggestion that he was speaking of two different groups of people. Indeed, the scriptural symbol he provided to illustrate his point referred to spiritual development within an individual: Jacob, wrestling with the angel, earned the name of Israel; and so the monk, wrestling with himself and the demons, will gain the reward of a contemplative life.[7]

The fact that one individual might engage in both 'the active life' and 'the contemplation of God' does not rule out the possibility, of course, that one enterprise was more worthy than, and subsequent upon, the other. Cassian was slow to modify his ideas; and we should not hasten his conclusions. Still in this first set of the *Conferences*, he introduced Paphnutius, as a contemporary example of just such a transition. Having overcome his vices, and having rooted in himself, through obedience to the teaching of his elders, the practice of all virtues, Paphnutius slowly progressed to a solitary life, 'so that he might cling, without fear of separation, to that Lord for whom he had longed while living amidst a throng of brethren: with no human company to hold him back, his union with God would be all the easier'.[8]

The rest of the Conference raises the example of this holy man to the level of ascetic theory. Cassian writes of three 'abrenuntiationes', which seem to represent three stages on the path from the coenobitic to the eremitic life; and the final sections of the Conference leave no doubt that this was his main intention. In praise of Paphnutius he says:

His words did us one favour in particular. We had brought to completion our first act of renunciation, striving for it with all our strength; and we thought that we had reached the peak of perfection. Now we came to realize that we had not even begun to imagine what heights a monk might climb to. We had learned a little, in community life, about this second act of renunciation; but, as for the third,—that which embraces all perfection, and which excels those two lower stages in

[7]The ref. to Jacob and Israel recurs, *Con.* xii. 11, symbolizing progress from 'continentia' to 'castitas', from struggle to self-possession.

[8]*Con.* iii. 1.

a great number of ways,—we had to admit that hitherto we had not even heard of it.[9]

Cassian and his companion Germanus had felt that leaving the world (their 'abrenuntiatio prima') was perfection enough. Paphnutius warns them to take further and full advantage of the coenobitic life, as a means of overcoming vice. Finally, their new insight into the value of contemplation is associated with the teaching of Paphnutius portrayed as an anchorite. The whole section shows that the coenobitic and eremitic lives were still distinct in Cassian's mind, although reference to personal progress, combined with the single portrait of Paphnutius, suggests again that they were distinct only as stages in the lives of individuals.[10]

However, in the third set of the *Conferences*, written somewhat later, Cassian definitely shifted his ground. He still laid theoretical emphasis on the excellence of the eremitic life; but in practice a more social asceticism had acquired a dominant position in his argument. In the Nineteenth Conference, the abbot John describes and explains a decision on his part to return from solitude to community life. He makes it clear that this was not a question of his worthiness: even the most saintly men run great risks in the solitary life.[11] As John unfolds the dangers of the desert, it becomes clear that Cassian is describing how a change of situation might force itself upon men similarly placed in his own day. The desert could become (as would-be hermits of the West would later find) 'a city that cannot be hid, though built on a desert mountain'.[12] Solitaries in Egypt faced distraction, 'so great a multitude of brethren rushed to visit them'; and, in the West, 'the more they try to lead their lives in hidden ways, the more their glory shines for all to see'.[13]

[9] *Con.* iii. 22.

[10] The examples presented by Marsili, *Giovanni Cassiano*, 67, do not affect my interpretation of *Con.* iii. 6 f., particularly when the passage is placed in the context of the Conference as a whole. The phrase 'tunc . . . quando . . . ' must imply development; and it is significant that, when talking of the third 'abrenuntiatio', Paphnutius appeals no longer to Abraham as a type, but to a new figure, Enoch.

[11] See *Con.* xix. 2.

[12] Eucherius of Lyon, *De Laude Heremi*, 36.

[13] *Con.* xix. 5; Eucherius, loc. cit. Eucherius himself may not have minded this publicity; but to allow hermits such accessibility involved a new interpretation of their role, which Cassian would resist: see below, pp. 183 ff.

It was not the world but the ascetic life itself that had despoiled the environment of hermits. With a growth in numbers, isolation became relative. Hermits received visitors, read books, and lived close enough to others to run the risk of pride (by comparing themselves with their fellows).[14] When, therefore, John attempts to define the coenobitic and eremitic lives, he touches more upon an orientation of mind, leaving aside the question of location, or the degree of association involved: 'The purpose of a community man is to mortify, to crucify, his every wish, and, in accordance with the saving demands of evangelical perfection, not to be anxious about tomorrow. . . . The hermit, on the other hand, achieves perfection by stripping his mind of all earthly things, and so—in so far as human weakness will allow—uniting it with Christ'.[15] The distinction is between those involved in the negative enterprise of dissociating themselves from the world, and those who look forward and away from themselves, towards the positive goal of union with Christ; and John emphasizes the difficulty of achieving success in either endeavour.

At the end of the *Conferences*, there is the same contrast between praise for the solitary life and grudging admission that the coenobitic vocation will claim the attention of most. Abraham demands that Cassian and Germanus withdraw as much as possible from the company of others. He is positively harried by their objections that his own way of life has exposed him to inevitable compromise. He is forced to admit that, following St. Paul, work must take precedence over meditation on the Scriptures. He agrees that the saintly hermits of his own day will never rid themselves of an admiring circle of visitors. At the end of the Conference, the coenobite and his characteristic virtues receive the closest treatment. 'Mortificatio', Abraham's main concern, must be based, he says, on imitation of Christ's obedient self-abnegation; and he adds that this is the particular mark of those 'who live in community, subject to the commands of an elder'.[16] The final aim (and this is, after all, the climax of

[14] *Con.* xix. 12.
[15] *Con.* xix. 8.
[16] *Con.* xxiv. 26.

Cassian's work) is not so much union with Christ as union with one's fellows–'to be loved by the brethren who share one's task'.[17]

In these key passages, therefore, it is possible to trace a development in Cassian's thought. In the early stages, he appears to have had in mind two distinct groups of people, pursuing their ideals side by side. Subsequently, he suggested that the two modes of life might be more accurately considered as possible stages in the lives of individuals. Finally, he surrendered to the historical development of asceticism, and agreed that the solitary life might not be practical, nor even desirable, in spite of its theoretical excellence.

[17] *Con.* xxiv. 26. See also 4, 7, 10–12, 19.

III

ADAPTING EGYPT TO THE WEST

Cassian's change of heart involved, to some extent, surrender to reality, but not a betrayal of principle. He had come to feel that the coenobitic life was necessary—not only as a noviciate, in which to overcome the more obvious vices, and to acquire the fundamental techniques of self-perfection, but also as a safeguard for the highest spiritual values, even for the life of contemplative prayer and inner purity. Moreover, Cassian knew his audience, their aspirations and their failings; and he felt that they needed protection, encouragement, and discipline, which only community life could provide. So his analysis of monastic life was not conducted in a vacuum: he gave an interpretation of ascetic values that was, in his opinion, loyal to eastern tradition, and yet suited to the needs of his western readers.[1]

He was at some disadvantage, legislating for ascetic experiments already under way; and his own emphasis on tradition may have been an attempt to counter the influence of other monastic teachers, promoting in Gaul customs from the East of which he disapproved. Traditions initiated further north by Hilary, Martin, and Sulpicius may have disturbed him: the extent to which he knew of them, or passed judgement upon them, is impossible to discover. Nearer home, however, Castor—formerly a monk, then bishop of Apt, who commissioned the writing of the *Institutes*—had begun to set up a monastery of his own, (it is not certain upon what pattern,) some time before he sought Cassian's advice.[2] Then a *Regula Orientalis*, written by one Vigilius, and heavily dependent on Pachomian sources, was circulating in Gaul around 420.[3]

[1] A major theme of Marrou, 'Le fondateur de Saint-Victor de Marseille: Jean Cassien', *Provence Historique*, xvi (1966), 297–308.

[2] *Inst.*, Preface, 2.

[3] On the possible connection with Cassian's work, see C. de Clercq, 'L'influence de la règle de saint Pachôme en Occident', *Mélanges d'histoire du moyen âge, dédiés à la mémoire de Louis Halphen* (Paris, 1951), 169–76.

The situation was confused. Not that Cassian was either ignorant or unsympathetic, as far as Pachomian ideals were concerned:[4] it was the instability of asceticism in Gaul that made him most anxious. This may have been partly because he was not yet sufficiently familiar with the customs and attitudes of the country: the art of combining mobility and piety was a longstanding mark of its religious men and women.[5] But a love of wandering eventually aroused anxiety in others besides Cassian. Even those most sympathetic sought to justify the practice very carefully—by appealing to a need, for example, to cast over a wide area when recruiting monastic postulants.[6] A wanderer like the young Honoratus, fleeing from fame, took with him a well proven ascetic, 'as one to guide him aright in the Lord, and protect his youth'.[7] The reason for this greater care may be connected with increasing pastoral concern (and not only in the minds of those less immediately connected with monasticism)—a matter to be discussed more fully[8]—; Eucherius of Lyon, for example, thought that mobility could undermine a man's power to intercede for others.[9]

These are only incidental references, but enough to remind us that it was within such a situation of variety and misgiving that Cassian formulated his own ideas about solitude and community discipline. It seemed to him that the ideal of ἀναχώρησις, the withdrawal of the anchorite from society, had been seriously misinterpreted in Gaul—not only because

[4] Chadwick is less confident, *Cassian*, 55-60.

[5] Jerome made the same mistake, criticizing his 'mother and daughter of Gaul' for wandering around the countryside with their friends and relations, *Ep.* cxvii. 6. One has only to think of Silvia of Aquitaine and Martin of Tours to see how wrong (or how hopelessly unrealistic in their criticism) he and others were. Ausonius shared, in his own way, this ability to combine piety and social ease:

Satis precum datum deo,
. . . .
Habitum forensem da, puer.
Dicendum amicis est ave
Valeque, quod fit mutuum.

Ausonius, *Ephemeris*, iv. 1, 4-6.

[6] Hilary of Arles, *Sermo de Vita S. Honorati*, 17. They needed to justify themselves, given opponents like Pope Leo: see his *Ep.* x. 5 (*PL* liv. 633A).

[7] Hilary, *Sermo*, 11 f.

[8] See below, pp. 212-20.

[9] If we can accept as his the *Homilia III ad Monachos* (*PL* l, especially 838C f.).

men were generally ignorant on the subject, but also because they seized upon solitude for its own sake, and refused to submit themselves to the judgement of others.[10] Almost the whole of Cassian's teaching on the eremitic life was a response to this situation. 'Aναχώρησις was, for him, a way of life much more settled, more confined by principle, by custom, and by sensitivity to the opinion and authority of other ascetics. It was in no way a licence for experiment or self-expression, and was entirely compatible with a narrowing of the opportunities open to ascetics, and with rigid and formal patterns of observance.[11] It was practical fear, therefore, that prompted Cassian to warn his readers against undertaking a solitary life too soon, and against setting up new communities, multiplying small and unstable monastic foundations, inadequately governed by men who lacked both experience and humility.[12]

Cassian addressed a western audience, therefore; a process of adjustment that can be detected at many levels of his work. He promised, in the *Institutes*, to modify the customs of Egypt, placing less emphasis on elements which, 'because of the harshness of the climate, or because of differing customs and the resulting obstacles, I have judged to be impossible in this part of the world, or at least burdensome and laborious'[13]—a tactful ambiguity, with implications that could not be avoided. He referred rather pointedly to 'the perfection of the Egyptians', and to their 'rigorous teaching and practice', which was, he said, 'beyond imitation'.[14] He felt that he himself was dealing with men who, 'because of their total neglect or halfhearted endeavour, are less acquainted with this degree of purity';[15] and he thought

[10] *Con.*, Third Preface; *Inst.* iv. 1.

[11] The liberating ideal of *Inst.* v. 4—'Although our religion has one end, there are various forms of commitment that focus religion on God'—is not denied but disciplined by the realism of *Con.* xiv. 6—'There are many ways to God; and so everyone should persist in that which he first took up, his mind fixed beyond recall upon his course: in this way he will bring one decision, at least, to completion'. Compare this with the increasing rigidity of Jerome's view, expressed in kindred terms; see above, p. 123.

[12] *Inst.* xii. 30; *Con.* iv. 20.

[13] *Inst.*, Preface, 9.

[14] *Inst.* iii. 1.

[15] Ibid. vi. 20.

there were few in his audience likely to have achieved such perfection that they were ready for the rigours of the solitary life, or liable to the dangers of spiritual pride.[16]

The *Conferences* make the same point, with a tone even more exasperated. Cassian deplores, but admits, the need to modify the teaching of the East:

If it should happen that anyone thinks these things impossible, or at least hard to bear, either for a person in his position, with his ambitions, or for a man anxious to contribute to the benefit, and share in the daily life, of others; then let him judge their value, not according to his own insignificant abilities, but rather according to the excellence and perfection of those who speak about such matters.[17]

His readers should remember, he says, that the desert setting of these *Conferences* was in part a key to the worth of their spiritual message: 'Because they had set themselves to live in that great emptiness, their perception was enlightened; and they pondered and spoke about things which, to those unfamiliar or unschooled in these matters, might seem impossible, simply because of the setting and lesser excellence of their normal lives'. He warned that, if the western ascetic wished to achieve the same, 'he must hurry to share their undertaking, with the same enthusiasm and daily practice: then he will find that what seemed beyond the capacities of man is not only possible but indeed most sweet'.[18]

Given this combination of pessimism and anxiety, it was inevitable that Cassian's assessment of the coenobitic life should be linked, to some extent, with the spiritual weakness he thought he saw around him. Sheer publicity, therefore, was to be the safeguard of virtue: the scrutiny of others would prevent backsliding, and spur a monk on to greater austerity and observance.[19] Cassian repeats the warning of the *Institutes*: one must not leave too hastily the formative environment of a coenobitic monastery.[20] Not only will vices worsen—'The more it is hidden, the more deeply will

[16] *Inst.* xii. 24.

[17] *Con.*, First Preface, 6.

[18] Loc. cit.

[19] *Inst.* vi. 3; *Con.* i. 20; v. 12. Weber points to this last passage as an example of how Cassian transposed eremitic values into a coenobitic context, *Stellung*, 107: it was not the hermit's lack of 'cenodoxia' that he praised, but the austerity of community life, enforced by human respect.

[20] *Inst.* viii. 18.

that serpent foment in the sickening man an incurable disease'—: the monk will also rob himself of the affectionate correction of his brethren.[21] Virtue must be tested before it is taken for granted; and there is no better trial than life in a community. Indeed, man has social qualities that demand a social schooling.[22]

Cassian had done more than resign himself to a regrettable need for the coenobitic life. In the Sixteenth Conference, which can be described as Cassian's own *De Amicitia*, he makes a deliberate attempt to define in much more positive terms the correct relationship between the ascetic and his fellow devotees; and the emphasis is unashamedly communal.[23] He begins by examining the failure of normal patterns in human association, and in particular their lack of permanence. He proposes in their place a new bond between men, unaffected by the changes and tensions of society: what he calls 'a type of charity that allows no weakness or division'. This bond is to be based upon 'similarity of virtues', which Cassian explains: 'Affection can remain unbroken only in those who share one purpose in life, one desire; who affirm or deny as one'.[24] In order to participate in this new brotherhood, therefore, the ascetic must rigorously conform to the accepted ideals of membership. Cassian wished above all to encourage a sense that the opinion of others is better than one's own. Such an attitude had been fundamental to an understanding of authority in traditional ascetic society; but here it is given a wider importance, in that it is supposed to govern also relationships between friends. A link was thus forged between authority and community. Cassian reminds his readers that they must submit themselves to the 'definitiones' of their fellows.[25] And what of the *seniores* in this

[21] *Con.* xviii. 8. There may have been a note of autobiographical guilt in this: Cassian later admitted that he and Germanus had stayed for too short a time under the discipline of their Palestinian community, *Con.* xix. 2, 11, 13; and see the comments of Paphnutius, described above, pp. 179 f.

[22] *Con.* v. 4; xviii 12 f.

[23] The Conference is given by a Joseph. Bousset thought that this was the same Joseph as is mentioned in G Eulogius 1—a master of the coenobitic life—: 'Das Mönchtum', 6; see above, p. 46. I cannot share Chadwick's disenchantment with this Conference as a whole, *Cassian*, 1st edn. (Cambridge, 1950), 107.

[24] *Con.* xvi. 3.

[25] Ibid. 6; compare the developments described above, pp. 69 ff.

'new society'? Provided the bond of friendship functioned as it should, they became little more than guardians of the bond itself–holding the ring, as it were, in a company of equals. The 'precept of the elders' was to take on the 'force of law', to ensure 'that none of us trusts in his own judgement more than in that of his brother'.[26]

[26] *Con.* xvi. 10.

IV

AUTHORITY

1. THE DECLINE OF THE CHARISMATIC MASTER

Cassian not only espoused, therefore, the cause of the coenobitic movement: he developed an interpretation of spiritual authority that responded to the needs of a coenobitic society. In this he maintained the tradition of the East. He portrayed the ascetic master as a man of experience[1] and insight;[2] a man deeply rooted in the Scriptures,[3] and inspired by God.[4] The master's example was to have, in Cassian's opinion, an even greater influence. He would teach his disciples, 'not with fine words', but 'on the basis of his own experience, by an example that can be trusted'.[5] When Cassian had first arrived in Egypt, Chaeremon had sounded a warning: 'The authority of a man intent upon forming others will never achieve results unless he is able to win the hearts of those who hear him by the successful example of his own labour'.[6] Cassian's audience in Gaul took the lesson to heart: for Honoratus, 'Great men suffer much: they are born to give example to others, and so teach them to suffer also'.[7] Probity of life, therefore, was a quality of leadership just as important for Cassian as respect for tradition.[8]

This emphasis on example, as well as on insight, Scripture, inspiration, and experience, recalls the development of monasticism in Egypt. But Cassian raised other points about authority that show he had moved into a world of doubt, compromise, and structural change. A fresh anxiety disturbs

[1] *Inst.*, Preface, 5; *Con.* xiv. 9, 14; xxi. 36.

[2] *Con.* i. 20; viii. 16.

[3] *Inst.* i. 7; *Con.* xiv. 16.

[4] *Con.* i. 23; vii. 7, 34; viii. 20; xviii. 3, 30; xxi. 9; xxiv. 1. Compare all these characteristics with those described above, pp. 21 ff.

[5] *Inst.* xii. 13.

[6] *Con.* xi. 4. Pinufius would repeat the point, xx. 1.

[7] Hilary, *Sermo*, 31.

[8] *Con.* ii. 11.

the ascetic group: a fear that the elders might sometimes mislead. This was a danger inseparable from the history of sin itself. The serpent in Eden, the erroneous counsellor *par excellence*, had lost his position of influence; but that did not save his disciples: 'Beware evil counsel, therefore: its author will be punished; but sin and punishment will be shared no less by him who is deceived'.[9] The risks were enormous: 'We should not follow, therefore, in the footsteps of every elder, nor accept what they say of the past, or of the course that we should take: attend only to those whom we know to have lived praiseworthy and proven lives in their younger days'.[10]

The admission that grey hairs might be a deceit of the devil is at least one step away from the original gerontocracy of Egypt. Even tradition was, for Cassian, a fallible touchstone. Sarapion's famous plaint, 'They have taken my God away from me', (following the promulgation of the *Paschal Letter* of Theophilus in 399,) impressed itself deeply on Cassian's mind—not merely because of Sarapion's venerable age, but also because of the terms of his objection to the patriarch's attack on anthropomorphic piety: 'To him this opinion seemed new'. Those present at the reading of the *Letter* had felt confident that God would soon rescue the old man from his ignorance;[11] but Cassian felt the need to explain away Sarapion's appeal to tradition, in a cause with which he himself (a follower of Origen) could never sympathize: 'You should not be surprised that a totally unlettered man could still be possessed or deceived by the habit of longstanding error. He was persisting, in fact, in the error of his own youth: his obstinacy sprang, not (as you suppose) from a sudden trick of demons, but from the ignorance of his early paganism'.[12] The intellectual lineage and religious temperament of many Christians would still have borne,

[9] *Con.* viii. 11. God's judgement was not always so impartial. Referring to Cyprian, and to the Council of Carthage of 256, Vincent of Lérins gave a dry warning: 'The masters were forgiven, the disciples were condemned', *Commonitorium*, vi (11). The same anxiety had inspired the *Commonitorium* itself: 'When you think a man a prophet, . . . when you have attached yourself to him with deep respect and love, it is a great trial for you, if he should suddenly introduce in secret ways harmful errors: you will not be able to detect them quickly, for you will be led on by your habit of thinking him your master of long standing', x (15).

[10] *Con.* ii. 13.

[11] *Con.* x. 3.

[12] Ibid. 5.

uncomfortably close to the threshold of consciousness, the marks of such 'gentilitas'.[13] Some basis other than heritage had to be found for a confident orthodoxy; and hence the importance of the cleric Photinus in this account—a deacon from Cappadocia, who explained to the brothers of Paphnutius's *congregatio*, 'in a long speech, supported by many quotations from Scripture', the faith of the eastern churches.[14] The ascetic group was allowing outside authority to teach and discipline its members.

Even attitudes to Scripture became tinged with misgiving.[15] It could no longer be taken for granted that masters would reproduce in their own behaviour the discipline and insight that the Bible contained—translating it, so to speak, from word to action, in a form at once impelling and readily available to disciples. The master would now interpret Scripture as a text to be discussed—a third and quite separable element between teacher and pupil.[16] He became 'one who sings with great learning the songs of God', exercising 'the patronage of the interpreter'; and Scripture itself became a work of reference, against which to check the opinions of men, and in which to find a literal blueprint for the organization of the ascetic life.[17]

Cassian's attitude to inspiration reflected this change of mood. He demanded keener appreciation of the fact that God's guidance and instruction would come most often through human mediation. Two anecdotes illustrate the conviction. Moses tells of two monks who resolved to eat only the food that God might give them. Wandering in the desert, their hunger increased, while the bountiful hand of God remained ominously withdrawn. Suddenly there chanced upon the starving pair a band of barbarians, who, moved with pity, offered them food. One of the ascetics, 'discernment coming

[13] The memory of classical authors learned in youth distracted Cassian himself from prayer, *Con.* xiv. 12.

[14] *Con.* x. 3.

[15] Compare this with similar changes in the East: Esaias, *Ascet.* XIII, 1; G Amoun of Nitria 2 (a late piece, according to Chitty, *Desert*, 79, n. 83).

[16] J.-C. Guy, 'Les Apophthegmata Patrum', *Théologie de la vie monastique*, 81.

[17] Respectively, *Con.* xviii. 16; viii. 3; vi. 2; ix. 9; and, in this last, Cassian uses the very order of Paul's words in I Tim. ii. 1 to indicate the acceptable pattern of growth in prayer.

to his aid', gladly accepted, 'thinking that the food was being given him by divine power'. The other rejected their help, obstinately clinging to his original decision.[18] Describing the conversion, secondly, of Helladius, Cassian showed how these divine and human agencies combined: 'Thanks to the inspiration of the Holy Spirit, he took the truly acceptable path of teaching almost before he had learned of it; and he wished to gain knowledge, not from his own speculations, but from what they [the desert hermits] might hand on to him'.[19]

This lesson was directed, it is true, at the disciple. Paul, struck to the heart by the voice of God on the road to Damascus, was also sent to Ananias for further instruction, 'in case anyone delude himself that he too, in the same way, should be formed only by the authority and teaching of God, and not rather by the instruction of the elders'. But there was a lesson here too for the elders themselves. Paul was driven, by the same humility, to travel to Jerusalem, 'so that the Gospel that he preached to the nations, assisted by the grace of the Holy Spirit, he might also discuss with his older fellow apostles, in more secluded and intimate fellowship'.[20]

The need for such consultation had, by Cassian's day, weakened the confidence of the fathers. Disciples were instructed to seek out those who harked back to masters of a former age;[21] who, like Moses, sought to confirm their own opinion, 'not only by examples drawn from their daily experience, but also by the judgements and debates of a former period'.[22] Moses himself regarded such self-effacing loyalty as essential to the virtue of 'discretio', judgement based on insight, the virtue that had been *par excellence* the mark of the ascetic master. Gone was the πληροφορία, the self-assurance of the inspired ascetic, and the unpredictable movement of the Spirit: 'This was considered to be the sole cause of man's downfall: lacking formation by the elders, they were totally unable to acquire that balance of

[18] *Con.* ii. 6.
[19] *Con.* First Preface, 3.
[20] *Con.* ii. 15.
[21] Ibid. 13.
[22] *Con.* i. 23.

mind that comes with inspired judgement'.[23]

The charismatic brilliance of the pioneer had therefore faded; and his successors, more drab, stood out less clearly against the background of monastic history. Cassian not only reflected but strengthened this process, by mounting an attack on the authority of the individual; by attempting to balance, against 'the will of a few men', the 'countless company of the saints'.[24] There is, in many parts of his work, a suggestion that authority springs from the group; and from the group seen, not only as a historical succession of authoritative leaders, but as a widespread pool of contemporary insight, experience, and expertise.[25] The ascetic society described by Joseph was based on bonds of love between equals; and, although the 'precept of the elders' could still be regarded as a 'divine oracle', its role (as we have seen) was to ensure, 'legali quadam sanctioni', 'that none of us trusts in his own judgement more than in that of his brother'. It had, in other words, a social effect, as if to suggest that the traditional *δύναμις*, the spiritual power of a master, might dominate an individual, but was less able to control the increasingly important problem of relations among his disciples.[26]

When Cassian came to write his third set of *Conferences*, he still paid court to the concept of *traditio*, but also stressed the value of 'successfully applied labour, born of long experience'.[27] Experience here does not refer to the enriched memory and well disciplined habits of an individual master, but to the enduring dedication of a group of men, who busy themselves with a familiar task. Cassian was addressing an audience that had, in a sense, lost touch with its past (or was less blessed than Egypt with a past to look to). But it knew what custom demanded; and so, in the final Conference, custom and the past (*consuetudo* and *antiquitas*) join hands, to make the pattern of Abraham's life an instantly available,

[23] *Con.* ii. 2. [24] *Inst.* i. 2.

[25] See A. de Vogüé, 'Le monastère, église du Christ', *Commentationes in Regulam S. Benedicti*, ed. B. Steidle (Rome, 1957), 37.

[26] *Con.* xvi. 10; see above, pp. 187 f. Eastern parallels were noted and discussed above, pp. 68 ff.

[27] *Con.*, Third Preface.

instantly recognizable model for the reader; an unreflective storehouse of doctrine and ritual that called for neither criticism nor experiment.[28] How ironic that 'antiqua consuetudo', from which the Christian and the ascetic had once successfully broken free, should now become the norm for this society of dedicated converts!

2. DISCIPLESHIP WITHIN THE COMMUNITY

A similar development, from the simplicity of early Egyptian communities to the complex formality of Cassian's day, can be traced in those passages that discuss the correct reaction of the disciple. Again, Cassian's emphasis is reminiscent of the East; his *point de départ*, trusting admiration. Yet the same elements of doubt and inquiry, and the need for adaptation, emerge as his arguments proceed.

Cassian eventually left to one side the problems of a monk's relationship with his spiritual guide. He discussed instead the sanctions, ideals, and practices that bound communities together. The first task of disciples, for example, is described as 'imitating behaviour' in the company of elders: 'stirred up by their daily exhortation and example', they must travel along 'the royal road built upon the apostles and prophets, and worn smooth by the footsteps of all the saints, and of the Lord himself'.[29] Here, theoretical respect for the past merged imperceptibly into imitation of ascetics both dead and living;[30] but the example of the perfect did more than stir up the observer: it came to possess the stereotyped quality of a 'propositi forma', a model enterprise.[31] For those who were 'following in the footsteps of the elders', imitation became, once again, a matter of conformity, if not of obedience—'We should not dare to do anything untried, nor make assessments on the basis of our own judgement'[32]—; and spiritual formation became drained of its colour and enthusiasm.

The Conference of the abbot John (already revealed as a sad but important essay in pessimism, describing one man's

[28] *Con.* xxiv. 8.
[29] *Inst.*, Preface, 4; *Con.* xxiv. 24.
[30] *Inst.* vii. 18.
[31] Ibid., iv. 23.
[32] *Con.* ii. 11.

symbolic exchange of heroic solitude for the ordered life of the coenobite)[33] freely admits that to imitate the virtue of great ascetics lies beyond 'the power of normal virtue': their achievements are to be taken 'less as an example than as a miracle'.[34] It is by the group as a whole that standards are to be formulated and enforced: 'The rule that binds all is to be drawn up on the basis of what most—indeed, what all—are able to perform'.[35] Freedom from the tyranny of law, the ambition of every ascetic, could now be purchased only at the price of living under rule. 'Where the Spirit of the Lord is', Cassian assured his readers, 'there is freedom'; but understanding of the passage he reserved for those 'who adhere strictly to the discipline of the active life'.[36]

Of course, obedience had played its part in the formation of Egyptian ascetics. It had been the fruit of a disciple's trust in his master.[37] Cassian recounted with no less approval the outstanding obedience of John of Lycopolis, who applied himself wholeheartedly to the most daunting tasks imposed upon him.[38] But such confidence could be based only on intimate knowledge of a spiritual director; on familiarity with 'the authority of his own virtue'.[39] Now, it was becoming a problem to grasp the full significance of a father's words, and to translate them effectively into action.[40] Only with 'a pure mind, enlightened by the Holy Spirit,' could a monk hope to grasp 'the deep and hidden mysteries' contained in the teaching of the elders; and the possession of such insight was either too remote a possibility, or too easily assumed.[41]

Hence the conviction that the path to discernment lay in humble submission to the opinion of others; 'and the first

[33] See above, p. 180.

[34] *Con.* xix. 8.

[35] Ibid. Cassian may have anticipated this in his suggestion, 'If we retain a measured sense of what is possible, then perfect observance will be found, even when people's abilities vary', *Inst.*, Preface, 9.

[36] *Con.* xxi. 34, referring to II Cor. iii. 17.

[37] See above, pp. 51 ff.

[38] *Inst.* iv. 24; see further in Appendix IV.

[39] *Con.* xxiii. 2.

[40] *Con.* xxi. 22. Compare this with a corresponding doubt in the East: 'I made my appeal to the elders, and they spoke to me concerning my soul's salvation, and I gained nothing from their words', Nau 223; see also Nau 183 f.

[41] *Con.* xiv. 9.

proof that you possess such humility is this: that you submit to the judgement of the elders, not only what you are to do, but also what you are to think'.[42] The *traditio* of the elders was now seen, not as a fountain of original insight, but as a static and negative scale against which to measure the opinions of others. Their judgement was no longer the only source of authority: the Law of God stood as a clear alternative, showing how the framework of sanctions and guidance had become not only more rigid but also more broadly based.[43] The ascetic had ceased, in fact, to be a questioner in the traditional style. He followed 'the instructions and judgements of the elders'; but he did so in the company of men 'who become perfect, not through the words of those who teach them, but by virtue of their own deeds'.[44] The obligations of obedience were expressed in less personal terms, and no longer depended upon response to the virtues of a superior.[45] Reverence for wisdom and old age continued to have its place; but equally important was a willingness to follow doggedly the demands of the life one had chosen.[46] Ascetics were also beginning to value more highly 'an old age made venerable by graces gained, rather than by years amounted: it is the splendour of a man's behaviour that counts, not the stiffness of his limbs'.[47]

Within the new society described by Joseph, obligations were still expressed in terms sufficiently similar to those that had bound disciples to their masters: 'He had no wish to obey his own commands, but rather those of his neighbour'.[48] But many of the masters were now dead; and not only had the dictates of authority changed from advice to judgement, and from guidance to command: it was a monk's

[42] *Con.* ii. 10. Compare Orsisius, *Liber*, 18: 'Cultivate humility and modesty, and regard each precept of the elders as a rule for the common life'. Before long, truly individual insight or opinion would be overruled by 'the general consensus', and dubbed disparagingly 'a limited opinion, proper to one person only, hidden and private', Vincent of Lérins, *Commonitorium*, xxviii (39).

[43] *Inst.* iv. 41.

[44] *Con.* xiv. 9.

[45] *Inst.* iv. 10.

[46] *Con.* xviii. 3.

[47] Hilary, *Sermo*, 11; see also the opinion of Eucherius about Hilary himself, *Vita Hilarii*, xi. Here again, it is possible to detect the first stirrings in the East: see above, pp. 50 f.

[48] *Con.* xvi. 6; see above, pp. 187 f.

brethren that brought these pressures to bear.[49] When Joseph spoke of brotherly love, he was not thinking of mere *agape* (a term that could include, according to him, the tolerance extended to one's enemies): it was rather διάθεσις that should govern the community—the penetrating, almost claustrophobic, intimacy of a tightly knit and isolated family.[50]

If the monk was now at the mercy of his fellows, Cassian maintained to the end that only obedience could hold in check so powerfully charged a network of relationships. The final aim, in the Conference of Abraham, had been union with ascetic companions: 'only monks can maintain everlasting unity among those who live together; only they possess, without division, all things'. But the sequel was no less important: 'This task is fulfilled worthily and faithfully only by those holy men who first submit themselves and all they possess with a ready devotion to the service of their fellows'.[51] Such were the rigorous privileges that brotherhood bestowed.

Asceticism had also acquired, for Cassian, the formality of an art. 'Scientia', 'ars', and 'disciplina' are terms that occur again and again in his text. The opening Conference sets the tone: 'Every art and discipline . . . has a certain *scopos* (that is, a point to be arrived at), and a certain *telos* (that is, its own special purpose). Keeping these in mind, the man who seeks with perseverance to master an art is able to bear any labour'.[52] Imitation of the fathers, therefore, and of their

[49] Loc. cit.

[50] *Con.* xvi. 14; see Marsili, *Giovanni Cassiano*, 5; and compare the use of διάθεσις in the East (above, p. 50, n. 103). A similar sense of unity, a sense of being drawn together, and at the same time ruthlessly controlled, must have been felt in the church at Arles, when Hilary preached in praise of the dead Honoratus—still the acknowledged master of both bishop and people. His authority, Hilary implied, was not that of a remote historical figure, whose teaching was mediated through long tradition: 'To us, you are a patron: you interpret our prayers, and make them acceptable [to God]'. Honoratus still saw into the souls of his people. This awareness placed both Hilary and his flock on one level—the level of discipleship, but also of awe—: 'Priest and people are here together: you command us all; you teach us all'. So they prayed 'with one breath for the intercession of their patron', Hilary, *Sermo*, 39. This was the attitude to the past already detected in the East (above, pp. 75 f.) and in Sulpicius (pp. 145 f.).

[51] *Con.* xxiv. 26. [52] *Con.* i. 2.

'cura' and 'industria', implies the concentration of the apprentice, watching a skilful craftsman. Whoever wishes to acquire expertise must apply himself to 'disciplina', and obey 'the commands and instructions of those masters most accomplished in workmanship or knowledge'.[53] This emphasis at the opening of the third set of *Conferences*, merely echoes the theme of intervening passages;[54] and it reflects, in only a slightly different form, the terminology of the *Institutes*.[55]

The implication is that, striving for, and eventually acquiring, the techniques of an expert, the ascetic can depend more on the fruits of his own experience: 'they become perfect by virtue of their own deeds'.[56] This was no longer a privilege reserved for recognized leaders. The relative novice, endowed with 'scientia naturalis', may submit all things (at least in matters of external discipline) to the judgement of his own conscience,[57] and need not be slow to admit that he has found experience instructive.[58] This emphasis on principles, on techniques that had little reference to the personalities involved, shows how the discipline of the spiritual life had come to depend less on the insight and authority of holy men, and more on a sense of corporate tradition, custom, and experience.

[53] *Con.* xviii. 2.

[54] *Con.* xii. 8; xiv. 1.

[55] Note the implication of clearcut principles in the phrase 'legitime decertare', *Inst.* vi. 5; vii. 20; viii. 5, 22; ix. 2; x. 5; xi. 19; xii. 32. Imitation of the expert would at one time have encouraged freedom and mobility. Cassian made an analogous point in *Inst.* v. 4: 'The monk who wishes to lay up spiritual honey must, like the wisest bee, garner each virtue from the man who possesses it most closely'. Weber points to the echo here of *V. Ant.* 3,—'If he heard that there was, in some place or other, a dedicated man, going there, he would seek him out, like the wise bee',—*Stellung*, 81 (and it may be important that Cassian's phrase 'apem prudentissimam' [i.e. superlative] reproduces the 'apis prudentissima' of Evagrius's trans., rather than the *σοφή* of the Greek, or the 'sapiens illa apis' of the earlier Latin trans.). Weber's point is that Cassian has transformed Antony's arbitrary habits into a maxim for all monks, showing how imitation became restricted by organization. Chadwick expresses doubt, without much argument, about a dependence of *Inst.* v. 4 on *V. Ant.*, *Cassian*, 98.

[56] *Con.* xiv. 9.

[57] Ibid. xx. 4; xxi. 22.

[58] Ibid. ix. 7; xxiv. 7; see also xii. 4—'It is by experience, as from a master, that we learn'.

V

MONKS AND THE WORLD

1. THE MONASTIC *élite*

Both the manner in which he defined his terms, coenobit and hermit, and the interpretation that he gave to authority, to the bonds and obligations demanded by asceticism, strongly suggest, therefore, that Cassian was most concerned with the order and development of the coenobitic life. He understood and described the manner of its growth, up to his own day; and he contributed to further change. Several of the points made so far—particularly his willingness to adapt tradition to a new audience, and his implication that authority had become more legalistic—raise the question of his own authority, and of his role as a writer; and this will be pursued.[1] But, bearing in mind the evolution described in Part One,[2] there is another feature of his work that must be examined first. By paying less attention to hermits, and by focusing on possibly more compromised, certainly more communal, types of asceticism, Cassian opened the way to a closer link between monastery and world; a world that not only tempted the ascetic, or distracted him, but that also made demands. To suggest as much is, certainly, to dissent from common opinion about Cassian;[3] but it is misleading to exaggerate the exclusive quality of his monasticism, and legitimate to ask whether he succeeded in maintaining whatever exclusive note he may have wished to introduce.[4]

[1] See below, pp. 221–34.

[2] Where I also moved from a discussion of authority within the community, pp. 49 ff., to a discussion of wider links, pp. 56 ff.

[3] Munz, for example, asserts that Cassian attached no value to 'the clergy's attention to society'; that he did not imagine that the church could 'remodel' society; and that his conception of 'Christian brotherly love' did not require men to 'save society from the ravages of the barbarian chieftains', 'John Cassian', 19. All three points are made with too much emphasis.

[4] One may respect the better-documented scepticism of J. M. Wallace-Hadrill: 'Whether they [the monks of Lérins and of St Victor's] thought Gallic society

Scattered throughout his works, there are signs of a desire on Cassian's part to preserve a division between monastery and world; and, taken as a whole, they do suggest an underlying prejudice. It is not only that Cassian directed his teaching, even in the *Institutes*, at those who sought perfection;[5] nor that he demanded of his readers that they embrace wholeheartedly one chosen vocation, and remain faithful to it throughout their lives.[6] He interpreted the whole history of asceticism in this light. He felt that, once the initial body of Christian believers had become numerous, a 'credentium multitudo', through widespread evangelization, then, because of 'that liberty that was allowed the Gentiles, in view of the weakness that sprang from their earlier beliefs', the conviction, enthusiasm, and observance of the Christian community had been undermined.[7] Faced with this degeneration, those who were 'mindful of that primitive perfection' were forced to withdraw from the cities, and from the company of those who had compromised: 'They remained in country places, hidden away, and began to put into practice, in seclusion, and in their own more perfect manner, those teachings which, as they remembered, the apostles had imparted to the whole body of the church'.[8]

Such people were, according to Cassian, the first coenobites. It was the *coenobium*, rather than the cell of the anchorite, that had first sheltered men from the world.[9] In the light of such a theory, ascetics could interpret their exceptional way of life as the Christian norm; as a way of life 'first, not only in time, but also by virtue of the grace it bestows; and to this very day we see its traces survive in the

worth the saving is an open question', *The Long-Haired Kings* (London, 1962), 35; but his opinion, even in its phraseology,is dependent on Chadwick, who had the grace to call it a 'guess', *Cassian*, 1st edn., 105. I would certainly accept, however, that there is no sign in Cassian of a wish to convert the barbarians themselves.

[5] *Inst.*, Preface, 3.

[6] *Con.* xiv. 6.

[7] Ibid. xviii. 5. Compare Salvian, *Ad Ecclesiam*, i. 1; *De Gubernatione Dei*, vi. 1.

[8] Loc. cit. For parallels to this reaction against *libertas*, see above, pp. 193 f., and below, p. 202.

[9] See de Vogüé, 'Monachisme et église dans la pensée de Cassien', *Théologie de la vie monastique*, 234. (He, too, rejects the possibility of finding a pastoral element in Cassian's writings.)

disciplined life of monasteries'.[10] Small wonder, then, that the world (an increasingly Christian world!) should seem peopled by men 'halfhearted and debased', far less likely to respond to the call of asceticism than even those 'more hardened by surrender to the flesh'.[11]

Against the laxity of this world, Cassian wished positively to protect his community. Even when apparently moved by the spirit of conversion, the world (in the person of the new monastic postulant) must be kept waiting at the door of the monastery, in order to prove its 'constantia'—the likelihood that such fervent impulse would be maintained.[12] Even when admitted, the postulant must live for a year with the pilgrims and guests. It was more important that the standards of the community should be protected, than that the dedication of the postulant himself should be sheltered from the influence of visitors from outside.[13]

Yet Cassian was beset by a problem facing all who make such emphases. The ascetic group needed recruits; and recruitment presupposed that there were people 'in the world' suited to this way of life. If the postulant was made to give proof of his 'constantia', it was because such virtue could, in some at least, be anticipated. It was not so much the world's capacity for virtue that Cassian wished to dispute, but rather the likelihood of its perseverance.[14] He was willing to admit that all Christians, members of one body in Christ, were faced with the general obligation to purify themselves of vice.[15] Those 'in the world' could still be men of prayer, he thought; family life, and the cultivation of the soil, could take their place with solitude and meditation on the Scriptures as activities indifferent in themselves—capable of

[10] *Con.* xviii. 5; see also *Inst.* ii. 5; *Con.* xxi. 30. Munz takes this as 'the basic assumption from which all of Cassian's arguments proceed', 'John Cassian', 2; but Cassian's arguments were neither neat nor conclusive.

[11] *Con.* iv. 19. Cassian emphasized, with a supporting piece of exegesis, that converts should be looked for mainly among the wholehearted pagan population.

[12] *Inst.* iv. 3. [13] *Inst.* iv. 7.

[14] Perseverance was the chief requirement in a novice in the East as well: see the famous competition in endurance between Antony and his disciple Paul, *HL* xxii; and the terminology of *HM* ix, 423A.

[15] *Inst.* v. 4; *Con.* xii. 2 f.

bringing a man to perfection, but equally dependent upon honest motive and a sense of purpose.[16] Formal monasticism, therefore, was only one method among many of living 'the practical life';[17] and this diversity of gifts in the church allowed men to achieve a certain 'integritas', without aspiring to (or obtaining) the 'scientia' of the contemplative monk.[18]

What set the monk apart, in Cassian's eyes, was not so much ability as nerve. The would-be ascetic placed a great deal at stake; and real professionals had little respect for those who committed themselves late in life.[19] Behind this scepticism lay a fear of backsliding: the man who had once embraced the ascetic life, and then turned away, involved himself in even greater danger, if not sin.[20] The only assured quality that the postulant possessed was a certain freedom, which sprang from his 'subjection of the flesh'. Like the early Christians, he graduated from the status of one bound by law to the greater freedom of submission to the teaching of the apostles.[21] But this achievement exposed him to further risk. The substitution of virtue for vice in the soul was as precarious an enterprise as the conquest by the Jews of the Promised Land. Victory in one battle was no substitute for lasting settlement: each advantage had to be pressed home, and the effort carried through to the end, until possession was complete. This freedom, therefore,–the initial expulsion of vice,–brought with it an openness, indeed an emptiness, of the self (as well as a readiness for fresh enterprise); and this the demons might easily turn to their own advantage, regaining possession of complacent converts.[22]

In what sense, therefore, did ascetics form an *élite*? Cassian

[16] *Con.* xxi. 14, 26.

[17] *Con.* xiv. 4; see Weber, *Stellung*, 110 (which refers to this passage, although the ref. is wrongly printed).

[18] *Inst.* vi. 18. 'Between the life led by the faithful in the world and that of ascetics . . . in community, there was no distinction of kind, but only of degree', G. M. Columbas, 'El concepto de monje y vida monástica hasta fines del siglo V', *Studia Monastica*, i (1959), 317; and both world and monastery would benefit from the doubt, as it were.

[19] *Inst.* iv. 30; *Con.* xx. 1–although they admitted that men who began from a position of weakness, even with the lowest motive, might achieve great things in the end, *Con.* iii. 5; see *HL* xviii; Weber, *Stellung*, 97.

[20] *Inst.* iv. 33.

[21] *Inst.* v. 11; *Con.* xxi. 20.

[22] *Con.* v. 25, referring to Matthew, xii. 43-5.

suggested that the brotherhood of man, represented and guaranteed by membership in the one body of Christ, would be experienced with greater intensity, and seen in sharper focus, the nearer one moved to the centre of the church—the ascetic group; the pool of light in a darkened world—; the more one became, in fact, 'faithful, sharing in our daily life'.[23] These men regarded themselves as 'the few', set aside from the 'multitude' of the world. While others had to rest content with belief and hope, they were the true friends, indeed the sons, of God, possessing the charity that belonged especially to God himself, and to those 'who have been stamped with the image and likeness of God'.[24]

They were also initiates, into a mystery that few others could penetrate. Even in the *Institutes*, Cassian made this exalted emphasis: ascetics strive to attain 'vera scientia', the true knowledge imparted by God's word, which brings them 'to the central mysteries of our private world; . . . and, as the Apostle says, he will bring to light for us the things now hidden in darkness, and will disclose the purposes of the heart'.[25] The theme is taken up in the *Conferences*. Isaac assures his questioners that they have already entered upon the 'penetralia', the 'interiora', the 'adyta'; and therefore, he says, in teaching them more about these matters, 'I do not fear an accusation of irresponsible betrayal [i.e. of secret teaching]'.[26]

This was the language of the mysteries; but Isaac gives an unexpected explanation of this privileged position; an explanation that goes far toward helping one to understand the more exposed quality of Cassian's monastic *élite*: 'A man comes closest to understanding when with prudence he can recognize what calls for inquiry; and he is not far from attaining knowledge when he has begun to realize what it is he does not know'. Nothing more was required, in order to gain entry to this inner circle of ascetics, than a certain curiosity, and the humble admission of ignorance.[27] So, although Cassian

[23] *Con.* xvi. 17. [24] *Inst.* iv. 38; *Con.* xi. 6. [25] *Inst.* v. 2.

[26] *Con.* x. 9; see also i. 1 (i.e., significantly enough, the opening passage of the work); *Inst.* v. 2, 36.

[27] *Con.* x. 9.; compare this with eastern anxieties about access to ascetic groups by outsiders, pp. 59 ff.

had begun with the suggestion that monastic teachers might run the risk of 'proditionis crimen' by imparting their wisdom 'haphazardly, to men who had no wish for it, or sought for it halfheartedly', he later considered that they should not seek for pupils among the virtuous or perceptive only, but rather among those 'who are weighed down with sorrow and grief, repenting their former misdeeds'.[28]

A similar transition from privilege to humility is revealed in Cassian's analysis of the Lord's Prayer. This he regarded as proper to men who had reached a 'higher state of perfection', since it placed them in an intimate relationship with God as their father. His interpretation of the phrase, 'Hallowed be thy name' suggests, again, a group of men set apart: 'Form us in such a way, Father, that we may deserve to perceive, to grasp, the extent of your holiness, or certainly to display that holiness in our spiritual lives. This we shall bring about most surely when men see our good works, and give glory to our Father who is in heaven'.[29] Not even the words, 'And forgive us our trespasses' could bring down a monk to the level of other men: they formed (like the prayer as a whole) part of those 'elevated and most sacred commands, given only to the holy and the perfect, no concern of evil or faithless men'.[30]

Nevertheless, Cassian's interpretation shows that 'the holy and the perfect' were not so remote from other men that they could not move them, at least by their example. Moreover, the structure of the prayer itself imposed on the monk discipline, as well as privilege, and pointed to a need for schooling and effort in the life of prayer: 'Unspeakable mercy of God: he not only gave us an example of how to pray, and

[28] *Con.* i. 1; xiv. 17. Compare this with the sarcastic remarks of Vincent of Lérins, addressed to an imaginary heretic: 'Learn on the sly, and privately: that's what you like. And again, when you have learnt, teach in hiding, in case the world hears you; in case the church finds out. For only a few are privileged enough to grasp the secret of so great a mystery', *Commonitorium*, xxi. The pressure of opinion such as this would have forced Cassian and his disciples to cultivate a very different type of *élite*.

[29] *Con.* ix. 18. Marsili, *Giovanni Cassiano*, 99 ff., points to a link with Evagrius, quoting from the translation of I. Hausherr, 'Le traité de l'oraison d'Evagre le Pontique', *RAM* xv (1934), 88. Evagrius is much more exclusive: 'Hallowed be thy name: that is to say, May thy name be hallowed among us, through being glorified by the nations on account of our good works. They shall say, "Here are the true servants of God" '.

[30] *Con.* xxiii. 18.

a teaching programme for our moral improvement acceptable to himself; but he also provided an opportunity for those who would ask his favour, and a way by which they could invite upon themselves the merciful and faithful judgement of God'.[31] Cassian's treatment of the Lord's Prayer, therefore, illustrates something of the tension between ascetics and the world. They were set apart, he thought, by their closeness to God; but this was a hard-won privilege: they could never escape from the need for discipline, nor ever cease to be capable of further improvement; and their sense of obligation was to some extent inspired by the expectations of lesser men.

2. WEALTH AND PATRONAGE

The monk was also supposed to be poor—another characteristic that could involve a contrast between ascetics and the world. Cassian's view of what might be called 'ascetic economy' was in theory simple enough: they wished only to give freely what they felt they had freely received.[32] 'To have nothing, and to be in no way anxious about tomorrow': such was the ideal.[33] Having surrendered all their property and wealth, and having taken upon themselves what Eutropius had called the 'stigmata Christiana',[34] ascetics claimed the status of true sons of the New Covenant; and their total renunciation was contrasted with the more measured, indeed more legalistic, generosity of laymen.[35]

But Cassian had glumly to admit that the impulse to give all created as many problems as it solved. Many had shaken off in one short moment the burden of avarice; but not only were they faced then with the more lasting problem of their other vices: they found themselves involved in persistent

[31] *Con.* ix. 22.

[32] Compare Pachomius, *Catech.*, 'My son, be merciful in all things. . . . Conduct yourself before God like one who sows and reaps, and you will gather into your granary the good things of God', trans. Lefort, 7.

[33] *Inst.* iv. 5.

[34] 'Bear with patience, I beseech you, the proof of your faith, which brands you as Christians—the poverty of the church', Pseudo-Jerome, *Ep.* ii. 4 (*PL* xxx. 48A). For the attribution to Eutropius, see J. Madoz, 'Herencia literaria del presbitero Eutropio', *Estudios Eclesiasticos*, xvi (1942), 27–54; and the comments of P. Courcelle, *Histoire littéraire des grandes invasions germaniques*, 3rd edn. (Paris, 1964), 303 f.

[35] *Con.* xxi. 5.

scruple and never-ending debate on how to support themselves thereafter.[36] Moreover, 'not to be anxious about tomorrow' took for granted, not only the providence of God, but also the generosity of men;[37] and the freedom to give all implied, as a subsequent support, the cooperative activity of a religious community, where at least a few were burdened with anxiety about food and clothing.[38]

As one would expect of a man schooled in the East, Cassian insisted that this living must be worked for: 'We must gain our daily bread by our own labours, not with the help of money tucked away'.[39] Two fears lay behind this statement, both of which reveal to what extent the issue of monastic poverty impinged upon that of contact with the world. There was, first, what Cassian would have regarded as a danger: the growing permanence and respectability of the monastery, and its ability to attract and preserve property and wealth. Sulpicius had written of the *nobiles* who entered Marmoutier, and had described the monasteries of Martin, built near towns, and patronized by bishops.[40] Cassian's own foundations had been under the protection of Proculus, and were within sight of Marseille; and he wrote for the patrons of similar communities.[41] He and the monks of Gaul were moving, in a sense, into what had been one of the traditional centres of power and self-assurance in the province, the town; and therefore, conscious of alien or more humble roots, they may have stressed on that account the importance of honest virtue and hard work (pleading, in their own terms, the excuses of Ausonius, 'scanty means, though enriched with books and learning').[42] But the earnest-minded *arriviste*, once he feels

[36] *Con.* v. 8. This was a major issue of the period: the contrast between the total renunciation of a Paulinus of Nola, and the more compromised dependence of a Sulpicius upon the security, if not the material benefit, of an estate. Compare the anxieties of Jerome above, e.g. pp. 115 f., 120 ff.

[37] A link made very forcibly by Orientius of Auch, *Commonitorium*, i. 195–8.

[38] Bacht, 'Antonius und Pachomius', 100. Orsisius made this very point, *Liber*, 21; and it was one of the reasons why John had abandoned the hermit's life: see above, pp. 180 f.

[39] *Inst.* vii. 18. Almost the whole of Book x makes a similar plea.

[40] *V. Mart.* vii. 1; x. 3–9; xvi. 6.

[41] See above, pp. 174 f., and below, p. 218.

[42] Ausonius, *Ad Gratianum, pro Consulatu*, viii, trans. H. G. Evelyn White, *Ausonius*, ii (London & Cambridge, Mass., 1961), 241. Compare Aurelius Victor,

at home, may give himself airs. Cassian was particularly angered, and alarmed, by those who made a misleading pretence of having sacrificed great opportunities in their commitment to the monastic life—he was indeed, as Rutilius had suspected of his colleagues, 'as much afraid to enjoy the gifts of fortune as to face its reverses'.[43] By entering monasteries, he said, monks may well have improved their state of life.[44] This was not an attack on men like Paulinus of Nola, for whom a real sacrifice may have been involved; but rather on those who, Cassian felt, indulged in a false and dangerous sense of achievement. When Sulpicius wrote the *Life of Martin*, Paulinus had seemed a lonely example.[45] Cassian gave the impression that now there was a whole band of would-be imitators, who felt that their zeal to join an established community was an adequate substitute for the less predictable gamble that Paulinus had been able to make.

There was a second fear, connected with the first. In a period that had witnessed, on the one hand, disruption (of the countryside in particular) by barbarian invasion, and, on the other, 'a growing subdivision of patronage', the urban bishops and the urban monks stood out as potential heirs to the roles of *patronus* or *defensor civitatis*.[46] Following the treaty with the Visigoths between Constantius and Wallia in 418, many had left the towns and retired (with Rutilius) to rebuild estates;[47] but others, less capable of forgetting or restoring 'the soul's wide plains, the courtyards of the heart,

Liber de Caesaribus, xx. 5; and see Syme, *Ammianus*, 104, n. 9. For the change of milieu in Ausonius's life that makes the comparison useful, see Hopkins, 'Social Mobility', *passim*.

[43] Rutilius Namatianus, *De Reditu Suo*, i. 443, trans. S. Dill, *Roman Society in the Last Century of the Western Empire*, 2nd edn. (London, 1925), 310.

[44] *Inst.* xi. 13.

[45] 'He was almost the only one in this age to have fulfilled the precepts of the Gospel', *V. Mart.* xxv. 4.

[46] L. Harmand, *Le patronat sur les collectivités publiques* (Paris, 1957), 462, and (for the background in general) 448-65. Wallace-Hadrill shows how easily Gallic loyalties, even that implied by *romanitas* itself, could seek new foci under pressure, *Long-Haired Kings*, 34; and how 'the old episcopal tradition of service to the *civitas*' stood to gain from such changes, 36. I have tried to pursue the matter, into the later period, in my 'In Search of Sidonius the Bishop', *Historia*, xxxv (1976), 356-77.

[47] See E. A. Thompson, 'The Settlement of the Barbarians in Southern Gaul', *JRS* xlvi (1956), 65-75.

the crumbling honour of a mind made captive',[48] wandered in search of protection and support. For these, the monasteries offered more than 'religious refuge': they were, in more senses than one, 'a comfort in life'.[49] Paulinus of Pella is their best known beneficiary. He reveals (after recounting the inroads of barbarians, and his own financial misfortune), 'Finally, impoverished, I decided to remain in Marseille. It was a city where many holy men were living, all of them dear to me, although my own property was small, a family possession, without much hope of fresh revenue'.[50] Cassian comments on the same situation, as it were from within the monastery. A Salvian, a Paulinus of Pella, a monk's relations in particular, might look to him for support in the midst of social disruption. Their plea of poverty and insecurity would, if it were heeded and satisfied, belie the monk's grand visions of renunciation, for they would be appealing to status and prosperity that he either took for granted, or preferred to ignore.[51]

Cassian was, to some extent, caught in a trap. He wanted to impose stability on the ascetic life of Gaul: at the same time, he wanted to avoid the suggestion that a settled existence need involve (as it often did in a secular context) the administration of property, with all its attendant privileges and responsibilities. Far from resolving completely Jerome's anxiety about the administration of estates, barbarian incursion had, for Cassian's ascetic, made the problem even more acute.[52] To offer some solution, Cassian tried to encourage an interior attitude of humility; a sense that independence had been lost, or surrendered, that survival alone was no longer possible, that a monk's trust must be placed entirely in the community.[53] This was the conviction behind a long

[48] *Epigramma Paulini*, 28 f.

[49] *Epigramma Paulini*, 102 modifies Griffe, 'La pratique religieuse en Gaule au Ve siècle, *saeculares et sancti*', *BLE* lxiii (1962), 259.

[50] Paulinus of Pella, *Eucharisticos*, 520-3.

[51] 'For they long to acquire wealth that they never before possessed, or at least persist in holding on to what they have; or else (even sadder) they want to see their money grow, under the pretext—which, they assert, is just—that they have an enduring obligation to support thereby either their dependents or their relatives', *Con.* iv. 20.

[52] See above, pp. 120 ff.

[53] *Inst.* xii. 25.

attack by Piamun on the monks called *Sarabaites*. Among other criticisms, he mentions their attitude to property. They are individualists. They dissociate themselves from the coenobitic movement, and continue to live in their own homes, concerning themselves with their personal affairs. This involvement Piamun interprets as mistrust of God's providence: 'They display a faithless anxiety, not only about tomorrow, but about many years to come; and they think God either deceitful or destitute'. In order to give to the poor, they save up the money that accrues from their labour. Piamun does not deny the importance of such generosity. He says of the genuine monks, 'it is for this reason, of course, that they struggle to exceed the demands of their rule of life in their daily works, so that anything left over, after the holy requirements of the monastery have been attended to, may be given (in accordance with the judgement of the abbot) to prisoners, travellers, the sick, and the needy'. But it is precisely the judgement of the abbot that makes the difference: it implies a background of coenobitic discipline, and offers the guarantee of a genuine authority. The *Sarabaites* engaged in similar activities, 'but not with the same belief and purpose'. Thus providence, the common life, humble obedience, and hard work all combined, under Cassian's hand, to bestow upon the monastery a capacity for patronage, while protecting the monk from the dangers of status.[54]

In his discussions on wealth, therefore, Cassian moved from a simple description of ideal behaviour to a careful analysis of the attitudes of mind that a monk should cultivate. The ascetic life, and in particular the poverty of the monastery, was the concrete expression of a point of view about the world. Riches in themselves were neither good nor bad—'They change from one to the other, according to the judgement and character of those who use them'[55]—; but purity of motive was the important consideration, and could be preserved only in the monastery, where, 'as the Apostle

[54] *Con.* xviii. 7. Compare Esaias, *Ascet.* XXII, 2b; note the link between wealth and providence in Augustine, *Ep.* clvii, especially 29; and see the debate in Salvian, *Ad Ecclesiam*, especially iii. 4 f.

[55] *Con.* iii. 9.

says, if we have food and clothing, with these we shall be content'.[56] By declaring himself in this way, by a visible and formal pattern of life, the monk would avoid being forced to extremes, and could maintain a balance between the distractions of property and the restlessness of the destitute. He could with justice expect sufficient food and drink (Cassian criticized only those who expected more).[57] At the same time, his labour need not be entirely divorced from the needs of more worldly men; and, faced with results of greed or inequality, he would be drawn to work for the welfare of others. Germanus, speaking with impatience about 'visits from brethren, calling on the sick, working with one's hands—yes, even showing kindness to pilgrims, and others who happen to visit us', bemoans the inconvenience and distraction involved; but his complaint suggests how frequently such demands were made.[58]

As a result, monks began to feel that, within the Christian community as a whole, they were being compelled more and more to accept the role of patron, and to bear the full burden of responsibility for those in need.[59] It was precisely here that the practical demands of compassion and justice merged into theological principle. The monk was drawn back from his chosen isolation precisely because he fulfilled an ideal proper to the church itself. One of the chief advantages of the coenobitic movement was its ability to organize, and maintain at an even and continuous pitch, the generous impulse of the convert.[60] But Theonas, in Cassian's text, goes further: retreat from the ideal of the common life had been a major factor in the decline of the early church; and it must become, for that very reason, a major incentive in the development of monasticism.[61] So the 'monastic history' that had seemed to mark off monastery from world did as much, in fact, to draw them together. The ideal church was not merely a model or type of the monastic life: numbed by habit

[56] *Inst.* vii. 29.
[57] *Con.* ix. 5.
[58] Ibid. i. 12 f.
[59] Ibid. xxi. 30.
[60] Nagel, *Motivierung*, 79.
[61] *Con.* xxi. 30.

and ease, the church was an organism to be reinvigorated by monastic zeal.[62]

The final Conference (by Abraham) reveals in a telling way how these issues claimed to the end the attention of Cassian. The dialogue opens with a declared intention, on the part of Germanus and himself, to establish a new relationhip with the world. They wish to live dependent on the generosity of others, (of their relations, in fact,) and so in some ways to increase their degree of isolation. Yet they want to convert others; and they want to do these things, not in the desert,—the traditional arena of self-perfection,—but in some new and untried setting.[63] They could hardly have been more radical.

In reply, Abraham urges upon them total withdrawal from the world. The conditions of the desert, he says, have been deliberately sought out, because of the spiritual fruit they are known to produce. Cassian and Germanus must avoid any form of activity that distracts them from a life of contemplation. But then Germanus, by his objections, (an integral part of Cassian's argument,) carries the dialogue into its second stage; and Abraham now attacks, instead, their desire to depend upon others for support. They must imitate Paul, by working for their living. They must imitate Antony, too, who withdrew to the desert—that demand Abraham maintains—; but the desert he now sees, not as a place of rest, but rather as a place where a man may escape from the rights and demands of property and ownership. Ascetics seek out 'the barren desert', because they are 'for that very reason subject to the law and mastery of no man'. The real foes are power and property.[64]

[62] See above, pp. 208 f. De Vogüé, in both 'Monachisme et église' and 'Le monastère, église du Christ', has done much to show the influence of the 'ecclesial model' on Cassian's understanding of the monastic life, without giving equal attention to the ways in which the model could be used in reverse. Cassian's interpretation of Acts, ii. 44 ff., which lay behind so much of monastic history as he saw it, depended on what he called 'the plain story unfolded by historical interpretation', which, as he said himself, readied a man for 'the labours of an active life', *Con.* viii. 3. Compare this, therefore, with *HM* vii, 413B, where the link between ecclesial and monastic models is also at issue: above, pp. 61 f.

[63] *Con.* xxiv. 1.

[64] *Con.* xxiv. 2 f., 12. Cassian may easily have made the point with a Gallic audience in view: he attacked those 'who take pride in nourishing themselves with what their relatives can offer them, or the fruits of their dependents' labour, or the produce of their own estates', 12.

Abraham seems to end the Conference with a sharp comparison between monastery and world: between sweet purity, and the turbulence of lust; between the peace and safety of the monk, and the dangers of secular life; between the freedom from anxiety that poverty bestows, and the restless worry and disappointment of the man of property. But, after prolonged assurance about the profit to be gained from a life of renunciation, both in heaven and in this world, Abraham ends on a sudden note of surprising realism:

You must agree, surely, that even in this those who serve Christ faithfully gain clear favour a hundredfold: for his name's sake, they are honoured by the greatest rulers; and, although they do not seek for themselves glory among men, they awaken the respect of judges and of those in power, even amidst the trials of persecution. Now might it not be that, if they had continued to live in the world, they would have seemed of little worth, despised (even by men of very moderate means) because of their lowly birth, or servile status? Having banded together, however, in the service of Christ, none of us would dare to insult another man's nobility; but nor would we hold against him the lowliness of his line: indeed, for the servants of Christ, the very shame that comes with humble estate (which others find cause for blushes and disgrace) bestows upon them a more glorious nobility.[65]

Faced either with wealth and power misused, or with the threatened collapse of an empire, Cassian would not rest content with the facile triumph of supposing that poverty in this world (voluntary, or *faute de mieux*) would guarantee a man dominion (over those less honest, or less generous) in the next.[66] He was more concerned to regulate the ways in which such poverty, when properly controlled, when linked with humble virtue, might usurp the machinery of allegiance that wealth had hitherto claimed as its own.

3. A PASTORAL ROLE

Neither virtue nor self-denial, therefore, could entirely separate the monk from other men. Moreover, it is dangerous (even if easy) to suggest that only a lack of definition in Gallic asceticism (the very shortcoming that Cassian tried

[65] *Con.* xxiv. 25 f. The final words reflected a widespread opinion: compare Hydatius on Paulinus of Nola, *Continuatio*, 81 ('made more noble by his conversion to God'), and G John Colobos 24 ('We honour the One, and everyone else honours us').

[66] Pseudo-Jerome (= Eutropius), *Ep.* v. 10 (see above, n. 34); Orientius, *Commonitorium*, ii. 335 f.

to counter) allowed the life of monks to spill over into pastoral activity.[67] Cassian's sense of order, crystallized and disseminated in literary form, at first to men who either were or would become bishops, controlled, rather than stifled, such developments. Monasteries had become, in Gaul as in the East, generators of enthusiasm, self-confidence, and reflective wisdom, seeking an outlet for spiritual power; and the sanctity of the ascetic, bearing fruit in a well-disciplined capacity for giving advice, and even in miraculous activity, was able to attract, and then to dominate, the hearts of men.

When he identified the sources of this power, and sketched out the network of motivation and authority by which it could be harnessed and set usefully to work, Cassian seemed mostly concerned with a field of spiritual force entirely contained within the monastery itself.[68] But his distaste for the admiration of outsiders, his suspicion of monks 'who proclaim themselves in public as exorcists', and his virtual prohibition of 'intercessiones ac visitationes piae', all suggest that, in spite of criticism, the current of power was being tapped or redirected by the world outside.[69]

Cassian doubted the value of spectacular power; but he could not shake off entirely the conviction of the age, that miracles were a sign of sanctity. Even pagans asked Abraham to prove by a miracle that he was indeed a *servus dei*; and such confidence was respected by a church that encouraged conversion in response to the wonderworker.[70] The true miracle, for Cassian, in the face of less openminded but similar taunts, ('What miracles did he do, this Christ of yours?',) was the ability of the ascetic to remain unmoved. Sanctity was at once the fruit and the basis of such inner strength and self-reliance; and the accomplished ascetic had no need

[67] G. Bardy, 'Les origines des écoles monastiques en Occieent', *Sacris Erudiri*, v (1953), 101.

[68] There are some passages (although see further below) where Cassian seemed to take for granted that miraculous power is bestowed primarily 'because of deserving sanctity', with no inevitable reference to its public effect, *Con.* xv. 1; and Paul's basketwork, for example,—which might have provided, in a less remote setting, money for the poor,—is thrown without scruple on the fire, undertaken 'solely to purify his heart and steady his thoughts', *Inst.* x. 24—although Chadwick suspected that this last story was an addition, *Cassian*, 46.

[69] *Inst.* v. 30; *Con.* i. 20; xv. 7.

[70] *Con.* xv. 1, 5.

of man's approval.[71] Yet, when a guarantee of sanctity was called for, and was hard to supply on any other basis, Cassian was not reluctant to point to more spectacular evidence. The decision of Theonas to leave his wife, for instance, (very much against her will,) was supported, in Cassian's opinion, not only by the 'judgement of the fathers', but also by 'the visible proofs of apostolic virtue' in his subsequent life: 'and in my opinion', Cassian added, 'the decision of so many holy men, pronounced on God's own initiative, cannot be mistaken, being confirmed, as I said above, by the most wondrous signs'.[72] So he could not ignore the fact that wonderworking, even when achieved 'by the intrigue and deceit of demons', might arouse and strengthen (even while misleading) the faith of the community, and stimulate the readiness of laymen to imitate and follow those whom they considered to be saints.[73] 'Although they did not exercise in any way the functions of clergymen', ascetics had become, 'without a word on their part, teachers of those who teach'.[74] A consideration of its pastoral relevance, therefore, and a sense of responsibility for its pastoral effect, was forced upon any monk anxious to maintain a correct understanding of ascetic virtue and spiritual authority.

Cassian illustrated his own convictions in this matter with a splendid story about the great Macarius.[75] A follower of the Arian bishop Eunomius has been leading the people of his neighbourhood astray; and Macarius is approached, 'by men of the Catholic faith', to expose the heretic, and silence him. This Macarius does by challenging the intruder to bring a dead man back to life. The villain withdraws from the contest, 'paralyzed with shame', and 'absolutely terrified by the knowledge of his own error and disbelief', fleeing from Egypt altogether while the hero, Macarius, brings off the promised miracle.[76] The pastoral motive is clearly expressed: 'The

[71] *Con.* xii. 13; xiii. 6; see also xvii. 23.
[72] *Con.* xxi. 10.
[73] Ibid. xv. 1.
[74] Hilary, *Sermo*, 13.
[75] *Con.* xv. 3.
[76] With the charming twist in the story, that Macarius condemns the dead pagan to live again only enough to promise him a Christian resurrection at the end of time. As for the Eunomaean, his loss of nerve in the face of such a challenge echoes the lack of confidence inwardly admitted by Martin's audience, *V. Mart.* xii. 4; xiv. 7; see above, p. 154.

blessed Macarius came upon the scene to save the simplicity of all Egypt from the shipwreck of error and despair'.

But there is another feature of the story, also with pastoral implications, that does not appear so clearly on the surface of Cassian's prose. Macarius is prompted to his task by 'catholici viri', 'men of the Catholic faith'; and in this vague phrase Cassian steered a middle path between other versions of the story. Rufinus, for example, placed these events in an entirely monastic context. Of the heretic he wrote, 'This man, with his great skill in speaking, distressed and alarmed many of the brethren living in the desert'; and he hinted at a similar limitation in the motives of Macarius himself: 'The holy man saw that the faith of the brethren was endangered'.[77] At least one other eastern text, however, described the miracle in a secular context; and, in place of Cassian's 'catholici viri', mentioned the local bishop, discussing at length the relation between the power of Macarius and the authority of the bishop himself. Cassian's use of the story may therefore have been more subtle than appears at first sight. He wished to show how Macarius had left his ascetic circle, in order to fulfil a public role; but he was nevertheless on the side of the angels, and may not have wanted ascetic power to fall too much under the surveillance of a bishop.[78]

How, then, did Cassian interpret the role of the clergy themselves; and what was his opinion about the involvement of monks in clerical life? All that has been said above, about the exclusive and exalted nature of monasticism in Cassian's

[77] *HM* xxviii, 452.

[78] See above, p. 64, n. 46. In the Greek (Preuschen, *Palladius und Rufinus*, 124 ff.), it is the bishop who takes the initiative, placing his faith in the power of Macarius. Macarius tries to avoid involvement, limiting himself to advice: he agrees to ask the heretic to make a declaration of faith, although he still insists that the bishop must tell the people what that faith is—such is not the task of ascetics. When it comes to the actual miracle, the bishop reassures Macarius that he will not be tempting God, because he will be strengthening the faith of the people—the pastoral motive is clear enough. Bishop and clergy join, by their prayers, in the act itself; but the bishop has little doubt where praise is due. He asks Macarius, after the miracle, the vital question: what does it *feel* like to be a wonderworker, and in particular to arouse men's admiration? These last words reveal how anxious he was about the possible misuse of power, and the threat it posed to his own authority.

eyes, and about the poverty of monks, betrays the extent to which he was unable to place a convincing barrier between monastery and world. The monk, as Cassian saw him, was exposed to danger and temptation; and yet, for the same reasons, he was available to others, open to their exploitation and demands. In the same way, therefore, the duties and privileges of clerical office were regarded as a snare, and yet accepted as a challenge that the monk could not avoid.

In this, as in all things, Cassian reflected the opinions of the East. Apphy and Netras had their counterpart in Cassian's text, as well as in that of Sulpicius–Archebius, the bishop of Panephysis. 'Throughout his life he preserved his vocation to solitude so rigorously', Cassian wrote, 'that in no way would he soften the severity of his past humility'.[79] Archebius himself was not so confident about his success as a monk turned bishop. When Cassian and Germanus, at the start of their visit to Egypt, approached him for guidance, he felt obliged to send them to other men: 'They will provide you with that which I, alas, have lost, and cannot, having lost it, pass to others; and you will learn from them, not by their words, but by the very example of their holy lives'.[80] Again, as in eastern texts, ascetics cast in a clerical role appear throughout the works of Cassian. Piamun he described as a presbyter; and he mentioned explicitly that Pinufius held that rank, while still remaining superior of a large community of monks.[81] The same is said of Paphnutius, who succeeded Isidore as presbyter in Scetis, and even attempted to appoint the deacon Daniel as his own successor in that office.[82]

These are all eastern examples, and bound up in Cassian's mind with the fact (which he deliberately brings to the notice of his readers) that the patriarch of Alexandria claimed jurisdiction over all the monasteries, as well as the churches, of his diocese.[83] But, although many of these references are

[79] *Con.* xi. 2; see above, pp. 64, 150 f. [80] Loc. cit.

[81] *Con.* xviii. 1; xx. 1.

[82] *Con.* ii. 5; iii. 1; iv. 1; xviii. 15. Cassian would surely have known Rusticus, eventually bishop of Narbonne, once a hermit, then a monk in the monastery of Proculus, son of one bishop and nephew to another, Griffe, *Gaule chrétienne*, ii, 220 f., 256; see also Marrou, 'Le dossier épigraphique de l'évêque Rusticus de Narbonne', *Rivista di Archeologia Cristiana*, iii/iv (1970), 331–40.

[83] *Con.* x. 2.

made in passing, Cassian included them with half an eye on Gaul. When he exhorted his readers to avoid both women and bishops, he spoke to a monastic audience very much subject to the patronage and control of ecclesiastical authority: Castor, to whom the *Institutes* were dedicated, was already a bishop when the words were penned.[84]

Only in the light of these developments is it possible to assess Cassian's more theoretical anxieties. To aspire to clerical office, he said, even 'under the pretext of offering spiritual help to others', was nothing less than an illusion of the devil.[85] The ideal monk will make himself difficult to run to earth, and keep himself sufficiently dirty to repel those who stumble upon him nevertheless.[86] Yet the challenge of the world's demand, if not of its admiration, drew even men like these from solitude. To covet priesthood 'through a desire for status' was clearly out of place; but to reject it when offered, Cassian said, might make a man no less guilty of pride, 'judging that office unsuited or unworthy for one of *his* former rank, one whose birth and career deserved better reward'.[87]

Within Cassian's lifetime, quite different criteria of worthiness had become attached to the office of bishop and priest. 'Promotion' to the episcopate from ascetic circles became increasingly common, and the two states of life were less harshly contrasted, while persistent opposition, even from the bishop of Rome, bore witness only to the popularity of a widespread development.[88] Of Honoratus of Lérins—the

[84] *Inst.* xi. 18. It is not known when Castor became a bishop; but he was addressed as such by Pope Boniface I in a letter of 419 (*Ep.* iii).

[85] *Con.* i. 20. For an even stronger condemnation of such attempts at 'aedificatio', see *Inst.* xi. 14—where, however, the phrase, 'likely to gain many souls, not only through the manner of his life, but also through his teaching and words' may suggest that 'conversatio', the example of a monk's life, could fulfil a pastoral purpose, even in situations less open to criticism.

[86] *Con.* iv. 11.

[87] Ibid. 20. Martin sailed very close to this wind: *V. Mart.* v. 2.

[88] Celestine, in his letter *Cuperemus* of 428 (*Ep.* iv), forbade the wearing of the monastic habit in church by those 'who did not grow up in the church, but came from another religious setting, bringing with them, into the church, the customs of their former way of life', 1 (2) (*PL* 1. 430B/431A). He also attacked example as a method of instruction: 'People need to be taught, rather than entertained: we should not impress them visually, but instil commandments in their minds', ibid. (431B). For Celestine, as for Cassian, the problem was to impose disciple-

recipient, if not the instigator, of Conferences xi to xvii (as Castor had been of the *Institutes*)—Hilary of Arles would say, 'Indeed he preserved monastic humility so completely in his priesthood that, even while enjoying the priesthood's rewards, he remained in every way a monk'.[89] Rigorous asceticism became the natural school of priestly grace, contradictions being overcome by the inner continuity of a humbled soul. Hilary himself owed his position as a leader of the Gallic episcopate, not to the importance of his see, but to his own powerful personality; and his epitaph would speak of him (linking the roles of priest and monk) as 'gemma sacerdotum plebisque orbisque magister'.[90] The same transition can be found in almost all the men associated with Cassian's work. Helladius the anchorite, mentioned in the Preface to the first set of the *Conferences*, probably succeeded Patroclus as bishop of Arles.[91] Eucherius, who shared a later dedication with his master Honoratus,[92] became bishop of Lyon in 434. If the Leontius of the *Conferences* was bishop of Fréjus, then Theodore, the monastic pioneer of Cassian's Third Preface, may have been his successor in that see.[93] Cassian's own background reflected the same ideals. He could have come to Marseille in the company of Lazarus—bishop of Aix, a former monk, and protégé of Proculus—;[94] and Proculus himself was succeeded by Venerius, a monk from his own monastery.

It is hardly surprising, therefore, that Cassian, for all his emphasis on sordid seclusion, should have made some concession to the 'wind of change'. The externals of asceticism, for example, should not wholly outrage men of the world, nor invite their ridicule.[95] Preaching, the task *par excellence*

ship in a school of orthodoxy—'Whoever wishes to be a teacher must first be a disciple', ibid. iii (4) (433A)—; and he feared the 'new brotherhood' of 'wanderers and outsiders', from which bishops might otherwise be drawn, ibid. iv (7) (434B). The letter confirms organization bypassed by events, and protects the vested interests of a clerical *cursus honorum*—see ibid. v especially. Compare, of course, the emphases of Siricius above, pp. 129 f.

[89] Hilary, *Sermo*, 16.

[90] *CIL* XII, 949b; see Griffe, *Gaule chrétienne*, i. 331.

[91] O. Chadwick, 'Euladius of Arles', *JTS* xlvi (1945), 200–5.

[92] *Con.*, Second Preface.

[93] Chadwick, *Cassian*, 38 f. See *Con.*, First Preface.

[94] See above, pp. 174 f.

[95] *Inst.* i. 10.

of bishops, was not wholly incompatible with self-improvement; and the priesthood itself could shame a man into virtuous behaviour.[96] 'Many are the fruits of repentance', Pinufius remarks, 'by which we atone for our transgressions'; and among them he includes the conversion of others.[97] Even at his most forceful, Cassian left room for compromise: 'Since even he who preached the Gospel—a labour so exalted and spiritual—did not demand free food for himself, (by appealing to the authority of our Lord's own command,) what should we do, when we have received no call whatsoever to preach the word, or to care for any soul but our own?'[98] The point was made (in the context of the Book as a whole) to counter any desire for financial support: not at the expense of saving others.

These are scattered admissions, and do not constitute a theory; but they reveal the chinks in Cassian's armour: read by men already accustomed to a greater degree of pastoral involvement, they would offer some justification for responding to the world's demand. It was hard, in any case, to make a firm distinction between brothers in the monastery and brothers outside. Even within the ascetic community, there were many unavoidable activities that called a monk away from prayer—visits from other ascetics, movement away from one's monastery, even the building of cells.[99] To leave the world was not to solve the problem of distraction. Virtue and composure were equally threatened, 'whether we attend to the needs of our brethren, or offer alms to the poor'.[100] Yet the visible structure of monasticism could be adapted when the need arose. Cassian praised the humility of a woman of noble birth in Alexandria, who attended to the needs of destitute widows, even though she, no less than the *Sarabaites*, (castigated in the very same Conference,) lived

[96] *Con.* v. 12. Celestine, maintaining his prejudice (above, n. 88), exclaimed, 'What will there be for you to do in the church, if these men [sc. the monks] do most of the preaching?', *Ep.* xxi. i (2) (*PL* l. 529B); yet the chief addressee of his letter, Venerius, had once been a monk!

[97] *Con.* xx. 8.

[98] *Inst.* x. 8, referring to the way in which Paul might have taken advantage of the dictum in Luke, x. 7, 'The labourer deserves his wages'.

[99] *Con.* xxiii. 5. [100] Ibid. 7.

in the city on her own resources; and Piamun could make the pointed comment on her case (lamenting thereby his own contrasting weakness): 'It is enough to shame us, we who cannot remain at peace unless buried away in caves, like wild beasts'.[101]

In the Seventeenth Conference, Joseph provided a key to Cassian's attitude on this matter of relations with the world: 'So we cannot assure ourselves of a deeply rooted charity unless, easing a little the proper demands of a rigorous and perfect life, we show a ready willingness to adapt ourselves to the needs of others'.[102] How far beyond the bounds of the ascetic circle would such generosity extend? It would depend, no doubt, on circumstances; but the admission had been made: the needs of others might sometimes claim more attention than strictness of life. In the light of such a principle, even Theonas could praise the generosity of Paul, who denied himself the vision of Christ for the sake of his people.[103]

[101] *Con.* xviii. 14
[102] Ibid. xvii. 19; compare *HL* lxviii.
[103] Ibid. xxiii. 5, referring to Philippians, i. 22–4.

VI

CASSIAN THE WRITER

1. BOOKS

Armed with these convictions, supported by this concept of authority, and set in the midst of so much potential activity, Cassian lived as a writer; and in his literary skill lay his chief contribution to the history of the ascetic movement. Yet, in spite of the reputation of Jerome and Sulpicius, to write for the instruction of others was still not taken for granted as the proper task of the ascetic teacher; and the author of works as formal and as detailed as the *Institutes* and *Conferences* would have felt self-conscious. Cassian was careful to present his work as no more than a secondary support for the authority of the monastic leaders to whom his books were dedicated.[1] He only wished, it seemed, to report on events and customs in another land; to provide almost an armchair pilgrimage, to save his readers from the dangers of a trip to the East.[2] He was also careful not to assert opinions as his own, but to claim dependence on oral tradition. This was justified, not only by the general structure of his work, which ostensibly reproduced conversations between masters and disciples, but by detailed and particular evidence of that dependence.[3] Any self-confidence that Cassian may have felt as a writer would have rested to a greater extent on his status as a living source of tradition: hence, at the beginning of the *Institutes*, his criticism of those writers 'who try to describe what they have heard, rather than what they have seen for themselves'.[4] His own chief claim to authority was that he

[1] e.g. *Inst.*, Preface, 3.

[2] *Con.*, Second Preface. So Cassian's books, in so far as they offered an alternative, were designed to be descriptive as well as instructive—a fact that links his work with the *Dialogues* of Sulpicius, and the *HL*.

[3] Weber, *Stellung*, presents some interesting examples and suggestions: see Appendix IV.

[4] *Inst.*, Preface, 7.

had been in the East, and had seen these men.

Yet ecclesiastical writers of this period did not regard themselves as the compromised custodians of a dying classicism. Writing, and therefore reading, followed upon their desire to communicate, and to broadcast new ideas.[5] Cassian was not, least of all in his own eyes, a mere stenographer, preserving *verbatim* an oral culture: he claimed a place in a literary tradition, already well established in the East. He knew, no less than Sulpicius, that his work represented a novel alternative to accepted methods of religious formation.[6] He told his readers that he had written these books, 'so that you may more easily lay hold of the teaching and formative discipline of the elders: by taking into your cells these *Conferences*, you will receive their authors also'.[7] To read them, in other words, (so Cassian hoped,) would be to enter into that dialogue of formation so typical of Egypt.

Nothing could alter the fact, in any case, that ascetic society was now more book-conscious than it had been. Moses complains to his hearers, 'There are many who treasure their books with such ardour that they will not allow anyone even to glance at them, let alone touch them, which gives rise to outbursts of anger, and even death'.[8] Clearly, it is covetousness that is condemned here, rather than possession: books have become a matter for compromise, as well as scruple. Writing to Valentinus of Hadrumetum, Januarius expressed the hope that, 'like imitators of God and Christ', the monks would read 'with all reverence, and a religious motive, . . . those things which the holy fathers . . . have written or collected in their books'; and the letter as a whole

[5] Christine Mohrmann, 'Le rôle des moines dans la transmission du patrimonie latin', *Mémorial de l'année martinienne*, ed. G. Le Bras (Paris, 1962), 194.

[6] *Con.*, First Preface, 1. Chadwick seems to suggest that Cassian was really recounting the *collationes* of desert fathers, *Cassian*, 3. He regards the *Conferences* in particular as an intermediate form between the oral discourses of the pioneers and the bald recollections of the *Apophthegmata*. Prolonged instruction was certainly a feature of early monasticism in the East—see *V. Pach.* I, 77; Nau 211—; but it seems likely that the *Apophthegmata* reproduce an equally primitive method of instruction. Cassian has created something new. Statements by Moses on distractions in prayer, *Con.* i. 17, are taken from Evagrius, and then woven into a literary argument, Weber, *Stellung*, 28. *Con.* ii is built on an appeal to G Antony 8, but in the light of Evagrius again, Weber, 42-50.

[7] *Con.*, Third Preface.

[8] *Con.* i. 6.

implies that more was involved than works of edification.[9] Even commentaries on Scripture, which Theodore assumes will be available,[10] were not the only sources upon which a monk might draw. Germanus openly admits to a knowledge of pagan history and custom, 'which we learned about, either in the course of our own reading, or through hearing it from others'; and Cassian allowed that those unable to inquire of firsthand witnesses about ecclesiastical affairs might turn to works of history.[11] This in itself suggests that the tradition of the church was valued, not only as a guide, but also as something richer in detail and longer in duration than could safely be preserved and interpreted by oral tradition alone. Cassian's insistence on respect for the past made writing inevitable in the preservation and development of the monastic movement.

It is possible to detect some of the particular anxieties for which Cassian catered as a writer. He hoped that his work would help to create a *milieu* 'in which monasteries will not be set up merely through the whim of this or that man leaving the world, but will endure, or be built to endure, on the basis of authority and teaching handed down by our elders to this present day'. He may have had in mind the fluid situation in Gaul itself, already mentioned; or he may have recalled the variety of ascetic experiments that he would have discovered, like Jerome, on his various travels, and which Palladius appeared to tolerate: whichever was the case, his aim was certainly to encourage uniformity based on tradition; and a written work was an excellent means to this end.[12]

This still left open, of course, the precise manner in which to use the medium. For Cassian did more than reproduce the dialogue between master and disciple. Germanus, for example, is often made to betray impatience with these long exhortations, and to demand instead a *formula*, a rule of

[9] G. Morin, 'Lettres inédites de s. Augustin et du prêtre Januarien dans l'affaire des moines d'Adrumète', *RB* xviii (1901), 252. The words 'imitators' and 'reverence' (*imitatores* and *veneratio*) show how traditional attitudes persisted in the new literary culture.

[10] *Inst.* v. 34.

[11] *Con.* xii. 4; *Inst.* ii. 5.

[12] *Inst.* ii. 3.

thumb, by which to encapsulate in memorable form the more extended teaching of the fathers. Such an anxiety would have been an essential prerequisite for the popularity of written rules.[13]

Another anxiety, found also by this time in the East, concerned a decline in the power of the spoken word, and a corresponding lack of confidence on the part of the fathers. Even old age itself, once the chief characteristic of an ascetic master, could be repudiated as a weakness.[14] Yet it was precisely these men, unsure of themselves and of their capacity to teach, who compelled Cassian (not to mention the compilers of the *Apophthegmata* and other such texts) to create a more enduring form of spiritual instruction; a corpus of literature in which they themselves would figure nevertheless as the chief exponents. The moment at which the ascetic tradition exchanged an oral for a written culture was precisely the moment at which it began to doubt its own insight and authority.

This new instrument of formation disrupted the old relationship that it claimed to reproduce in another form—the relationship between master and disciple. Cassian had insisted on a need for secrecy; a need to restrict the teaching of the fathers to an audience inspired by the highest motives.[15] Yet, once that teaching was written, the reins of tight control slipped from the fingers of the masters themselves. Such control was not relinquished without a struggle. Januarius, writing to Valentinus, praised 'the caution with which you exercise your authority, the warnings which your love impels: no brother should take up and read whatever text or book may come his way, since his heart may not be ready yet to understand it'.[16] Ambrose, long before, inspired by a

[13] The role of Germanus in Cassian's dialogues (for such they are)—particularly his interjections, which seem designed either to carry the argument to a further stage or to raise objections (such as Cassian may have anticipated in his readers)—may be compared to the role of Gallus and others in the *Dialogues* of Sulpicius. R. R. Voss, *Der Dialog in der frühchristlichen Literatur* (Munich, 1970), discusses the form of Sulpicius's work, 308-14; but not that of Cassian.

[14] See above, pp. 189 f., 196.

[15] *Con.* i. 1.

[16] Morin, 'Lettres inédites', 253. The phrase 'ne *passim* accipiat . . . codicem' reproduces exactly the force of the word in *Con.* i. 1, 'si *passim* vel nolentibus eam vel tepide sitientibus exhiberet'; see above, p. 204.

similar motive, had tried to restrict the act of reading to the level of intimate dialogue—in that case, between himself and the author.[17] Cassian may have hoped that a similar intimacy would develop between himself and his readers, so that, like true disciples, they would enter into the mind of their master. Like Honoratus, he would have wished his writings to rest, 'not on desks or in cupboards, but in the storehouse of the heart'.[18]

But writing brought with it more impersonal qualities. The *Conferences* could be interpreted, by reader and writer alike, as an independent support, even a substitute, for the traditional authority of the abbot.[19] They buttressed the increasing stability and formality of the monastic life. The great legend of the angel, for example, (who, according to some texts, gave Pachomius his famous *Rule*, although Cassian places the story in a more general framework,) strikes at the root of traditional ascetic authority, and does so in the name of the written word. Cassian referred to the story in the course of an attack on personal initiative, stressing the importance of respect for the past.[20] Yet the event described is quite arbitrary and ahistorical: the *Rule* is dictated, rather than developed on the basis of experience; and its continuity, its capacity to endure, is that of a written text, guaranteed by sudden supernatural intervention, rather than by the tradition of the fathers. Such a tale could have achieved popularity only at a time when oral teaching had begun to make less impact.

We are brought back, in fact, to Germanus's concept of *formula*. Oddly enough, Isaac agrees to supply one, so that no one may feel denied the possibility of achieving

[17] 'When he read, his eyes travelled across the page and his heart sought into the sense, but voice and tongue were silent. . . . Perhaps he was on his guard lest [if he read aloud] someone listening should be troubled and want an explanation if the author he was reading expressed some idea over-obscurely', Augustine, *Confessions*, vi. 3, trans. Sheed, 82 f.

[18] Hilary, *Sermo*, 22.

[19] *Con.*, Second Preface; xxiv. 26.

[20] *Inst.* ii. 4. For Cassian's use of the legend, see Chadwick, *Cassian*, 58–60. Oddly enough, when Cassian recounted how Cham had perpetuated knowledge of the magic arts by writing them down (an obscure tradition), he was quick to dismiss the supposed intervention of angels in this event as a mythical addition, *Con.* viii. 21.

perfection of heart simply on account of his lack of letters.[21] Did this imply that the pseudo-dialogue of the written *Conferences* had already outlived its usefulness, or at least its popularity, destined to survive only in the more rigid structure of a *Regula Magistri*?[22] Not entirely: lack of letters, 'inperitia litterarum', on Isaac's lips, could refer backwards in time, to the simplicity of early ascetics, just as much as forward, to herald some supposed period when monks would have time only for commands rather than instruction, for observance rather than formation. But a new note *had* been sounded during Cassian's lifetime—in the phrase of Januarius, for instance: 'As your own measured judgement may allow, let a monk take and read what he can grasp with ease'.[23] This more formal tendency would render obsolete, or at least change radically, the *collatio* in the old style, with its individual quality, and its reference to the needs of particular persons. After Chaeremon has spoken at length on chastity, Germanus interrupts, again with some impatience:

> We wish you to instruct us, teaching us with the fullest argument, how we should set about safeguarding [our chastity], and how long we shall need to acquire or perfect it. Only then can we believe its achievement possible, and bestir ourselves to seek it for the length of time required. For we shall think it in some ways beyond the reach of those bound by the flesh, unless it is clearly explained to us what particular drill we should follow, what direction we should take, in order to arrive at our goal.[24]

Chaeremon has his answer, his *formula*, ready. Abstain from idle conversation, from anger, and from worldly care; eat only two *paxamatia* a day, and drink such water as you need; sleep no more than three or four hours: then, trusting in God rather than in yourself, six months should bring you victory. With what ominous ease such a brief and clearcut distillation of experience could become a

[21] *Con.* x. 14.

[22] In the *Regula Magistri*, a dialogue form is used, the 'interrogatio discipuli' alternating with the words of the master (which are introduced with the significant phrase, 'The Lord replied through the master'). For the influence of Cassian on the *Regula*, see B. Capelle, 'Cassien, le Maître et saint Benoît', *RTAM*, xi (1939), 110–18. Eucherius, *Instructiones ad Salonium*, may represent an intermediate example (*PL* 1. 773–822).

[23] Morin, 'Lettres inédites', 253.

[24] *Con.* xii. 14.

changeless and impersonal principle![25]

2. THE CHURCH AS A MONASTERY: CASSIAN'S *DE INCARNATIONE*

Yet Cassian the writer was concerned with more than abetting a transition from spoken exhortation to written rule. With a personal history of at least potential involvement in the public affairs of the church, he was drawn by the wider issues of the day. There were in his writings two processes at work in this regard. He took note of controversy beyond the monastic sphere; and yet his awareness was such that he allowed his response to mould his argument at the level of ascetic theory. He did not turn from ascetic studies simply to make incidental reference to an unconnected debate. Wide-ranging concern lay beneath the surface of all his work: and he allowed these interests to prompt ascetic speculations that might not otherwise have emerged in the course of his argument.

When called upon, for example, to write the *De Incarnatione*,–when given the opportunity of a specific controversy,–Cassian showed a striking ability to develop, in a polemical text, ideas on ascetic discipline and the monastic life. His arguments against Nestorius, (patriarch of Constantinople, later to be condemned for heresy at the Council of Ephesus in 431,) even though marshalled in the service of dogma, reflected the principles and customs of ascetic society, and showed how the teaching of the *Institutes* and *Conferences* (on authority in particular) could be used in a pastoral context. In this way he maintained the traditions of Martin of Tours and Victricius of Rouen, combining ascetic zeal with polemic on behalf of orthodoxy.[26]

Cassian presented both himself and the authorities to whom he appealed in the guise of ascetic masters. He wrote of himself as an 'incantator', mediating 'the power of the prophets, and the God-given vigour of the Gospel message'.[27]

[25] Loc. cit. Weber points to a link with Evagrius here, and concludes, 'A specific reply like this from the Abbot Chaeremon shows that it is only one step from here to a legally binding rule: Cassian is the immediate precursor of the rule', *Stellung*, 84 f.

[26] See above, p. 149 f. The basic *unity* of Cassian's work is strongly emphasized by Chadwick, *Cassian*, 1st edn., 165.

[27] *De Inc.*, Preface, 3, thus echoing *Con.* ii. 11; xviii. 16; see above, pp. 191 f.

Moreover, he addressed his readers, not only as a teacher in his own right, but as the disciple of Chrysostom; as one whose confidence was based on links with authentic tradition. 'The stream depends upon its source', he wrote, 'and whatever men may think the work of the disciple must all redound to the honour of the master'.[28] He wished, like Vincent of Lérins, to write 'impelled by trust and loyalty, like one who tells of another: not with the rash confidence of a self-appointed pioneer'.[29] So he betrayed the sense of dependence on the past that had entirely inspired his interpretation of monastic history and ascetic discipline.[30]

Turning to his authorities, he described Paul as 'the teacher of the churches', inspired by God—'There dwelt in him all the richness of God's word and counsel'.[31] To the Fathers of the Church, commenting on the riches of Scripture, he ascribed a 'plenissima brevitas', an ability to say all in a few words—precisely the quality found in ascetic masters of the desert.[32] This enabled them to compile, in the light of Scripture, a *σύμβολον*, a concentrated and memorable corpus of Christian teaching, inspired by God himself; 'In this way, like a faithful father, he takes account of the waywardness of his sons, or of their lack of learning'.[33] *Σύμβολον* Cassian translated as *collatio*, forging yet another link between pastoral and ascetic treatise; and he emphasized the connection by this accompanying reference to God's providence, which echoed faithfully the methods of guidance and government recommended by himself.[34]

For the moment, however, Cassian gave primacy to the pastoral motif. He regarded the *De Incarnatione* as more

[28] *De Inc.* vii. 31.

[29] *Commonitorium*, i. For Vincent's own concern with authority, see above, p. 190, n. 9. This does establish a link between the two men: both, for all their chosen solitude, were engaged in public debate; and there is no need to contrast them, in the manner of Chadwick, *Cassian*, 95: see rather J. Madoz, *El concepto de la tradición en s. Vicente de Lérins* (Rome, 1933), 54, 65.

[30] *De Inc.* iii. 1.

[31] Ibid. iv. 3.

[32] Ibid. vi. 4; see above, pp. 19 f.

[33] *De Inc.* vi. 3; compare this with the remarks made above about *formula*, pp. 223 f., 225 f.

[34] *De Inc.* vi. 4; compare this especially with points made in the Thirteenth Conference, below, pp. 233 f.

important than his ascetic works; and he said that he would not have taken up the pen in any case, 'unless forced by a bishop's command'.[35] He desired God's inspiration, only to guarantee the pastoral effect of his words; and he asked Christ to bless these his seven books, (as he had blessed the five loaves and two fishes,) 'so that, just as you strengthened the hungry with that food, so, with this book, you may bring back to health those who now suffer in weakness'.[36]

Two particular themes show the *De Incarnatione* to be imbued with the principles of ascetic authority. First, Cassian tried to force upon his opponents the sense of being involved in a wider community. He wanted to *shame* them into orthodoxy—pointing, for instance, to the repentance of former Pelagians, using the example of one group in the church to foster virtue in another.[37] He wanted Nestorius to submit to the corporate authority of that community: 'A belief that is shared by all has an authority of its own that makes the truth clear beyond doubt'.[38] Neither Nestorius nor he himself need be forced, he thought, to find authority in the past alone. They were members of a believing society that owed its cohesion, not to a demand for submission, but to the ability of its members to communicate one with another, and to engage in fruitful debate.[39] The church was presented, therefore, as a society that demanded of its members (like the ascetic community itself) consistency, as well as continuity. Cassian felt able to respect, for example, Arians who adhered to the faith of their parents, their baptism, their Christian education: for Nestorius, however, 'born in a Catholic city, brought up in the Catholic faith, given new birth by Catholic baptism', there was no such excuse.[40]

[35] *De Inc.*, Preface, 2. This puts Cassian's relations with Castor, for example, in a new light: perhaps he responded as much to Castor's episcopal authority as to his needs as a monastic pioneer.

[36] *De Inc.* v. 2.

[37] Ibid. i. 5. This may have been one motive, at least, for asserting close links between the errors of Pelagius and those of Nestorius; see Chadwick, *Cassian*, 137 f., 142 f., and J. Plagnieux, 'Le grief de complicité entre erreurs nestorienne et pélagienne: d'Augustin à Cassien par Prosper d'Aquitaine?', *REA* ii (1956), 391–402. I do not think that Cassian need have depended entirely on Prosper for whatever prejudice he may have had; see above, pp. 174 f.

[38] *De Inc.* i. 6.

[39] Here one must recall Joseph's 'new society': see above, pp. 187 f., 196 f.

[40] *De Inc.* vi. 5.

Cassian demonstrated, in a second theme, further pastoral implications of his concept of authority. He recalls at one point the declaration of faith made by Peter—a declaration of faith in the divinity of Christ[41]—; and he asks the apostle to inspire in himself and his readers an understanding of this doctrine. He then makes as if to repeat the answer of Peter himself to this demand:

> Why do you ask of me in what way men should bear witness to their faith in the Lord? You know how I did so myself. Read the Gospel: there you will find my declaration, and you will have no need of me in person. Indeed, I am there in my act of faith: had it not been made, I myself would possess no authority; and what authority I have stems entirely from that faith itself.[42]

This emphasis on the spoken word, and on the faith of the speaker, rather than on his status, reproduced exactly the attitude of Cassian (and of the Desert Fathers) to the authority of the ascetic master. Yet, with increasing stress on the coenobitic life, governed more by rule than by personal influence, it was the teaching itself of the holy man,—the 'confessio', the 'doctrina',—that carried greatest weight. Prophets, apostles, even the Fathers themselves, now remote in the past, became haunting, ever-present symbols of traditional values, rather than a visible force in the lives of believers and disciples. Dissociated from his 'persona', the teaching of the ascetic master (as of the theologian) acquired an authority of its own. Preserved in texts, (like the Gospels themselves,) this disembodied 'confessio' reached an audience, and underwent an interpretation, over which the holy man himself no longer had control.[43]

But the practical and pastoral effect of this emphasis was no less important. Cassian regarded office in the church, and the authority that went with it, as entirely dependent on the content of a man's teaching, and on the faith that inspired it. For this reason, error had undermined the very priesthood of Nestorius: 'Having lost faith in the Creed, you have lost everything that you ever were: the life-giving signs that bring you priesthood and salvation depend on the truth of the

[41] Referring to Matthew, xvi. 16.

[42] *De Inc.* iii. 2.

[43] Compare the atmosphere described at the end of Part One, pp. 74 ff.; and recall remarks made above about Cassian as a writer, pp. 221 ff.

Creed'.[44] There was a link, therefore, between office and orthodoxy, between personal salvation and priestly power; but faith was the basis of authority: to deny or undermine the teaching of the church was to repudiate the source of spiritual power itself.[45]

3. THE THIRTEENTH CONFERENCE: PORTRAIT OF AN ABBOT

The same ability to comment on two worlds in the language of one overriding insight and conviction—the world of the monk, and the world of controversy—appears in Cassian's treatment of freedom and grace. Again, he did not limit himself to the occasional barbed reference or parenthetic attack. The passages that raise the issue, and the Thirteenth Conference in particular, form part of a broad debate: a debate about the basis and effect of authority; intended to achieve more than a solution of theological controversy.[46] It is true that Cassian took particular issue with Augustine, and joined with his contemporaries in their 'semi-Pelagian' attempt to reformulate the principles at stake;[47] but he shied away from theoretical extremes, rejecting as much the arguments of Pelagius himself.[48] Yet his own position owed little to cautious logic or skilful compromise in argument. His great fear was that experience would not play a sufficient part in the formulation of theological positions; and the Thirteenth Conference itself ends with a studied declaration on this point: Cassian appeals, in ascetic terms, to the guidance of those 'who assess the greatness of grace or the puny power of the human will, not in longwinded phrases, but in the wake of their own experience'.[49]

The message of the Thirteenth Conference is inseparable

[44] *De Inc.* vi. 6.

[45] Ibid. 6, 18.

[46] Munz was right to suggest that Cassian was no systematic theologian, 'John Cassian', 1; but he fails to credit him with *any* sense of purpose. Chadwick would prefer to substitute 'ethics', where I have 'authority', *Cassian*, 120: I think Cassian was more specific.

[47] Cassian never mentions Augustine by name; but Prosper read him in this light: *Ep.* ccxxv. 3 (in the Augustinian corpus). See Chadwick, *Cassian*, 19 f., 37, 112, 127 ff.

[48] See virtually the whole of *Inst.* xii, especially 4, 11: the phrase, 'He judged himself like to God' may be linked directly with *De Inc.* i. 3.

[49] *Con.* xiii. 18.

from its structure. Cassian allowed his interpretation of the problem to be moulded entirely by his conception of proper debate. In the opening passages, God's influence is seen as a major factor in human activity, affecting especially 'the first movements of a will that is becoming holy'.[50] But then, instead of putting forward a sharply contrasting statement in defence of human freedom,[51] Cassian undermines with greater subtlety his own original statement. God in his goodness responds, he writes, to a certain 'spark of goodwill', which he either finds or kindles in men's hearts.[52] Having thus secured his base, (or perhaps a line of retreat,) Cassian makes another bold move. Instead of referring to Scripture in support of his case, he freely admits that the Bible is contradictory, and quotes extensively to show that this is so. The texts assert nothing, he writes, but that man is free, and yet in need of God.[53]

Cassian was now able to make his most characteristic contribution to the whole debate. The apparent conflict, he writes, between human freedom and the power of God, is not a conflict between the integrity of the human will and some force outside itself. Whatever conflict there may be is interior to each individual: a conflict between the undoubted power of the will and its no less evident weakness. He also explains more fully his determination to attach equal importance to these conflicting elements of human experience: 'They are both in harmony; and I think it is only just to pay equal attention to both, arguing the matter with religious deference: otherwise, if we deny to man one or the other of these qualities, we shall seem to go beyond the limits of what the church believes'.[54]

In a third stage of the argument, Cassian begins to discuss

[50] Particularly forceful is the phrase, 'He initiates what is good, follows it through, and brings it to perfection in us', *Con.* xiii. 3.

[51] As he had in other passages: e.g. *Inst.* vii. 1, 3; xii. 14; *Con.* i. 15.

[52] *Con.* xiii. 7.

[53] Ibid. 9.

[54] *Con.* xiii. 10 f. Chadwick contrasts the method of this Conference with that of the *De Inc.* The first, he says, makes little appeal to church authority, the second a great deal, *Cassian*, 120. The reference here to a 'regula fidei' must undermine that suggestion. Even more ominous is the link between a formal 'regula' and the less tangible but more personal concept of 'pietas' (here translated 'religious deference').

this inner tension in the context of the Fall. The effect of the Fall, he writes, was not to obscure in man the knowledge of good, instilled in him by God, but to heighten his awareness of evil. In this way, Cassian brilliantly translated his own psychological insight into the scriptural terms understood by his opponents. What effect did this transformation achieve? First, Cassian betrays his motive: 'So we have to be careful not to attribute to the Lord all the merits of the saints in such a way that nothing is ascribed to human nature but what is evil and an obstacle to goodness'.[55] Then he reveals how he wishes to apply his new understanding of Genesis to the psychology of the ascetic life: 'There can be no doubt that there is by nature in every soul the seed of virtue, planted there by the goodness of the Creator; but that seed cannot grow to perfection, unless stimulated with the help of God'. 'The seed of virtue' provides a much firmer and more optimistic basis for the spiritual life than the fragile hope of a 'spark of goodwill'.[56]

But what was the chief concern in Cassian's mind, implied by his statements on freedom and grace? He wished to create an image of divine authority that did not clash with the image of human authority demanded by his interpretation of the ascetic life. In the *Conferences*, especially, God plays the role of the ideal abbot. Several phrases emphasize the point: God is a 'kindly doctor', who awakens within us these seeds of virtue; and, faced with intransigence, or dulled enthusiasm, 'he moves our hearts with lifegiving encouragement, and so restores, or brings into being, goodwill within us'.[57] He exerts this influence, not only 'according to each one's capacity', but also 'according to his faith'—demanding, in other words, the trust of a disciple in the wisdom of his master.[58] God does not call upon his power and prescience to impose straight lines on the graph of human progress, but allows himself to follow the variable curve of individual ambition and ability.[59] He must therefore influence his

[55] *Con.* xiii. 12. This was to some extent the anxiety of Jerome, in the *Adversus Iovinianum*; see above, pp. 107 f., 128 f.

[56] Loc. cit. Jerome used the same phrase, when translating Orsisius, *Liber*, 6.

[57] *Con.* xiii. 7, 11 f.

[58] *Con.* xiii. 15.

[59] *Con.* xvii. 25.

creatures in a variety of ways, adopting a very human pose, and revealing the gentle skill of the ascetic master:

> We can see how God achieves the salvation of the human race. Those who wish for it, and thirst for it, he stirs up to more ardent endeavours; others less willing he compels. At one time he will help towards fulfilment those things which he sees we long for to our advantage; at another he will prompt for the first time that holy desire, and give us the power to begin or continue good works.[60]

Behind this image of God lay Cassian's firm belief in authority based on persuasion; a belief that demanded the possibility of merit and reward: 'When a man is persuaded, rather than commanded, his deeds gain him profit; but what is left undone is no cause for punishment'.[61] The Christian ascetic lived in an age set free by Christ, neither bound by law nor impelled by fear of retribution: 'Christ arouses our free will by counsel rich in both power and healing; and he sets us alight with a longing for perfection'.[62] Fired, therefore, by his own admiration for those who taught, 'not in longwinded phrases, but in the wake of their own experience',[63] Cassian perceived, not only the model for his method in controversy, but also the model for his conclusion to the controversy itself. The implications had come full circle. Not only did Cassian's God take on the guise of abbot: Cassian's abbot was called upon to school himself as a fitting mediator for the influence of God.

[60] *Con.* xiii. 17. Compare the similar phrases of Paphnutius, *Con.* iii. 10, 19—noting in particular, in the first passage, that terms like 'vocatio', 'inspiratio', 'magisterium', and 'inluminatio' in no way rule out the possibility that God's actions might be mediated through ordinary circumstance: they represent patterns of influence that depend for success entirely on the response of the subject. This was the understanding of providence that would find its echo in the *De Inc.*—see above, p. 228.

[61] *Con.* xxi. 14—again, an echo of Jerome; see above, n. 55. Cassian had made the same point at the beginning of *Inst.*, Preface, 9 (and see *Con.* xix. 8); but one is reminded also of Augustine—not only the famous epigram, 'Give what you command, and command what you will', but also another passage in the *Confessions*, discussing the problems of human judgement, (to be linked, therefore, with *City of God*, xix. 6,) and ending with the phrase, 'He is said to judge only of those things in which he has also the power to correct', xiii. 23.

[62] *Con.* xxi. 5.

[63] Ibid. xiii. 18.

EPILOGUE

THE NEXT GENERATION

Cassian is difficult to summarize; and there is no denying the contradictions in his work. While formulating concepts of authority and discipline that cater for the coenobite, and encourage the development of corporate monasticism, he continues to plead the supreme value of the eremitic life. While advocating attitudes that prompt the monk to involvement with the world, and equip him for pastoral endeavour, and the exercise of priestly authority, he still defends the esoteric—the maintenance of an exclusive group, governed by arcane principle.

It was not that Cassian was unable to make up his mind on these issues. He felt it was impossible, or rather imprudent, to commit himself in public on one side or the other. For he had a deep sense of obligation to the past, to the 'traditio maiorum'; and this would have urged upon him the need for fidelity, a fidelity embracing many potentially conflicting traditions. It would have been immensely difficult for any man in his position, or in his period, to repudiate or ignore the practice of heroes so recently dead, so powerful a force in the memory and life of their disciples. Cassian may have wished, for his own part, to discipline the ascetic enthusiasm of his adopted province; but he had to be careful not to reject in the process the original ideal of ἀναχώρησις, now (in his eyes) subject to abuse. There would have been a need for caution, too: caution in the face of criticism by the followers or successors of Brictius (Martin's heir, and enemy, in Tours) or Vigilantius (criticized by Jerome)—men opposed to ἀναχώρησις in every sense. Cassian was, in any case, a diplomatic man. Having subscribed to the teaching of Origen, he may have had a past to live down: he took great care, in his ascetic works, to attack no one by name; and, over a period of fifteen years, (during which, to judge by his writings, he must have acquired a considerable reputation,) he was able to move from the status of a protégé of Proculus —a man not exactly *persona grata* in the eyes of Rome, not to mention his colleagues nearer home—to become the collaborator in controversy, if not the friend, of Leo the Great himself.

Nevertheless, there is in Cassian's work a drawing together of the threads of development identified here in the East, and following through the writings of Jerome and Sulpicius. The values of the hermit are not only described in the *Institutes* and *Conferences*,—prayer, self-mastery, and closeness to God,—but woven into the daily life of the coenobite. Ascetic values in general are analysed and recommended by Cassian in such a way as to make very clear their possible application to a world beyond the monastery, with needs and aspirations that differed only in degree from those of monks. This had happened, to some extent, in the writings of Jerome and Sulpicius. What makes Cassian particularly important is that his work has an obvious unity. These threads are drawn together by one man, impelled by one purpose; and Cassian's relative success in this respect provides a point of focus in the development of monastic history that is in some ways more convincing than the emphasis of Sulpicius, in whose work there is always a suspicion of division between himself, the retiring ascetic, and Martin, the 'apostolic man'. Moreover, Cassian's essay in ascetic theory was destined to exert a more rigorous influence, and to survive in a written form that was quite independent of the reputation, not only of its author, (who was, indeed, almost forgotten,) but also, to some extent, of the other figures portrayed in his pages. The *Institutes* and *Conferences* stand as a complete and entirely literary creation, exerting upon their readers the influence of a rule of life.

For this reason, the study of early monastic history reaches, with Cassian, a *point de départ*, rather than a conclusion. Ranging over a hundred years or more of ascetic development and influence, the survey given here represents a species of aerial photography. Just as patterns are revealed by the camera in flight,—in the varying height of crops, in the uneven lie of the land,—(patterns impossible to observe at ground level, and pointing, perhaps, to archaeological sites below,) so the historian, taking a broad view, can discover trends that extend beyond the bounds of individual biography: such are the trends described here towards social complexity, pastoral involvement, and dependence upon literary forms. But the insight gained is no more than an invitation to return over the same ground, first surveying the surface, and then, perhaps, digging deeper, in the light of patterns revealed from the more distant viewpoint.

There is more that could be said, therefore, about monks in Egypt: not so much about their spectacular but (to the historian) relatively familiar intrusions upon public affairs, (the destruction of temples, the forcing of the issue over Origen, the lynching of Hypatia,) but about the relationship between Egyptian bishops and the monks from among whom they were often drawn. There is more that could be said about the development, during the fifth century, of an *urban* monasticism in Egypt, somewhat estranged from the desert. There is more, a great deal more, that could be said about Jerome: not only about his ecclesiastical ambitions, but about his own relationship with Egypt and the writings of Pachomius, the development of monasticism in Palestine, and some less familiar aspects of his character as a polemical writer and biblical exegete. More could be said about the circle at Aquileia. There are links to be made between this analysis and the history of Pelagianism, which involved spiritual direction, the setting of ascetic standards, a certain withdrawal from the 'official' church, and a great predilection for privately circulated literature. Basil and Chrysostom are examples of the 'monk-bishop': pastoral men, but with great secular influence, who left behind them an extensive and important corpus of ascetic and liturgical texts. They had their western counterparts, to some extent, in Ambrose and Augustine: men similarly dedicated to the ascetic life; similarly involved in developing an understanding of the office of bishop; similarly the inspiration of ascetic rules, and of hagiography. Finally, there is more that could be said about Martin of Tours: about the schism in the Gallic church during and immediately after his lifetime, and its relation to controversy on the issue of asceticism; and about the progress and influence of the cult of Martin in later years. All these people and places were marked by changes in the understanding and use of sanctity and power, therefore; changes that affected the course of church history in many ways still open to investigation, still not clearly understood, taking place precisely during that period when churchmen, with a new sense of freedom, laboured to capture the allegiance of a new pagan empire.

There is also in Cassian an invitation to the future. Reading him, ascetics in the West would have looked, as it were, through a window, on to the whole field of monastic development from Antony to their own day. The historian, however, can see that his work acted more as a lens, a kind of prism in reverse, capturing the diverse colours, the diverse traditions of the ascetic life, and focusing them in a concentrated ray of light upon the religious imagination of the West. He constitutes, therefore, a *point de départ* in another sense. He marks the beginning, perhaps more than Sulpicius, of a tradition that reaches at least to Gregory the Great, and, in Ireland and Germany, far beyond: a tradition that linked more and more firmly the practice of ascetic virtue and the preaching of the Gospel. This is the tradition represented, at the level of monastic experiment, by Cassiodorus and Benedict, and by the early *Regulae* of the Benedictine movement. At the level of the episcopate, it was a tradition that inspired not only the many bishops who emerged from the monasteries of Lérins in the middle years of the fifth century,—Faustus of Riez, for example, or Lupus of Troyes,—but also men like Caesarius of Arles or Gregory of Tours. It was most of all a literary tradition, and culminated in Gregory the Great himself: a monk, a bishop, and a missionary; a lawgiver, and a hagiographer.

These are the invitations and the possibilities, therefore; and to press the matter further would be to write another book. The survey of Egypt given here, the tracing of themes in Jerome, Sulpicius, and Cassian, and swift glances aside at men such as Basil and Augustine, should reveal, at least, an understanding of tradition, cooperation, discipline, authority, and obedience which, when permanently formulated, and made more readily available in written form, would teach a man 'already holy in the eyes of all' how to become 'a man of power as well, a true successor of the apostles'.

APPENDICES

APPENDIX I

GREEK, COPTIC, AND LATIN LIVES OF PACHOMIUS[1]

The link between Dion. and II is in dispute. Lefort considered that Dion. translated a Greek text similar to, possibly the source of, II; and that this earlier text was the first Greek life of Pachomius.[2] Chitty made a more careful comparison of the two, and considered that II had been a model for Dion., subsequently modified; a conclusion echoed by Veilleux.[3] Peeters mentioned an added complication: the influence of *HL* on the sources of Dion.[4]

Both Chitty and Lefort came to their conclusions against the background of wider controversy. When he edited the Greek lives, Halkin pointed out that there was nothing in II that could not have come either from I or from the *Paralipomena.*[5] Among elements of I *not* found in II, he mentioned passages about Theodore, and about events following the founder's death.[6]

Lefort appealed to these 'omissions' to make a contrary emphasis, claiming them as evidence that II was more primitive; but, Chitty pointed out, 'the Theodoran chapters omitted in [II] are fewer than those retained, and are also fewer than those omitted which do not concern Theodore'.[7] Chitty also asked if anyone could prove that the first biography *must* have been of Pachomius alone:[8] he stressed the importance of *De Oratione*, 108 (probably by Evagrius, and therefore prior to his death in 399), with its phrase, *βίοι τῶν Ταβεννησιωτῶν μοναχῶν.*[9]

These points robbed Lefort of proof, but did not prove themselves that II was late. Other matters raised by Halkin strengthened the contrary opinion. II does not reproduce I, 17, 98 f., where the biographer apologizes for bothering readers with matters of little importance. Such apology would have made sense where existing but unfamiliar material was being presented to a non-Pachomian audience. More

[1] The prefix '*V. Pach.*' has been omitted through this appendix.

[2] Lefort, *Vies*, pp. xxvii–xxxviii; lxxxvii f.

[3] Chitty, 'Pachomian Sources Reconsidered', *JEH* v (1954), 56–9; Veilleux, *Liturgie*, 32.

[4] P. Peeters, 'Le dossier copte de s. Pachôme et ses rapports avec la tradition grecque', *AB* lxiv (1946), 262.

[5] Halkin, *Vitae Graecae*, 55*.

[6] Ibid. 58*.

[7] Lefort, *Vies*, p. xxxix; Chitty, 'Pachomian Sources Reconsidered', 63.

[8] Chitty, op. cit., 48.

[9] Ibid. 39, 65; see *PG* lxxix. 1192A.

interesting is the relation between II and the *Paralipomena* (which many accept as an early attempt to establish or maintain a written tradition—although Peeters warned of its apparent dependence on a long history of anecdote).[10] Whenever II relates material found in both I and the *Paralipomena*, it is, according to Halkin, the latter that is followed.[11] The only exception is II, 17, where the phrase, *δότε τόπον τῷ ἀνθρώπῳ θεοῦ* echoes I, 18, while all other elements in the passage appear to depend on *Paralipomena*, 14; but this is a phrase that might easily have been preserved by oral tradition alone.

Reading Lefort, some of these suspicions are strengthened further. He approached the matter more by undermining I—'clearly a compilation'[12]—; and he pointed to passages apparently derived from the *Paralipomena* that suggested piecemeal construction.[13] Chitty countered these points by arguing that all the *Paralipomena* could have been based on independent oral tradition, with no literary relation to I; that I could, even so, have been in existence when that oral tradition emerged; and that all existing apophthegmata about Pachomius could have been drawn from I, rather than *vice versa*.[14]

Chitty described as subjective Lefort's feeling that I was a compilation; and he was unimpressed by Lefort's examples of muddled chronology and varied spelling of names.[15] Chitty's more general argument—that II depended on I—is less satisfactory. He described as 'clear indications of the secondary document' the alleged tendency of II to use lengthy phrases, to pile up quotations from Scripture, to show concern for style, and to emphasize narrative less than edification.[16] These judgements are no less subjective than those of Lefort, dependent on Chitty's defence of 'the principle, followed in an earlier generation by Ladeuze and Dom Cuthbert Butler, of preferring in general the shorter and more factual account of an event to the longer and more picturesque'.[17]

When he examined the passages where the two lives either correspond or diverge, Chitty betrayed the uncertainty of the whole procedure: 'If we allow that [II] may, apart from pure omissions, have modified the order and contents of [I] sometimes by substitution . . . and sometimes by transposition . . . the grounds for supposing that [II] used [I] in an uncompleted form disappear'.[18] But he still had to admit that 'parallelism' was 'unmistakable' for only the first fifty-four chapters of II; no more than 'reasonably demonstrable' for

[10] Peeters, 'Le dossier copte', 264.
[11] Halkin, *Vitae Graecae*, 58* f.
[12] Lefort, *Vies*, p. xxxviii.
[13] Ibid. pp. xlvi–xlviii.
[14] Chitty, 'Pachomian Sources Reconsidered', 48–54.
[15] Chitty, op. cit. 65 f.
[16] Ibid. 60.
[17] Ibid. 45.
[18] Ibid. 60.

the next thirty; and merely 'vaguer' for the rest. He maintained a negative note in his final judgements: 'There is nothing to prove that the author of [II] had not [I] in its complete form before him, and some evidence to suggest that he did'.[19] This leaves a great deal frustratingly obscure. Veilleux has accepted that I may be the oldest Greek text;[20] but he is undoubtedly correct in asserting that its status can be assessed only in relation to Coptic and (equally important) Arabic sources (see below).

On the second major issue, priority of Greek or Coptic, even Halkin never pleaded the absolute originality of I. He expressed the frustration that (to my mind) still endures: 'It is impossible to reconstruct the original form of the Greek texts'.[21] He did insist, however, that the first life of Pachomius must have been in Greek, working on the assumption that no Copt would have been educated enough to attempt the task in his own language.[22] Yet this still allowed him to suppose that the writers of the first Greek lives could have been bilingual, and could have drawn upon *oral* Coptic material.[23] He thought, in addition, that the earliest Greek corpus could then have been translated very quickly into Coptic—and revealed, by his explanation, the roots of his prejudice (shared in some ways by Peeters): 'With this model before their eyes, educated native monks would have been cured of that inborn impotence which had prevented them from giving literary form to that confused mass of memories and false legends which they felt pressing in upon them'.[24] This could still imply, however, that all our existing Greek texts were heavily influenced by a written Coptic tradition.

Lefort followed up Halkin's hints at a Coptic background to I. By analysing supposed 'copticisms' in the Greek, Lefort was not trying to prove that Coptic written material had been plentiful before the compilation of *any* Greek biography, but to discover more about the compiler of I. His attempts were criticized, not without some justice, by Festugière.[25] In any case, copticisms would not automatically suggest, as Chitty had already pointed out, that I had been *translated*, even in part, from a Coptic original.[26] So Lefort was making a separate point when he suggested that, if one *were* looking for a primitive Coptic life, dating possibly from the fourth century, S^1 would be an obvious choice.[27] His argument here *was* subjective, as he admitted (and it became positively dangerous when he compared the structure of S^1 with Theodore's account of the life of Pachomius in Bo, 194: S^1 *is* built on such a pattern; but can one be sure independently that Bo preserved

[19] Chitty, 'Pachomian Sources Reconsidered', 65.
[20] Veilleux, *Liturgie*, 34 f.
[21] Halkin, *Vitae Graecae*, 89*.
[22] Ibid. 90*.
[23] Halkin, op. cit. 89*, 101* f.
[24] Ibid. 103*; see Peeters, 'Le dossier copte', 277.
[25] Festugière, *Moines d'Orient*, iv, 2, 125 f.
[26] Chitty, 'Pachomian Sources Reconsidered', 70 f.
[27] Lefort, *Vies*, p. lxxii.

fourth-century tradition?). The investigations of Veilleux have made the suggestion more secure.[28]

Lefort attempted, finally, to link primitive Greek and primitive Coptic traditions, as he conceived them to be. It was particularly on this issue that Chitty took up arms. His criticism was negative once more. Instead of putting forward an alternative theory, based on fresh evidence, he again asked a question: had anyone yet proved that I must have been based on Coptic material?[29] He made the general point that everything (with one exception) common to the Greek, Latin, and Syriac texts on the one hand, and the Coptic texts on the other, could be found in I.[30] Seeking external evidence of a fourth-century date for I, Chitty argued that there had been an early MS. corpus that bound together I, the *Paralipomena*, and the *Letter of Ammon.*[31] After alleging, with persuasive argument, that these 'early Greek' texts were historically more accurate on some points than sources in Coptic, he suggested that much other material could have been derived from such a corpus—not only apophthegmata and I, but also Coptic texts that followed (when there had been apparent 'choice') I rather than the *Paralipomena.*[32]

However, when it came to passages in which Lefort had felt that I had drawn upon Coptic versions, Chitty merely repeated his suggestion that Lefort had made a subjective assessment, and asserted the superiority of his own impressions, which were entirely contrary.[33] Behind his brief but technical analyses lay a wider conviction: 'The freedom from emphasis either on sex or on vision or on miracle seem to the present writer (as it seemed to Ladeuze) one of the most refreshing characteristics of [I], and one of the strongest evidences of its early date'.[34] The same suppositions dominated his later article:

> The strongest argument for the priority of [I] over the surviving Coptic and Arabic documents lies in its retention of an earlier, more sober intellectual atmosphere, and a positive spiritual teaching, which suggest an age when paganism, with its false miracles, was still a very present reality. There is a guardedness in regard to miracles and visions which tends later to be discarded.[35]

This judgement deserves respect: it was not so much the conclusion to detailed documentation, as the fruit of many years familiarity with the sources.

Nevertheless, it seems in no way disrespectful to the memory of Chitty and Lefort to suggest that, while their scholarly achievements were considerable, their argument lost its momentum. Having thoroughly ground away the grains of evidence seemingly available, the academic mill was spinning free. On the specific point of the general relation between Greek and Coptic sources, it was Veilleux who carried

[28] Veilleux, *Liturgie*, 40 f.

[29] Chitty, op. cit. 47.

[30] Chitty, 'Pachomian Sources Reconsidered', 39.

[31] Loc. cit.

[32] Ibid. 46.

[33] Ibid. 67 ff.

[34] Chitty, op. cit. 69.

[35] Chitty, 'Pachomian Sources Once More', 56 f.

the matter further.[36] His conclusions, by his own admission, were still tentative, and they will undoubtedly encourage further debate; but the task will be lengthy and demanding: Ruppert is content to accept his argument.[37] The basic contention, already mentioned, is that priority cannot be decided merely by comparing Greek and Coptic documents: it is the Arabic tradition that betrays a pattern of dependence. Briefly, the suggestion is this: S^1 lies at the root of the biographical tradition. Two other primitive documents—a short life of Pachomius, and a life of Theodore (linked, perhaps, with S^{10})—combine to form a source for both Bo and I. Other sources are of secondary value, although S^3 must command respect.

[36] Veilleux, *Liturgie*, especially 49-107.
[37] Ruppert, *Pachomianische Mönchtum*, 3 ff.

APPENDIX II

GREEK AND LATIN VERSIONS OF THE *HISTORIA MONACHORUM* AND THE *LIFE OF ANTONY*

Comparison of Greek and Latin versions brings to light intriguing differences. The state of the Greek texts in the fourth century cannot be discovered with complete confidence;[1] but it is worth presenting a few examples (from among many) of the variations found, and useful to speculate with care about what the differences might signify.

1. THE *HISTORIA MONACHORUM*

(a) *HM* i, 395BC = (Gk) i. 20.

John emphasizes the value of reading the prophets; and the Latin continues, 'Qui utique ob hoc in omnibus Dei ecclesiis recitantur, ut exampla vitae hominibus, non de longinquis et peregrinis locis quaerantur, sed domi unusquisque et apud se habeat quod debeat imitari': in the Greek, *πανταχοῦ δὲ εἰσιν οἱ ἄξιοι θαύματος καὶ ἐπαίνου οἱ τοῦ θεοῦ προφῆται καὶ ἀπόστολοι οἱ ἐν ταῖς ἐκκλησίαις ἀναγινώσκονται' οὓς δεῖ μιμεῖσθαι.* The Latin states that the Bible is *read* in *private*: the Greek suggests that it is *heard* in a *liturgical* context. Might this reflect a contrast between the domesticated ascetics of the western aristocracy and the monastic communities of Egypt (now—*c*. 400—more closely involved in the worship of the church)?

(b) *HM* i, 404BD = i. 62 f.

John admits that men 'in the world' may achieve a degree of goodness. He refers to 'opera bona', 'actus religiosi et sancti', and in particular to 'hospitalitas', 'caritatis ministeria', and 'misericordiae ac visitationes'. Then, by contrast, he refers to ascetics, 'qui vero in exercitio mentis desudat, et spiritales intra semetipsum excolit sensus, longe illis superior iudicandus est'. He gives a general exhortation: 'quietem silentiumque diligite, et scientiae operam date, atque exercete vosmetipsos, ut frequenti collatione mentem vestram puram exhibeatis Deo'. This last is represented thus in the Greek: *τὴν ἡσυχίαν μεταδιώξατε πρὸς τὴν θεωρίαν ἀεὶ γυμναζόμενοι, ἵνα καθαρὸν κτήσησθε νοῦν τῷ θεῷ προσευχόμενοι*; and, of the good man 'in the world', the text says, *πρακτικὸς γὰρ καὶ ἐργάτης ἐστὶν τῶν ἐντολῶν, ἀλλὰ περὶ τὰ γήϊνα ἀσχολεῖται.* The ascetic, on the other hand, is described as *κρείττων γε μὴν τούτου καὶ μείζων ὁ θεωρητικός.* The Greek has developed a technical vocabulary to distinguish the active from the contemplative life,—the vocabulary of Evagrius of Pontus,—whereas the Latin does not

[1] See above, pp. 14–16.

yet possess the precise terms that Cassian would later propagate in the West.

(c) *HM* xv, 434B–435A = xiii. 7-10.
John (not of Lycopolis) has had a vision of an angel, and has become 'repletum scientiae et doctrinae gratia'.[2] The angel, speaking of gifts of the Spirit, says, 'et caelestis cibi, id est verbi et scientiae suae, tibi abundantiam donat'. John is then commanded to visit other ascetics, 'aedificare eos in verbo et doctrina Domini'.

In the Greek also, John has a vision, but not with this effect. The Latin words underlined above, with their implication of teaching authority, represent a considerable addition to the meaning of the text.[3]

Paragraph 10 of the Greek, however, suddenly opens, out of the blue, *ἀποκαλύπτετα δὲ αὐτῷ ποτε περὶ τῶν αὐτοῦ μοναστηρίων*. Latin and Greek then proceed together; but the Greek word *αὐτοῦ* is a little more possessive than the Latin 'de vicinis monasteriis'. The Latin gives a more coherent picture of development in John's career.

2. THE *LIFE OF ANTONY*

There are, of course, two Latin translations to compare with the Greek: the early, anonymous version, edited by H. Hoppenbrouwers (referred to here as L), and that of Evagrius of Antioch, printed beneath the Greek text in Migne (and referred to here as E).

(a) *V. Ant.* 5 (*PG* xxvi. 848B; Hoppenbrouwers, 78-81)
The Greek discusses how an ascetic might resist sexual fantasies: *ὁ δὲ τὸν Χριστὸν ἐνθυμούμενος, καὶ τὴν δι'αὐτὸν εὐγένειαν, καὶ τὸ νοερὸν τῆς ψυχῆς λογιζόμενος*. These phrases are reproduced in L, but omitted by E, who passes on (with the rest of the Greek) to fear of hell as a motive for rejecting temptation. This may have been a chance omission by E, or a failure in the MS. tradition. On the other hand, E may have felt that, in spite of *δι'αὐτὸν*, the Greek supplied too exalted or 'humanist' a picture of man's ability to achieve perfection. Jerome maintained more balance: 'facile rumpit haec vincula amor Christi et timor gehennae'.[4]

(b) *V. Ant.* 7 (*PG* xxvi. 853A; Hoppenbrouwers, 82-6)
τότε γὰρ ἔλεγεν ἰσχύειν τῆς ψυχῆς τὸν τόνον, ὅταν αἱ τοῦ σώματος ἀσθενῶσιν ἡδοναί. The contrast *τόνος/ἡδοναί* is between a quality of soul and a passing failure at bodily level (reproduced by the 'voluptates' or 'voluntates' of L[5]). E reads, 'Asserebatque sensum animi sic posse reviviscere, si corporis fuisset impetus fatigatus'. 'Impetus' has a more substantial ring than *ἡδοναί*, and implies (as the Greek does not) that inner liberation depends on a weakening of the body. It represents more the sentiments of Daniel: *ὅσον τὸ σῶμα θάλλει, τοσοῦτον ἡ ψυχὴ*

[2] See above, p. 42.
[3] Not given sufficient weight by Festugière, 'Le problème littéraire', 277.
[4] Jerome, *Ep.* xiv. 3.
[5] See Hoppenbrouwers, *La plus ancienne version latine*, 31.

λεπτύνεται· καὶ ὅσον τὸ σῶμα λεπτύνεται τοσοῦτον ἡ ψυχὴ θάλλει.[6] This harsher emphasis was repeated by Jerome: 'nobis non corporum cultus . . . sed animae vigor quaeritur, quae carnis infirmitate fit fortior'.[7]

(c) *V. Ant.* 14 (*PG* xxvi. 864 f. Hoppenbrouwers, 96-9)
Antony emerges from the Roman fort, after years of ascesis, *ὥσπερ ἐκ τινος ἀδύτου μεμυσταγωγημένος καὶ θεοφορούμενος*; and the Greek continues, *ἀλλ᾽ὅλος ἦν ἴσος, ὡς ὑπὸ τοῦ λόγου κυβερνώμενος, καὶ ἐν τῷ κατὰ φύσιν ἑστώς*. L is merely muddled here; but E seems to have been more calculating in his omissions: 'temperata mens aequali ad cuncta ferebatur examine'. He passes over, in particular, the implications of *κατὰ φύσιν*.[8]

(d) *V. Ant.* 55 (*PG* xxvi. 924B; Hoppenbrouwers, 149-52)
Ἕκαστος τὰς πράξεις, Antony says, *καὶ τὰ κινήματα τῆς ψυχῆς, ὡς μέλλοντες ἀλλήλοις ἀπαγγέλλειν, σημειώμεθα καὶ γράφωμεν· καὶ θαῤῥεῖτε, ὅτι, πάντως αἰσχυνόμενοι γνωσθῆναι, παυσόμεθα τοῦ ἁμαρτάνειν, καὶ ὅλως τοῦ ἐνθυμεῖσθαι τι φαῦλον.* The key word is *ὡς*—*ὡς μέλλοντες ἀλλήλοις ἀπαγγέλλειν*: it makes the exercise *imaginary*. The ascetic must *pretend* that others know his vices, and thus shame himself to a higher standard of behaviour. This is reproduced by L, with the phrase, 'quasi iudicantes proximis nostris'. E, on the other hand, takes the situation literally: 'necnon dicebat magnam esse ad virtutem viam, si singuli vel observarent quid agerent, vel universas mentium cogitationes fratribus referrent'. It is not clear whether E misunderstood the sense of the Greek, or chose to ignore it; nor, indeed, whether the Greek was subsequently changed, or whether E wished to adapt the *Life* to a more coenobitic situation.[9]

(e) *V. Ant.* 88 (*PG* xxvi. 965C; Hoppenbrouwers, 186 f.)
Πόσαι δὲ καὶ μνηστῆρας ἔχουσαι παρθένοι, καὶ μόνον ἀπὸ τοῦ πέραν ἰδοῦσαι τὸν Ἀντώνιον ἔμειναν τῷ Χριστῷ παρθένοι; in E, 'ad eius conspectum ab ipso pene thalamo recedentes, in ecclesiae matris gremio consederunt'. The phrase, 'in ecclesiae matris gremio', much more institutional than *τῷ Χριστῷ*, would have corresponded more closely to the experience and aspirations of the 'Aquileia circle', and of the Roman aristocracy. It may, indeed, have been an 'Aquileian phrase': compare the words of Jerome, addressed to Chromatius, 'ille [sc. Bonosus] inter minaces saeculi fluctus in tuto insulae, hoc est ecclesiae gremio'; and Chromatius himself saw the church as a mother.[10]

[6] G Daniel 4.
[7] Jerome, *Ep.* liv. 10.
[8] See Chitty, *Desert*, 4.
[9] See Dörries, 'Die Vita Antonii', 383.
[10] Jerome, *Ep.* vii. 3; Chromatius, *Sermo* xxxiii. 4 f.

APPENDIX III

THE MONASTIC TEACHING OF EVAGRIUS OF PONTUS

My purpose here is not to question the emphases of other commentators. Evagrius was a mystic, a master of spirituality. The portrait given by A. Guillaumont is accurate, and points to an important feature in Evagrius's life and teaching; and Marsili was undoubtedly justified in linking Evagrius, seen in this light, with Cassian.[1] I only wish to recall[2] that Evagrius had very practical things to say about the ascetic life; that he reflected, in doing so, features of asceticism outlined above, in Part One; and that his ability to combine the mystical and the practical in this way may denote and explain a similar breadth of purpose in Cassian, his pupil.[3]

Evagrius portrays an *élite,* the privileged recipients of esoteric wisdom.[4] But he does not take their excellence for granted: they must remember that virtuous laymen are better than negligent monks, and be careful not to give scandal to those who remain 'in the world'.[5] The ascetic group was subject to the rule of a master, the spiritual guide and constant companion of his disciples, a living witness to the value of experience.[6] He was also 'God's heir', imparting to his own 'children' the λόγος of God himself: a word that must be respected and obeyed.[7] Ascetics were dominated by the power of the word;[8] but they also

[1] A. Guillaumont, *Les 'Kephalaia Gnostica' d'Evagre le Pontique* (Paris, 1962); Marsili, *Giovanni Cassiano*.

[2] With Bousset, *Apophthegmata*, 304; and R. Draguet, 'L'"Histoire Lausiaque", une oeuvre écrite dans l'esprit d'Evagre', *RHE* xlii (1947), 39.

[3] The sources (to which I do no more than point) are as follows: (a) The *Practicus* (henceforward *P*), ed. A. Guillaumont (Paris, 1971): this provides a more just arrangement of the two collections in *PG* xl. 1221D–1236C; 1244B–1252C, together with certain parts of the *Antirrheticus*, ibid. 1272A–1276B; and it implements the principles first laid down by J. Muyldermans, 'La teneur du *Practicus* d'Evagre le Pontique', *Le Muséon*, xlii (1929), 74–89. (b) The *De Oratione* (henceforward *DO*), attributed to Nilus of Ancyra, *PG* lxxix. 1165–1200; and read in the light of I. Hausherr, 'Le traité de l'oraison d'Evagre le Pontique', *RAM* xv (1934), 34–93; 113–70. (c) *Evagriana Syriaca* (henceforward *ES*), ed. and trans. J. Muyldermans (Louvain, 1952). (d) *Nonnenspiegel und Mönchsspiegel des Euagrios Pontikos* (henceforward *NS* and *MS* respectively), ed. H. Gressmann, *Texte und Untersuchungen*, xxxix/4 (Berlin, 1913), 143–65.

[4] *P*. Preface.

[5] *MS* 34, 78, 113.

[6] *MS* 73; *ES* xi. 41.

[7] *MS* 1, 88.

[8] *DO* 74; *MS* 126.

valued a sense of tradition, and the continuity of monastic teaching. Experience gained in the past was as potent a force as the instruction of their present masters; and those now dead were regarded as patrons, whose prayers would protect the living monk.[9]

It was a society based on *ἀναχώρησις*, and in particular upon a flight from the body;[10] but this definition of withdrawal allowed scope for social development. Evagrius considered hermits superior, because they exposed themselves to the full force of demonic attack; but, precisely because of their isolation, precisely because they were no longer surrounded by material objects, the demons were compelled to attack them on an inner front, through their *λογισμοί*.[11] This inner battle with temptation came to be regarded as the typical task of the monk in his cell.[12] Evagrius also did as much to bring together as to divide the active and the contemplative: 'They meet together, with the Lord in the midst of them'.[13]

Together with a certain stripping away of the material world, there was an emphasis on poverty: 'Keep with you nothing but your cell, your cloak, your tunic, and the Gospels'. All other possessions must be given away at once, for the benefit of the poor—and one monk even sold his Gospels.[14] It is a dangerous temptation, says Evagrius, to imagine that one should not depend upon others for support.[15] Nevertheless, opportunity must be maintained for further generosity. The impulse to surrender worldly goods creates the proper atmosphere for prayer;[16] but it is also an enduring fulfilment of initial conversion, which will have quite practical effects, such as the service of the sick.[17] There must have been, therefore, some form of monastic property, *τα ὑπάρχοντα τῆς μονῆς*, upon which the generous monk could draw, in order to give to others.[18] In one passage, Evagrius says that ascetics should show generosity by giving food to those in need: in this way the poor, for a time at least, would have shared in the life of the monks, objects of monastic patronage.

Evagrius's monk, therefore, was not cut off completely. In order to cultivate, again, the proper atmosphere for prayer, he must remain at peace with his brothers, and must visit them frequently, eating in their company.[19] Evagrius makes more than occasional reference to the dangers of anger (a threat to prayer), implying that the contemplative

[9] *P*, Preface, 91, 100.
[10] *P* 52.
[11] *P* 5, 48.
[12] *P* 28; compare points made above, pp. 44-9.
[13] *MS* 121; compare 132.
[14] *P* 18, 97; *ES* i. 11; viii. 3.
[15] *P* 9; *ES* i. 2.
[16] *DO* 17; compare *P* 20.
[17] *P* 91; *MS* 53.
[18] *MS* 75.
[19] *DO* 21; *MS* 15.

life, as he understood it, was to some extent exposed to the distractions of society.[20] Nor was charity merely a matter of maintaining peace of mind: Evagrius understood the need for genuine sympathy.[21] He suggested that closeness to God could lead to greater closeness among brethren; that increasing perfection in prayer could draw a man back into the company of others: 'The monk is a man set apart, more than any other; and yet at one with all men'.[22]

This relatively social group was subject, not only to the authority of masters, but also to a rule. Evagrius echoed Pachomius, suggesting that the perfect will have no need of *νόμος*.[23] Yet he hints at the potential division between inner and visible obedience (and so, in another sense, between the active and the contemplative life): the mere keeping of commandments is no guarantee of spiritual strength, unless balanced by an understanding that springs from contemplation.[24] He writes of the ascetic *κανών*, even while pleading for adaptability.[25] He betrays a striking fear of judgement: 'Woe to the lawless man [*ἀνόμῳ*] on the day of his death'.[26]

Evagrius showed, too, a concern for the influence of the priesthood in ascetic society. He attempted to distinguish between priests, who purified monks through the celebration of the mysteries, and ascetic masters, who prepared them for battle with the demons.[27] But any monk with a reputation for sanctity, attracting disciples and admirers, could easily attribute his charismatic power to the supposed possession of priestly qualities.[28] Priests, properly regarded, interceded by their prayers for the rest of the community; but ascetics as a whole also enjoyed, with Evagrius's consent, an intercessory role.[29]

[20] *P* 25, 93.
[21] *MS* 87.
[22] *DO* 124.
[23] *P* 70; see above, p. 71.
[24] *P* 79.
[25] *P* 40.
[26] *MS* 22.
[27] *P* 100.
[28] *P* 13. For a possible link with Cassian, *Inst.* xi. 14, discussed above, p. 217 n. 85, see Marsili, *Giovanni Cassiano*, 92.
[29] *P* 100; *DO* 39, 122; see Hausherr, 'Le traité de l'oraison', 73 f., 152.

APPENDIX IV

CASSIAN'S DEPENDENCE ON ORAL TRADITION: SOME EXAMPLES

With regard to *Inst.* iv. 24,[1] Weber suggests that the examples of obedience given in the passage, referring as they do to men who were living eremitic lives, had been recast by Cassian, to make them more relevant to coenobites.[2] Comparing it with G John Colobos 1, he says, 'Wonder-working is the characteristic of the hermit: blind obedience is indispensable for community life'. This is to assume that Cassian knew the story as we now have it in G, or in Sulpicius, *Dial.* i. 19, with the subsequent flowering of the dry stick that John had been ordered to water; and that Cassian deliberately omitted this element. It is possible, however, that he reproduced an earlier, less miraculous version of the story[3]—in which case, his emphasis on obedience may just as much reflect the values of the desert hermits. Cassian was certainly not dependent on the later version of Pelagius and John, *Vitae Patrum*, V, xiv. 3: they follow the Greek, independently of Cassian.

Inst. iv. 27, similar to G Sisoes 10, may also depend on Cassian's memory of an oral tradition.[4]

I am not happy with Weber's suggestion that the dictum at the end of *Con.* vii. 23—'sedete in cellulis vestris et quantum libitum fuerit manducate et bibite atque dormite, dummodo in eis iugiter perduretis'—depends on a version of the Latin apophthegma, *Vitae Patrum*, V, vii. 27.[5] Cassian's words, 'sedete in cellulis vestris', are much closer to Greek equivalents, such as Nau 195;[6] but, since many of these, in their present form, are no more likely to be contemporary with (or earlier than) Cassian himself, his own statement may, again, reproduce an oral tradition.

Even more uncertain is the link forged by Weber between *Con.* viii. 15 f. and *Vitae Patrum*, V, v. 39.[7] He asserts that it is hard to decide which text depends on which, and therefore suggests an *Urform* for the pair. Nau 191, the Greek equivalent, (which Weber does not mention,) is no more likely as an *Urform*; and it is quite possible that here Cassian

[1] See above, p. 195.
[2] Weber, *Stellung*, 40, 111 ff.
[3] Chadwick, *Cassian*, 21.
[4] Weber, op. cit. 40.
[5] Weber, *Stellung*, 21.
[6] See above, p. 44.
[7] Weber, op. cit. 92.

has drawn upon an oral tradition only later transposed into Greek and Latin apophthegmata.

The most famous link between Cassian and the *Apophthegmata Patrum* concerns the dying words of John of Lycopolis, *Inst.* v. 28.[8] Both Bousset and Weber suggest that G Cassian 5 is dependent on the *Institutes*, rather than their source.[9] This might help to explain why the Latin equivalent, *Vitae Patrum*, V, i. 10, is so different from Cassian's text. G reproduces the *structure* of *Inst.* v. 28, while Pelagius and John reflect the *vocabulary* of G. The same is true of *Inst.* v. 27, to be linked with G Cassian 4 and *Vitae Patrum*, V, iv. 24. *Vitae Patrum*, V, iv. 25 is also connected with Cassian: *Con.* ii. 11. Weber is sure that Cassian's is the primary text: there is, again, a Greek equivalent, possibly intermediate between the two Latin versions, and not in G; but about its significance Weber will only speculate.[10] The conclusion must be, therefore, that Cassian, recounting the deathbed scene of John, could easily have been calling upon memory alone, without recourse to written sources.

[8] See above, p. 24.
[9] Bousset, *Apophthegmata*, 72; Weber, *Stellung*, 101.
[10] Weber op. cit. 103, n. 172.

BIBLIOGRAPHY

This is a selective list, incorporating all works cited in the text, together with some others that have contributed directly to the formulation of ideas and arguments. Major historical commentaries on late antiquity have been omitted, together with some treatments of early monasticism that are either entirely narrative descriptions or superseded by other works included.

Some texts are quoted under both author and editor, where this seemed likely to make reference more easy. In addition to individual articles taken from them, collections of articles, *Festschriften*, and *mélanges* are quoted under their titles, unless they form volumes in a periodical series, or contain papers all by the same author.

A: SOURCES

Ammianus Marcellinus, *Rerum Gestarum, quae supersunt*, ed. V. Gardthausen (2 vols., Stuttgart, 1967).

Antony, *Letters*, trans. G. Garitte from his own edn. *Lettres de saint Antoine, version géorgienne et fragments coptes, CSCO* cxlix, scriptores Iberici, 6 (Louvain, 1955).

Apophthegmata Patrum, alphabetical collection, *PG* lxv. 72–440.

Apophthegmata Patrum, anonymous collection, nos. 133–369, ed. F. Nau, 'Histoires des solitaires Egyptiens (MS Coislin 126, fol. 158 sqq.)', *ROC* xiii (1908), 47–57 (Nau 133–74); 266–83 (Nau 175–215); xiv (1909), 357–79 (Nau 216–97); xvii (1912), 204–11 (Nau 298–334); 294–301 (Nau 335–58); xviii (1913), 137–40 (Nau 359–69).

Athanasius, *Apologia contra Constantium, PG* xxv. 595–642.

—— *Apologia de Fuga Sua, PG* xxv. 643–80.

—— *Vita Antonii*, s.v. *Vita*.

Augustine, *Confessions*, ed. M. Skutella, revised H. Juergens and W. Schaub (Stuttgart, 1969).

—— *De Civitate Dei*, ed. B. Dombart and A. Kalb, with minor amendments, *CC*, ser. lat. xlvii, xlviii (2 vols., Turnhout, 1955).

—— *De Moribus Ecclesiae Catholicae, PL* xxxii. 1309–44.

—— *Enarrationes in Psalmos*, revised edn. D. E. Dekkers and I. Fraipont, *CC*, ser. lat. xxxviii–xl (3 vols., Turnhout, 1956).

—— *Letters, PL* xxxiii; *CSEL* xxxiv, xliv, lvii, lviii.

Ausonius, *Opuscula*, ed. R. Peiper (Leipzig, 1886).

Cassian, *Conlationes* [*Conferences*], ed. M. Petschenig, *CSEL* xiii (Vienna, 1886).

—— *De Incarnatione Domini contra Nestorium*, ed. M. Petschenig, *CSEL* xvii (Vienna, 1888), 235–391.

Cassian, *De Institutis Coenobiorum et de Octo Principalium Vitiorum Remediis* [*Institutes*], ed. M. Petschenig, *CSEL* xvii (Vienna, 1888), 3-231.

Celestine I, Pope, *Epistolae et Decreta, PL* l. 417-618.

Chromatius of Aquileia, *Sermons*, ed. R. Etaix and J. Lemarié, *CC*, ser. lat. ixA (Turnhout, 1974).

Chronica Minora I and II, ed. Th. Mommsen, *MGH*, auct. antiquiss. ix, xi (new edns., Berlin, 1961).

Codex Theodosianus, ed. Th. Mommsen (Berlin, 1905).

Concilia Galliae, 314-506, ed. C. Munier, *CC* ser. lat. cxlviii (Turnhout, 1963).

Cyril of Scythopolis, *Vita Euthymii*, s.v. *Vita*.

Dionysius Exiguus, *Vita Sancti Pachomii*, s.v. *Vita*.

Epigramma Paulini, ed. C. Schenkl, *CSEL* xvi (Vienna, 1888), 503-8.

Esaias of Scetis, *Asceticon*, ed. R. Draguet, with separate comm. and trans., *Les cinq recensions de l'Ascéticon syriaque d'abba Isaie, CSCO* cclxxxix-ccxc, ccxciii-ccxciv, scriptores Syriaci, 120-3 (Louvain, 1968).

Eucherius of Lyon, *De Laude Heremi*, ed. C. Wotke, *CSEL* xxxi (Vienna, 1894), 177-94.

Eunapius of Sardis, *Vitae Sophistarum*, ed. J. Giangrande (Rome, 1956).

Eutropius Presbyter, *Letters* = Pseudo-Jerome, *Epp.* ii, vi, xix, *PL* xxx.

Evagrius of Antioch, *Vita Antonii*, s.v. *Vita*.

Evagrius of Pontus, *De Oratione, PG* lxxix, 1165-1200.

—— *Evagriana Syriaca, textes inédites du British Museum et de la Vaticane*, ed. and trans. J. Muyldermans (Bibliothèque du Muséon, xxxi; Louvain, 1952).

—— *Nonnenspiegel und Mönchsspiegel des Euagrios Pontikos*, ed. H. Gressmann, *Texte und Untersuchungen*, xxxix/4 (Berlin, 1913), 143-65.

—— *Practicus*, ed. A. and C. Guillaumont, with introd., trans., and comm., *Evagre le Pontique, Traité pratique ou le moine* (Sources chrétiennes, clxx, clxxi; Paris, 1971).

Gennadius, *De Scriptoribus Ecclesiasticis*, lxii, *CSEL* xvii (Vienna, 1888), pp. cxv-cxvi.

Hilary of Arles, *Sermo de Vita Sancti Honorati*, ed. S. Cavallin, *Honorati et Hilarii, Vitae Sanctorum* (Skrifter Utgivna av Vetenakapssocieteten, i; Lund, 1952).

Hilary of Poitiers, *Ad Constantium, PL* x. 557-64; 563-72.

—— *Contra Auxentium, PL* x. 609-18.

—— *Contra Constantium Imperatorem, PL* x. 577-606.

Historia Monachorum in Aegypto, Greek text ed. A.-J. Festugière (Subsidia Hagiographica, xxxiv; Brussels, 1961).

—— Latin version by Rufinus, *PL* xxi. 387-462.

Hydatius, *Continuatio*, ed. Th. Mommsen, *Chronica Minora*, II, q.v.

Innocent I, Pope, *Epistolae et Decreta, PL* xx. 463-612.

Isaiah of Scetis, s.v. Esaias.

Januarius, *Letter* to Valentinus of Hadrumetum, ed. G. Morin, 'Lettres inédites de saint Augustin et du prêtre Januarien dans l'affaire des moines d'Adrumète', *RB* xviii (1901), 247-53.

Jerome, *Adversus Iovinianum, PL* xxiii. 211-338.

—— *Altercatio Luciferiani et Orthodoxi, PL* xxiii. 155-82.

—— *Apologia adversus Libros Rufini, PL* xxiii. 397-492.

—— *Comm. in Ep. ad Galatas, PL* xxvi. 331-468.

—— *Comm. in Ep. ad Titum, PL* xxvi. 555-600.

—— *Comm. in Isaiam*, ed. M. Adriaen, *CC* ser. lat. lxxiiiA (Turnhout, 1963).

—— *Contra Vigilantium, PL* xxiii. 339-52.

—— *De Spiritu Sancto, PL* xxiii. 101-54.

—— *Epistolae*, ed. I. Hilberg, *CSEL* liv (Vienna, 1909), lv (1912), lvi (1918).

—— *Opera Homiletica*, ed. G. Morin, *CC* ser. lat. lxxviii (Turnhout, 1958).

—— *Vitae*, s.v. *Vita.*

Life, s.v. *Vita.*

Nau, F., Anonymous collection of apophthegmata, s.v. *Apophthegmata.*

Orientius of Auch, *Commonitorium*, ed. R. Ellis, *CSEL* xvi (Vienna, 1888), 205-43.

Orsisius, *Liber*, ed. A. Boon, *Pachomiana Latina* (Bibliothèque de la Revue d'Histoire Ecclésiastique, vii; Louvain, 1932), 109-47.

Pachomius, *Catéchèse à propos d'un moine rancunier*, trans. from his own edn. L. Th. Lefort, *Oeuvres de saint Pachôme et de ses disciples, CSCO* clx, scriptores Coptici, 24 (Louvain, 1956), 1-26.

—— *Praecepta*, etc. [*Rule*], ed. A. Boon, *Pachomiana Latina* (Bibliothèque de la Revue d'Histoire Ecclésiastique, vii; Louvain, 1932), 13-74.

—— *Vitae Pachomii*, s.v. *Vita.*

Palladius, *Dialogus de Vita Sancti Johannis Chrysostomi*, ed. P. R. Coleman-Norton (Cambridge, 1928).

—— *Historia Lausiaca*, ed. with introd. and comm. C. Butler, *The Lausiac History of Palladius*, ii (Texts and Studies, ed. J. Armitage Robinson, vi/2; Cambridge, 1904).

Paulinus of Milan, *Vita Beati Ambrosii*, s.v. *Vita.*

Paulinus of Pella, *Eucharisticos*, ed. W. Brandes, *CSEL* xvi (Vienna, 1888), 289-314.

Possidius, *Vita Augustini*, s.v. *Vita.*

Prosper of Aquitaine, *Epitoma de Chronicon*, ed. Th. Mommsen, *Chronica Minora* I, q.v.

Regula Magistri, ed. with introd. and comm. A. de Vogüé (Sources chrétiennes, cv-cvii; Paris, 1964-5).

Rufinus, *Historia Ecclesiastica*, ed. Th. Mommsen, in *Eusebius Werke*, ii/1-3 (Leipzig, 1903, 1908-9).

—— *Historia Monachorum*, q.v.

Rutilius Namatianus, *De Reditu Suo*, ed. with introd., French trans. and comm. J. Vessereau and F. Préchac (Paris, 1933).

Salvian, *Ad Ecclesiam*, ed. F. Pauly, *CSEL* viii (Vienna, 1883), 224-316.

—— *De Gubernatione Dei*, ed. C. Halm, *MGH*, auct. antiquiss. i/1 (Berlin, 1887).

Serapion of Thmuis, *Letter*, ed. with Latin trans. R. Draguet, 'Une lettre de Sérapion de Thmuis aux disciples d'Antoine (A.D. 356) en version syriaque et arménienne', *Le Muséon*, lxiv (1951), 1-25.

Siricius, Pope, *Epistolae et Decreta, PL* xiii. 1131-94.

Sulpicius Severus, *Dialogi*, ed. C. Halm, *CSEL* i (Vienna, 1866), 152-216.

—— *Vita Martini*, s.v. *Vita.*

Theodore, *Catéchèses*, ed. L. Th. Lefort, *Oeuvres de saint Pachôme et de ses disciples, CSCO* clx, scriptores Coptici, 24 (Louvain, 1956), 38-61.

Victricius of Rouen, *De Laude Sanctorum, PL* xx. 443-58.

Vincent of Lérins, *Commonitorium*, ed. R. S. Moxon (Cambridge, 1915).

Vigilius, *Regula Orientalis, PL* 1. 373-80.

Vita Ambrosii (Paulinus of Milan), ed. with introd., Italian trans. and comm. M. Pellegrino (Rome, 1961).

Vita Antonii (Athanasius), *PG* xxvi. 837-976.

—— Latin trans. (Evagrius of Antioch), printed beneath the Greek text in *PG.*

—— Latin trans. (anon.), ed. H. Hoppenbrouwers, *La plus ancienne version latine de la vie de saint Antoine par saint Athanase* (Nijmegen, 1960).

Vita Augustini (Possidius), ed. with introd., Italian trans. and comm. M. Pellegrino (Alba, 1955).

Vita Euthymii (Cyril of Scythopolis), ed. E. Schwartz, *Texte und Untersuchungen*, xlix/2 (Berlin, 1939), 3-85.

Vita Hilarii, ed. S. Cavallin, *Honorati et Hilarii, Vitae Sanctorum* (Skrifter Utgivna av Vetenskapssocieteten, i; Lund, 1952).

Vita Hilarionis (Jerome), *PL* xxiii. 29-54.

Vita Malchi Monachi Captivi (Jerome), *PL* xxiii. 53-60.

Vita Martini (Sulpicius Severus), ed. with introd., French trans. and comm. J. Fontaine, *Vie de saint Martin* (Sources chrétiennes, cxxxiii-cxxxv; Paris, 1967-9).

Vita Melaniae, Greek text ed. with introd., French trans. and comm. D. Gorce, *Vie de sainte Melanie* (Sources chrétiennes, xc; Paris, 1962).

Vita(e) Pachomii, Greek texts ed. F. Halkin, *Sancti Pachomii Vitae Graecae* (Subsidia Hagiographica, xix; Brussels, 1932).

—— Bohairic Life,ed. L. Th. Lefort, *Sancti Pachomii Vita Bohairice Scripta, CSCO*, scriptores Coptici, textus, ser. iii, t. 7 (Paris, 1925).

Vita(e) Pachomii, Sahidic texts, ed. L. Th. Lefort, *Sancti Pachomii Vitae Sahidice Scripta, CSCO*, scriptores Coptici, textus, ser. iii, t. 8 (Paris, 1933).
—— Bohairic and Sahidic texts trans. L. Th. Lefort, *Les vies coptes de saint Pachôme et de ses premiers successeurs* (Bibliothèque du Muséon, xvi; Louvain, 1943).
—— Latin trans. (Dionysius Exiguus), ed. H. van Cranenburgh, *La vie latine de saint Pachôme, traduite du grec par Denys le Petit* (Subsidia Hagiographica, xlvi; Brussels, 1969).
Vita(e) Patrum, systematic Latin trans. of some of the *Apophthegmata Patrum* (Pelagius and John), *PL* lxxiii. 851-1062.
Vita Pauli (Jerome), *PL* xxiii. 17-28.

B: SECONDARY WORKS

Adnès, A. and Canivet, P., 'Guérisons miraculeuses et exorcismes dans l'"Histoire Philothée" de Théodoret de Cyr', *RHR* clxxi (1967), 53-82; 149-79.
Andrieu-Guitrancourt, P., 'La vie ascétique à Rouen au temps de saint Victrice', *RSR* xl (1952), 90-106.
Antin, P., 'Hilarius Gallicano cothurno attolitur', *RB* lvii (1947), 82-8.
—— ' "Simple" et "simplicité" chez saint Jérôme', *RB* lxxi (1961), 371-81.
Antonius Magnus Eremita, ed. B. Steidle (Studia Anselmiana, xxxviii; Rome, 1956).
Arbesmann, R., 'Fasting and Prophecy in Pagan and Christian Antiquity', *Traditio*, vii (1949-51), 1-71.
Aubin, P., *Le problème de la conversion* (Paris, 1963).
Auerbach, E., *Literary Language and its Public in Late Latin Antiquity and in the Middle Ages*, trans. R. Manheim (London, 1965).
Babut, E.-C., *Saint Martin de Tours* (Paris, 1913).
Bacht, H., 'Antonius und Pachomius: von der Anachorese zum Cönobitentum', *Antonius Magnus Eremita* (q.v.), 66-107.
—— 'L'importance de l'idéal monastique de saint Pachôme pour l'histoire du monachisme chrétien', *RAM* xxvi (1950), 308-26.
—— 'Pakhôme et ses disciples', *Théologie de la vie monastique* (q.v.), 39-71.
—— *Das Vermächtnis des Ursprungs, Studien zum frühen Mönchtum*, i (Studien zur Theologie des geistlichen Lebens, v; Würzburg, 1972).
Bardy, G., 'Les origines des écoles monastiques en Occident', *Sacris Erudiri*, v (1953), 86-104.
Bartelink, G., 'Observations de critique textuelle sur la plus ancienne version latine de la Vie de saint Antoine par saint Athanase', *RB* lxxxi (1971), 92-5.
Baynes, N. H., 'Alexandria and Constantinople: a Study in Ecclesiastical Diplomacy', in his *Byzantine Studies and Other Essays* (repr. London, 1960), 97-115.

Bell, H. I., 'Athanasius: a Chapter in Church History', *Congregational Quarterly*, iii (1925), 158–76.

—— *Jews and Christians in Egypt, the Jewish Troubles in Alexandria and the Athanasian Controversy* (British Museum, 1924).

Benoit, F., 'Le *martyrium* rupestre de l'Abbaye Saint-Victor', *CR*, 1966, 110–25.

Boon, A., *Pachomiana Latina* (Bibliothèque de la Revue d'Histoire Ecclésiastique, vii; Louvain, 1932).

Bousset, W., *Apophthegmata, Textüberlieferung und Charakter der Apophthegmata Patrum; zur Überlieferung der Vita Pachomii; Euagrios-Studien* (Tübingen, 1923).

—— 'Das Mönchtum der sketischen Wüste', *ZK* xlii (1923), 1–41.

Bowersock, G. W., *Greek Sophists in the Roman Empire* (Oxford, 1969).

Brown, Peter, 'Approaches to the Religous Crisis of the Third Century A.D.', *EHR* lxxxiii (1968), 542–58; repr. in his *Religion and Society in the Age of Saint Augustine* (London, 1972), 74–93.

—— 'Aspects of the Christianization of the Roman Aristocracy', *JRS* li (1961), 1–11; *Religion and Society*, 161–82.

—— *Augustine of Hippo* (London, 1967).

—— 'The Patrons of Pelagius: the Roman Aristocracy between East and West', *JTS*, n.s. xxi (1970), 56–72; *Religion and Society*, 208–26.

—— 'Pelagius and his Supporters', *JTS*, n.s. xix (1968), 93–114; *Religion and Society*, 183–207.

—— 'The Rise and Function of the Holy Man in Late Antiquity', *JRS* lxi (1971), 80–101.

Butler, C., *The Lausiac History of Palladius* (Texts and Studies, ed. J. Armitage Robinson, vi/1 and 2; Cambridge, 1898, 1904).

—— *Palladiana, an Examination of R. Reitzenstein's Monograph Historia Monachorum und Historia Lausiaca* (Oxford, 1921).

Cameron, A., 'Rutilius Namatianus, St Augustine, and the Date of the *De Reditu*', *JRS* lvii (1967), 31–9.

Capelle, B., 'Cassien, le Maître et saint Bénoît', *RTAM* xi (1939), 110–18.

Cavallera, F., 'L'héritage littéraire et spirituel du prêtre Eutrope (IVe–Ve siècles)', *RAM* xxiv (1948), 60–71.

—— *Saint Jérôme, sa vie et son oeuvre*, i/1 and 2 (Spicilegium Sacrum Lovaniense, études et documents, i and ii; Louvain, 1922).

Chadwick, O., 'Euladius of Arles', *JTS* xlvi (1945), 200–5.

—— *John Cassian*, 1st edn. (Cambridge, 1950); 2nd edn. (Cambridge, 1968).

Chastagnol, A., *La préfecture urbaine à Rome sous le Bas-Empire* (Publications de la Faculté des Lettres et Sciences Humaines d'Alger, xxxiv; Paris, 1960).

Chitty, D., 'Abba Isaiah', *JTS*, n.s. xxii (1971), 47–72.

—— *The Desert a City* (Oxford, 1966).

—— 'A Note on the Chronology of the Pachomian Foundations', *Studia Patristica*, ii, Papers presented to the Second International Conference on Patristic Studies, held at Christ Church, Oxford, 1955, ed. K. Aland and F. L. Cross = *Texte und Untersuchungen*, lxiv (Berlin, 1957), 379-85.

—— 'Pachomian Sources Once More', *Studia Patristica*, x, Papers presented to the Fifth International Conference on Patristic Studies, Oxford, 1967, ed. F. L. Cross = *Texte und Untersuchungen*, cvii (Berlin, 1970), 54-64.

—— 'Pachomian Sources Reconsidered', *JEH* v (1954), 38-77.

Columbás, G., 'El concepto de monje y vida monástica hasta fines del siglo V', *Studia Monastica*, i (1959), 257-342.

Commentationes in Regulam Sancti Benedicti, ed. B. Steidle (Studia Anselmiana, xlii; Rome, 1957).

Courcelle, P., *Histoire littéraire des grandes invasions germaniques*, 3rd edn. (Paris, 1964).

—— 'Paulin de Nole et saint Jérôme', *REL* xxv (1947), 250-80.

—— 'Possidius et les *Confessions* de saint Augustin', *RSR* xxxix (1951), 428-42.

—— *Recherches sur les Confessions de saint Augustin* (Paris, 1950).

Crouzel, H., 'Origène, précurseur du monachisme', *Théologie de la vie monastique* (q.v.), 15-38.

Crum, W., 'Inscriptions from Shenoute's Monastery', *JTS* v (1903-4), 552-69.

Danielou, J., *Études d'exégèse judéochrétienne* (Théologie historique, v; Paris, 1966).

Daumas, F., 'L'activité de l'Institut Français d'Archéologie Orientale durant l'année 1965-66', *CR* 1966, 298-309.

—— 'Les travaux de l'Institut Français d'Archéologie Orientale pendant l'année 1966-67', *CR* 1967, 436-51.

De Clercq, G., 'L'influence de la règle de saint Pachôme en Occident', *Mélanges d'histoire du moyen âge, dédiés à la mémoire de Louis Halphen* (q.v.), 169-76.

Delehaye, H., 'Saint Martin et Sulpice Sévère', *AB* xxxviii (1920), 6-136.

De Mendieta, E. D. Amand, *L'ascèse monastique de saint Basile* (Maredsous, 1949).

—— 'La virginité chez Eusèbe d'Emèse et l'ascétisme familial dans la première moitié du IVe siècle', *RHE* l (1955), 777-820.

Dempf, A., 'Evagrios Pontikos als Metaphysiker und Mystiker', *Philosophisches Jahrbuch*, lxxvii (1970), 297-319.

De Vogüé, A., 'L'anecdote pachômienne du "Vaticanus graecus" 2091. Son origine et ses sources', *RHS* xlix (1973), 401-19.

—— 'Monachisme et église dans la pensée de Cassien', *Théologie de la vie monastique* (q.v.), 213-40.

—— 'Le monastère, église du Christ', *Commentationes in Regulam Sancti Benedicti* (q.v.), 25-46.

—— 'Les pièces latines du dossier pachômien: remarques sur quelques publications récentes', *RHE* lxvii (1972), 26-67.

De Vries, W., 'Die Ostkirche und die Cathedra Petri im IV. Jahrhundert', *OCP* xi (1974), 114-44.

Diesner, H.-J., 'Possidius und Augustinus', *Studia Patristica*, vi, Papers presented to the Third International Conference on Patristic Studies, held at Christ Church, Oxford, 1959, ed. F. L. Cross = *Texte und Untersuchungen*, lxxxi (Berlin, 1962), 350-65.

Dion, J. and Oury, G., *Les sentences des pères du désert: les apophthegmes des pères (recension de Pélage et Jean)*, trans. with introd. by L. Regnault (Solesmes, 1966).

Dörries, H., 'Die Vita Antonii als Geschichtsquelle', *Nachrichten der Akademie der Wissenschaften in Göttingen*, phil.-hist. Klasse, 1949, 359-410.

Draguet, R., 'Le chaptire de l'*Histoire Lausiaque* sur les Tabennésiotes dérive-t-il d'une source copte?', *Le Muséon*, lvii (1944), 53-145; lviii (1945), 15-95.

—— *Les cinq recensions de l'Ascéticon syriaque d'Abba Isaïe*, ed. with introd. and trans., *CSCO* cclxxxix, ccxc, ccxciii, ccxciv, scriptores Syriaci, 120-3 (Louvain, 1968).

—— 'L' "Histoire Lausiaque", une oeuvre écrite dans l'esprit d'Evagre', *RHE* xli (1946), 321-64; xlii (1947), 5-49.

—— 'Notre édition des recensions syriaques de l'"Ascéticon" d'abba Isaïe', *RHE* lxiii (1968), 843-57.

Duval, Y.-M., 'L'éloge de Théodose dans la *Cité de Dieu* (V, 26, 1): sa place, son sens et ses sources', *Recherches Augustiniennes*, iv (1966), 135-79.

—— 'Sur les insinuations de Jérôme contre Jean de Jérusalem: de l'Arianisme à l'Origènisme', *RHE* lxv (1970), 353-74.

Festugière, A.-J., *Antioche païenne et chrétienne: Libanius, Chrysostome et les moines de Syrie* (Bibliothèques des Ecoles Françaises d'Athènes et de Rome, cxciv; Paris, 1959).

—— *Les moines d'Orient* (4 vols., Paris, 1961-5).

—— 'Le problème littéraire de l'Historia Monachorum', *Hermes*, lxxxiii (1955), 257-84.

Florovsky, G., 'The Anthropomorphites in the Egyptian Desert', *Akten des XI. Internationalen Byzantinisten-Kongresses, München, 1958*, ed. F. Dölger and H.-G. Beck (Munich, 1960), 154-9.

Fontaine, J., 'Une clé littéraire de la Vita Martini de Sulpice Sévère: la typologie prophétique', *Mélanges offerts à Mlle Christine Mohrmann* (q.v.), 84-95.

—— *Sulpice Sévère, Vie de saint Martin*, ed. with introd., French trans. and comm. (Sources chrétiennes, cxxxiii-cxxxv; Paris 1967-9).

—— 'Vérité et fiction dans la chronologie de la Vita Martini', *Saint Martin et son temps* (q.v.), 189-236.

Frank, K. S., 'Gehorsam und Freiheit im frühen Mönchtum', *Römische Quartalschrift*, lxiv (1969), 234-45.

Frend, W. H. C., 'The Winning of the Countryside', *JEH* xviii (1967), 1-14.

Garitte, G., 'A propos des lettres de saint Antoine l'ermite', *Le Muséon*, lii (1939), 11-31.

—— 'Un fragment grec attribué à saint Antoine l'ermite', ed. with comm., *Bulletin de l'Institut Historique Belge de Rome*, xx (1939), 165-70.

—— *Lettres de saint Antoine, version géorgienne et fragments coptes*, *CSCO* cxlix, scriptores Iberici, 6 (Louvain, 1955).

—— *Un témoin important du texte de la vie de saint Antoine, la version latine inédite des archives du Chapitre de saint Pierre à Rome* (Brussels, 1939).

—— 'Le texte grec et les versions anciennes de la vie de saint Antoine', *Antonius Magnus Eremita* (q.v.), 1-12.

Gorce, D., 'Comment travaillait saint Jérôme', *RAM* xxv (1949), 117-39.

Gordini, G., 'Origine e sviluppo del monachesimo a Roma', *Gregorianum*, xxxvii (1956), 220-60.

Gribomont, J., 'L'influence du monachisme oriental sur Sulpice Sévère', *Saint Martin et son temps* (q.v.), 135-49.

—— 'Saint Basile', *Théologie de la vie monastique* (q.v.), 99-113.

Griffe, E., 'Cassien a-t-il été prêtre d'Antioche?', *BLE* lv (1954), 240-4.

—— 'L'Epigramma Paulini, poème gallo-romain du Ve siècle', *REA* ii (1956), 187-94.

—— *La Gaule chrétienne à l'époque romaine*, 2nd edn. (Paris, 1964-6).

—— 'La pratique religieuse en Gaule au Ve siècle, *saeculares* et *sancti*', *BLE* lxiii (1962), 241-67.

Guillaumont, A., *Les 'Kephalaia Gnostica' d'Evagre le Pontique* (Patristica Sorbonensia, v; Paris, 1962).

—— 'Un philosophe au désert: Evagre le Pontique', *RHR* clxxxi (1972). 29-56.

—— 'Premières fouilles au site des Kellia (Basse-Egypte)', *CR* 1965, 218-25.

—— 'Le site des "Cellia" (Basse-Egypte)', *Revue Archéologique*, 1964, ii, 43-50.

Guy, J.-C., 'Les Apophthegmata Patrum', *Théologie de la vie monastique* (q.v.), 73-83.

—— 'Le centre monastique de Scété dans la littérature du Ve siècle', *OCP* xxx, 1 (1964), 129-47.

—— *Jean Cassien, Institutions cénobitiques*, ed. with introd., French trans. and comm. (Sources chrétiennes, cix; Paris, 1965).

—— *Jean Cassien, vie et doctrine spirituelle* (Paris, 1961).

—— 'Note sur l'évolution du genre apophtégmatique', *RAM* xxxii (1956), 63-8.

—— *Recherches sur la tradition grecque des Apophthegmata Patrum* (Subsidia Hagiographica, xxxvi; Brussels, 1962).

—— 'Remarques sur le texte des Apophtegmata Patrum', *RSR* xliii (1955), 252-8.

Hagendahl, H., *Latin Fathers and the Classics, a Study on the Apologists, Jerome and other Christian Writers* (Studia Graeca et Latina Gothoburgensia, vi; Goteborg, 1958).

Halkin, F., 'L'Histoire Lausiaque et les vies grecques de saint Pachôme', *AB* xlviii (1930), 257-301.

—— *Sancti Pachomii Vitae Graecae* (Subsidia Hagiographica, xix;

Brussels, 1932).
Halphen, L., s.v. *Mélanges*.
Harmand, L., *Le patronat sur les collectivités publiques, des origines au Bas-Empire* (Paris, 1957).
Hausherr, I., 'Spiritualité monacale et unité chrétienne', *OCA* cliii (1958), 13-32.
—— 'Le traité de l'oraison d'Evagre le Pontique', *RAM* xv (1934), 34-93; 113-70.
Holl, K., 'Die schriftstellerische Form des griechischen Heiligenlebens', *Neuen Jahrbüchern für das klassische Altertum*, 1912, 406-27.
Hopkins, M. K., 'Social Mobility in the Later Roman Empire: the Evidence of Ausonius', *CQ*, n.s. xi (1961), 239-49.
Hoppenbrouwers, H., *La plus ancienne version latine de la vie de saint Antoine par saint Athanase* (Nijmegen, 1960).
Hunt, E. D., 'Palladius of Helenopolis: a Party and its Supporters in the Church of the Late Fourth Century', *JTS*, n.s. xxiv (1973), 456-80.
Jullian, C., 'La jeunesse de saint Martin' ('Note gallo-romaine, 47'), *REA* xii (1910), 260-80.
—— 'Remarques critiques sur les sources de la Vie de saint Martin' ('Notes gallo-romaines, 93-5'), *REA* xxiv (1922), 37-47; 123-8; 229-35.
—— 'Remarques critiques sur la vie et l'oeuvre de saint Martin' ('Notes gallo-romaines, 96-9'), *REA* xxiv (1922), 306-12; xxv (1923), 49-55; 139-43; 234-50.
Kellia 1965, ed. R. Kasser (Recherches suisses d'archéologie copte, i: Geneva, 1967).
Kelly, J. N. D., *Jerome, his Life, Writings, and Controversies* (London, 1975).
Kemmer, A., 'Gregorius Nyssenus estne inter fontes Joannis Cassiani numerandus?', *OCP* xxi (1955), 451-66.
Kirk, K. E., *The Vision of God* (London, 1931).
Klauser, Th., s.v. *Mullus*.
Klejna, F., 'Antonius und Ammonas, eine Untersuchung über Herkunft und Eigenart der ältesten Mönchbriefe', *Zeitschrift für katholische Theologie*, lxii (1938), 309-48.
Labourt, J., *Saint Jérôme, Lettres*, ed. with introd., French trans. and comm. (Paris, 1949-63).
Leclercq, H., 'Primuliac', *DAGL* xiv, 2 (1948), 1781-98.
Leclercq, J., 'Saint Jérôme, docteur de l'ascèse, d'après un centon monastique', *RAM* xxv (1949), 140-5.
Lefort, L. Th., *Oeuvres de saint Pachôme et de ses disciples*, ed. and trans., *CSCO* clix-clx, scriptores Coptici, 23-4 (Louvain, 1956).
—— 'Les sources coptes Pachômiennes', *Le Muséon*, lxvii (1954), 217-29.
—— *Les vies coptes de saint Pachôme et de ses premiers successeurs* (Bibliothèque du Muséon, xvi; Louvain, 1943).
Leloir, L., 'Essai sur la silhouette spirituelle du moine d'après la collec-

tion arménienne des Apophtegmes', *Revue des Études Arméniennes*, n.s. v (1968), 199–230.
Lemaitre, I., 'La contemplation chez les grecs et autres orientaux chrétiens', *RAM* xxvi (1950), 121–72; xxvii (1951), 41–74.
Lorenz, R., 'Die Anfänge des abendländischen Mönchtums im 4. Jahrhundert', *ZK* lxxvii (1966), 1–61.
Lorié, L., *Spiritual Terminology in the Latin Translations of the Vita Antonii* (Latinitas Christianorum Primaeva, xi; Nijmegen, 1955).
Luck, G., 'Die Form der Suetonischen Biographie und die frühen Heiligenviten', *Mullus* (q.v.), 230–41.
Lütcke, K.-H., *'Auctoritas' bei Augustin* (Stuttgart, 1968).
Madoz, J., *El concepto de la tradición en s. Vicente de Lérins* (Analecta Gregoriana, v; Rome, 1933).
—— 'Herencia literaria del presbítero Eutropio', *Estudios Eclesiásticos*, xvi (1942), 27–54.
Mähler, M., 'Denys le Petit, traducteur de la Vie de saint Pachôme', *La vie latine de saint Pachôme*, ed. H. van Cranenburgh (q.v.), 28–48.
Mâle, E., *La fin du paganisme en Gaule et les plus anciennes basiliques chrétiennes* (Paris, 1950).
Malone, E., *The Monk and the Martyr* (Studies in Christian Antiquity, xii; Washington, 1950).
Marrou, H.-I., 'Le dossier épigraphique de l'évêque Rusticus de Narbonne', *Rivista di Archeologia Cristiana*, iii–iv (1970), 331–40.
—— 'Le fondateur de Saint-Victor de Marseille: Jean Cassien', *Provence Historique*, xvi (1966), 297–308.
—— 'Jean Cassian à Marseille', *RMAL* i (1945), 5–26.
—— 'La patrie de Jean Cassien', *OCP* xiii (1947), 588–96.
Marsili, S., *Giovanni Cassiano ed Evagrio Pontico* (Studia Anselmiana, v; Rome 1936).
Mélanges d'histoire du moyen âge, dédiés à la mémoire de Louis Halphen (Paris, 1951).
Mélanges offerts à Mlle Christine Mohrmann (Utrecht-Anvers, 1963).
Mémorial de l'Année Martinienne, M.DCCCC.LX–M.DCCCC.LXI, Seizième centenaire de l'Abbaye de Ligugé, Centenaire de la découverte du tombeau de saint Martin à Tours, ed. G. Le Bras (Bibliothèque de la Société d'Histoire Ecclésiastique de la France; Paris, 1962).
Mertel, H., *Die biographische Form der griechischen Heiligenlegenden* (Munich, 1909).
Meslin, M., *Les Ariens d'Occident, 335–430* (Patristica Sorbonensia, viii; Paris, 1967).
Mohrmann, Christine, 'Note sur la version latine la plus ancienne de la Vie de saint Antoine par saint Athanase', *Antonius Magnus Eremita* (q.v.), 35–44.
—— 'Le rôle des moines dans la transmission du patrimonie latin', *Mémorial de l'Année Martinienne* (q.v.), 185–98.
—— s.v. *Mélanges*.

Momigliano, A., 'La libertà di parola nel mondo antico', *Rivista Storica Italiana*, lxxxiii (1971), 499-524.

—— 'Popular Religious Beliefs and the Late Roman Historians', *Popular Belief and Practice*, ed. G. J. Cuming and D. Baker (Studies in Church History, viii; Cambridge, 1972), 1-18.

Morard, Françoise-E., 'Monachos, moine. Histoire du terme grec jusqu'au 4e siècle. Influences bibliques et gnostiques', *Freiburger Zeitschrift für Philosophie und Theologie*, xx (1973), 329-425.

Morin, G., 'Lettres inédites de saint Augustin et du prêtre Januarien dans l'affaire des moines d'Adrumète', *RB* xviii (1901), 241-56.

Mulders, J., 'Victricius van Rouaan: leven en leer', *Bijdragen, Tijdschrift voor Philosophie en Theologie*, xvii (1956), 1-25.

Mullus, Festschrift Theodor Klauser, ed. A. Stuiber and A. Hermann (Münster, Westf., 1964).

Munz, P., 'John Cassian', *JEH* xi (1960), 1-22.

Murphy, F. X., *Rufinus of Aquileia (345-411): his Life and Works* (The Catholic University of America Studies in Mediaeval History, n.s. vi; Washington, 1945).

Muyldermans, J., *A travers la tradition manuscrite d'Evagre le Pontique* (Bibliothèque du Muséon, iii; Louvain, 1932).

—— 'La teneur du Practicus d'Evagrius le Pontique', *Le Muséon*, xlii (1929), 74-89.

Nagel, P., *Die Motivierung der Askese in der alten Kirche und der Ursprung des Mönchtums = Texte und Untersuchungen*, xcv (Berlin, 1966).

Nautin, P., 'Études de chronologie hiéronymienne', *REA* xviii (1972), 209-18; xix (1973), 69-86; 213-39; xx (1974), 251-84.

Nock, A. D., *Conversion, from Alexander the Great to Augustine of Hippo* (Oxford, 1933).

Olphe-Galliard, M., 'Les sources de la Conférence XI de Cassien', *RAM* xvi (1935), 289-98.

—— 'Vie contemplative et vie active d'après Cassien', *RAM* xvi (1935), 252-88.

Palanque, J. R., 'Les dissensions des églises des Gaules à la fin du IVe siècle et la date du Concile de Turin', *RHEF* xxi (1935), 481-501.

—— 'La *Vita Ambrosii* de Paulin: étude critique', *RSR* iv (1924), 26-42; 401-20.

Paschoud, F., *Roma Aeterna: études sur le patriotisme romain dans l'Occident latin à l'époque des grandes invasions* (Rome, 1967).

Peeters, P., 'Le dossier copte de saint Pachôme et ses rapports avec la tradition grecque', *AB* lxiv (1946), 258-77.

Penco, G., 'Il concetto di monaco e di vita monastica in Occidente nel secolo VI', *Studia Monastica*, i (1959), 7-50.

—— 'Osservazioni preliminari sui caratteri dell'antica letteratura monastica', *Aevum*, xxxv (1961), 220-46.

Peterson, E., 'Zur Bedeutungsgeschichte von παῤῥησία', *Reinhold-Seeberg-Festschrift* (q.v., s.v. Reinhold), i, 283-97.

Petit, P., *Libanius et la vie municipale à Antioche au IVe siècle après*

J.-C. (Bibliothèque archéologique et historique de L'Institut Français d'Archéologie de Beyrouth, lxii; Paris, 1955).

Pichery, E., *Jean Cassien, Conférences*, ed. with introd., French trans. and comm. (Source chrétiennes, xlii, liv, lxiv; Paris, 1955–9).

Plagnieux, J., 'Le grief de complicité entre erreurs nestorienne et pélagienne: d'Augustin à Cassien par Prosper d'Aquitaine?', *REA*, ii (1956), 391–402.

Preuschen, E., *Palladius und Rufinus: ein Beitrag zur Quellenkunde des ältesten Mönchtums* (Giessen, 1897).

Priessnig, A., 'Die biographische Form der Plotinvita des Porphyrios und das Antoniosleben des Athanasios', *BZ* lxiv (1971), 1–5.

Prinz, F., *Frühes Mönchtum im Frankenreich, 4. bis 8. Jahrhundert* (Munich, 1965).

Quibell, J. E., *Excavations at Saqqara*, ii, 1906–7 (Cairo, 1908); iii, 1907–8 (Cairo, 1909); iv, 1908–9, 1909–10 (Cairo, 1912).

Regnault, L., *Les sentences des pères du désert*, introd., s.v. Dion.

Reitzenstein, R., 'Des Athanasius Werk über das Leben des Antonius: ein philologischer Beitrag zur Geschichte des Mönchtums', *Sitzungsberichte der Heidelberger Akademie der Wissenschaften*, phil.-hist. Klasse, V (1914), viii.

—— *Historia Monachorum und Historia Lausiaca: eine Studie zur Geschichte des Mönchtums und der Begriffe Gnostiker und Pneumatiker* (Göttingen, 1916).

Rothenhäusler, M., 'Das innere Leben des Zönobiten nach Jh. Cassian und die Regel des hl. Benedikt', *Vir Dei Benedictus* (q.v.), 276–92.

Rousseau, P., 'Blood-relationships among Early Eastern Ascetics', *JTS*, n.s. xxiii (1972), 135–44.

—— 'Cassian, Contemplation, and the Coenobitic Life', *JEH* xxvi (1975), 113–26.

—— 'The Formation of Early Ascetic Communities: Some Further Reflections', *JTS*, n.s. xxv (1974), 113–17.

—— 'In Search of Sidonius the Bishop', *Historia*, xxv (1976), 356–77.

—— 'The Spiritual Authority of the "Monk-bishop": Eastern Elements in Some Western Hagiography of the Fourth and Fifth Centuries', *JTS*, n.s. xxii (1971), 380–419.

Ruppert, F., *Das pachomianische Mönchtum und die Anfänge klösterlichen Gehorsams* (Münsterschwarzacher Studien, xx; 1971).

Saint Martin et son temps, mémorial du XVIe centenaire des débuts du monachisme en Gaule, 361–1961 (Studia Anselmiana, xlvi; Rome, 1961).

Sauneron, S., 'Fouilles d'Esna (Haute-Egypte): monastères et ermitages'. *CR*, 1967, 411–18.

Schäublin, C., 'Textkritisches zu den Briefen des Hieronymus', *Museum Helveticum*, xxx (1973), 55–62.

Seeberg, R., *Reinhold-Seeberg-Festschrift*, i, ed. W. Koepp (Leipzig, 1929).

Serra, M., 'La carità pastorale in s. Gregorio Nazianzeno', *OCP* xxi (1955), 337–74.

Seston, W., 'Remarque sur le rôle de la pensée d'Origène dans les origines du monachisme', *RHR* cviii (1933), 197-213.

Simon, M., *Verus Israel, étude sur les relations entre Chrétiens et Juifs dans l'empire romain, 135-425*, 2nd edn. (Paris, 1964).

Spanneut, M., 'Evagre d'Antioche', *DHGE* xvi (Paris, 1964-7), 102-7.

Steidle, B., ' "Homo Dei Antonius": zum Bild des "Mannes Gottes" im alten Mönchtum', *Antonius Magnus Eremita* (q.v.), 148-200.

Stroheker, K. F., *Der senatorische Adel in spätantiken Gallien* (Tübingen, 1948).

Studer, B., 'A propos des traductions d'Origène par Jérôme et Rufin', *Vetera Christianorum*, v (1968), 137-55.

Syme, R., *Ammianus and the Historia Augusta* (Oxford, 1968).

Tailliez, F., 'βασιλικὴ ὁδός—les valeurs d'un terme mystique et le prix de son histoire littérale', *OCP* xiii (1947), 299-354.

Taylor, J., 'St Basil the Great and Pope St Damasus I', *Downside Review*, xci (1973), 262-74.

Thélamon, F., 'L'empéreur idéal d'après l'*Histoire Ecclésiastique* de Rufin d'Aquilée', *Studia Patristica*, x, Papers presented to the Fifth International Conference on Patristic Studies, held in Oxford, 1967, ed. F. L. Cross = *Texte und Untersuchungen*, cvii (Berlin, 1970), 310-14.

Théologie de la vie monastique (Théologie, xlix; Paris, 1961).

Thompson, E. A., 'The Settlement of the Barbarians in Southern Gaul', *JRS* xlvi (1956), 65-75.

Van Cranenburgh, H., *La vie latine de saint Pachôme, traduite du grec par Denys le Petit* (Subsidia Hagiographica, xlvi; Brussels, 1969).

Van Molle, M. M., 'Aux origines de la vie communautaire chrétienne, quelques équivoques déterminantes pour l'avenir', *Supplément de La Vie Spirituelle*, lxxxviii (1969), 101-21.

—— 'Confrontation entre les règles et la littérature pachômienne postérieure', *Supplément de La Vie Spirituelle*, lxxxvi (1968), 394-424.

—— 'Essai de classement chronologique des premières règles de vie commune connue en chrétienté', *Supplément de La Vie Spirituelle*, lxxxiv (1968), 108-227.

—— 'Vie commune et obéissance d'après les institutions premières de Pachôme et Basile', *Supplément de La Vie Spirituelle*, xciii (1970), 196-225.

Van den Bosch, J., *Capa, basilica, monasterium et le culte de saint Martin de Tours* (Latinitas Christianorum Primaeva, xiii; Nijmegen, 1959).

Veilleux, A., *La liturgie dans le cénobitisme pachômien au quatrième siècle* (Studia Anselmiana, lvii; Rome, 1968).

Verheijen, L., 'La vie de saint Augustin par Possidius et la *Regula Sancti Augustini*', *Mélanges offerts à Mlle Christine Mohrmann* (q.v.), 270-9.

Villain, M., 'Rufin d'Aquilée et l'histoire ecclésiastique', *RSR* xxxiii (1946), 164-210.

—— 'Rufin d'Aquilée: la querelle autour d'Origène', *RSR* xxvii (1937),

5-37; 165-95.
Vir Dei Benedictus, ed. R. Molitor (Münster, Westf., 1947).
Von Balthasar, H. Urs., 'Die Hiera des Evagrius', *Zeitschrift für katholische Theologie*, lxiii (1939), 86-106.
Vööbus, A., *History of Asceticism in the Syrian Orient: a Contribution to the History of Culture in the Near East*, i, *The Origin of Asceticism and Early Monasticism in Persia, CSCO* clxxxiv, Subsidia, 14 (Louvain, 1958); ii, *Early Monasticism in Mesopotamia and Syria, CSCO* cxcvii, Subsidia, 17 (Louvain, 1960).
Voss, B. R., *Der Dialog in der frühchristlichen Literatur* (Studia et Testimonia Antiqua, ix; Munich, 1970).
Wallace-Hadrill, J. M., 'Gothia and Romania', in his *The Long-Haired Kings* (London, 1962), 25-48.
Weber, H.-O., *Die Stellung des Johannes Cassianus zur ausserpachomianischen Mönchstradition: eine Quellenuntersuchung* (Beiträge zur Geschichte des alten Mönchtums und des Benediktinerordens, xxiv; Münster, Westf., 1961).
White, H. G. Evelyn., *The Monasteries of the Wadi 'n Natrun*, ii, *The History of the Monasteries of Nitria and Scetis* (New York, 1932).
Wilmart, A., 'Une version latine inédite de la Vie de saint Antoine', *RB* xxxi (1914), 163-73.

INDEX

Texts are listed both independently and under the names of their authors; but *Lives,* specifically, are listed also under the names of their subjects. For individual ascetics listed alphabetically in *Apophthegmata Patrum, see* desert fathers. Friends, acquaintances, or correspondents of Jerome are followed by * (for example, Asella*). Modern authors are cited only where there is discussion or dispute.

Abraham, 'abbot' in *Con.*, 181–2, 193–4, 197, 211–13
Ambrose, bishop of Milan, 88–90, 93, 112, 145, 153, 157n29, 224–5, 237; *Life of* (by Paulinus of Milan), 95, 144, 162–3
Amoun of Rhaithou (Tor, near Suez), Egyptian ascetic, 26–7, 27n36
Antioch: schism at, 104–7, 107n36, 174
Antony of Egypt, xvii, xx, 20–22, 24–5, 24n25, 36n13, 65, 163, 201n14; relations with secular world, 38n21, 44–5, 60–61, 163; view of ascetic history, 22–4; demons, 34, 47–8; visions, 27–8; compared with Pachomius, 22, 34–6, 134n3; events after death, 72; *Life of,* 14–16, 38, 45, 47n85, 69, 72, 83, 85–6, 92–5; impact of *Life of* on Augustine, 92–5; impact of *Life of* on Cassian, 198n55, 211; impact of *Life of* on Jerome, 69, 105, 133–7, 144; impact of *Life of* on Sulpicius, 69, 79, 95, 144, 148, 156n23. *See also* Evagrius of Antioch
Apollonius, ascetic in the *Historia Monachorum,* 41
Apophthegmata Patrum, 12–14, 21, 26n35, 30n56, 33, 39, 45, 49n94, 60n23, 69–73, 222n6, 224, 254–5
Aquileia, 87, 90, 100, 102, 250. *See also* Chromatius, bishop of Aquileia; Fortunatianus, bishop of Aquileia; Valerian, bishop of Aquileia; Jerome: in Aquileia
Arcadius, emperor: legislation on monks, 10
Archebius, bishop of Panephysis (Nile Delta), 151n48, 216
Arius, bishop of Panopolis (Akhmîm), 64–5
Asella*, 110, 112
Athanasius, archbishop of Alexandria, 66–7, 81–3, 85, 104, 143–4. *See also* Antony of Egypt: *Life of*
Augustine, bishop of Hippo, 46, 48n88, 82n8, 92–5, 112, 119, 127, 149n37, 153, 157n29, 209n54, 223n9, 231, 234n61, 237; *Life of* (by Possidius), 95, 145, 161n1, 162
Aurelius Victor, 102n11, 134n4, 206n42
Ausonius, 184n5, 206
Auxentius, bishop of Milan, 86, 88

Babut, Ernest-Charles, 144n7, 154n13, 154n15, 156n26
Bacht, Heinrich, 35n7
Basil, bishop of Caesarea, xi, xii, 25, 81–2, 104–5, 149, 237
Blesilla*, 110
Bonosus*, 100–101, 115n6, 250
Bousset, Wilhelm, 40n37, 51n111, 187n23
Brictius, bishop of Tours, 159, 235
Brown, Peter, ix, xii–xiii, xviii
Burton-Christie, Douglas, xix n41
Butler, Cuthbert, 16n28

Cassian, John: biographical details, 17, 25, 65, 169–76, 187n21, 211–12; as a cleric, 172, 174–5; restlessness, 172–3, 187n21; relations with John Chrysostom, 17, 169–73, 175, 228; compared with Jerome, 122, 132, 138n24, 172–5, 185n11, 208, 233n55, 234n61; compared with Martin of Tours, 183, 227; on authority and obedience, 189–98,

Cassian, John (*cont.*)
231–4; on contemplation, 177–80, 201–2, 211, 228; and controversy over teaching of Origen, 171–2, 190–91; on freedom and grace, 202, 231–4; on miracles, 213–15; on monastic history, 192–4, 200–201, 210–11; on paganism and its literature, 190–91, 201, 223; on Scripture, 179, 180n10, 189, 191, 223, 228, 232; as a writer, xix, xxiii, 69, 79, 95, 133, 146, 169, 221–34; as forerunner of monastic rules, 194–8, 225–7, 227n25, 236; his audience, 199–205, 222–3; *Institutes*, 185n11, 231n48, 236, 253n28, 254–5; *Conferences*, 225–7, 227n 25, 227n27, 231–4, 234nn60–61, 236, 254–5; relation between *Institutes* and *Conferences*, 185n11, 213n68, 225n20, 234n61; *De Incarnatione*, 170–71, 173, 227–31, 232n54, 234n60; later reputation, 226, 235–9. *See also* Antony of Egypt: *Life of;* charism of the word; Evagrius of Pontus; Germanus, Cassian's companion; hermits and coenobites: Cassian on the superiority of the latter; pastoral engagement, ascetics': Cassian and
Castor, bishop of Apt, 183, 217, 229n35
Cavallera, Ferdinand, 107n36, 115n7
Celestine I, bishop of Rome, 217n88, 219n96
Chadwick, Owen, 169n2, 170n7, 184n4, 187n23, 198n55, 213n68, 222n6, 228n29, 231n46, 232n54
charism of the word: among early eastern ascetics, 19–21, 23–4, 26–7, 30, 37, 52–63, 69–70; Sulpicius and, 146, 152; Cassian and its decline, 189–95, 224–5, 230
Chin, Catherine, xxi n46
Chitty, Derwas, 14n18, 28n45, 29n54, 35n7, 87n29, 243–7
Chromatius, bishop of Aquileia, 46n78, 89–90, 250
Chrysostom, John, archbishop of Constantinople, 17, 82n9, 169–74, 228, 237
Clark, Elizabeth A., xxv–xxvi
Constantius II, emperor, 84–6, 104, 134
Courcelle, Pierre, 115n7
Cyprian, bishop of Carthage, 112, 123, 190n9
Cyril, archbishop of Alexandria: and attacks on Orestes and Hypatia, 10–11

Damasus I, bishop of Rome, 88, 104–12
Delehaye, Hippolyte, 144n7, 154n13, 154n15
Demetrias*, 123–4
desert, as literal *locus* of ascetic endeavour, xi, xviii, xxv, 11, 40, 44, 93–4, 100, 109
desert fathers listed alphabetically in the *Apophthegmata Patrum:* Agathon, 48–50; Ammoes, 50; Ammonas, 46; Amoun of Nitria, 21, 27n36; Anoub, 52–3; Arsenius, 25–7, 59–60, 71, 163; Ephraim, 29n51; Eulogius, 46; Isaac of the Cells, 63n40; Isidore of Scetis (Isidore "the Priest"), 21, 62–3, 216; John Colobos (John the Dwarf), 21; Longinus, 49; Macarius of Alexandria, 13n12, 62; Macarius "the Egyptian," or "the Great," 13, 13n12, 21, 24n25, 37, 44, 47, 53,
62–3, 64n46, 214–15; Pambo, 21, 29, 40, 60, 60n23, 75, 163; Paul "the Simple", 20; Poemen, 46, 50, 52, 156–7; Sisoes, 26–7. *See also* Antony of Egypt; Evagrius of Pontus; Paphnutius
De Vogüé, Adalbert, 14n15, 16n26, 200n9, 211n62
Dorotheus, presbyter at Antinoe (Sheikh Abada), 62
Dörries, Hermann, 38n21, 45n70, 47n85
Draguet, René, 14n18, 38n25, 71n14
Duval, Yves-Marie, 107n36

Epiphanius, bishop of Salamis (Cyprus), 87n27, 108, 130–31, 136, 149
Esaias of Scetis, 14, 24, 46, 48–9, 54, 71, 209n54
Eucherius, bishop of Lyon, 180n12–13, 184, 196n47, 218, 226n22
Eunapius, 9–11, 56
Eusebius, bishop of Caesarea, 90
Eusebius, bishop of Vercelli, 85, 87
Eustathius, bishop of Antioch, 104

Eustathius, bishop of Sebaste (Armenia), 149
Eustochium*, daughter of Paula*, 101, 108–10, 116, 120, 123–4
Eutropius (Pseudo-Jerome), 205, 212n66
Evagrius of Antioch: translator of the *Life of Antony*, 15n19, 45n70, 94–5, 100, 106, 133, 136, 198n55, 249–50
Evagrius of Pontus (northeastern Turkey), 25–6, 37–8, 38n20, 243, 248, 251–3; and Cassian, 171, 177, 204n29, 222n6, 227n25
example as basis of ascetic instruction, 20–21, 24–6, 31, 36–9, 69–70, 111, 126, 128, 134. *See also* Cassian, John: on authority and obedience

Fabiola*, 102n16, 115n6, 117
Faou (Faw Qibli, Thebaid), Pachomian monastery at, 22, 32, 64n50
Festugière, A.-J., 16n27, 31n67, 47n85, 71n14, 81n5, 245, 249n3
Fontaine, Jacques, 149n39, 151n46, 154n13, 154n15, 155n20, 157n28, 159n37
Fortunatianus, bishop of Aquileia, 102n11
Frank, Georgia, xxvi
Furia*, 116, 118

Gennadius of Marseille, 169
Germanus, Cassian's companion, 172, 180–81, 187n21, 210–11, 216, 223–6
Geruchia*, 121
Goehring, James E., x–xi, xviii
Gould, Graham, xix n41
Gregory, bishop of Nazianzus, xiii, xxi, 25, 107
Gribomont, Jean, 149n39
Griffe, Élie, 172n16, 208n49
Guy, Jean-Claude, 170n8

Halkin, François, 38n25, 243–5
Heliodorus*, bishop of Altinum, 102–4, 106, 126
Helladius, bishop of Arles, 178, 192, 218
hermits and coenobites: transition from first to second, xi–xii, xvi, xviii–xix, 17–18, 21, 31, 33–49, 143, 148, 159; Cassian on the superiority of the latter, 177–82, 184–7, 194–202, 210, 236
Hilarion, Life of. See Jerome: his *Lives*
Hilary, bishop of Arles, 184nn6–7, 196n47, 197n50, 218
Hilary, bishop of Poitiers, 83–7, 92, 102n11, 148–50, 150n42, 155n18, 175. *See also* Jerome: relations with (writings of) Hilary, bishop of Poitiers; Martin, bishop of Tours: relations with Hilary, bishop of Poitiers
Historia Monachorum, 15–17, 21, 38n20, 40n35, 61, 81, 94, 211n62, 215, 248–9
Holl, Karl, 15n20
Honoratus of Lérins, bishop of Arles, 184, 189, 197n50, 217–18, 225
Hor, ascetic in the *Historia Monachorum*, 40–41, 73
Horsiesius, successor of Pachomius. *See* Orsisius
household asceticism, 80–81, 89–91, 106n30, 223, 248. *See also* Jerome: on household asceticism

Innocent I, bishop of Rome, 169, 173–4
Iovinianus. *See* Jerome: relations with Iovinianus
Isaiah, Isaias of Scetis. *See* Esaias of Scetis
islands, ascetics on, 100, 115, 115n6, 148–9

Januarius, correspondent in the 'Hadrumetum Affair', 222–4, 226
Jeremias, monastery of (at Saqqara), 23n20, 30, 55, 57n6, 75
Jerome: scholarly reassessment of, xix, xxi, xxiii; early life, 93, 101, 143; in Antioch, 100–101, 106–7, 111, 130, 133; in Aquileia, 87, 100, 102, 115, 126; in Bethlehem, 114, 173–4; in Chalcis, 101–6, 109, 113, 119, 133–5; in Constantinople, xx, 107, 118, 172–3; in Rome, 81–3, 108–13; enduring concern with the city, 116–20, 122–5, 135–6; attitude towards Gaul, 118, 120–22, 131–2, 144, 184n5, 206n36, 208; relations with Augustine, 119; relations with Damasus, 88, 104–5, 107–8;

Jerome (*cont.*)
relations with Demetrias, 123–4; relations with Eusebius, bishop of Vercelli, 87; relations with Eustochium, 101, 108–10; relations with (writings of) Hilary, bishop of Poitiers, 86–7, 102, 144; relations with Iovinianus, xix, 108n40, 119–20, 128–9, 233n55; relations with John, bishop of Jerusalem, 86–7, 115n10, 119, 130–31; relations with (indirectly) Sulpicius Severus, 122, 132, 136, 144; relations with Theophilus, 131; on ascetic exile, 102–3, 106–7, 114–16, 120–22, 126, 131, 138–9; on household asceticism, 83, 87, 106–7, 110–12, 115–17, 120–21, 123–4, 135, 143–4; on learning and the classical tradition, 101–2, 126–8, 132; on Origen, xx, 118–19, 125; on ascetics and pastoral engagement, xix, xxiv, xxv–xxvi, 87n27, 103–4, 106–7, 111, 122, 125–32, 143–4; on his own priesthood, xix–xx, 106–7, 130; on virginity, 107, 109–10, 112, 117, 128–9, 135–6; his *Lives*, 95, 106, 133–9, 143–4; his translations of Pachomian material, 16, 233n56
John, 'abbot' in *Con.*, 180–81, 194–5, 206n38
John, bishop of Jerusalem. *See* Jerome: relations with John, bishop of Jerusalem
John Cassian. *See* Cassian, John
John Chrysostom. *See* Chrysostom, John, archbishop of Constantinople
John of Lycopolis, 20n8, 37, 38n20, 73, 90, (in *Con.*) 195, 255
Joseph, 'abbot' in *Con.*, 187–8, 193, 196–7, 220
Jovinian. *See* Jerome: relations with Iovinianus
Julian, emperor, 84n13
Jullian, Camille, 150nn41–2

Kellia, Egyptian monastic settlement (al-Muna, south of Nitria), 21, 42, 62
Kelly, J. N. D., 107n36, 119n29, 127n11
Klingshirn, William E., xiv
Krueger, Derek, xxvi

Laeta*, mother of the younger Paula, 119–21
Latopolis (Esneh), 22; Synod of, *see* Pachomius: at Synod of Latopolis
Lazarus, bishop of Aix: disciple of Martin of Tours, 174, 218
Lefort, Louis Théophile, 31n64, 243–7
Leo I, bishop of Rome, 173, 184n6, 236
Leontius, bishop of Fréjus, 218
Leyser, Conrad, xiv, xxiii
Libanius of Antioch: on Christian ascetics, 10
Liberius, bishop of Rome, 88
Lorenz, Rudolf, 87n29

Madoz, José, 228n29
Malchus, Life of. See Jerome: his *Lives*
Marcella*, 108
Marrou, Henri-Irénée, 169n2, 173n18
Marsili, Salvatore, 170n7, 180n10
Martin, bishop of Tours: early ascetic experiments, 115n6, 148–9; relations with Hilary, bishop of Poitiers, xx, xxi, 86, 148–9, 155n18; relations with other clergy, 155–6, 175; his enduring asceticism, xxi–xxii, 148–51, 206; on authority, 152–6, 164–5; on bishops and pastoral engagement, xii, xxi–xxii, 148–51, 159, 162–5, 206, 217n87, 237–8; and demons, 122n54, 145n11, 152, 154–5, 158; disciples, character and formation of, 161–3; literacy, 147, 150n42; miracles, 156–60, 163; on pagans and their temples, 152–4, 158; visions and dreams, 145n11, 152, 156; *Life of* (by Sulpicius Severus), 79, 145–7, 151, 157n29, 158–60, 164–5
Melitius, bishop of Antioch, 104
Mierow, Charles, 103n19
Mulders, J., 150n42
Munz, Peter, 170n7, 199n3, 201n10, 231n46

Nagel, Peter, 44n61
Nepotianus*, 115, 119, 126–9, 132
Nestorius, archbishop of Constantinople, 171, 174, 227, 229–31
Netras, bishop of Pharan (southern Sinai), 64, 216

Nitria, Egyptian monastic settlement (el-Barnudj, eastern Delta), 21, 36, 62

obedience: among desert fathers, 51–5; in Cassian (as feature of coenobitism), 179, 181, 194–7. *See also* Pachomius: on authority and obedience
oral tradition and literary record, 13, 145–6, 254–5. *See also* texts as vehicles of ascetic influence
Orientius, bishop of Auch, 206n37, 212n66
Origen, controversy over teaching of, xx. *See also* Cassian, John: and controversy over teaching of Origen; Evagrius of Pontus; Jerome: on Origen; Theophilus, archbishop of Alexandria: repudiation of Origen in A.D. 399
Orsisius, successor of Pachomius, 22, 32, 67, 69; *Liber,* 54, 57, 61, 72, 74–5, 196n42, 206n38, 233n56

Pachomius: early asceticism, 22–4, 56–8; comparison with Antony, 34–6, 56; on authority and obedience, 30, 34, 51–3, 69, 253; consideration for the weak, 70–71; on priesthood and pastoral engagement, 56–9, 63–4; pessimism about successors, 23, 51–2; at Synod of Latopolis, 30–31, 65, 104n24; visions, 27–30, 156n25, 246; *Lives of,* 17–18, 28n46, 31n64, 31n67, 32n69, 35, 56–8, 64n50, 72–3, 75–6, 82n8, 243–7; *Rule,* 15–16, 45–6, 54–5, 69, 74; *Rule* and associated vision, 38–9, 41, 225; Latin *Life* (by Dionysius Exiguus) and his standing in the West, 18, 69, 183–4
Palladius, bishop of Helenopolis (Bithynia prima), 25, 38n20, 65, 106; *Dialogue,* 169–73; *Lausiac History,* 16–17, 64n46, 70, 71n14, 106n30, 138n25, 146, 223
Pammachius*, 116–17, 120
Panopolis (Akhmîm), Pachomian foundation at, 22. *See also* Arius, bishop of Panopolis
Paphnutius, 21, 27, 40; in *Con.,* 63n44, 171–2, 179–80, 187n21, 191, 216, 234n60
pastoral engagement, ascetics', xviii–xix, xxiv–xxvi; among eastern ascetic pioneers, 56–67; in the West, 82–3; Cassian and, 151n48, 169, 211–20, 230–31. *See also* Jerome: on ascetics and pastoral engagement; Pachomius: on priesthood and pastoral engagement
Patlagean, Evelyne, xi n6, xxv
Paul, Life of. See Jerome: his *Lives*
Paula*: patron and associate of Jerome, 108, 116
Paula, daughter of Laeta, 119–21, 123
Paulinianus, brother of Jerome, 87n27, 107n33, 130–31
Paulinus, bishop of Antioch, 104, 106, 108, 130
Paulinus, bishop of Nola, 94, 115, 118, 127, 139, 158n33, 206n36, 207, 212n65
Paulinus of Milan. *See* Ambrose, bishop of Milan: *Life of*
Paulinus of Pella, 208
Pelagius and Pelagianism, xix, xx, 174, 229; controversy reflected in Cassian, *Con.* xiii, 231–4
Phbow, Pachomian monastery at. *See* Faou
Possidius, bishop of Calama. *See* Augustine, bishop of Hippo: *Life of*
Preuschen, Erwin, 16n28
Priscillian, bishop of Avila, xx, xxi
Proculus, bishop of Marseille, 122, 126, 175, 206, 216n82, 218, 236

Rapp, Claudia, xiv–xv, xviii
Rebenich, Stefan, xxi
Reitzenstein, Richard, 15n20, 16n28, 41n43
Rubenson, Samuel, xvii n37, xviii
Rufinus of Aquileia, 16, 79, 81, 89–91, 93, 119. *See also Historia Monachorum*
Ruppert, Fidelis, 51n113, 247
Rusticus: correspondent of Jerome, 121
Rusticus, bishop of Narbonne, 122, 131, 216n82
Rutilius Namatianus, 115n6, 207

Salvian of Marseille, 200n7, 208–9
Salvina*, wife of *comes* Nebridius, 118
Sarabaites, 209, 219
Sayings of the Desert Fathers. See Apophthegmata Patrum
Scetis, Egyptian monastic settlement (Wadi el-Natrun, Delta), xvi, 11, 21–2, 36, 53, 69–70, 178
Scripture, ascetic use of: among desert fathers, 20n4, 30, 32, 36n14, 41, 73–5; in the West, 100–101, 121, 127, 132, 152. *See also* Cassian, John: on Scripture
Serapion, bishop of Tentyra (Dendera, Thebaid), 64
Serapion, bishop of Thmuis (Tell el-Timai , Delta), 24n25
Seston, William, 27n43
Shenoute of Atripe, founder of the White Monastery (Sohag), x, xv, xvi–xvii
Siricius, bishop of Rome, 129–30, 217n88
Stancliffe, Clare, xxii
Stewart, Columba, xxii
Sulpicius Severus: as disciple of Martin, xxi, 50n99, 143–6, 206–7, 206n36, 236; as writer, 133, 136, 144–7, 221n2; *Dialogues*, 145, 147, 157n29, 159–60, 224n13, 254. *See also* Antony of Egypt: impact of *Life of* on Sulpicius; Jerome: relations with (indirectly) Sulpicius Severus; Martin, bishop of Tours: *Life of*
Syme, Ronald, 108n41, 132n1

Tabennesis, Pachomian monastery near Seneset (Kasr es-Sayad, Thebaid), 22, 32, 65
texts as vehicles of ascetic influence, xxiv–xxvi, 12, 43, 55, 68–76, 92–5, 135, 145–6, 165. *See also* Cassian, John: as forerunner of monastic rules; Pachomius: *Rule*
Theodore: successor of Pachomius, 22, 31–2, 38, 50, 53, 57, 66–7, 69, 72–6
Theodore, bishop of Fréjus, 218
Theodosius I, emperor: legislation concerning monks, 10; as Christian emperor, 90
Theophilus, archbishop of Alexandria, 59–60, 65, 66n61, 131, 153n8, 170; repudiation of Origen in A.D. 399, 10, 17, 26n33, 65, 68, 171–2, 190
tradition, formation of ascetic, 22–4, 33–49, 71–6, 86. *See also* Antony of Egypt: view of ascetic history; Cassian, John: on monastic history

Valentinian I, emperor, 88
Valerian, bishop of Aquileia, 87, 102n11, 126
Van Molle, M. M., 16n26, 51n113
Veilleux, Armand, 16n26, 243–7
Venerius, bishop of Marseille, 218, 219n96
Victricius, bishop of Rouen, 150n40, 227
Vigilantius, 120–22, 159, 235
Vigilius, *Regula Orientalis*, 183
Villain, Maurice, 81n5
Vincent of Lérins, *Commonitorium*, 190n9, 196n42, 204n28, 228
visions. *See* Antony of Egypt: visions; Martin, bishop of Tours: visions and dreams; Pachomius: visions
Vitae Patrum. See Apophthegmata Patrum

Wallace-Hadrill, J. M., 199n4
wandering ascetics, 40, 43–5, 48–9, 105–6, 160, 164–5. *See also* Cassian, John: restlessness; Jerome: on ascetic exile
wealth and patronage, 59, 109, 117, 124, 134–5, 137–8; Cassian on, 205–12
Weber, Hans-Oskar, 169n1, 170n7, 198n55, 254–5
Wessel, Susan, xiv, xxiii
Williams, Megan, xxi n46

www.ingramcontent.com/pod-product-compliance
Ingram Content Group UK Ltd.
Pitfield, Milton Keynes, MK11 3LW, UK
UKHW010256240525
458861UK00002B/21